W9-CAY-767

Praise for *When the Meadow Blooms*

"With its pastoral setting and reflective characters, this cozy read explores the uncertainty present in every new beginning."

Booklist

"*When the Meadow Blooms* by Ann H. Gabhart is an engaging tale of heartache, first loves, and spiritual lessons that leave the reader entertained and educated."

Interviews & Reviews

"*When the Meadow Blooms* is a touching, wholesome story about second chances and the possibility we all have for growth."

Manhattan Book Review

Praise for *Along a Storied Trail*

"Fabulous! This beautifully written book brings a little-known part of American history to life with characters so real they leap off the pages into readers' hearts and linger there long after the last page is turned."

Amanda Cabot, bestselling author of *Dreams Rekindled*

"Adventure, a romantic triangle (or two!), plus an unexpected natural disaster roil up, spilling into a dramatic, heart-pounding conclusion. *Along a Storied Trail* might be Gabhart's best book yet."

Suzanne Woods Fisher, author of *The Moonlight School*

"This is a story of resilience that is not only representative of the 1930s, but a story of resilience that we so deeply need in our times."

Susie Finkbeiner, author of *The Nature of Small Birds* and *Stories That Bind Us*

"Gabhart's skillful use of period details and the Appalachian landscape lend plenty of atmosphere to accompany the lessons of hope, compassion, and fortitude amid hardship. This is her best historical inspirational yet."

Publishers Weekly, starred review

"Gabhart crafts an absorbing story that deeply explores the rich tradition of storytelling."

Booklist

7/23

WITHDRAWN

ALBERT WISNER PUBLIC LIBRARY
ONE McFARLAND DRIVE
WARWICK, NY 10990
(845) 986-1047
www.albertwisnerlibrary.org

In the
SHADOW
of the
RIVER

Books by Ann H. Gabhart

In the
SHADOW
of the
RIVER

ANN H. GABHART

Revell

a division of Baker Publishing Group
Grand Rapids, Michigan

© 2023 by Ann H. Gabhart

Published by Revell
a division of Baker Publishing Group
Grand Rapids, Michigan
www.revellbooks.com

Printed in the United States of America

All rights reserved. No part of this publication may be reproduced, stored in a retrieval system, or transmitted in any form or by any means—for example, electronic, photocopy, recording—without the prior written permission of the publisher. The only exception is brief quotations in printed reviews.

Library of Congress Cataloging-in-Publication Data
Names: Gabhart, Ann H., 1947– author.
Title: In the shadow of the river / Ann H. Gabhart.
Description: Grand Rapids, MI : Revell, a division of Baker Publishing Group, [2023]
Identifiers: LCCN 2022034075 | ISBN 9780800741723 (paperback) | ISBN 9780800744601 (casebound) | ISBN 9781493441327 (ebook)
Subjects: LCGFT: Novels.
Classification: LCC PS3607.A23 I52 2023 | DDC 813/.6—dc23/eng/20220722
LC record available at https://lccn.loc.gov/2022034075

Scripture used in this book, whether quoted or paraphrased by the characters, is taken from the King James Version of the Bible.

This book is a work of fiction. Names, characters, places, and incidents are the product of the author's imagination or are used fictitiously. Any resemblance to actual events, locales, or persons, living or dead, is coincidental.

Published in association with Books & Such Literary Management, www.booksandsuch.com.

Baker Publishing Group publications use paper produced from sustainable forestry practices and post-consumer waste whenever possible.

23   24   25   26   27   28   29   7   6   5   4   3   2   1

To my family with love and gratitude
for all the life scenes we have shared

All the world's a stage,
And all the men and women merely players:
They have their exits and their entrances;
And one man in his time plays many parts.

William Shakespeare, *As You Like It*

Chapter

1

JACCI REED'S MOTHER shook her awake, then put her fingers lightly over Jacci's lips.

"Shh. We have to get off the boat." Her mother's eyes were wide in the light of the lantern she held.

Jacci wanted to ask why, but instead she sat up and felt for her shoes with her toes.

Her mother shook her head and pulled her off the bed. "No time." But she didn't fuss when Jacci grabbed her sock doll.

Her mother left the lantern on the table without even blowing it out. At five, Jacci had been warned so often about a candle or lantern being upset and catching the boat on fire that now she feared the room might explode in flames before they got out of the door.

Her mother led Jacci out into the passageway. "Not a sound." She sounded scared.

Jacci's mother never got scared. She was always the one to

help Jacci not be afraid when thunder boomed over the river or floods made the steamboat bounce in funny ways. So now Jacci bit her lip and didn't cry out when her mother squeezed her hand so tight her fingers hurt. The fear coursed between their hands and Jacci's heart pounded up in her ears. Maybe the boat was on fire already and they would have to jump in the river to escape.

But she didn't smell smoke as she hurried to keep up with her mother's fast steps. Her nightgown flapped against her legs. Her mother never let her go out on the steamboat deck without putting on a dress. Ever.

She couldn't swim. Maybe she wouldn't have to. They were at the dock. She'd watched the crew tie up their steamboat earlier and listened to the roustabouts sing while they unloaded barrels and crates. She'd stayed hidden up on the top deck while the fancy men and women headed out down the gangplank. The women wore hats with ribbons and feathers. The men carried gold-knobbed canes.

Even better than that was the sound of a calliope drifting down the river that meant a showboat was on the way. When it docked right beside their boat, she clapped her hands. She never got to go to the shows, but she loved to watch the actors coming and going. Sometimes they played music and sang.

By the time the river swallowed up the sun, people were streaming up onto the boat to see the show. She did so wish she could be one of them, but her mother would never allow that. Instead she had found Jacci and made her go to bed.

Now as Mama hurried her up to the main deck, Jacci could hear music spilling out of the showboat. Lively music and then laughter.

Sometimes when she watched a showboat tied up next to their boat, she laughed too when she heard laughter, even though she had no idea what was funny. She didn't feel like doing that now. Not with her mother so afraid.

A man stepped out of the shadows in front of them. Her mother shoved Jacci behind her.

"You can't get away." The man's voice was low, as if he didn't want anyone but her mother to hear him. "Just let me have the kid and nobody will have to get hurt."

"No. She's mine." Her mother's voice sounded strained.

"That's not what I've been told," the man said.

"You've been told wrong."

"Lisbeth says different."

"Lisbeth?" Jacci's mother breathed out the name as her whole body stiffened against Jacci. "You're lying."

Jacci peeked out from behind Mama's skirts. She could see the man's smile in the moonlight, and she wanted to jerk free from her mother and run hide. She knew plenty of great hiding places on their boat. But what if it really was on fire?

The man laughed. "I think we know who has been lying."

He was barely taller than her mother and had on fancy passenger clothes. Not what the crewmen wore.

Her mother held Jacci behind her and jerked her small gun out of her pocket with her other hand. "Get out of the way."

The man laughed. "What do you think you're going to do with that?"

"Whatever I have to." Mama's voice sounded so cold, so wrong, that Jacci shivered.

The man rushed toward her mother and knocked the gun out of her hand. There was a flash of metal in his hand.

Her mother made a choked sound. "Run, Jacci."

But Jacci couldn't leave her mother. She dropped her doll and grabbed the gun off the deck. She'd seen men shoot at things on the riverbanks. She knew how they spread their feet to stand steady while they held their guns out in front of them. She did that now as the man pushed her mother away from him so hard she landed against the railing. Jacci pointed the gun at him and pulled back the trigger.

The gun made a popping sound, only a little louder than the plop of a fish jumping up from the river and falling back in. The man looked confused as he turned toward Jacci. Then, still staring at her, he sank to a sitting position on the deck, his hands pressed against his middle.

Jacci shook so much she couldn't hold on to the gun. It clattered to the deck once more. She looked at her mother doubled over against the rail. "Mama?"

As if the sound of Jacci's voice gave her strength, her mother straightened up. Her voice was weak but back to sounding like Mama. "Get the gun."

Jacci did as she was told while she tried not to look at the man still sitting there with that funny look on his face.

"Socks." Her doll had slid over close to the man. She hesitated, then took a step toward it.

"No." Her mother grabbed Jacci's shoulder to yank her back as the man lurched toward her. "I'll make you a new one."

The man said something as he fell back, but Jacci couldn't understand what it was. His voice sounded all bubbly and wrong. She wished the moon would go behind a cloud so she couldn't see his face.

Mama's hand was wet and sticky now and her grasp weak instead of hard the way it had been.

"Where are we going?" she asked as they went down the gangplank to the wooden dock and then onto the grass.

"The showboat."

Jacci wanted to be happy about that. She'd always wanted to go on a showboat and see what made people laugh. But now she wasn't sure she would ever laugh again. Her mother's breath was ragged, and when she stumbled over a rock, she groaned. Jacci put an arm around her to try to hold her up.

They went up the stage plank toward the music. Happy music. Horns and drums and a piano. Her mother's steps slowed until she was barely moving. Jacci wanted to run, but she couldn't leave her mother.

"Do you still have the gun?" Mama said.

Jacci held it out.

"Throw it in the river."

When Jacci started to drop it over the side, her mother stopped her. "Not here. On the other side. Throw it as hard as you can." She pushed Jacci away from her and leaned on a post. "Don't let anybody see you. Be fast."

Applause and cheers came from inside the theater. Jacci ran through the shadows around the deck. She was scared to be away from Mama, but she had to do what she said. After she slung the gun into the river, she raced back to where her mother hung on to the post as if that was all that kept her from falling.

But when she saw Jacci, she pushed away from the post and they went past the empty ticket booth. A few people passed by them, but they were too busy laughing and talking to pay any attention to Jacci and her mother.

Inside a big room with rows and rows of seats, a crowd of people moved toward the front where men and women in frilly costumes smiled and waved from a stage. Some lanterns glowed bright there while others along the wall flickered with only enough light to see the way between the rows of seats. A man came toward them, stopping now and again to turn up the lantern flames.

Her mother followed the crowd toward the stage, but stopped when she got close to the man in the aisle. She called out to him. "We need to see Tyrone Chesser."

The man looked at her and then at Jacci. He took a step back. "Freaking fishworms. What's happened to you?"

Jacci looked down at her gown. It was red with blood.

Chapter

2

IRENA BRACED HER LEGS against one of the seats. She wanted to give in to the pain and collapse, but she couldn't. Not until she made sure Jacci was safe. Her father could do that for her. If he would.

When she saw the *Kingston Floating Palace* tying up beside their steamboat earlier, she'd been irritated. She had no desire to see her father, an actor on the showboat, but if he noticed their steamboat's name, he would come over to look for her.

To pretend he cared. Maybe he did care for the ten minutes he would smile and ask how she was doing. He might have a pocketful of candy for Jacci. Or he might not. He never claimed to be her grandfather, and so Irena had never used that name with Jacci. He was Tyrone Chesser to them both. Not father. Not grandfather. Those titles were earned with more than an hour here and there through the years.

But now as she took small breaths and tried not to allow the fear that was even worse than the pain of the knife lodged in her side to overcome her, she thanked the Lord for bringing the two boats side by side.

The young man took one of the lanterns off the hook on the wall and held it up. His eyes were wide. He was really more boy than man. Probably one of the Kingston family.

"You need a doctor," he said.

"First get Tyrone." The lights were dimming, but then Irena realized she was what was fading. She couldn't faint yet. "Please."

He turned toward the stage and started to yell something. She reached out a hand to stop him. "Quietly. Don't want a scene."

"Right," the boy said. "Here, let me help you."

He moved to put his arm around her, but Jacci stayed plastered against Irena between them. Irena gave Jacci a little push away. "It's all right, sweetheart. Run up on the stage and get your grandfather Tyrone."

Maybe it was time he earned the title.

Jacci looked up at her and then did as she was told, threading her way between the audience members waiting to talk to the performers. Nobody appeared to give the barefoot girl in a nightgown stained with blood a second look. Perhaps they thought she was in costume, part of the cast.

Irena hoped she would know which one was Tyrone. They hadn't seen him for several months, but he was an impressive-looking man. Broad through the chest, with a noble bearing, especially when holding court in front of his fans. His hair was going gray, but now it might be black with some combed-in dye for whatever part he was playing. In the showboat dramas, he often took the role of the villain of the piece. Those characters always seemed to have dark hair.

She looked toward the stage, but her vision was too fuzzy to see him. She leaned on the youngster, who blanched at the sight of the knife hilt in her side, but he buoyed up his nerve and slipped around to her other side to support her as they slowly made their way down the aisle.

"What happened?" he asked.

"An accident," she said.

He didn't believe her. She knew that, but he didn't ask more. For that, she was grateful. He was probably thinking he would know the whole story eventually. Nothing stayed secret among a showboat cast. But she needed it to be secret. One thing sure, she'd see that no one ever knew Jacci pulled the trigger to shoot that man. No one could ever know that.

She hadn't known who the man was. A hired hand most likely. But Lisbeth wouldn't have sent him. Irena could never believe that. Lisbeth had loved Jacci, even if she held her only for those few weeks. Poor, dear Lisbeth.

Irena pushed away thoughts of her friend. She needed all her concentration to keep moving her feet. She had to stay alive long enough to talk to her father. Long enough to make sure Jacci never told anyone about firing that gun. Long enough to be sure her daughter was safe.

And she was her daughter. No one would dispute that even if the man did live to claim otherwise. She did hope the man didn't die, in spite of the fact she had been ready to shoot him. Would have shot him if he hadn't knocked her gun away before she could pull the trigger.

Oh please, Lord, let him not have seen us boarding the showboat. But then, what if he wasn't alone? The thought sent a quiver through her as she began to lose her grip on consciousness.

"Hold on a little longer." The boy tightened his hold under her shoulders, not realizing the piercing pain that brought her. "We're almost backstage."

Then Tyrone was in front of her, his face tight with concern. "Irena."

She looked from him to Jacci beside him and tried to focus on her child's face, but black nothingness swallowed her.

Irena had no idea how much time had passed when she swam up out of the black toward the light. She wasn't even sure she was alive. Maybe the light was heaven. She had a feeling of floating in the depths for a moment.

She'd felt that once before. The time Kelly had taught her how to swim. She'd wanted him to teach Jacci too, but he said she was too young at only two. That Irena would have to teach her when she was older.

He had been surprised when she asked him to teach her. "Why do you want to swim?" he'd asked. It wasn't something women did.

"I am a maid on a steamboat. Steamboats sink or catch fire. I intend to have a way to escape with Jacci."

She was glad he didn't point out that her small cabin was deep in the steamboat where she'd have little chance of escape if either of those things happened. She wanted to believe it possible, but only if she could swim.

Irena smiled at the memory of the swimming lessons as she lingered in this between-sleep-and-waking time or perhaps life and death. It was one of her best times with Kelly. They had been few enough. Not that Kelly wasn't kind, even affectionate, but just never there. He was always chasing after the next big pot he'd win at the gambling tables on this or that steamboat while she stayed steady on the *Mary Ellen*.

He would have taken her with him had she insisted. While they might not have a real marriage, he didn't mind putting up a believable front. But Jacci needed steady. It wasn't uncommon for the river to separate a man from his family, even when there was nothing pretend about the ties.

Kelly was handsome, with wavy hair more blond than brown and light blue eyes that flashed like sunlight off river water when he smiled. They had found a preacher to marry them in a little country town along the river. Dove Creek. Before Jacci was born. It had to be.

She pushed that thought aside and let the floating feeling take her back to Kelly holding her up in the water, showing her how to move her arms and legs. When he moved his arms out from under her and she began to sink, he would hold her up again until she finally began to understand what she needed to do to stay afloat. He had made her strip off her long skirt and swim in her bloomers. Told her should she ever need to jump into a river to do the same. Modesty was a bad reason to drown, he said.

She tried to remember how long it had been since she'd seen Kelly. Months now. In early spring, he'd come aboard the *Mary Ellen* and stayed through a few landings before another steamboat drew him away. That time he needed money. Sometimes, not as often, he gave her money, which she always saved for the next time he needed it. She could get by on her maid's pay.

She wished she could see him one more time. To thank him for being Jacci's father even if it was all pretend. It was glorious pretend. Maybe with all her playacting she was more like Tyrone than she'd ever thought.

Tyrone. That was his voice she heard. Calling her name. She swam on up toward the light. Not heaven. She knew that as soon as pain engulfed her. She hadn't died. Yet.

She tried to be glad. She was glad when she thought of Jacci. She pushed open her eyelids and moistened her dry lips. "Jacci."

Hands pushed her down when she tried to sit up. Gently. Tyrone's hands. His face loomed over her. "She's fine. Sleeping."

"Where?" Again she attempted to raise her head to see her.

"On a pallet across the room."

Irena sank back on the pillow. The bed was narrow. The room small. "Where are we?"

"In my room on the showboat."

"We're moving." She could feel the river under the boat.

"Yes. We untied before dawn. Thought it best, considering."

He looked tired as if he hadn't slept. She should thank him, but the words stuck in her throat. She'd best wait until he promised more than one night watching over her.

She tried to move again, and this time pain made her gasp. Before, with all her thoughts on Jacci, she'd been able to ignore the pain. She lay back, shut her eyes, and took tiny breaths. Even those hurt.

Tyrone didn't say anything, perhaps thinking she had gone back to sleep. The boat creaked and then a whistle sounded. She didn't know whether it was the showboat's whistle or a steamboat they were passing. Not the *Mary Ellen*. She knew the sound of its whistle. That was a relief.

She had no idea what time it was. Morning at least. Maybe later, according to how long she'd been floating in unconsciousness. Dim light filtered in through a tiny window high on the wall over the bed, but the candle lit on the bedside table was still needed. At last her ears picked up the sound she most wanted to hear. Jacci's even breathing in sleep.

Her hand felt heavy when she lifted it up to feel her middle. The knife was gone. Of course it was. They wouldn't have left it sticking out of her even if pulling it free killed her. Either way, a person couldn't live with a knife in her side. Bandages were under the shift that was all that covered her. That wasn't any matter. Tyrone was her father, whether he'd ever acted much like one or not.

"The doctor said it would be best if you stayed still for a spell," Tyrone said.

"Doctor? Where'd you find a doctor?" she said.

"One of the boys took off into town after him, but turned out he was already on his way down here. Seems somebody got shot over on the *Mary Ellen*."

"Did he die?"

"Can't say for sure. Did you want him to?"

Irena glanced at Tyrone and then back at the ceiling. "Why would I want that?"

"That's generally why a person shoots somebody."

"I didn't shoot anybody."

"So that wasn't his knife sticking in you?"

She could feel Tyrone staring at her, but she didn't look at him. "I was careless. Fell on the knife in one of the rooms I was cleaning."

Tyrone sighed. "I suppose that's as good a story as any."

"Did the doctor tell you how badly hurt the man was?" She had to know if he was dead.

"He wasn't dead when the doctor first saw him. He had them carry him back to his house before he came to see to you. Figured a lady should take precedence. The boy told him how you were bleeding. Gave young Kingston quite a scare. All that real blood and not the fake stuff in our plays."

"I'm sorry, but I didn't know what else to do. I had to think of Jacci."

"It's about her, isn't it?" Tyrone said.

She ignored his question and asked one of her own. "Did the doctor think I'd live?"

Tyrone hesitated too long before he answered. "Yes."

She looked at him then with as much of a smile as she could muster. "I thought you were a better actor than that. Tell me what he really said."

"I think you're the one acting, but all right." He moistened his lips. "He said as long as an infection didn't set in, you had a chance. That you were in the Lord's hands and I should pray."

"You were never much for praying. That was Mother."

"I've been doing some practicing. All night." He leaned over and took one of her hands in his. "I've never been much of a father to you, but I sincerely do not like seeing you lurk around death's door."

Her heart softened a bit toward him then. Enough to say the

thanks she needed to say. "Thank you, Tyrone. I'll aim to back away from that door if I can, but if I can't, will you promise to take care of Jacci?"

His hand went stiff in hers. "What about that man you married? Kelly whatever his name is."

"Kelly Reed." Irena shook her head a little. "You wouldn't wish a gambler's life on a little girl, would you?"

"I'm not sure a showman's life would be much better." He pulled his hand away. "What do I know about little girls?"

She just stared at him without saying anything. To his credit, he didn't turn his eyes away from her.

He did shut them for a long moment before he pulled in a deep breath. "I won't desert her. Even if I have to take a wife."

"Make sure she's a kindhearted one and not some actress without a brain to her head."

"How you talk. Actresses and actors alike are some of the finest people you'll ever come across and have no lack of brains or kindness." He glared at her. "Marelda has a heart of gold."

"Is she in line to be Mrs. Tyrone Chesser?"

"Oh no. Marelda is Dan Kingston's wife, the mother of three boys, along with mothering every person who sets foot on her boat, even an old codger like me. She wanted to sit with you through the night, but I insisted she go sleep and let me do my fatherly duty with you."

"That's kind of you."

"But you should tell me the truth."

He reached for her hand again, but she tucked it under the blanket covering her. "I haven't lied to you."

He sat back with a little snort of exasperation. "Your whole life has been a lie ever since you and Lisbeth came up with that plan years ago. I warned you then you'd live to regret weaving such a web of lies."

"We did what we had to for Jacci."

"There had to be a better way."

"No. We had no other choice." Not after Jason died, but she didn't say that aloud.

Her father had never known the whole story. Lisbeth thought it better that way. So many tragedies piled one on another. Would her death be yet one more? The pain burned inside her to make her believe that definitely possible.

She must have groaned because Tyrone's voice changed. "The doctor left a draught to help with the pain." He put his arm under her shoulders and lifted her enough to take a few sips of the bitter drink he held to her lips. Then he wiped her face with a cool cloth. "Rest, my daughter. Sometimes we have no choice but to play the roles we're given."

His caress was so gentle that tears spilled out of her eyes. "That's all I've ever done."

Chapter

3

IRENA TURNED HER FACE to the wall to hide her tears. She had done what she thought she had to do when Lisbeth came to her for help. Together they had come up with a desperate plan and one that held as much risk for Irena as for Lisbeth. Perhaps more, as it was turning out.

Of course, she had no idea what Lisbeth was enduring. Being married to Griffith Giles could not be easy. She hadn't wanted to marry him. She was in love with Jason Charles. If only he had known Jacci was on the way before Lisbeth's father sent him on a fool's errand to New Orleans. He intended to get him away from Lisbeth, but not soon enough as it turned out.

Still grieving over the sudden death of her mother, Lisbeth couldn't fight her father. He demanded she marry Griffith Giles, a local politician years older than her. Griffith had aspirations of importance and power in elected offices. Her father had plans to increase his fortune. A state senator in his pocket to push favorable bills through legislature would make that easier. Lisbeth Bridwell was key to both their plans. With

Coleman Bridwell's deep pockets and a beautiful wife by his side, Giles could begin his climb to higher offices.

Lisbeth might have found the courage to escape the net her father and Giles wanted to trap her in if not for tragedy striking when the boilers of the steamboat Jason was on exploded. Jason was one of the casualties. In a way, Lisbeth was as well.

She hid the fact that she was carrying Jason's baby for six months, blaming her vapors and ill health on the thought of marriage. She convinced her father she needed a few months to adjust to the idea of becoming Mrs. Griffith Giles. Away from both him and Griffith Giles.

She concocted an elaborate story of visiting a friend of her mother's in Boston as a way of dealing with her grief over her mother's death. Her mother had attended a finishing school there. Lisbeth demanded that neither her father nor Griffith contact her during this time.

There was no friend in New England. Lisbeth boarded a train to Boston, but she disembarked in Louisville, where she sent a message to Irena begging for help.

Irena had been working as a maid and cook's assistant on the *American Princess* steamboat for almost a year. Her mother had died of a lung ailment and Irena had no suitors. While she wasn't ugly, beauty eluded her. Worse than that, she had little patience with the rites of courtship. Her mother said she expected too much from the few who had come seeking her favor. Perhaps her mother was right or perhaps witnessing the glitter of Lisbeth's life made her think above her station.

But it seemed better to take a job on a steamboat to at least go places, whether she could enjoy those places or not. At least she would see them from a steamboat deck. If her mother had been alive to see her board the *American Princess* for the first time, she might have been distraught at the thought of Irena following her father to a life on the river. Perhaps she had inherited his wanderlust.

At any rate, when Irena got the message from Lisbeth, she couldn't refuse her friend. They weren't social equals. Irena's mother had been a seamstress for Lisbeth's mother. During fittings and times when Irena's mother worked on the dresses at the Bridwells' big house, Lisbeth and Irena had become unlikely friends.

"Please let me hide in your rooms until I have the baby," Lisbeth asked when Irena found her on the dock, as out of place as a hen attempting to float with ducks.

"I don't have rooms. Only a tiny room with a bed, a chest, and one chair." Irena couldn't imagine Lisbeth even visiting her in such a place. She was used to a four-poster bed with featherbeds she never had to fluff and a separate dressing room with mirrors. Servants built fires in her fireplace, carried water to her for washing, and took away the nighttime necessary pot. "You'll feel like you're in a prison cell."

"It will be less a prison than my house." Lisbeth's violet blue eyes were sad but without tears. Always Lisbeth had wept copious tears over things that seemed nothing to Irena. A broken necklace string that could be easily repaired. Curls that wouldn't hold in her black hair. A dress in a darker color than she had wanted. But now her sorrow went beyond tears.

When Irena hesitated to answer, for there was barely room for one in her maid's quarters, Lisbeth had gripped Irena's hands. "You are my only hope."

But there was no hope in her eyes or thought of the future except to hide away from her father until after the baby came.

A week went by and then another. Irena feared every day someone would discover she was hiding a passenger in her room and they would both be put off the boat. She smuggled food to Lisbeth, claiming the river air made her extra hungry. Sometimes she was reduced to surreptitiously snagging uneaten food from the plates she collected from the passengers' tables. Lisbeth had to eat. For the baby.

The baby. Lisbeth seemed to have walled off thought of actually having a baby in her arms soon. What then?

At the end of the third week, Irena sat down on the bed beside Lisbeth and asked that very question. They had to whisper or converse on paper. They couldn't be heard. Sometimes Irena sang to hide any extra noises, but now she whispered. "What do you intend to happen after the baby comes?"

Lisbeth's whole body seemed to droop as she mouthed the words so softly that Irena had to lean in to hear her. "I will go back home and marry Griffith Giles."

"With the baby?"

Lisbeth jerked back from Irena, her eyes wide, as she shook her head. "I can't take the baby."

Irena continued to look at her without blinking. "Then are you going to leave him on a church's step in a village we pass?"

"What?" Lisbeth's hand went to her swollen abdomen. "I couldn't do that. Not to Jason's son."

They had spoken of the child only as a boy, as though they knew what couldn't be known. Irena wanted to back away and not push truth at Lisbeth. She had suffered so much already, but some things couldn't be hidden forever. Babies were one of those things.

A silence filled with more than words wrapped around them for what seemed like minutes. At last, Lisbeth moistened her lips and spoke. "I thought . . ." She hesitated before she went on. "I thought you would keep him."

Irena pushed away from Lisbeth and stood. She paced back and forth in the small room. She should have expected as much, but how could Lisbeth ask her to destroy her life?

She didn't look at Lisbeth. She didn't want to see her begging eyes.

Finally, Lisbeth whispered, "You love him. I know you do."

Truth was in those words. She had put her hand on Lisbeth's tummy and felt the baby kick. She had laid her ear against

Lisbeth's skin to try to hear the tiny heartbeat. But she couldn't claim the baby as her own.

She stopped in front of Lisbeth. "No one would believe he is mine." She turned sideways and smoothed down her skirt. "I'm slim as a post."

"Some women don't show early. They keep pulling up their waistbands to let their skirts hide being in the family way." Lisbeth's whisper was weak, as though she knew her words were foolish.

"That may be, but I'm not married."

"Nor am I," Lisbeth said.

"But you will be."

"Griffith would never accept Jason's child as his own. He'd find a way to be rid of him." Lisbeth shuddered and again held her belly as though to shield her baby from that danger.

Irena shut her eyes and pulled in a long breath. What Lisbeth said might be true, but how could she expect Irena to throw away any chance of having a respectable life? A fallen woman with not so much as a whisper of a serious suitor. Even if she claimed being widowed, how could she care for a baby and keep working?

She opened her eyes and looked straight at Lisbeth. "It's impossible."

"Don't say that." Lisbeth reached toward her. "I can send you money."

Irena shunned her touch. "Money cannot solve every problem."

"But it can help. Please, Irena." She stood up and captured Irena's hands. "We have time. We can pray for an answer."

Irena didn't pull away from her. She knew her thoughts were unkind, but she let them become words anyway. "Maybe you should have said those prayers before you got with child."

"Yes." Lisbeth stepped back as though Irena had slapped her. "But please don't judge me. When you fall in love, you'll understand how such feelings can attack you and cause you to stumble."

Irena fought against feeling sorry for her. "An unwed mother with a child has little chance of finding love."

"And I will never know it again. I don't regret the love that made this baby. And while I will be made to pay for my sin, the baby I carry is innocent of any wrongdoing."

"Yet he will pay the same as you."

"Not if you will be his mother."

"How can I protect him from the things people will say if he has no father?"

"I don't know, but I believe the Lord will not punish him for my wrong. I believe if we pray, an answer will come."

What could she do but bend her will to Lisbeth's and hope the Lord would bend his ear down to hear their prayers?

Perhaps he had if she could believe he would choose a gambler to achieve his purposes. To give them reason to hope, but hope did come in with Kelly.

The crashing notes of the showboat's calliope pulled Irena back to the present and her pain. The bitter draught her father had given her earlier must have worn off. She turned her head to look at the table. The glass was there, but her body screamed at her when she attempted to reach for it. Better to lie still and concentrate on breathing.

Irena was alone. She knew without looking that Jacci wasn't in the room, but she looked anyway. The pallet on the other side of the room had been folded up and pushed into a corner. The door, partially open, allowed sunlight to sneak through the boat and filter fingers of light into the room. The boat was docked. It rocked gently under her as the river rolled past.

The sound of horns and drums let her know everyone on board was marching into whatever village might be nearby. The showboats always paraded into the towns to draw out comers for their evening show. Surely Tyrone hadn't taken Jacci with them, but perhaps it was best if he had. Irena had no way to protect her. *Dear Lord, watch over her.*

The parade to the town or village wouldn't last long. An hour perhaps. Then someone would be back to check on her, to make sure Jacci was all right if she wasn't with Tyrone and was instead watching from the top deck as she did so often on the *Mary Ellen*. Irena hadn't been able to stay with her all the time then either, but others of the crew had kept an eye out for the child to be sure she was safe.

They might not have escaped the night before if not for one of the cabin boys telling her someone had been asking about a dark-haired child of five. She had no idea how the man had found her or why anyone even would want to all these years later. The child was no danger to them now. To Griffith Giles. She had never been a danger to him. Only to Lisbeth if he found out, and they had been very careful not to let him find out.

The only people on earth who knew besides Lisbeth and herself were Tyrone and Kelly. Tyrone might have thought Irena foolish to play such a part in Lisbeth's tragedy, but he would have never betrayed her. He would act out the play with them whether he liked the script or not.

That left Kelly.

She didn't want to believe it of Kelly either, but if there was a gambling debt. If he had one drink too many. If he didn't believe there was any physical danger, only danger to reputations and fortunes. He had always been something of that mind from the beginning.

At the time, when they were all together, Lisbeth told him how mistaken he was. She tried to impress on him how upset Griffith would be should he discover his wife had a child before they married. Before she was wed to anyone. A child out of wedlock was something to be hidden. Not only for the mother's reputation but also for the child. If he wouldn't think of her, he had to think of the baby.

The baby was always Lisbeth's first thought. That was why she had invited Kelly into their room that night. Irena's heart had almost stopped when she opened her door after finishing her cleaning duties to find him there.

Irena shut her eyes and was back in that room, staring at him while barely able to keep standing on her trembling legs. They had surely been found out and would be put off at the next landing.

The man, decked out in a fancy suit, was so handsome in a rakish way that the sight of him might have stolen Irena's breath had her fright not already done so. Then anger rose up in her to burn away her fear. He wasn't a large man, but he filled her small room to overflowing. There was no way he and Lisbeth could have spoken to one another or moved around without being heard.

Lisbeth smiled, held a palm toward Irena, and whispered, "I will explain."

Irena didn't say a word but grabbed the pad of paper they often used to converse. Her hands were shaking so that she splattered a bit of the ink. She blotted it away and printed out the words. *Why did you let him in?*

Lisbeth took the pad and pen. Her hands were steady as she wrote. *He's here to help.*

Irena looked from the words to the man sitting in their one chair as if he owned the room. Little wonder that Lisbeth was in the situation she was if she was willing to entertain men in her bedchamber. Not her bedchamber. Irena's. She would be the one to pay for Lisbeth's foolishness.

Lisbeth stood up to take Irena's hands. She pulled her over to sit beside her on the bed. "Don't be angry, Irena," she whispered into her ear. "You will like Kelly."

Irena threw another look at the man. She knew his type, one of those who rode the steamboats not to get from here to there, but to gamble along the way, fleecing unwary passengers with his skill in cards. Such men were easy to pick out. Some were older than this man, but they all had an air about them. She had seen plenty like him on the steamboats, but never expected one to invade her room.

She wished him gone, but then what if someone saw him leaving her room? Could she come up with a convincing story?

"He's a gambler," Irena hissed.

"Trust me." Lisbeth clutched Irena's hand. "He's the answer to our prayers."

Chapter

4

Jacci hit the tambourine against her leg as she marched along beside her grandfather. He had awakened her with a shushing sound that made Jacci's heart leap in her chest because it was so like her mother waking her the night before. But Tyrone merely didn't want her to disturb Mama, who was sleeping again.

They tiptoed out of the room into a breezeway, where Marelda shrugged as she held out a pair of pants and a boy's shirt. "I only have boys. No girls, but I'll make you a dress. Until then you can pretend you're a boy in a play."

After Jacci got dressed, Marelda combed the tangles out of Jacci's long black hair and said, "A little girl shouldn't call her grandfather by his given name. It's not proper."

"Tyrone doesn't care," Jacci said.

"Well, he should, and whether he does or not, I do. Here on my boat you can call him Grandpa Tyrone."

"Grandpa?" Tyrone flinched as though the sound of the word hurt his ears. He let out an exaggerated sigh. "That sounds more than dreadful, but Queen Marelda is the boss on this floating palace. If she says it, then it must be done."

"I'm glad you understand that, Duke." Marelda pointed the comb at him. "And don't you forget it." But she was smiling before she started gently working out more tangles in Jacci's hair.

"Duke?" When Jacci twisted to look behind her, the comb yanked at her hair. But she needed to see if that man had found her.

"Easy, child," Marelda said as Tyrone chuckled. "Your grandfather played a duke in so many of our dramas that he earned the name."

"Oh. Then I could call him Duke too," Jacci said.

"Now, there's a name I could live with. Anything without 'grandpa' attached."

"Duke. I guess that will work." Marelda shrugged and went back to work on Jacci's hair. "But Grandpa or Grampus would have been better."

"Grampus? Surely you jest, my queen."

Marelda was nice. The night before, she washed Jacci as if she was covered with something as ordinary as mud instead of her mother's blood. The woman hadn't asked questions, just murmured about the curls in Jacci's black hair and how she'd feel better in the morning. After she gently helped Jacci put on a soft shift, she tucked her into a small bed. Jacci pulled the cover up to her chin and acted like she was asleep.

The woman stood by the bed a moment before she moved away. The door opened and closed. Jacci opened her eyes and looked around. She was alone. She slid out from under the covers and tiptoed out of the room.

She didn't know where they had taken her mother, but she would find her. The night didn't scare her. At least not much. She was more afraid of shutting her eyes and seeing the man's face after she had pulled the trigger on the gun. She was glad she'd thrown it in the river.

The half moon gave enough light for her to find the stairs. She knew she had to go down at least one flight. She scooted back into the shadows when she saw someone coming toward her. She was good at staying out of sight. She did it all the time while exploring on their steamboat.

When she came out on the forward deck, she shivered when she saw the *Mary Ellen* beside the showboat. The man might be on the deck where they left him. He might be staring across at her, seeing her there in the moonlight. Her breath came fast as she ran to get somewhere out of his sight.

The first door she came to led back into the big room with the stage where all the people were earlier. With no windows and the lanterns gone, the dark was thick around her. She stood still and tried not to be afraid. She slipped out on the *Mary Ellen* in the dark all the time to see the stars. But what if the man followed them to the showboat and was waiting for her?

Voices drifted back to her from somewhere ahead. Not the man's voice. Perhaps Tyrone. He'd know where her mother was. She scooted her feet forward a step, then two, and banged into something. A seat. She remembered running past rows of seats when she went to find her grandfather. Feeling her way from one row to another, she moved forward.

When she got to the first row of seats, she hesitated. She couldn't remember how she'd climbed up on the stage earlier. There were lights then. She no longer heard the voices now. A few rays of light came from somewhere beyond the stage, but it wasn't bright enough to show her how to get there.

She stumbled down a few steps into a place with more chairs, but they were scattered around. Not in rows. When she bumped into something that fell with a clank, her heart bounded up into her throat. She didn't know why she was afraid to make any noise, but she was.

She blinked and could see a little better in the near darkness.

The chairs all had some kind of instruments on them or beside them. Of course. The showboat had a band. She picked up the horn and put it on one of the chairs, then retraced her steps to climb out of the band's sunken place.

The people were talking again, the voices louder. This time she was certain one of them was Tyrone. She slid her hand along the edge of the stage and finally found steps. As she started to climb up them, someone grasped her shoulder. She shrieked and kicked to get away.

"Easy, kid." A man's voice, but he didn't sound like the man on the *Mary Ellen.* "Where do you think you're going?"

"To see my mother." Jacci stopped fighting. She made her voice sound as strong as she could, the way she'd heard her mother talk to people when they weren't doing what she thought they should.

Then Marelda was there with a lantern, kneeling down in front of her. "You should have stayed in bed."

"I have to be with Mama."

Marelda closed her eyes as if she needed to summon some extra patience. Jacci's mama did that sometimes too.

"I suppose you do." Marelda opened her eyes and looked up at the man holding Jacci. "It's all right, Dan. I'll take care of her."

"Sorry, kid." The man turned loose of Jacci and patted the top of her head. "Didn't aim to scare you. I guess it's little wonder you're jumpy. Did you see whoever did this to your mother?"

"Not now, Dan." Marelda spoke up before Jacci could answer.

"It might be good to know," the man said.

"Her mother told Gabe it was an accident."

"Even Gabe didn't believe that." The man made a noise of disbelief. "We should send for the local sheriff."

The man sounded so angry that trembles shook through

Jacci as she looked from him to Marelda. Why would her mother call the man hurting her an accident?

"Duke asked us not to," Marelda said.

"When did you ever listen to him?"

She didn't answer the man's question. "He's the same as family, he's been with us so long."

"Family? We didn't even know he had a daughter."

"Yes, but now we do. Let it be." Marelda pulled Jacci into a hug. "You're scaring the child."

"We don't want to be crossways with the law."

"We're on the river. We'll abide by river law."

"What is that?"

"Taking care of our people. Doing what we do best. Putting on shows." She leaned back and ran her hand softly over Jacci's face. "Taking care of this child. Talk to Duke. He'll tell you moving on is best for her."

Jacci kept her head down, but she could almost feel the man staring at her. Finally, he breathed out a heavy sigh. "All right, Marelda, but it could mean trouble lying in wait for us on down the river."

"If so, we'll do our best to steer around it."

Jacci waited until the man's footsteps went away before she looked at Marelda. "Am I trouble?"

"Don't worry, baby. We'll work things out." Marelda kissed her cheek.

"Please, can I see Mama?"

"When the doctor leaves, but she might not know you're there. She's in a sleep."

In a sleep. That sounded different than sleeping. Jacci let the woman pull her into her lap as she sat down right on the floor and leaned back against the wall. There were other doors around them, all closed.

Marelda must have noticed her looking at them. "The actors' dressing rooms."

"Are they in them?"

"Not now. They went down to eat something and talk about the play."

"And about Mama and me?"

"Maybe. At least those who saw you."

"Is Mama going to be all right?"

Marelda looked at her without saying anything for a long moment before she answered. "We'll have to see what the doctor says."

But they didn't tell her what the doctor said after he left. Marelda handed her over to Tyrone. He took her hand in his and tried to smile at her, but his lips trembled too much. So it wasn't a real smile. He always smiled when he came to visit them. Sometimes her mother didn't smile back at him but looked mad instead. That never kept Tyrone from laughing and telling them stories about being on the river.

Marelda piled some blankets and a pillow on the floor across from where her mother was in a sleep. Not sleeping. In a sleep. Jacci knew that was different. The trembles started up in her again when she looked at her.

Marelda gave her another hug and said she could go back with her to the other bed, but Jacci shook her head. She was scared when she looked at her mother lying so still, but she had to be there in case she woke up. She curled up on the pallet and tried to hear her mother breathing, but the creak of the boat shifting in the river was too loud.

Tyrone leaned down and tucked a blanket around her. "Sleep, child. I'll keep watch over your mother."

Jacci's eyes did feel heavy. "Promise to tell me if she wakes up."

"That might not be for a while."

He didn't wake her the way she asked. Instead, the sound of him and Mama talking woke her. She started to get up, but something about their voices stopped her. Instead, she lay very still to pretend to sleep, the way she had earlier in Marelda's room.

She almost got up when her mother asked about her, but then she was asking about the man. The man Jacci shot. His face was right there in the dark in front of her again, freezing Jacci in place. She had to shoot him. He hurt her mother. But why did her mother lie about what happened? That must mean it was something she should keep secret. She and her mother sometimes played keeping secrets. Mama said other people didn't need to know everything about them. Even Tyrone.

But then Tyrone saying it was about her sounded like one of those secrets that maybe he did know and Jacci didn't. What did that mean and why hadn't her mother answered him?

Fear clutched her heart when Tyrone talked about death's door. Her mother couldn't die. Tears slid out of her eyes and down her cheeks, but she didn't move to wipe them away.

She was glad when they started talking about Kelly. She loved Kelly. Whenever he showed up on their steamboat, even Mama smiled a lot, although she always warned Jacci not to expect him to stay. He was like Tyrone, coming and then gone again.

But who was Lisbeth? She'd heard Kelly and her mother talking about her once, but Mama waved away her question asking who she was, just saying she was a girl she used to know. But Kelly had sounded so serious talking about her that day, and Mama had cried. Lisbeth must be another secret, but not one Mama would tell Jacci.

Now as she marched along beside Tyrone in the parade, Jacci had the secret of pretending to be a boy. She hit the tambourine against her leg to make it jingle in time with the horns and drums. Marelda had wound Jacci's hair up on top of her head and stuffed a hat down over it.

"Best to look all the way like a little boy," she had said. "Although I've never seen a boy as pretty as you. If Duke can teach you to sing or dance, the people will love you."

"I don't know about that, Marelda," Duke said. "Her mother won't want her in show business."

"I can't imagine whyever not." Marelda stood back, looked at Jacci, and nodded as though satisfied with what she saw. "Not a better business to be in, going around making people happy by putting on a show for them."

"You don't have to convince me," Duke said. "Only Irena."

"Give me time. I'll have her doing a mother-daughter song act."

"I hope so." A worried look settled on Duke's face.

Marelda's smile faded as she put a hand on his arm. "I'm praying. Captain Dan's praying. Aunt Tildy is praying in the kitchen and you know she can pray a storm off the river. I'm thinking even you might be praying."

"I've been getting some practice at it." Duke looked down at Jacci. "You best be adding some prayers to ours, Princess. I'm sure your mother taught you about praying."

"You'll have to pray while we're marching. Time to get our parade underway," Marelda said. "I'll go up top and hit some keys on the calliope to let the townsfolk know we're on the way. Hunt up a tambourine for your girl there, Duke."

So, Jacci tried to pray as she hurried alongside Duke. He was blowing a trumpet. The man who had helped her and Mama last night played a drum. Not a man after all. Just a tall boy with a big smile on his face while he beat on his drum like that was the most fun he'd had all summer. He gave Jacci a funny look, as if he had no idea who she was and that maybe they'd picked up a new boy somewhere along the river.

That made Jacci want to giggle. She bit her lip and swallowed hard. She was supposed to be praying, not laughing. But how could she pray with all this music around her and none of it sounding anything like church music? She should have stayed back on the showboat with her mama. Then maybe she could have prayed.

She knew some prayers. One her mama taught her to say at night. *Watch over me while I sleep and thank you for the blessings you let me keep.* But that wasn't right for now, although she did want the Lord to let her keep her mama.

Then Mama was helping her memorize the Lord's Prayer. If only she could remember it now, she might be able to sing the words in her head along with the music, even if it didn't sound very prayerlike.

She sighed and let her steps lag. Duke looked back at her and motioned with his horn for her to keep marching. The boy with the drum stepped over close to her and said, "Gotta keep up, kid. Can't stop the music."

She hurried to catch up with Duke, who gave her a nod without missing a note. With a shake of the tambourine, she decided the Lord might not mind a little jingling along with a prayer.

"Our Father, who art in heaven," she whispered the words. Nobody could hear what she was saying. Not with all the noise of the parade. But her mother said the Lord heard every prayer no matter what else was happening.

She couldn't remember the next line, so she skipped ahead. "Give us our daily bread. And make Mama better so she can eat it with me. And forgive me for shooting that man." Maybe that would make the man's face stop jumping up in her head whenever she shut her eyes.

She looked around at the drummer. He was behind her now, but he didn't look like her words had drifted back to him. That was good. Some prayers weren't for others to hear. She said the next line a little louder. "For thine is the power forever."

Other words were supposed to be in there, but all she could remember was power. Power was what she wanted. The Lord's power to make her mother better. She finished with the blessings the way her mother always told her to.

"Bless Mama. Bless Duke. That's Tyrone, if you didn't know.

I just started calling him Duke. Bless the captain of the boat and help him guide it right. Bless the drummer boy behind me. Bless the people watching our parade. Bless Marelda. Bless Mama's friend, Lisbeth. Bless Daddy Kelly."

She hit the tambourine against the heel of her hand while she tried to think if there was anyone she'd forgotten to ask blessings on. It helped to say those other names. Even Lisbeth's. Whether she knew who she was or not, she could need blessing.

Mama would say everybody needed blessing. So maybe Jacci should have asked for blessings for herself too. She thought about the man on the *Mary Ellen*, but she skittered her thoughts away from him and said, "Amen."

After she went a few more steps, she added more to the prayer even though she had already said amen. "Please let Daddy Kelly come find us."

Daddy Kelly didn't come find them very often, but whenever he did, her mama always did a lot of smiling. Jacci needed to see her mama smile. She might smile if she saw Jacci dressed up like a boy. As soon as she got back to the showboat, she would run and show Mama her boy clothes. She'd even leave on the hat. Maybe her mama would be awake. She needed her to be awake. It scared Jacci too much to look at her mama so still and white.

Chapter

5

"WE'RE ALL GAMBLERS in this game of life," Lisbeth had told her when Irena had accused Kelly of being a gambler.

How right she surely was, Irena thought now as she stared up at the ceiling over the bed in her father's showboat room. If only she could get up, but even the slightest movement sent pain ripping through her. She needed a chair to grab hold of to pull herself up. None were in reach. She tried to draw in a deep breath, but the pain made her take tiny sips of air instead.

She focused on the sun streaks finding their way into the room through the window and the door. A reason to rejoice. She was still alive. But for how long? A chill shook her even though her face felt hot to the touch. Not a good sign. Her mother had done the same before she died. But she had lingered awhile with Irena's care. Perhaps Irena could linger too and have more time with Jacci.

What should she tell her if that time was short? Maybe nothing. Maybe all the secrets should stay unknown. She had sometimes wondered aloud to Kelly what would be best to tell her when she was older, but Kelly claimed ignorance could be bliss.

"Why mess up the kid's head?" he said. "She has you for a mother and me for a sometimes daddy."

Sometimes was right, but it had worked the way he and Lisbeth said it could.

Even now when she thought about it, Irena was still amazed Lisbeth had talked Kelly into such a crazy plan. A marriage. Of convenience. In name only.

Irena remembered everything about that night, from the way the lantern light had thrown shadows on the wall to how Kelly watched them with a face she couldn't read. A gambler's poker face.

"Listen to me." Lisbeth gripped Irena's hands. "Kelly is the Lord's answer."

"You think the Lord would send us a gambler?" As soon as Irena whispered the words, she hoped this man named Kelly hadn't heard them.

Nobody was outside the Lord's love, but that didn't mean people shouldn't try to live right. And what about Irena? Lying every day, continually fretting she was going to get caught in her web of deceit. She stared at Lisbeth, knowing she was ready to wrap more threads of lies around them.

But Kelly did hear her. He took the pad and wrote swiftly. He ripped the page out of the book they used and leaned forward in the chair to hand it to Irena. He was that close, but the room was too small for him to separate more from them.

He had dipped the pen into the inkpot more than once and written in sweeping cursive. He obviously had no idea of thrift of ink or paper.

The Lord loves maids. The Lord loves fallen women. The Lord loves babies. Might not the Lord have a bit of love left over for a lowly gambler?

The words angered her and shamed her at the same time. She was very tired. The day had been long, the work hard, and the constant fear of being found out taxing. She wanted to go out of the room and walk on the deck to let the river breeze calm her. Lisbeth held on to her as if guessing her desire to escape whatever plan they had made.

"Kelly has agreed to marry you."

Lisbeth's words slammed into her. "Agreed?" Irena forgot to whisper as she choked out the word. She looked at the man who had given up his poker face for a confident smile as though he held all the aces. She turned back to Lisbeth and lowered her voice. "I don't remember asking."

"Of course, you didn't. I did." Lisbeth shook Irena's hands.

"Why would he agree to such a plan?" Her heart thundered in her chest and her breath was shaky. How could Lisbeth expect this of her?

"He knew Jason." Lisbeth's eyes filled with tears as they did every time she mentioned Jason. "He was with him on the steamboat when . . ." She turned loose of Irena's hand to jerk a handkerchief from her sleeve to catch the overflow of tears.

The man scooted his chair even closer to the bed, scraping it on the wooden floor. Not a sound to be a concern if overheard. A woman alone in a room might move a chair.

He at least understood the need for quiet. He didn't exactly whisper but spoke in a low mumble that would surely blend in with the sound of the paddle wheel churning through the river.

"Jason and I grew up in the same little town in western Kentucky. He went one way with gambling on horse trading which I take it is how he met and fell in love with the beautiful Lisbeth. I, on the other hand, went a different way, gambling on my ability to size up the other men playing cards around a table."

When Irena started to say something, he held up a hand to stop her. "Approve or not, I never cheat. I'm an honest gambler if there is such a thing."

Irena could feel her face stiffening into disapproval and rubbed her hands over her cheeks. She needed to close her ears to Lisbeth's insane plans and find a way to kick him out of her room without anyone seeing him.

But she hadn't kicked him out. The three of them had planned late into the night. Or rather Irena had listened to the plans Lisbeth had already made.

"I can't marry a stranger." Irena spoke those words often, but it was as if they disappeared like mist burned off the river by the sun.

They turned the lantern very low to save the oil. She studied this man willing to marry her without even the exchange of names. She didn't know how Lisbeth had arranged it, how she had found him or he had found her. Lisbeth claimed it was more than coincidence. That instead Kelly was the Lord's providence.

It was true that at times when the room closed in on Lisbeth, she dressed in Irena's clothes, covered her black hair, and went out on the deck for air. Always in the gray of dawn but never for long and with the promise of speaking to no one. She only stayed the few minutes a maid might have to spare before her workday started. She could have chanced upon Kelly. Gamblers played the night away and then slept through the day.

"No one will ever believe a man like him would marry someone like me." Irena had kept her eyes away from him. He was a dandy. A very handsome dandy. She was a maid. A very plain maid.

"My dear lady," he had said when he overheard her whispers to Lisbeth. "I am an honorable man, even if a gambler. If I get a lady, no matter her station in life, in the family way, I will take responsibility and do what I can to shield an innocent babe from the barbs that might come his way without a known father."

"This is crazy." Irena stared straight at him then.

"I will not argue that truth, but for my friend Jason and this woman he loved so truly and for his child, I will embrace this somewhat, as you say, crazy plan."

"Embrace? And will you expect to embrace me?" Irena asked.

He seemed to try not to smile and failed. "Not unless the embrace is desired, my lady. But a kiss when we are pronounced man and wife might be necessary to convince the officiate of the truth of our binding vows."

Binding. How could she do this? How could she not? Lisbeth would leave the baby with her, and whether the child was hers or not, others would think it so. She would be the fallen woman. The captain would not let her continue to work on his boat. Then what would she do?

That too Lisbeth had figured out. "The next landing is Dove Creek. Kelly says there is a small village there. You and Kelly will do what is necessary to marry. Then I will become Irena and you will be my sister." She hesitated a moment before going on. "Not Lisbeth. You can pick a name."

Irena choked back a laugh for fear of falling into hysterics. "I have a name."

"And you will have it back in a few months."

Kelly spoke up. "Violet. You look like you could be a Violet."

"That's a flower," Irena said.

"It is," he said. "A delicate one in appearance, but its sweet flowers hide how tough it really is. Frosts freeze it. Cows eat it. People walk on it. No matter what comes its way, that little purple bloom pops up again to decorate the grass every spring."

"What do you know about flowers?" She kept her voice cross. She wasn't about to let him know how his words made her want to smile.

He did smile. "I haven't always been a riverboat gambler." He raised his eyebrows at her. "And I doubt you've always been a riverboat maid."

"Or someone floating on a runaway raft of disaster."

"It won't be a disaster," Lisbeth whispered, gripping Irena's hands again. "It will be good and I am glad to have you for a sister, Violet."

With a whirlpool of misgivings, she stepped onto that raft being swept down the river in the flood of Lisbeth's plans.

She didn't know how Lisbeth arranged it all. Kelly helped, but Irena walked around in a daze, simply doing whatever they said she must. Kelly found a house to rent in Dove Creek. Not in the town but out in the country. Irena quit her maid job, claiming a sister in the family way needed her help. That much was true enough, except at times Irena felt she was more in need of help than Lisbeth.

Kelly and Lisbeth began calling her Violet right away, and Irena felt unmoored with the loss of her name. At the same time, with Lisbeth's encouragement, she often caressed the baby in Lisbeth's womb and began to feel as if she really was the one expecting the baby and not only through their pretense of changing names.

The small house had no conveniences. Water had to be drawn from a well. When cold weather came, fires would have to be kept in fireplaces. They did, at least, have a small cooking stove in the kitchen. Kelly reverted to his country upbringing and split wood they bought from a neighbor. Even more amazing, he stayed with them as they awaited the birth of the baby, except for a couple of times when the river call was too great. Even then he was gone only a week before coming back to act the part of a faithful husband eagerly awaiting the birth of his first child. Their marriage wasn't an act. She was legally the wife of Kelly Reed whether they shared a marriage bed or not. He appeared to delight in calling her Mrs. Reed with a teasing smile. Lisbeth laughed whenever she heard him.

Irena didn't laugh. She was too intent on hiding the truth that she wished being called Mrs. Reed wasn't a laughing matter. In spite of her best efforts, she not only felt like a mother awaiting her first child, she could not stop falling for the man acting the role of the baby's father. Her heart jerked sideways every time he smiled at her.

At the same time, she had no illusions his pretend marriage feelings would ever change to anything real.

The baby came in August. It was good they were in the house then. They could have never hidden the sounds of birth in her maid's room on the riverboat. Lisbeth had a hard labor. Irena wanted to send for a doctor. She had no idea how to deliver a baby. She was an only child, and Lisbeth had been kept away when her brother was born.

Lisbeth refused the thought of a doctor. She said they should wait for nature to take its course, but sometimes nature claimed both a mother and child when birthing was not easy.

"Maybe it will be best if I do die." Lisbeth's voice had been weak.

"But think of the baby." Irena was ready to go to war for the baby.

Kelly saved them once again. He found a black woman who knew about birthing and cared nothing about who was the mother and who was the wife. How he found her, Irena never knew. It didn't matter. Perhaps it was again the Lord's providence.

Norah was an angel of mercy. She eased a squalling baby girl into the world. She kept Lisbeth from fading away. In a way she smacked both of them into life. She paid no attention to Lisbeth's tears or how she didn't want to look at the baby.

"You is gonna live for this little chile," she said and put the baby to Lisbeth's breast.

Lisbeth stroked the baby's cheek with a trembling finger as she continued to weep. "I didn't know it would be so hard."

"Birthing ain't no easy thing," Norah said.

But Irena knew that wasn't the hard part Lisbeth was feeling. She refused to give the baby a name. "Better she doesn't have a name for me to carry in my heart," Lisbeth said whenever Irena asked what she wanted to name the baby. "You can name her when I'm gone. Then she'll be yours."

"But that will be weeks. Maybe months. You can't go back until you've recovered."

"I'll never recover," Lisbeth said. "I may lose the signs of birth on my body, but never on my heart."

"Then stay with me. We'll raise her together," Irena said.

Lisbeth had looked around at the cabin with walls covered in newsprint and rough-sawed boards for a floor. Irena knew she was thinking of her home. The big house. The flowing dresses. The servants to take care of her every need. "And how would we survive, Violet?"

She never stopped calling Irena Violet. Even after the baby came and Irena asked her to.

"I could take in sewing. Kelly would help."

They were in the kitchen. Lisbeth sat in a hickory-bottomed chair by the table as she nursed the baby. Irena was at the stove cooking the greens Norah claimed would build back Lisbeth's strength.

Lisbeth was silent so long, Irena looked around at her. She was studying the baby she held against her breast. "I keep wanting to see Jason when I look at her, but I don't."

"She looks like you," Irena said.

"How can a baby look like anyone?"

"I don't know, but she is going to be you made over."

"Oh, I hope not. Not for her sake."

"But you're beautiful. Why wouldn't you want her to have that same beauty?" Irena went over to stand beside Lisbeth and watch the baby nurse.

"So many ways to be beautiful," Lisbeth murmured. "You like that violet Kelly named you for. Norah with her kindness in helping us. Kelly with his good humor. My pretty face, the least important way of all."

"Your beauty is more than skin deep."

"I wish I could believe that." The baby pulled away from Lisbeth's breast and blew a milk bubble. "Take her. My arms are trembling."

Irena wiped her hands on her apron and lifted the baby away from Lisbeth. She put her to her shoulder and patted her back to make her burp.

"I can't stay here with you. With her," Lisbeth said. "We'd have no money. Only if I go back will I have a way to send money for her."

"Kelly—"

Lisbeth held up a hand to stop her. "We couldn't depend on Kelly."

"But he loves her."

"Yes, I think he does. As much as he is able. But you named the problem when we started down this road together. He's a gambler. Not a father. Not a husband. You know that is true even if you do wish it different." She shook her head a little as she watched Irena hold the baby. "I'm sorry I have done this to you."

"I'm not. Not now."

"I know. She's your baby. Forever yours."

"She will always be yours too." Irena held the baby down to touch Lisbeth's cheek.

"Not in ways that will ever matter to her." She turned away from the baby's touch.

Irena lifted the baby back up. "I can tell her about you. The sacrifices you made. The love you carry for her in your heart."

"No." The word came out harsh. Lisbeth took a breath. "I'm sorry, but you must never do that. It might not be safe for her. Griffith . . ." She looked away for a moment before she moistened her lips and went on. "You don't know men like my father and Griffith. You must promise to keep my secret even from her. Let her be truly yours and only yours."

Lisbeth's eyes stayed dry, but Irena's filled with tears for her friend. "Then at least give her a name."

"That's for you to do too."

And so the baby had no name until Kelly came back from one of his river trips. He had stayed for the birth and a week more, but then a steamboat whistle had called him back to the river.

He took the baby as soon as he came into the house. "What did you name her?"

"We haven't," Irena said when Lisbeth stayed silent.

"She's three weeks old. Yesterday. She needs a proper name. Baby Reed won't do for our daughter." He winked at Irena and then looked at Lisbeth. "You have surely thought of names."

Lisbeth merely stared back at him without speaking. Finally, Irena said, "Lisbeth says I must name her and I say she should."

"Women. Who can understand them?" Kelly held the baby out to look at her. "Well, if you won't name her, I will. How about Violet after her mother?"

"No." Irena and Lisbeth spoke the word at the same moment.

Kelly frowned at them and then talked to the baby. "I don't know what's the matter with them, daughter mine. Violet is a wonderful name. But all right. We'll try something else." He was quiet a moment as he studied the baby who seemed to be studying him in return. "If you don't like a flower name, how about the name of a jewel. This little girl is definitely a jewel. Hmm. How about Ruby?"

Even before Irena and Lisbeth spoke against that name, he went on. "No, that doesn't sound right. You need something more, my little one. A rare jewel. I know. Jacinth. Jacinth Reed. That's it. Jacci for short. The most beautiful baby girl ever born."

At that moment, Jacci became Irena's child by a man she had never kissed, if one didn't count the brush of lips they'd shared after the preacher pronounced them man and wife. Lies layered on lies, but somehow those lies held them all together.

The memory of those early years with Jacci in the bare-bones little cabin comforted Irena now. They were the happiest of her life. Only later after Lisbeth quit sending money—or if she did, Kelly gambled it away instead of bringing it to Irena—did she go back on the river to once more work on the riverboats.

While she didn't know what danger Lisbeth feared for her daughter, somehow Irena felt safer with the river running under her feet. Jacci had learned to love the river as much, and sometimes Kelly found them on the *Mary Ellen*.

But the danger, known or unknown, had caught up with them. Would it have come to violence if she hadn't pulled out the gun Kelly had given her? But the man threatened to take Jacci. For what reason she did not wish to imagine. Surely they didn't intend to harm the child. Whoever they were. Griffith Giles? Lisbeth's father? Could Lisbeth have simply wanted her daughter returned to her? The man wouldn't have had to kill Irena if that were the truth, but then perhaps he would. Irena would have never given up Jacci willingly, even if Lisbeth herself had come for the girl.

Whatever the truth, she feared she would have to give up Jacci. To trust her life and safety to another. She feared she might have only days to be sure her daughter was safe from more danger. Could she trust Tyrone to have changed enough to be a loving father?

Chapter

6

WHEN THEY CAME BACK to the showboat after the parade, Jacci ran ahead of everyone straight to see her mother. She was almost bursting with so much to tell her about the music and how the people followed along beside them.

In the little town, they had stopped to play a song, and while she didn't know what it was, her feet wanted to dance along with the tune as she tapped the tambourine against her hand. Then Captain Dan told the people about the night's show. A play. Singing. Dancing. Acrobats.

Her mother surely wouldn't say she couldn't watch. Duke would be one of the stars in the play. He laughed and told Jacci he always played the part of the villain. He didn't look much like a bad guy to her as he played his horn and smiled at everybody. Captain Dan also said Duke would be doing something he called a dramatic reading. That sounded good.

Her mama had to be awake so she could tell her everything.

Wind tried to sweep off the hat hiding her hair as she raced up the stage plank, but Jacci clamped a hand down on top of it. Her mother might not even recognize her in this getup, the way the boy playing the drums hadn't.

This time when the giggle wanted to bubble up out of her, Jacci didn't stop it. Her mother would laugh too. Her mother liked to laugh.

But then her mother didn't look like laughing about anything as she lay so still on the bed. Jacci hesitated in the doorway. "Mama." Jacci's voice was shaky.

Mama turned her head to look at Jacci. When she seemed to have a hard time smiling, tears pricked Jacci's eyes, and all the wonderful things she'd wanted to tell her slid away. She backed up a step. Maybe she should go for Duke or Miss Marelda. Her heart pounded up in her ears the same as it had last night on the *Mary Ellen* when she and her mother were running through the dark.

"Jacci? Is that you?"

That made Jacci remember her boys' clothes. "I look funny, don't I? Miss Marelda said she didn't have any girls' clothes. So I had to pretend I was a boy when I went with Duke in the parade."

"Duke?" Mama moistened her lips.

"Tyrone. Miss Marelda said I couldn't call him Tyrone. That I should call him 'Grandpa' or 'Grampus' or something like that." The words tumbled out of Jacci. "You should have seen his face when she said 'Grampus.'"

"I can imagine." Mama started to laugh but then went stiff.

Jacci took a step into the room before she stopped. "Do you hurt, Mama?"

"A little." Mama reached a hand out toward her. "Come here."

Jacci tiptoed over to the bed. She felt better when Mama touched her cheek.

"You can dress up like a boy, but you're still my beautiful little girl." Mama smiled as she tapped the hat's narrow brim. "You need a girl's hat."

"I guess so, but it was fun pretending to be a boy." When Jacci snatched off the hat, her hair fell down around her shoulders.

"Maybe that's what we should have always done."

"Done what?"

"Never mind. It was a silly thought," Mama said. "Can you push that chair over here with the back against the bed?"

That seemed strange, but she did as Mama said.

"Now sit in the chair."

"But I can't see you."

"It's only for a minute."

Jacci sat down but twisted around to watch her mother grabbing on to the slats on the back of the chair to pull herself up. Mama groaned as she slid her legs out from under the blanket and sat up. She was breathing too fast and her face was whiter than the pillowcase.

"Should I go get Duke?" Jacci jumped out of the chair and hopped back and forth from one foot to the other. She didn't know what to do.

"Not yet." Mama shut her eyes for a long moment, but when she opened them again, she smiled and looked more like Mama. "So, Tyrone told you to call him Duke. Sounds like him."

"Better than Grampus, he said."

"What did Miss Marelda say to that?"

"She called him Duke first. He sometimes pretends to be a duke in their shows, she said."

"Sit beside me." She patted the bed. "Just don't bounce too much."

Jacci climbed onto the bed as easy as she could. Mama made a funny sound that made Jacci want to jump back out on the floor, but Mama put a hand on her arm. It was good to have Mama touch her. For a few moments, they didn't say anything. Touching was enough.

Then Jacci asked, "Why don't you call him Papa or Father?"

"I guess he thought it was too much like Grampus. So I just called him Tyrone like my mother did."

"Even when you were my age?"

"Even then."

"Miss Marelda wouldn't have liked that," Jacci said.

"I guess not." Her mother made a noise that might have been a teeny laugh. "But he was never a papa like my friends had. My mother said he was married to the river instead of her, and there was no use in us expecting anything different."

"You say Daddy Kelly is like that too."

Her mother held her breath and eased her arm around Jacci. "He is. But he does love you. Never forget that. And I love you with all my heart. Always and forever. No matter what happens."

"I know. I'm glad you're my mama." Jacci tried to snuggle closer to her mother but jerked back when her mother gasped.

"It's all right, sweetie, but we'll have to wait on hugging until I'm better." Mama squeezed Jacci's hand before she pointed at the glass on the table beside the bed. "If you will get that medicine for me, it will help. And stuff the pillow up behind me against the wall."

Jacci did as she said, but she didn't get back on the bed. Instead, she settled down on the floor and leaned her head against her mother's knee.

Mama stroked her head. "Such beautiful hair."

"Was your hair black like mine when you were a little girl?"

"No. I've always had brown hair."

"If I keep being a boy, I should cut it off short."

"Putting on boys' clothes doesn't make you a boy except in a pretend way."

"It's fun to play pretend, isn't it?" Jacci said.

"I suppose as long as you never forget who you really are." Her mama's voice sounded funny.

Jacci looked up at her. Tears were sliding down Mama's cheeks. "Don't cry, Mama. I won't forget. I promise."

"I know you won't." Mama sounded tired.

"Can I watch the show tonight?" Jacci said. "Unless you want me to stay here with you."

Her mother brushed off her cheeks with a corner of the sheet. "I'll be resting, so yes, go to the show and then you can tell me all about it tomorrow."

"Oh, thank you, Mama." Jacci jumped up and started to hug her mother, but stopped when she remembered about no hugs. "When you feel better, Miss Marelda said we could do a mother-daughter song and dance. Duke didn't think you would, but Miss Marelda says their shows make people happy. That's good, isn't it?"

"Happy is good," Mama said, but she didn't look happy, even if her lips were turned up in a smile.

Duke spoke from the doorway. "There you are, you little scamp of a boy," he said with a laugh.

"Oh, Duke, I'm not really a boy."

"Well then, scoot on up to Miss Marelda's rooms. She's waiting there so she can turn you back into a girl with the proper trappings."

Mama caught her hand and squeezed it again. "I'll think about what song we can sing, but you'll have to do the dancing."

Jacci laughed and twirled to make her hair fly out around her before she ran past Duke to go to Miss Marelda's rooms.

The sound of Jacci's laughter drifting back to Irena did as much to help her ignore the pain as the bitter draught she'd just swallowed. But her head was spinning and she felt as if a red hot poker was stuck in her side.

"You shouldn't have sat up without someone to help you." Tyrone moved the chair and eased her back down in the bed.

"I wanted Jacci to stop looking so afraid."

"Did it help?"

"Not much."

"I can understand," he said. "It scares me to look at you."

She had to smile at that. "If I look that bad, I guess you best not show me a mirror."

"I'll be sure to take them all out of this room."

She brushed her hand through her hair. "Hide the mirrors, but a comb might help."

"A woman worrying about her looks has to be a good sign."

"I haven't worried about my looks for years," Irena said. "Little use trying to produce beauty where there is none."

"Nothing at all wrong with your looks, Irena. You've always been pretty enough to steal any man's heart. You could have found a proper fellow to wed without the least trouble, were you not already tied to a man who doesn't respect the bonds of marriage."

"If it didn't hurt to laugh, I would be doing so now," Irena said. "You faulting another man for not respecting his marriage vows."

"I never loved another besides your mother. She was my one and only love."

"Other than the river and the stage."

"Well, there are those two." He scooted the chair around and sat down. "I won't deny that."

"Mother had no chance against them."

"She never tried to hold me away from the river. She was a good woman." He let out a sigh. "Why didn't you send for me when she got sick?"

"She told me not to. She wanted you to remember her living, not dying."

"But you had to remember," Tyrone said.

"Yes, and now you will have to remember the same about me. As will Jacci." Irena shut her eyes a moment, wondering if screaming would help. Or weeping.

"Don't give up so easily. You're a fighter. You can come through this."

"If the Lord sends me a miracle." She had never been one not to face the truth.

"He sent you as a miracle for Jacci," Tyrone said quietly. "He could send another for her."

Irena opened her eyes and smiled then. "You are that miracle now, Father."

"Father." He almost whispered the word. "I don't think I've ever heard you call me Father. Not even when you were Jacci's age."

"You didn't want me to."

"Do you think that has changed? That I want you to now?"

Irena hung on to her smile as she reached to touch him. "I don't know, but maybe I'm the one who has changed. And maybe I hope you are changed too. That you can be a grandfather to Jacci even if she never calls you Grampus."

"Grampus." He made a face. "A perfectly awful word. I'm not sure I'd agree to play the part of grampus even in a play."

"I'm not asking you to play a part." The draught was beginning to push her toward sleep, but she fought to stay alert for a little longer. "She needs someone to watch over her."

"What about the man who claims her as his daughter? He does, doesn't he? That was the plan you came up with."

"Not me. Lisbeth." Irena pushed the words out through the fog gathering in her head. "It was a good plan."

"It was a terrible plan." He frowned. "For you."

"But not for her."

"You mean for Lisbeth. Got her off the hook."

"No, not Lisbeth. Jacci."

"I can find Kelly."

She forced her eyes to stay open as she fought off the fuzziness trying to claim her. She had to finish this in case the Lord demanded her presence before she could bring herself back to the surface of life. She intended to wake up again, to see Jacci and tell her one more time how much she loved her, but she couldn't be sure it would happen with the way her breath seemed harder and harder to pull in and let out.

"You can't give her to Kelly. He might love her. I think he does, but he would gamble away her future."

"I might act it away."

"You're settled here. Marelda told me you were the same as family. Let Jacci be part of that family too."

"She'll be pulled into the show. Her feet already want to dance to the music. You should have seen her in the parade."

"Then so be it. Keep her with you." Irena thought she spoke the words aloud, but she couldn't be sure as the room faded away. "Not Kelly. You, Father."

Chapter

7

Jacci ran halfway up the steps to Miss Marelda's rooms before she remembered the hat she'd left by her mother's bed. She didn't want Miss Marelda to think she lost it, so she scurried back to get it. The sound of her mother and Duke talking the same way they had the night before made her stop outside the open door instead of going on in to grab the hat off the floor.

What was that her mother said? About having to watch her mother die? And then Jacci heard her name. That made Jacci scoot back a step to lean against the wall beside the door. Out of sight. Her heart felt funny inside her chest. Mama said she needed a miracle.

Jacci knew what miracles were. Mama read her Bible stories about the Lord doing miracles. He made people see and walk, and once he even brought a little girl back to life after everybody said she was dead. Everybody but Jesus.

She wanted to run on into the room and make sure her mother hadn't forgotten those stories about how miracles happened. But then Mama said that name she'd said last night.

Lisbeth. She didn't know why hearing that name made her freeze. It had to be how her mother and Duke said it. Or was it the way they said her name? Jacci. As if somehow her mother needing a miracle was because of her. Because of that man. That man she had shot.

He might need a miracle like her mother. Jacci didn't know whether she should hope he got one or not, the way she wanted her mother to get the miracle she said she needed. The more she thought about it, the more confusing it all was.

On the *Mary Ellen*, she knew places to hide while she tried to figure out things, but not here on the showboat. At least not yet. Besides, she didn't want to hide from her mother or from Duke. If only they had hidden from that man. She slid down the wall and sat flat on the floor to wait until they quit talking. She still had to get the hat.

She started to put her hands over her ears to block out their voices, but then Duke said something about finding Kelly. That made her ears perk up. She wanted to jump up and say, oh yes, he should. Kelly wouldn't let Mama die. He would laugh and everything would be better, at least until he went away. Mama was right. He would go away again.

But Duke had always gone away too. Mama was the one who always stayed. What would Jacci do if she went away? Jacci put her forehead down on her knees as tears filled her eyes. A while ago she'd been marching with Duke and ready to laugh at anything, and now she couldn't even smile.

She was so full of her misery she didn't notice when her mother and Duke stopped talking. The boat rocked a little under her as she heard people moving around in a room across from her. She pulled her legs up closer to her body to make herself as small as possible to keep anybody from noticing her.

But Duke did see her when he came out of the room.

"What are you doing, Jacci? I told you Marelda wanted to

see you, and if Queen Marelda wants to see you, then you must attend."

Jacci started to keep her head down on her knees, but she couldn't pretend to be invisible when he was talking to her. She looked up at him without saying anything.

"Oh, Jacci." His face changed to look as sad as she felt. He slowly lowered himself down until he was sitting right beside her on the floor. He puffed out a breath. "It's farther down here than I thought it would be. You may have to fetch one of the acrobats to help me up."

She just looked at him. She wasn't sure who might be an acrobat or even exactly what an acrobat did.

"Don't look so worried." He patted her knee. "If I can't get up, I'll crawl somewhere."

In spite of the fear of losing her mother that had shut her in a black somber place, she almost smiled at the thought of Duke crawling instead of walking. "I'll help you up," she said.

He peered over at her. "You do look very strong for your size."

For a while then, they both just sat there not saying a thing or even looking at one another while the boat shifted slightly under them.

When Duke finally spoke, it wasn't what Jacci expected him to say. She thought he would ask why she was crying or tell her she shouldn't sneak around listening to people's private talk. Or fuss at her for not going to Miss Marelda's room. Instead, he asked, "Do you like the river?"

He didn't give her time to answer as he went on. "I do. I've loved the river since I first floated a raft out on it when I wasn't much older than you." He kept staring at the wall across from them. "The water took me somewhere."

"Where did you want to go?"

"Anywhere, as long as I was moving. That's the river. Always moving. Out in the middle of the ocean they say sometimes the water will get still as glass and a ship can just stay there without getting anywhere. No wind. No waves." He smiled then. "But on a river like the Ohio or the Mississippi, the water keeps moving, taking you along with it."

He bent his legs and rested his arms on his knees to sit the same as she was and didn't look so out of place there on the floor beside her.

"Mama and me like the river too," she said. "Mama says there's always something to see, that the river wakes up different every morning."

"Estelle couldn't keep her from inheriting the wanderlust."

"Estelle?"

"That was your grandmother, God rest her soul."

"Mama tells me stories about her. She died before I was born."

"That she did. Much too soon, it was. She was a wonderful lady, but she had no use for floating on a river. Liked her feet on solid ground. That came from being a farmer's daughter, I think." He was silent a moment before he went on. "I expected your mother to be the same."

"Oh." Jacci said. "What's wanderlust?"

"Wanting to see what's around the next bend. Never being totally happy except on the move to somewhere new."

"But Miss Marelda said you'd been here with them a long time."

"Longer than I ever expected, to be sure, but maybe as long as the river is running under this showboat, that's wanderlust enough for me now in my old age."

"Are you really, really old?" She looked over at him. He did have gray, almost white hair and wrinkles around his eyes.

"Compared to you, I am. More than half a century."

She tried to figure out how old that would make him, but she didn't know what a century was.

He must have noted her frown, because he said, "No need

worrying over numbers. Just know it's too many for you to count on your fingers and toes, but I'm sure you can count your years on your fingers. How many would it take?"

"Five." She held up her hand with all the fingers and thumb showing. "I'll be six in August."

"That old already." He stared down at her as if trying to decide if she was telling the truth. "How the years pass by. I remember you as a babe in arms the first time I saw you. Even then you had that black hair and those blue eyes. You were a beauty from day one."

"Mama says how we look isn't as important as what we do."

"Beauty can have its advantages, but your mother is right. Right living is more than skin deep."

That made Jacci remember what she'd done on the *Mary Ellen* the night before. The words to tell Duke about that jumped up to her mouth, but she didn't let them out. She wanted to, but she remembered about her mother making her throw the gun in the river. That and not telling about the man stabbing her must mean she didn't want anyone to ever know. But she needed to ask Mama if that meant Duke too. Maybe he could tell her if she'd done the right thing.

So, instead of telling about the man, she said, "I don't want Mama to be hurt."

"I know." He reached over and put his hand over hers on her knee.

The next words sneaked out before she could stop them. "Is she going to die?"

She wanted him to say no, but he didn't. He pulled in a slow breath and let it out. "I won't lie to you, Jacci. I don't know. I hope not, but I don't know."

A lie would have been better, but then, her mother said a lie was never better.

He pulled her over against him and held her close. She laid

her ear against his chest and felt his heart beating deep and steady. "If Mama dies, can I stay with you forever?"

"Don't you worry about that. I will always be your Grampus Duke."

She pulled away to look at him then. "Grampus Duke?"

"Why not?" He smiled. "If I'm going to play the part, I have to have the name. Don't you like it?"

"Uh-huh." A smile sneaked up on her as she said the name again. "Grampus Duke. Miss Marelda will laugh."

"That she will."

"Mama will too," Jacci said.

"Indeed, I fear you speak the truth." He let out an exaggerated sigh. "But a man must play the role given him."

"What role do I have?"

"Hmm. We need to consider that." He studied her a moment as though searching for the perfect answer. "What role do you think you might most like to play? A vagabond boy as you did in the parade today? A twinkle-toed dancer? A riverboat captain?"

That last made her giggle. "I'm too short. I can't see over the wheel."

"Then a riverboat captain in the making."

"I'd rather be an actor like you."

"A life of pretend." Something changed in the way he looked at her for a moment, but then his smile was back. "Not the worst kind of life, but I know the perfect role for you."

"What?" She got up on her knees to look him straight in the face.

"A princess. A showboat princess."

That made her laugh. "Mama will think that's too uppity."

"No, no," he said. "She knows you're a princess."

"Does that make her a queen?"

"That is a bit of an incongruity." He rubbed his chin.

She frowned a little. "What is that?"

"Something that won't exactly work. Only one queen allowed per showboat and Queen Marelda has that role nailed down."

"Oh."

"Don't look so disappointed. A good playwright can always come up with a rewrite to make things work out."

"Are you a playwright?"

"I am for this play we're writing." He pretended to write in the air. "I know. A queen can play hostess to a visiting queen. So that can be your mother. A queen from another kingdom."

"Then what kingdom will I belong to?"

"Both, of course. You will be the best kind of princess, one who rules wherever she goes. Except of course for the queens. Even a princess must do what the queen requests." He raised his eyebrows at her. "And I do think a certain Queen Marelda requested your presence."

"I came back to get my hat and then . . ."

"We won't worry about the 'and then.' We will just continue on from here in this play we're in. Now help me up and we will be about playing our roles."

She hopped up and took his hands to pull him up.

He didn't have any trouble getting to his feet. "I guess I didn't need you to fetch the acrobats after all. You are as strong as I thought. That's good. A princess must be strong. No matter what happens."

Jacci nodded. "Should I go get the hat?" She peeked around Duke into the room where she could see her mother sleeping.

"I'll get it. You've made Queen Marelda wait long enough already."

Jacci started away, but then she turned back to him. "Can I really call you Grampus Duke?"

"If the princess so desires."

"Can I ask you something else?"

"You do seem to be in a questioning mood, but ask away.

Perhaps I will have a worthy answer in spite of being an old grampus." He made a face.

She bit her lip.

"A hard question, is it?" His eyebrows peaked again.

What if he was upset when he knew she had been eavesdropping? But she did want to know. She pushed out the question. "Did Lisbeth make Mama get hurt?"

The look on his face changed. Any hint of a smile was gone and the wrinkles around his mouth got deeper. "How do you know about Lisbeth?" His voice sounded different, as though the mention of Lisbeth had spoiled their easy time together.

"You and Mama were talking about her." She decided not to tell that she'd heard Mama and Kelly talking about this Lisbeth once too. Duke hadn't sounded as if he liked Kelly much.

"So we were. We should have remembered little pitchers have big ears."

She'd heard her mother say that, so she knew what it meant. "I'm sorry. I didn't aim to listen. I just heard you."

"Of course you did. On a showboat, one hears everything that goes on." He didn't sound upset now, but he still hadn't answered her.

She wanted to ask about Lisbeth again, but instead she simply watched Duke, who lifted his gaze away from her to stare out toward where the river would be rolling past the tied-up showboat, even if they couldn't see it from where they were standing.

"Lisbeth." He spoke at last, looking down at Jacci. He was smiling, but it wasn't the good smile of minutes ago. "She was your mother's friend. She wouldn't hurt her."

"Does Mama wish she was here?"

"No, she wouldn't wish that. As far as I know, she hasn't seen or heard from her in years. Maybe because your mother took to the river." He put his hand on Jacci's head and his smile was better now. "I myself never met Lisbeth. I've only heard your mother speak of her."

"Will Mama tell me about her?"

He tilted his head and was quiet for so long that Jacci wished she had a way to take back her question.

He finally asked a question of his own instead of answering hers. "Why do you want to know about this Lisbeth?"

"I don't know." She didn't know why she wanted to know. She simply knew she did. "Is she a secret?"

"Not a secret, no. Just someone who is no longer part of your mother's life, but you are right. Your mother is the one to ask if you want to know more." He pointed a finger at her. "But it would be best not to trouble her with such questions until she's feeling better."

"You talked about her. About Lisbeth."

"So I did, but I asked no questions." He leaned down to look directly at Jacci. "Sometimes questions can be too hard to answer."

"All right." She tried to keep her lips from trembling, but she didn't quite succeed. "Was she mean to Mama? This Lisbeth."

"Nothing like that. Your mother might say she gave her the best gift ever."

"What was that?"

"A chance for love."

"With Daddy Kelly?"

"That might be. Some chances work out better than others."

"Will I ever see Daddy Kelly again?" He always found them on the *Mary Ellen*, but now he wouldn't know where they were. Her eyes filled with tears.

"There, there, Princess. No need for tears. You are on this palace of a showboat and the time is almost here to put on a show. An actor or actress has to sweep all worries away to play their parts."

"I don't have a part."

"You will, my girl. Never fear about that. Queen Marelda will be sure to find a part for you before we get too far down the river once she has a costume ready. So run on up and see what she has in mind for you." He turned her toward the stairway and gave her a gentle push. "Hurry now. The show must go on, and everybody loves a show."

Chapter

8

Everything else faded away as Jacci watched the show from a spot beside the piano close to the stage. She was swallowed up by the story. She almost didn't know Duke in his black coat and hat, with a scowl twisting his face when he rushed out from behind the curtains to demand the pretty lady in the play pay her rent or he'd put her out on the street. In the cold and rain.

Jacci shivered when the sound of wind whistling came from somewhere at the back of the stage. She was ready to join in with the boos from the crowd until Grampus Duke turned sideways to wink at her. He warned her he would be acting the evil part and the hero would knock him down but that she was to remember it was all pretend.

Pretend. She knew about pretend. Sometimes her mother played pretend games with her, but she'd never been to a show before, if she didn't count what her mother said were shows all around them on the *Mary Ellen*. Mama liked to tell her stories about the people on the boat and the silly things they did or said.

Those were real things, but the show playing out on the stage was all pretend. That didn't keep tears from coursing down her cheeks when the pretty girl was sure her true love had deserted her. She'd heard her mama crying in the night like that when Kelly went away.

She cheered and cheered along with the crowd when the hero saved the girl from the clutches of the terrible landlord and they happily embraced. But that wasn't the end of the fun. After the actors and actresses took a bow, Captain Dan came out to promise more entertainment from the cast. Not another play but singing, dancing, and something he called "vaudeville."

First out were the acrobats. Miss Marelda played so loud the piano bounced beside Jacci while some men tumbled and did flips. A woman holding up a bright-colored parasol over her head walked across a wire high above the stage. When she wobbled, everybody gasped. After she rushed on the last few steps to the safety of a little platform, Jacci sighed with relief.

Gabe, the redheaded boy who had played the drums in the parade, jumped down off the stage to take his mother's place at the piano while she sang a silly song that had the audience laughing. By the last verse, people in the crowd sang along with her on the chorus. Jacci didn't think she'd ever seen anybody look any happier than Miss Marelda as she bowed to crashing applause.

But her part in the show wasn't over. Gabe kept playing while Captain Dan pulled a rabbit out of his hat and scarves from his nose. Then Jacci watched in amazement as he waved his wand and Miss Marelda floated up off the stage. Just as quick as the rabbit disappearing, they cleared the stage to let the pretty lady from the play sing a sad song that made Jacci's heart feel heavy.

Then they were all laughing again as Miss Marelda, back at the piano, matched her music to whatever the boys were pantomiming onstage. The crowd loved it when they pretended to ride bucking broncos and fell off. But the scene that got the most laughs was the redheaded boy pretending to be a girl while another boy went down on one knee to propose. When the third boy came to push the other boy away from his girl, fisticuffs broke out until the boy pretending to be the girl grabbed a broom and chased them both away.

After that foolishness, Duke stepped to the middle of the stage to take on the appearance of a real duke instead of the villain he was earlier. In his introduction, Captain Dan said Duke would do a dramatic reading, but Duke didn't have a book in his hands. He simply started telling a story. Nobody tried to shout him off the stage now as the people hung on his every word.

Jacci took silent little breaths and sat stone still to listen as his voice wrapped around her like a warm blanket. When he talked about the stars shining so brightly over the two lovers in his story, she felt as though she were on the top deck with the night sky settling down around her. The happily-ever-after ending made her tingle with delight.

When he took a bow as the audience clapped and whistled their approval, Jacci couldn't help it. She raced up the steps at the side of the stage and ran to hug him.

He looked surprised for a moment, but then he took her hands and began dancing her around the stage. Miss Marelda started playing a waltz and the crowd cheered even louder and stomped their feet. Duke winked at her and did another bow. Jacci held out the skirt Miss Marelda had made for her and did a curtsy, then Duke grabbed her hand again and together they danced off the stage.

Later, after all the people were gone, they gathered in the galley area to drink coffee and tea and talk about the show. Grampus Duke said show people needed that time to come down off a performance high no matter how the show went.

"Looks like we've got us a scene stealer." Gabe sat down beside her. Freckles covered his nose and cheeks and his red hair curled around his ears. His voice went from low to squeaky in a second. "You're a changeable scamp. A little boy this afternoon and a dancing girl tonight."

Now that the excitement was over, Jacci worried she might be in trouble for running up on the stage. She looked away from Gabe's grinning face to peek over at Miss Marelda and Captain Dan. Even if she'd only been on the showboat a couple of days, she knew they were the bosses.

"I-I'm sorry," she said. "I won't d-do it again."

"None of that talk," Captain Dan said. "Folks loved it. We'll have to practice something for you and the Duke."

"And you need more sparkle," Miss Marelda said.

Jacci hunched up her shoulders. "I can smile more."

"Don't you worry your head over that," Gabe said. "You sparkled just fine. So bright I doubt anybody even noticed the old guy with you." He poked Duke's arm.

"Alas, I fear you are right, young Kingston, but if I am to be out-sparkled, then my girl here is a fine one to do so." Duke softly touched Jacci's head. "Queen Marelda means a sparkle or two on your costume. Could be we can come up with a tiara for your head, Princess."

Jacci didn't know what that was, but it sounded pretty.

"Princess." Gabe leaned his chair so far back the front legs came up off the floor. He clasped his hands over his heart. "You call Ma a queen. We all call you Duke. I'm thinking you should call me Prince."

"Don't be thinking over yo'self, Gabe." A little black woman with more wrinkles than Grampus Duke set a cup of hot cocoa in front of Jacci. She held another cup in the air. "You mind your manners with this little girl or you won't be getting this other cup of sweet chocolate."

Gabe dropped the front of his chair back down on the floor

with a clunk. "You wouldn't treat a prince that way, would you, Aunt Tildy?"

She gave him the cup, but she wasn't through with him. "I'm thinking those big brothers of yours is more likely the princes around here." She nodded over toward two older boys at a different table. "They ain't always makin' trouble like a certain redheaded rascal I know." She planted her hands on her hips and gave him a look.

"But you love me, Aunt Tildy, don't you?"

She continued to stare at him without even smiling. "I'm thinking you act more like a baby barely out of knickers sometimes than a boy going on fourteen."

"Tell him, Aunt Tildy." Captain Dan laughed.

"You can count on me doin' that, Captain." She kept her dark eyes on the boy and shook her finger at him. "You leave this little child alone. She's got enough troubles without your pestering ways."

That made Jacci remember her mama, and she felt bad for laughing and dancing while her mama couldn't do the same. She blinked back tears.

"I'm praying for your mama, sweet child," Aunt Tildy said.

That was good. She looked like she'd be more practiced at praying than Jacci. "Will you pray for a miracle?" Jacci kept her voice so soft that Aunt Tildy leaned toward her to hear. "Mama says she needs a miracle."

"The good Lord hasn't finished givin' out those miracles." The little woman's voice was almost as soft as Jacci's. "That's the very thing I'll do my best to pray down for her." She raised her voice then to let everybody hear. "I was up there with her a while ago. Sleepin' sound. That's when healin' can happen. When a body is sleeping."

"Aunt Tildy can pray up sunshine in the middle of a downpour," Duke said.

Other voices joined in agreeing with that, and even Gabe

nodded his head and said, "She sure as anything can." Then as if he knew Jacci needed to think of something besides how she hadn't prayed enough for her mama, he went on. "She makes the best cocoa on the river too. So take a sip before it gets cold."

She did take a drink, and the actors began talking about the show again and where they would be for the next show on down the river. After Jacci drank every drop from the cup, she slipped out of her chair and eased toward the door. Duke smiled to let her know he saw her, but he didn't stop her. He knew where she needed to be.

Mama was still asleep. Jacci hoped Aunt Tildy was right about the healing part. She knew she was right about the praying part. So Jacci got down on her knees beside her mama and whispered her prayer so she wouldn't wake her up.

"Our Father in heaven." She started the prayer the same as she had in the parade. "Please let Mama have a miracle. I promise to pray every day and do whatever Grampus Duke or Miss Marelda says I should. Please don't let dancing in a show be bad." She hesitated a few seconds and then went on. "And make Mama try to get better."

She wasn't sure why she said that last. Of course, her mother would try to get better. Her mother had to get better.

She looked up at her mother's face. "Mama." If only she would open her eyes and smile at Jacci.

Miss Marelda came into the room and put her hand on Jacci's shoulder. "Come, Princess, it's time for you to get some sleep."

"I'm not sleepy," Jacci said, even though her eyes felt heavy.

"A dancer needs her sleep." She reached for Jacci's hand. "Duke and Aunt Tildy will take turns watching over your mother tonight."

"Can't I sleep here on the floor the way I did last night? Please, Miss Marelda."

"No, dear. We fixed you a room right next door. The room is

smaller than this one where Duke usually sleeps, but we put a cot in there for you, and Duke will be sleeping in the bed when he's not sitting with your mother. If you wake up, you can peek in and see your mother if you need to, but I don't want you sleeping on the floor again."

Jacci hid her sigh as she stood up. Grampus Duke said she had to do what Queen Marelda said, but she stayed by Mama's bed. "May I kiss Mama before I leave?"

"Of course."

"Will she know?"

"I'm sure she will know in her heart."

Jacci touched her lips to her mother's cheek. It was hot and dry feeling. "Why is she so hot, Miss Marelda?"

"She has a fever." Miss Marelda touched Mama's forehead. "I'll tell Aunt Tildy to bring some cool water to bathe her face. That will help."

Jacci stared at her mother. "Please, please get well," she whispered.

Miss Marelda hugged Jacci then before she took her hand again and led her over to the next room. She helped her take off her dress and put on a soft shirt to sleep in. "Hop in bed and I'll tuck you in."

The cot was small but fine for Jacci. It felt good having Miss Marelda pull the covers up around her and then stroke her hair away from her face.

"Thank you, Miss Marelda."

"Miss Marelda sounds much too formal since you are part of our showboat family now." She tapped her cheek with her finger as though that would help her think.

"Duke calls you Queen Marelda."

She laughed. "He's the only one I let get away with that. So no Queen Marelda for you. How about Aunt Marelda?"

"I've never had an aunt."

"Everybody needs an aunt or two."

"I only have Daddy Kelly."

"Daddy Kelly?" Aunt Marelda frowned. "He wasn't the one who hurt your mother, was he?"

"Oh no. Daddy Kelly would never hurt Mama."

"Where is he?"

"I don't know. On a steamboat somewhere, I think. Mama says he comes and goes like the silverfish in the spring." Jacci blinked back tears. "I wish he was here now. He knows how to make Mama smile."

"And cry too, I wager," Aunt Marelda said.

"Only when he leaves," Jacci said, taking up for him.

"Right." She shook herself. "Tell you what. At our next landing I'll put out a message for him to come."

"Can you do that?" Jacci grabbed Aunt Marelda's hand.

"I can." Aunt Marelda smiled and squeezed Jacci's hand. Her smile faded as she went on. "But we can't be sure he will get the message and come."

"He will." Jacci knew he would.

"You could be right. News on the river can sometimes travel faster than a raft in a flood. So we can hope."

Jacci did hope as the showboat stopped at a different landing each day to put on their show, but Kelly didn't come. Her mother would get better if he did. Jacci was sure of it. But now her mother kept getting worse. Sometimes she was awake enough to talk to Jacci. Other times her eyes would be open, but she would be talking crazy things.

Whoever was sitting with Mama when that happened would shoo Jacci out of the room, but once Jacci heard her say Lisbeth. She still hadn't asked Mama about Lisbeth. She couldn't until she got better.

Jacci had a full skirt now of shiny red material. Her white blouse was made of some kind of sparkling material that flashed in the lights. Aunt Marelda put a big red bow in her hair. By the third stop, she and Grampus Duke had a whole act to themselves, with her asking him questions like why the moon was yellow and him giving crazy answers like it was made of cheese. Or how deep was the river and Duke saying if somebody in China dug a hole down far enough, the river might just drain right away into the rice paddies on the other side of the world.

Each time after they did a question and answer, Gabe hit two cymbals together and they did what Duke called a soft-shoe shuffle dance. At the end they danced off to disappear behind the curtains while the crowd clapped and clapped.

The play was the same at every stop, but Jacci never tired of watching it. She did get used to Duke putting on his character, as he liked to say, and turning into a villain. Every night at the end of the show after she drank her hot cocoa in the galley with the other actors and actresses, she went to say a prayer and kiss her mother good night before she went to bed. And each time she begged her to get better.

Then after Aunt Marelda tucked her in to bed and tiptoed away, Jacci would pray that Kelly would come. But the days passed without him coming.

Chapter

9

TIME STOPPED MEANING anything to Irena. She often didn't know if she was awake or dreaming. She felt soft kisses and fought through folds of darkness to come to the surface to see Jacci. The words of her child begging her to live penetrated her fever fog, but even when she did think she woke enough to talk to Jacci, she was never sure if it was real or a dream.

At least if those moments were dreams, they were happy ones. Other nightmares mocked her for the many lies she'd told. Claiming Jacci as her own. Pretending a marriage she wished was real. Loving her daughter so fiercely that she feared even trusting her to the Lord.

Perhaps that was her biggest wrong. Fearing to surrender it all to the Lord. She hadn't neglected Jacci's spiritual education. She read her Bible stories. Taught her to pray. And now she was saying those prayer words for Irena. All because Irena had taken her back on the river.

At the time, Irena told herself she had to, but she could have found another way. A better way. If she'd taken in more sewing jobs, she might have earned enough to stay in the little house, even after she no longer got money from Lisbeth. She could have divorced Kelly and accepted the attentions of another man. A few in the neighborhood had given her hopeful interest.

She could have done many things, but instead she had taken Jacci back on the river because that was where Kelly was. She should have put up a better wall against his charms. She had pretended such a wall, but her heart had betrayed her.

The way he had genuinely cared for Jacci had destroyed her defenses against loving him. Not that he truly loved her enough to give up his gambler's life and be a proper father. Irena had never known a proper father herself.

Then again, perhaps her father had always loved her more than she thought. He did show love now as he was often at her bedside when she was able to pull herself away from the darkness that lurked, constantly ready to claim her. She could tell by his eyes he had no hope of her survival. Nor did the others who came to her bedside, Marelda with her kind words and Aunt Tildy with her gentle hands and sweet prayers. The only one who clung to hope was Jacci.

Dear Jacci. For her, Irena did try to get better, but a raft could not float against the river current. This raft of life and death she rode had no poles to push it to the safety of the shallows where she could tie up to the willows and linger awhile. Then again, perhaps the rush down the river to her destination was the one of safety. Everlasting safety.

The current did slow. The Lord's gift to her, with time to do what she could to protect Jacci. When she came awake, truly awake, in the dark of the night, Tyrone was sleeping in the chair beside her bed. Another gift that he was there instead of Aunt Tildy or Marelda. In the flicker of the lamp on the bedside table, she could see how he'd aged. When he was awake, he ordered his face in ways to keep that truth shadowed. He was a talented actor, taking on whatever character worked best for him and those around him.

She prayed he would take on the loving grandfather character and that it would be more than a role in a play, but a lifetime part.

"Father." Her voice was hoarse, barely recognizable to her own ears.

He was instantly awake, leaning toward her. "Irena. Do you need more medicine?"

"No. The time for medicine is past, I think."

He looked hopeful for a moment before she shook her head slightly. "The Lord is giving me these few minutes. His blessing."

"I want him to bless you with years, not minutes."

"I know." She reached to touch his hand. "But the minutes are good. I need your promise that you will always see that Jacci is loved and safe."

"I love her already," Tyrone said.

"But will it be a steady love? A lasting love?"

He didn't hesitate. "Yes. But I'm not young. No one knows how many days they're given."

"Sometimes when something happens, a person can guess." Her mouth was almost too dry to talk. "Is there water without the draught mixed in?"

"Here, my daughter." He gently lifted her up enough to sip the water.

She smiled when he called her daughter. Had he ever done so? She couldn't remember. Such a shame that they made this loving connection too late. But then, perhaps the time was perfect. "You will have help with Marelda."

"Yes. We can love her as you ask, but I don't know what to fear for her. How can I protect her when I don't know the dangers she faces?"

"I'm not sure of them either. Lisbeth's husband must have

found out about the child. How, I don't know, but Griffith Giles is a man with political ambitions. He must fear Lisbeth's indiscretion will somehow be used by his opponents."

"Surely he could mean no harm to the child."

"His man was willing to harm me to get to her, for what purpose I can't imagine. But there was no mistaking his intent." *"Give me the child."* The words circled in her head. She pulled in a breath that brought the pain. She ignored it. "I don't know more."

"Does Kelly?"

The very mention of his name brought a wave of regret. She pushed it away. She wouldn't dwell on the regrets. They had shared lies, it was true, but they had also shared laughs and love for Jacci. She was worth whatever sacrifices Irena had made. Even this last one. "I don't know."

"Was he part of this? The man finding you?"

The same suspicion had tickled her mind, but she did not let it stay then or now. "No."

Tyrone sighed. "You love him, don't you?"

"Yes." The time for denial had long passed.

"Marelda sent out a message for him to find us."

"She shouldn't have done that. It would be better if he doesn't come." She was sure of that, even though the thought of seeing him again had haunted her fevered dreams. She lifted up off the pillow to clutch Tyrone's hand. "If he comes, you must not let him take Jacci. Promise me."

"He is legally her father. I might not be able to prevent it."

"But you must. She would not be safe with him." She sank back on the pillow. "Tell him I gave her to you. That it was my last request. He'll abide by that. He's not a bad person. He will want to do what's best for Jacci. And best is for her to lose herself here in this showboat family."

"Don't give up, Irena. Your play may not be over yet."

"I suppose that is true. Not in the way you mean, Father,

but I feel peace in whatever happens next. The next act, you might say. I feel the Lord knows my heart and has forgiven my wrongs."

He looked ready to say something, but when Irena shook her head slightly, he pulled in a shaky breath and didn't speak.

Irena broke the silence between them. "Where is Jacci?"

"In the room next to this."

"Bring her to me."

"She'll be asleep."

"She can go back to sleep here with me." She managed to hold in a groan as she scooted over to make room. "I need to hold her. Please."

"I can refuse you nothing, but I fear it will cause you pain." He stood up.

"The joy of holding her will wipe away the pain." As he started to turn away from the bed, Irena reached for his hand. "Wait. I have no idea how much time has passed. Are we still on the Ohio?"

"We are. Four shows since you came aboard."

"A show a night." She smiled at how he counted the time that way.

"Except Sunday."

She dropped her hand away from his. Five days. Where would that put them on the river? Maybe near enough. "Does that make us close to Dove Creek? I went to a church there when Jacci was a baby. It's built on a hill with a graveyard that overlooks the river."

He pulled in a breath and closed his eyes as though her words hurt him. After a moment, he opened his eyes to look at her with a sad attempt at a smile. "We aren't far from there. Two more stops, I think."

"That will do then. I was happy there."

While he went to get Jacci, Irena prayed for a clear head a little longer. She had things to tell Jacci. Nothing about the truth. That, someone else would have to tell her after she was older. Perhaps she should have written it down for her, but on the other hand, why would she ever have to know? Lisbeth had given her up. Completely. Jacci would have a new life here as part of the Kingston family. Part of their show.

Jacci came to her, rubbing sleep from her eyes. "Mama?"

She did look so like Lisbeth, but hundreds of little girls had black hair and eyes as blue as violets. Irena wouldn't think about Lisbeth and what she might be enduring if Giles had found out about her baby. Irena had done her part. Now she had a last act to play with Jacci. She smiled at the thought that she was sounding like Tyrone as she invited Jacci to get into the bed beside her. How many times had they slept cuddled like this in the little bed in her room on the *Mary Ellen*?

"Can we hug again now?" Jacci asked.

"For a little while." Irena bit her lip to keep from crying out as the little girl crawled up beside her. "Turn your back to me so we can nestle like two spoons." She wrapped her arms about her child, treasuring the feel of her warm little body and the tickle of her hair against her chin.

She looked up at Tyrone. "Go rest, Father. Jacci will fetch you if I need anything."

"I will, Grampus Duke. I promise."

"Grampus?" Irena had to laugh even if it did hurt.

"Not a thing wrong with being called Grampus." He lifted his chin and walked out of the room as if exiting the stage.

Jacci giggled. "Aunt Marelda said Grampus was a good grandfather name. Do you think it is too?"

"I do. And now you have a grampus and an aunt."

"And an uncle. Aunt Marelda says Captain Dan is my uncle, but I can still call him Captain. Everybody does. Even Gabe and he's the captain's son." Jacci twisted around to look at Irena's face. "That's all right, isn't it?"

"It's better than all right. It's wonderful. A little girl needs lots of family."

"But you'll always be my mama."

"Yes." Irena laid her hand over Jacci's heart. "And never, ever forget how much I love you."

"I love you too, Mama. I'm glad you tried to get better."

Irena let silence fall between them for a moment. She had to find the best words. "I have tried, Jacci, but sometimes no matter how you try, you can't always make what you want happen."

"But Aunt Tildy and me, we prayed for a miracle. Grampus Duke said he would too."

"Miracles come in all sorts of ways. One of them is being here on this showboat with your Grampus Duke." She had to smile again at the name. She no longer had the first doubt that Tyrone would be everything she hoped he would be for Jacci. "Another is the way love stays with one forever. My love will always be right there in your heart whenever you need me." She gently tapped Jacci's chest.

Jacci pulled Irena's hand up and kissed it. "Will my love always be in your heart too?"

"Oh yes. Forever and ever."

"Will you come watch me dancing with Grampus Duke? He says I have twinkle toes."

"I'll always be watching over you, whether you see me there or not." Irena blinked back tears. "Now, go to sleep and dream the best dreams, little Twinkle Toes."

"I'll dream about you dancing with me when you get better." Jacci sounded half asleep already.

"And I'll dream the same." She stroked Jacci's head and knew when she relaxed back into sleep. "Thank you, Lord, for this time," she whispered even as she felt her own consciousness slipping away.

She was on the raft again, but this time the river wasn't raging as it pushed her along. Instead, the water was a beautiful emerald color with the gentlest of currents. She floated easy now. Far ahead down the river, a light glowed like a thousand candles. She wasn't there yet, but she would be soon. A peace settled in her. She was loved and forgiven.

Chapter
10

MAMA WAS TRYING TO GET BETTER. She told Jacci she was, and Mama wouldn't lie to her about something like that. About anything.

When morning came, her mother's arm around her felt too heavy. Jacci slipped out from under it to get up.

"Mama," she said.

Her mother didn't wake up and say good morning the way she always had on the *Mary Ellen*. Her eyes stayed closed, but Jacci could hear her breathing. It sounded sort of funny, but that was probably because of her being hurt.

Jacci kissed her cheek that didn't feel as hot this morning. "Good morning, Mama. Sweet dreams." That was what her mother told her sometimes. The sleeping would make her better so she could watch Jacci dancing with Grampus Duke.

When Grampus Duke came in the room, Jacci wanted to tell him about Mama watching them that night, but he didn't give her time. He looked at Mama and shooed Jacci out of the room. "Off with you. We can talk later. I need to see to your mother now."

At the door, she looked back at him. He wasn't doing anything for Mama. He was just standing beside her bed. Maybe waiting for her to wake up and tell him she was better.

After she ate breakfast, Jacci climbed up to the top deck and watched Captain Dan in the pilothouse guiding them down the river. The sun was beating down, but the wind off the river kept it from scorching her skin. After a while, she went back to see if Mama was awake, but Aunt Tildy blocked her way through the door and said it would be better if she didn't bother her mama right then.

"Is she sleeping?" Jacci peeked around Aunt Tildy.

"She is." She turned Jacci away from the room. "Sleeping. Now go watch the river. We'll be where we are going to tie up for the show tonight soon."

That hadn't dampened Jacci's spirits. Hadn't Aunt Tildy called that sleep the healing kind? A little while later, Aunt Marelda's calliope music sounded especially cheerful as they pulled in to a new dock and put out the stage plank for the parade into the town.

She danced along with the rest of the crew, shaking her tambourine. Gabe pounded on his drum beside her. The same as that first parade, she was dressed up like a boy. Grampus Duke said that would keep her from getting her dancing clothes muddy. She had other clothes now. She wouldn't have had to wear the dancing skirt, but she liked wearing the britches and, as Grampus said, playing a role even in the parade.

Grampus Duke didn't do the parade. Gabe said he had stayed with Jacci's mother so Aunt Tildy could get their meal ready. They always ate a few hours before the show.

When they got back to the showboat, a doctor from the village was there seeing her mother. So Gabe took her back on land to play with the kids he knew from other summers the showboat stopped here. He claimed he had friends at every stop up and down the river and that soon she would too.

They hadn't even taken time to eat on the boat but grabbed a couple of apples and hunks of cheese before they ran back on shore where some children waited for them with big smiles. A girl Jacci's age laughed when Jacci told her about pretending to be a boy. They ran off into the woods where they climbed trees and played tag, things Jacci had never done. All the time she kept thinking about her mother watching her in the show that night.

When the sun started sinking in the western sky, Gabe found her in the woods. "We'd better get back to the boat to get ready for the show or both of us will get a tanning."

When she asked Gabe what a tanning was, he laughed and said she didn't want to find out. He'd grabbed her hand to run back to the boat. She didn't have time to go see if her mother was getting ready for the show, but she imagined Aunt Tildy helping her get dressed.

Later as she watched the play from the side of the stage and waited for her act with Grampus Duke, she tried to peer out into the crowd. But the lanterns all around the stage kept her from seeing faces. Finally, when Grampus Duke took her hand and led her out on the stage, she could feel her mother watching them. When they danced off the stage, Jacci was almost floating. It was the best day ever.

After the show was over, she started to run down off the stage to hunt for her mother, but Grampus Duke put his hand on her shoulders to stop her.

She tried to pull away from him. "I've got to go find Mama."

He held on tight. "She's not out there."

"She promised she'd watch me."

"Come on, Princess, back to the greenroom."

"But you always stay out here and talk to everybody," Jacci said.

"Tonight I need to talk to you and not them."

Grampus led her through the curtains back to the greenroom, where everybody waited for their turn to go do their acts. Costumes were draped across chairs where the actors had to make quick changes. The juggler's pins, the acrobat's unicycle, Captain Dan's magic hat on top of the gaily painted little table, and the cage holding two bunnies lined the wall. The room was a joyful mess of all the ways they had made people laugh and cheer.

In the light of the lanterns hung along the wall, Grampus Duke's face looked very tired. All the good feeling drained out of Jacci as he sat down and pulled her up on his lap. He'd never done that. He'd hugged her and sat beside her and lifted her in the air when they were dancing, but she'd never sat on his lap. She wanted to push away from him and run find somewhere to hide, but instead she sat very still.

"Your mother—" he started.

She pushed her words out fast in front of his. "She said she would watch us dance and do our act. That she would watch over me. She told me that last night. And she did tonight. I know she did."

His voice gentled. "And she will watch over you always." His eyes looked damp. "But now she will be watching over you from heaven."

"No." Jacci put her hands over her ears. "I don't want her to be in heaven. I want her to watch from here."

"So did I, but she couldn't."

He tried to hug her, but she pushed away from him as she demanded, "Why couldn't she? Why couldn't she have a miracle?"

"I don't know." He rubbed his hand up and down Jacci's back but didn't try to pull her close again. "I guess miracles aren't up for the ordering just because we want one."

Jacci's head drooped, and her voice was quiet now. "She said you and the showboat were a miracle for us. For me."

"We were there when she needed us," he said. "That was providential, if not miraculous."

Jacci didn't know what providential meant, but it didn't sound as good as miraculous. She leaned against Grampus Duke then and let him hold her. "I didn't shoot that man soon enough."

Grampus Duke's arm around her stiffened. "You didn't what?"

"Shoot that man." Jacci shivered. "He scared me."

"You shot somebody?" Grampus Duke sounded as if he wasn't sure he could believe what she said. "Who?"

"The man that hurt Mama. He wouldn't let us go past him. Mama pointed her gun at him and told him to leave us alone, but he didn't listen. He ran at her and made her drop the gun. I picked it up and shot him."

"How did you know how to shoot a gun?" Grampus Duke still sounded doubtful of what she was saying.

"It's easy. You just pull back on the trigger. Daddy Kelly showed Mama how when he gave it to her, and I sometimes saw men shooting things on the banks from the steamboat."

"Where's the gun now?"

"I threw it in the river. Mama told me to."

"I see."

"She said I should forget that man."

"That would be best."

"But I can't forget how he looked at me." Jacci shivered again. "He scared me."

"It's all right," Grampus Duke said. "We're far down the river now away from him."

"Why did he want to hurt Mama?" Tears jumped into Jacci's eyes.

"I don't know."

"Did I do something wrong? That's why Mama died?"

"No, no. None of what happened is your fault, Princess. None of it." Grampus Duke stroked her back again. "It wasn't your mother's fault either. She would have done anything for you."

"She said she would always love me. That her love would be in my heart." Tears trickled out of Jacci's eyes. She put her hand on her chest where her mother had touched the night before.

"And so it will. My love is right there beside it. Don't you ever forget that."

Jacci felt panic squeeze her heart. "You aren't going away like Mama, are you?"

"Oh no. I'll be right here with you."

"Will we still dance?" Jacci stared down at her feet. She didn't know if she should ever dance again.

"Of course we will."

"I wanted to dance with Mama the way Aunt Marelda said. A mother-daughter dance."

"Now you can dance for her." He gave her another little hug.

"But she won't see me."

"Not as we expect, no. But who knows the powers of heaven? For certain, she will be with you in everything you do."

"Can I go see her?" She wanted to, but she didn't want to at the same time. What if she didn't look like Mama anymore?

"Yes, I'll go with you, but one more thing." He stood up. "Captain Dan says a man came aboard while we were doing the show. I haven't seen him, but I think it could be Kelly."

"Daddy Kelly?" Excitement rose inside Jacci, but then sadness smothered it. "He's too late."

"To see your mother, yes, but not too late to see you." He squeezed her hand. "You'll like that, won't you?"

Jacci nodded a little, and let Grampus Duke lead her toward the room where her mother was. She wanted to see her and to see Kelly. She really did, but at the same time her feet started feeling heavier and heavier. She'd never seen somebody dead.

chapter
11

THEY STOPPED IN THE DOORWAY. Kelly was on his knees beside her mother's bed and he sounded as if he might be crying. "I'm so sorry, Irena. I should have stayed with you. Protected you." He laid his head down on her mother's chest. "I did love you. Both you and Jacci. I'm so very sorry."

"Daddy Kelly?" Jacci's voice was barely over a whisper.

He twisted around toward her with tears running down his cheeks. She'd never seen Kelly when he didn't look ready to smile, but now he looked as sad as she felt. He stood then and held out his arms to her.

When she hesitated, Grampus Duke gave her a little push. Two seconds later she was sobbing in his arms. He picked her up as though she weighed nothing and held her tight. Her tears let up a little and she peeked over his shoulder at Mama. A white sheet covered her up to her chin. Her face looked so calm that Jacci almost believed she might wake and sit up. But she had coins on her eyelids. Jacci didn't know why.

Kelly wiped his cheeks off on his sleeve and handed Jacci his handkerchief. "There, there, little one."

"Why didn't you come sooner, Daddy Kelly? Mama would have tried harder if you'd been here."

"Tried harder to what?"

"To get better."

"Oh, little one, I'm sure she tried with everything in her to get better for you, but sometimes it isn't meant to be." He carried Jacci away from the bed and seemed to notice Grampus Duke for the first time. He nodded toward him. "Mr. Chesser."

"Mr. Reed," Grampus Duke said in return.

Jacci looked between them. They were both frowning.

"I'm sorry," Kelly said.

"Yes." Grampus Duke sounded cross.

"I loved her," Daddy Kelly said.

"Did you?"

"Not at first, but later. Not as much as I should have, but I did love her. She was . . ." He hesitated as if searching for the right words. "She was so strong. So good."

"Yes." Now Grampus Duke only sounded sad. "We both failed her."

"I should have done better for her."

"Did you betray her?"

Daddy Kelly gasped a little and went stiff, as though Grampus Duke's words were rocks that hit him. "I would have never done that."

"Even if you needed to pay off a gambling debt."

"I would have died first." Daddy Kelly's face was fierce as he stared at Grampus Duke. Then he took a breath and held Jacci closer. "This is not the time to speak of this."

Grampus Duke lowered his head. "You're right, but we need to talk before you leave."

"You're not leaving already, are you, Daddy Kelly?" Jacci tightened her arms around his neck.

As if she'd suddenly gotten too heavy to hold, Daddy Kelly

set her down. "No, little one. Not as long as the captain and your grandfather say I can stay. At least until after."

"After what?" Jacci asked.

"Your mother's funeral." He looked back at Grampus Duke. "Is there a plan for that?"

"She told me there's a church at Dove Creek."

"That's just down the river. Dear Irena, she always had a way of making things easier for everyone. Even now."

"It's not easy for everyone." Grampus Duke was looking at her.

"I will do my best to make sure things are as easy as they can be for her."

"She stays with me." Grampus Duke stepped closer to reach for Jacci's hand.

"She's legally my child."

"Legally?" Grampus Duke made a disgusted sound. "Nothing legal about any of it. But all that aside, do you aim to raise her at the gambling tables?"

"I can change my ways," Daddy Kelly said. "Besides, who are you to talk anyway? You've never shown all that much concern before for either of them. And what kind of life can she have on a showboat?"

"A very good one. Irena wanted her to stay here with me as part of our showboat family. It was her last request."

They seemed to forget Jacci between them as they faced off, appearing ready to come to blows. She looked between them, not sure what to do. Her mother would know, but her mother couldn't help her now. Then again, hadn't her mother said she would always be with her? Jacci touched her chest over her heart.

She stamped her foot and stood as tall as she could. "Grampus Duke. Daddy Kelly. Stop fighting. Mama would not like it."

"Grampus Duke?" Daddy Kelly suddenly sounded ready to laugh. "You're letting her call you Grampus?"

"She likes it." Grampus Duke shrugged with the beginnings of a smile too. "And she's right. Irena wouldn't like us having words, with her daughter here between us."

"Maybe we should ask Jacci what she wants."

They both looked at Jacci, who peeked toward her mother's body on the bed behind them. "I want my mama." Tears dripped down her cheeks. Her legs felt shaky and she wanted to lie down on the floor and just go to sleep. Make it all a dream.

"Come, Princess." Grampus Duke took her hand. "You're tired. Let's put you to bed. Morning will be time enough to sort everything out."

She looked back at Daddy Kelly.

"Your grandfather is right," he said with a little smile. "I'll be here when you wake."

Bright sunlight was sneaking its way through the boat when Jacci woke the next morning. Grampus Duke's bed was empty. The blanket wasn't even rumpled. He must have sat with her mother. Maybe both he and Daddy Kelly had stayed with Mama. Jacci thought she should have stayed awake to make sure they didn't fight. About her.

They would ask her again what she wanted. What did she want? Other than to wish her mother hadn't gotten hurt. She sat up with a sigh. Her mother would tell her wishes didn't always come true. For certain, no matter how hard she wished it, her mother wouldn't come back to life.

Her heart hurt as that truth stabbed through her. As she pulled on her dress, she tried to figure out what she should wish, but her head felt too fuzzy to think.

She didn't even glance toward her mother's room to see if Daddy Kelly or Grampus Duke was there. Instead, she climbed up to the top deck and lay down on her stomach at the very edge to stare down at the water rippling past them.

She loved the feel of the boat moving through the river. Mama had too. Sometimes when Mama wasn't working, the two of them would find a spot away from the busy passenger decks on the *Mary Ellen* and watch the river. Her mother would point out birds swooping down over the water or turtles sunning on logs at the edge of the river. They would laugh when fish leaped up out of the water as if trying to fly and then left a splash ring when they fell back in.

A fish did that now, its belly glittering in the morning sunlight. Then she spotted a cow at the edge of the river getting a drink with a calf beside it. On down the way, another calf was all alone. That's how Jacci felt. All alone.

She didn't look when she heard someone walking behind her. She didn't want to talk to anybody. She just wanted to lie there in the sun and stare down at the river. Maybe whoever it was would not notice her there.

But of course, he did.

"Hi, little one, I've been looking all over for you. Had almost decided you'd jumped ship."

She raised her head to look at Daddy Kelly. "I can't swim."

"Then you need to learn. An important skill for someone living on a boat." He squatted down beside her. "I'm surprised your mother didn't teach you. She was keen to learn herself."

"She was going to." She looked back down at the water.

"I taught her, you know." He sat down and peered over at the river too. "What are we watching?"

"Whatever there is to see."

"Your mother used to say that. She took life as it came." He was silent for a minute before he spoke again. "Do you want me to go away?"

"No." She sat up then and leaned against him. She didn't want him to go away, but he would. He always did.

He combed his fingers through her hair. "Your hair is a tangle."

"I forgot to brush it when I got up."

"The wind off the river can fix it for you." He kept gently stroking her hair. "You had beautiful black curls the first time I saw you."

"When was that?"

"Not long after you came into the world. You were beautiful then and beautiful now."

"Mama used to tell me my hair was pretty too, but last month she said she wished my hair was brown like hers." Jacci twisted her head around to look at Kelly's face. "I asked her why, but she said it was a silly thought."

"She was probably worrying about how all the young men would be chasing after you when you got older." Kelly smiled. "That's all."

"I liked her hair. She let me comb it at night and was teaching me how to braid it." She looked at Kelly's hair sticking out around the hat he wore. "Your hair isn't like Mama's, but it is sort of brown too. How come I don't have brown hair?"

"I'm sure somebody along the way in your family had these same beautiful wavy black tresses to pass down to you." He ruffled her hair then. "My ma used to tell me the Lord gives us our looks and we have to make the best of it. You came out pretty good there and I didn't do so badly myself."

She relaxed against him again. Sitting there in the sun with him helped her not think about her mama never combing her hair again.

After a few moments of silence, he said, "We're going to be at Dove Creek in a little while. Do you remember living there?" When she shook her head, he went on. "That's where you were born. You started walking and talking there."

"What was my first word?"

"Da-da, of course." He laughed.

"Did you live there too?" She looked up at him.

"Some of the time." Kelly stared off at the trees along the

riverbank. "It was a pretty place. Out in the country. You and your mother were happy there."

"I don't remember."

"You were very young. I think you were three when your mother took you back on the river."

"Why didn't we stay in the country?"

"I'm not sure. Perhaps because she needed a job." He sighed. "I had a run of bad luck and didn't have enough money to give her. She should have married someone else."

"She loved you."

"Love can get in the way of good sense, for sure."

"Did you love her?"

"Not enough. Never enough, but I do love you enough."

"How much is enough?"

"Enough to do what is best. Your grandfather says you like it on the showboat."

"I wanted Mama to like it too."

"Maybe she would have. She had a pretty voice. I remember her singing to you when you were a baby. She might have been a star in the show. That would have been better than being a maid and a cook's help on the *Mary Ellen*." He frowned as he said that last.

"I dance with Grampus Duke."

Daddy Kelly's cross look changed to a smile. "He told me. Says you are a natural talent."

She shrugged. "I just let my feet follow the music Aunt Marelda plays."

"Aunt Marelda? Grampus. Seems you've found family here." He tightened his arm around her. "That's good. Your Grampus says your mother wanted you to stay with him. Now with time to think about it, that does seem best."

"You could stay too," Jacci said. "You could dance with me."

"I don't know about that. I don't think I'm meant for the stage. My place is on a steamboat rather than a showboat. But

I'll find a way to visit from time to time to watch the prettiest girl in the show."

"I don't think my feet can dance today."

"No, I guess not. Besides, Captain Kingston says no show tonight. We're going to tie up and see about having your mother's funeral at the little church on the hill. Then they're staying another day to let the show go on. Your grandfather says the locals would be disappointed if there was no show. But first we'll do right by Irena."

So late that afternoon as the sun was going down, they stood around the grave in the little church's cemetery. Daddy Kelly had gone ashore and arranged it all, even to a box to put Mama in and a wagon to take her up the hill to the church. When they lowered Mama into the ground, Jacci started breathing too fast.

Grampus Duke leaned down to whisper in her ear. "She's not in there, Princess. Her spirit is free and in heaven now with the angels."

She looked up to see if she could see her. The sun slipped out of sight and sent a burst of color up across the sky. Even if she couldn't see her, Mama might be right there in all that brightness. By the time they got back to the showboat, the first star of the evening was shining over the showboat and then dozens more started twinkling in the sky.

The next night the show went on. Jacci didn't dance. Instead, she sat cuddled against Kelly and watched from the audience.

"I'll be watching you next time," he said.

But before the next show, he was gone. He didn't even say goodbye, but then he never did. Mama always said that was how Daddy Kelly avoided tears but that she could count on him coming back again someday.

Grampus Duke wasn't mad at him for leaving either. He said Daddy Kelly had come when they needed him to help bury her mother at Dove Creek. Jacci liked thinking about them living there in a cabin together and being happy.

So she wasn't mad at him either, even though she was going to tell him to say goodbye next time. She would promise not to cry. She didn't want to go with him. She was home on the *Kingston Floating Palace*. A week after Mama died, Grampus Duke started teaching her a new song and dance.

Chapter

12

JACCI REED LOVED THE FEEL of the wind off the river as she stood at the bow on the middle deck of the new *Kingston Floating Palace*. Captain Dan had commissioned the building of this new showboat last year to be ready for their run down the rivers as soon as the danger of ice was past. The auditorium had twice the seating capacity of the old showboat, with room for up to seven hundred people. The walls were a marvel of ornate mirrors and crimson wall coverings, and the padded seats were a vast improvement over the hard wooden chairs and benches on that first *Floating Palace* what seemed so many years ago.

This showboat was the third for the Kingston family. Her family, whether her name was Kingston or not.

Of course, Duke was truly family. Grampus Duke. Her little-girl name for him popped into her mind and brought a smile. When she was thirteen, she had dropped the Grampus and simply called him Duke the same as everybody else on the showboat. Over the years, they had perfected a vignette act to perform after the featured play. He acted as her dancing instructor while chasing away her romantic suitors. They sang a duet, with her pining for love while he was determined to see her married to a wealthy man who could give her everything. Everything but love. The scene ended with Duke defeated and her dancing away with the man she loved. It was billed on their show card as "The Duke and the Princess."

Much of it wasn't pretend. He had been her instructor and protector, frowning away any romantic advances from cast members or young men in the audience.

Just last week, Gabe had teased her. "You're going to be the prettiest girl to ever end up an old maid."

"You're one to talk." She had laughed. "You're what now? Twenty-nine. I think that's well along the way to being a confirmed bachelor."

"No, no. I'm only twenty-eight. In the prime of life, but alas, the girls do seem to run the other way when I come around." He sighed. "It's this red hair of mine. Scares them away."

"Come, come. I've seen the way girls line up to have you be the one to escort them off the boat. I'll wager you've kissed a girl at every stop along the river."

"That's the trouble. The captain never stops the showboat long enough for the second kiss."

She smiled now, remembering how he had pulled a long face. Gabe had always been able to make her laugh from the time she came on the showboat at five when he was thirteen. He became her big brother, although he reminded her time after time that she wasn't really his sister.

Her smile faded. She sometimes worried that he might leave the showboat the way his older brothers had. Jacci didn't know what Captain Dan and Aunt Marelda would do without him. Or Duke either.

Duke was showing his age. Going on seventy, although he

would never admit to any age. He sometimes forgot his lines in the plays now. Some of those new to their cast of actors this season were grumbling, especially Cameron Drake, their lead male actor. But Gabe was the director and he would hear no criticism of Duke. Plus, he made sure Jacci was in every scene with Duke so she could cover for him when he bungled a line.

Perhaps she and Duke should leave the showboat. Find a place to live onshore. She stared down the river. What would it feel like not to have the river running under her? Even in the off months, she and Duke always wintered where they could see a river outside their lodgings. While they stayed busy attending productions in land theaters and thinking up new songs for their own acts, they counted down the days until they would be back on the showboat.

Captain Dan went up the Kanawha for the first months of spring, but now they were on the Ohio again. Eventually, they would stop at Dove Creek, as they did every summer. She would climb up the hill to the little church and put flowers on her mother's grave.

A stone chiseled with IRENA CHESSER REED, 1856–1881, BE-LOVED WIFE AND MOTHER marked the place now. Kelly must have had it put there during one of his flush times when he was winning at the gambling tables.

Her heart hurt when she thought about her mother. She remembered so little about their years together. Duke assured her they were very happy and that her mother had loved her without measure.

Enough to die for her. He didn't say that, but those last days with her mother stayed in her memory. How could she ever forget shooting the man who stabbed her mother? Her mother made her throw away the gun and told her to forget she had ever pulled a trigger. But she couldn't forget. The image of the man's face as he clutched his middle after she shot him still surfaced in her nightmares and gripped her with fear.

With the dark around her, especially on nights that lacked the light of the moon, her heart would pound and make her want to get up and run. She knew not to where. Just away from the feeling that something bad would eventually catch up with her. The man with his threats and knives might still be out there hunting Jacci.

Duke knew about the man, about the gun, about what she had done, but whenever she tried to talk to him about it, he claimed too many years had passed to bring up those old worries. At times she persisted, in hopes that if she knew why the man had tried to take her from her mother, she could at least understand the fear that haunted her.

"Worry not, Princess." Duke always threw out his hands as though slinging her worries away on the river water. "You're safe here with our showboat family. We have disappeared on the river, you and I. There is nothing to fear. Not now."

Not now. Obviously she had much reason to fear then. Whenever she insisted she needed to know more, he would shrug and put her off by saying he didn't have the answers she wanted. That Kelly was the one to ask.

Kelly. Her father. Her mostly absent father. He came in and out of her life like the glint of sunlight on still river water that shimmered and disappeared at the first rivulet. She had asked him. More than once. But each time he shifted and guided her questions away as easily as a gust of wind blowing a butterfly off course.

He, the same as Duke, said she should forget that night. That she didn't have to worry about that man anymore. Or anything, Kelly said. She was safe with the Kingstons. Yet, she noted that her real name was never printed on the show bills. She was always Princess Kingston. Duke said that was a good show name for her.

In fact, once Kelly told her it might be best if she stopped ever saying her name was Reed and to use the name Kingston all the time. He had caught up with them on a stop along the Kentucky River when the spring floods had let them take their showboat to some new landings.

His words had stabbed her heart. She was twelve at the time, that awkward age between being a little girl and a young lady. She'd stared at him in the dark night air and spoke without thinking. "Why? Don't you want to be my father?"

"No, no. I'll always be your father, although a poor one I've been. Your mother was right to want you to stay with your grandfather. She knew me too well, I suppose."

The two of them had been standing by the showboat's railing after the show. Kelly stared out at the dark water as though he didn't want to meet Jacci's eyes.

"Then why don't you want me to use your name? My name. What's wrong with it?"

He had run his hands back and forth on the rail. "Not a thing. Jacinth is a beautiful name, although I did vote for Violet, after your mother."

"Violet?" Jacci frowned. "But my mother's name was Irena."

"I know, but I called her Violet sometimes. She was so like the pretty little flower. Looking so delicate but being tough to make it through some hard times."

"But she didn't make it through. She died."

"She did. Forgive me, little one, I've wandered back in my memories to a time you wouldn't know about."

"I would like to know about it." Jacci had grabbed the chance to ask Kelly those questions Duke didn't want to answer or couldn't answer. "Do you know why that man attacked Mama? What did he want?"

"Some questions don't have answers. And some things are better forgotten." He had hugged her then, as though he had just noticed it was nearing midnight. "I better hurry to find my group or I may be left behind."

And just like that he was gone. Once again.

Jacci hadn't begged him to stay longer, although it always made her sad to see him disappear down the stage plank into the night. She'd been surprised when Kelly showed up at that stop in Kentucky so far from his usual stomping grounds on the Mississippi.

Gabe told her Kelly was with an attractive woman in the audience. Not Mrs. Kelly Reed. Jacci had asked him straight out if he was married.

He had laughed. "Oh no. I never expect to marry again. Then I never expected to marry at all. I'm not cut out for family life as you well know."

Jacci couldn't deny the truth of that. Not then and not now.

She sighed. Perhaps he and Duke were right about the questions with no answers. She should remember her mother and forget the tragedy of her death. But the shadow of it hung over her even now. Maybe more, now that she was twenty. A person should know about her past. She should know the reason for her sorrows.

"You're looking awfully glum for such a fine morning. Did the crew make too much noise getting us underway and disturb your beauty sleep?"

She turned to see Gabe smiling at her. His red curls peeked out from under his cap.

Before she could say anything, he went on. "Not that the star of the show has need of any extra beauty treatments."

"You've got a silver tongue this morning, Captain Gabe. If you're down here, who's guiding us along the river?"

"You know Captain Dan. You can't keep him away from the pilothouse. He chased me off the wheel. Said he knows this river like the back of his hand. He thinks he's still thirty-something instead of creaking around at sixty."

She laughed. "Captain Dan is hardly at the creaking-around stage. He'd give you what for if he heard you saying that."

"True enough. So it can be our little secret."

"Secrets." Jacci echoed him. "Do you ever think there are too many secrets?"

"Not me." Gabe made a face. "I think nothing stays secret long on this showboat. Except of course what I just said about my father. He'd load me off at the first landing, pull up the stage plank, and leave me there if he knew I called him old."

"That secret is safe with me." Jacci looked back out toward the river. "But everyone is getting older."

"You're thinking about Duke." The smile in his voice was gone.

"Cameron said he must be senile." She hated the very sound of the word.

"What's Cameron Drake know? He's just an actor we picked up for the season." Gabe scowled. "Could be he's the one we need to boot off the boat."

"He's a good actor. The audiences love him."

Some of the cast and crew had been part of the Kingstons' shows for years, but a few new people came aboard each season. Cameron Drake was one of those, and so far hadn't seemed to fit into the showboat's family of players. He was an excellent actor who played the lead opposite her in their current drama, a new production Gabe had gotten the rights to from a playwright in New York. They had changed it, added more humorous moments and a little less romance.

"They could love me in the part just as much," Gabe said.

"Then why did you hire him on?" Jacci asked, smiling again. "You are directing the play. You did pick the parts and the players."

"The captain found him. Thought it was a stroke of luck, but that was before the man started acting like he owned the stage."

"It's good for the lead actor to own the stage."

"Stop taking up for him." Gabe gave her a cross look. "I thought you were griping about him and what he said about Duke."

"I don't know that I was griping exactly. It hurts, but I fear it's true. Duke is forgetting his lines, even in those skits we've done forever."

"He still knows his songs. That's good enough." Gabe put his arm around her. "We'll manage the rest."

She leaned against him for a moment. "Thank you, Gabe. I don't know what Duke would do without the *Floating Palace*. He's been part of it for years."

"And so have you. Fifteen years."

She pulled away to look at him. "How do you remember that?"

"Easy. I can add and subtract. I was thirteen when you came aboard and, well"—he hesitated—"I'm older now."

She laughed. "So am I. That old maid you always claimed I would be."

"Hardly that."

"I bet Aunt Marelda had two children by the time she was my age."

"Only one. And look where that landed her. On a showboat for life."

"She loves it and so do you," Jacci said.

"How about you, Jacci? Do you love it?"

"I can't imagine any other life."

"That might be because you were five when you became part of the Kingston players. You have no memory of any other life."

"I have a few. Wisps of things before Mama died. But that was on a steamboat. You were born on a showboat, weren't you?"

"Yes, but we're talking about you. Not me," he said. "I was born to playacting and river running. You were sort of forced into it."

She turned to grasp the railing and stare down at the river. "Do you remember that night, Gabe? When we came on the showboat? Mama and me."

"How could I forget that?" His voice changed. "Your mother, you covered with blood."

"Mama's blood." She kept her gaze on the water. "Do you know anything about what happened or why?"

"I don't."

"Would you tell me if you did?" She glanced over at him.

"I wouldn't lie to you, Jacci. You know that."

When she looked back at the river and didn't say anything, he went on. "Not about anything important. Why is this worrying you now?"

"I don't know. Mama has just been on my mind." She looked up and stared down the river now. "I guess because I've been thinking about Dove Creek."

"Where she's buried. That was such a sad time." He moved up beside her on the rail. His shoulder brushed hers, but he didn't put his arm around her again. "I cried. I thought I was too old to cry at thirteen, but I cried. I've learned since then that maybe a guy never gets too old to cry."

"You have always been the best brother."

"No, no. I keep telling you not a brother. A friend."

She smiled. "Yes. A forever friend."

"That I would hope." For a minute they were silent with the only sound the chug of the towboat pushing the showboat down the river and crows cawing as they flew overhead.

He broke the silence. "What does Duke tell you about that night?"

"He tells me to forget it. To embrace the present and not let what can't be changed haunt me. But I keep remembering him asking Mama if it was all about me?" She looked over at him. "How can I forget that?"

"I don't think you can. Any more than I can forget how scared I was standing there with your mother while you went to get Duke." Gabe pulled in a breath and let it out slowly. "Maybe you should ask Duke again. Tell him what you just told me."

She looked away again, this time up at the clouds floating across the very blue sky. "I'm not sure he would remember now. Cameron is right. He is forgetting everything."

chapter
13

EVER SINCE GABE COULD REMEMBER, the gathering of the cast after the shows was his favorite time of any day. He loved how they shared stories about what happened during the performance. They nearly always had some laughs over things people said when they came up to talk to them after the last act. If something had gone awry, they commiserated with the hapless cast members or admired them for being quick on their feet to find a way to fix things so the audience never knew.

They put on a show every livelong night, so things were apt to go sideways now and again. The juggler's pins might seem to have a mind of their own and land on the poor fellow's head instead of in his hands. A comic turn was all it took to have the crowd laughing when something like that happened.

The right kind of laughter had a way of saving the show. The last thing any of them wanted was for somebody to throw rotten tomatoes toward the stage or, even worse, rocks at the showboat after the show. The people expected value for their admission money, and that was something the Kingstons aimed to give on the *Floating Palace*.

Whatever happened, good or bad, they talked it out over coffee in the galley area. Aunt Tildy always had some kind of sweets cooked up for them. They needed energy boosters after putting on a show.

Gabe figured he used up the most energy of all, trying to keep things rolling along and all the players satisfied enough to stay with them on to the next landing. His father used to do the peacekeeping before he gave that over to Gabe. Now he was content just being the one to signal the *Little Ruby* stern-wheeler towboat to push them on down the river where new crowds waited to be entertained.

But tonight as the cast gathered in the galley to drink coffee or tea and eat Aunt Tildy's molasses cookies, Gabe struggled to hang on to his good humor. They'd had a good night. The theater was packed, and his mother said most comers paid their tickets in coin instead of produce.

Since the economic downturn in 1893, a lot of the country folks bartered their admission with bacon, eggs, a sack of corn, or other vegetables from their garden. The last couple of seasons, they couldn't always count on a sold-out show. But times were getting better.

The take tonight didn't have anything to do with Gabe having to force a smile as he broke his molasses cookie into little pieces. No, that was Cameron Drake. Solely due to their handsome leading man.

Gabe's father had found Drake in Cincinnati. "A lucky encounter," he'd said when he brought him aboard the new showboat. Gabe had been of like mind then, after the actor who had traveled with them the last five summers tumbled off a stage somewhere down south and broke his leg.

That had given a whole new meaning to the "break a leg" wish for an actor, Benton had said in his letter that found its way to them at the last minute while they were expecting him to show up to round out their cast. Benton had always been ready with a joke. A great guy to have aboard. Gabe was remembering him more fondly every day.

He couldn't fault Cameron's acting ability. He was as good as they'd ever had on the boat, but he could fault plenty of other things. Like how he was way more hands-on in the final scene with Jacci in their play. The scene did call for an embrace but not one that lasted a full minute. Gabe had half a mind to rewrite the scene. Let Jacci's character, Penelope, go off with the villain. That would be a twist for sure, and Penelope would have more chance of happily ever after with him.

Disgruntled. That was the word his mother would use for how Gabe was feeling. It didn't help that Cameron had his chair pulled over close to Jacci's. The chair Gabe usually took. They all had their places. The man knew that was where Gabe sat every night after the show. Before Cameron sat down, he had shot a grin over at Gabe, who was helping Aunt Tildy with the coffee.

He'd had other actors or crew members through the years that had been hard to like. On a showboat, everybody lived all season in close quarters. Not much privacy unless the players wanted to stay shut up in their little rooms. But Gabe had never wanted to pitch anybody overboard and steam on down the river without a glance back. Until now.

"You've 'bout wore that cookie out." Aunt Tildy sat down at the table beside him.

There were four tables in the dining area of this new boat. More room than they'd ever had on the old showboats. And a bigger crew. That meant more work for Aunt Tildy, who was showing her age. Gabe had told his mother they needed to hire on somebody to help her, but Ma said she and Gabe could be the extra help. Ma counted her pennies, and after the expense of the new showboat, she was counting them twice.

"Besides," she had said. "You know how Aunt Tildy is with her kitchen. She doesn't like anyone cooking but her."

He looked across at his mother on the other side of the room, chatting up their new act, the ventriloquist, Perry Wilson. Gabe wondered if he was talking for himself or his dummy, Corky, propped on his lap. Nobody ever saw him without one of his dummies, either Corky or Cindy. He expected people to greet them the same as him.

Aunt Tildy noticed the direction of his glance. "He's different, that Perry. Had me searching in my cupboard for a mouse until I figured out he was throwing his voice. Makin' some kind of squeak. I knew it was his doin' when that mouse let out a laugh instead of a squeak."

"I guess you gave him what for and sent him on his way." Gabe finally put a piece of cookie in his mouth.

"No indeedy. I sat him down at the table with that little doll of his and made him peel a pan of onions for the stew." Aunt Tildy nodded her head a little and raised her eyebrows at Gabe. "Ain't nobody gonna be pullin' a trick on me without havin' to pay. If anybody was to know that, it would be you."

Gabe had to laugh at her words, in spite of Cameron leaning way too close to Jacci as though telling her a secret. "That's for sure. I've cried my remorse tears over a bucket of onions many the time."

She reached over and patted his hand. "But you've got over your pesky ways." She smiled. "Mostly."

Aunt Tildy was another of the showboaters who was more family than crew. The same as Duke. He couldn't fathom how many meals the little black woman had cooked for them over the years.

"Well, I do try to keep from having to peel those onions."

"You need to get married. Have us some more redheaded rascals to keep us hopping around here."

"Nobody will have me, Aunt Tildy," Gabe said.

She looked straight at him with no smile showing. "Leastways not the one you's wantin' to note you, I'm thinking."

"A showboater doesn't stay in one place long enough to do any courting." He tried to brush off her comment.

"Captain Dan seemed to do all right with his courting. Found him a woman as crazy about showboating as he is. It's been a fine thing riding these rivers with the likes of you-uns."

"You aren't thinking on turning into a landlubber on us, are you? We couldn't go down the rivers without you."

"Comes a time for us all." She looked over at where Duke and Jacci were sitting. "Me and the Duke are pilin' on a lot of years. I figure he might have done left us if'n it weren't for Jacci."

"Could be the other way around. Him keeping her aboard."

"I'm thinking not. She got showboat fever early on." Aunt Tildy's face changed as she lowered her voice. "I still remember that poor little thing after her mama died. I'd find her hidin' in some of the funniest places. Back behind the rabbit hutches. Standing wrapped in the stage curtains. And sometimes thinkin' she was hid right in plain sight, stretched out flat at the edge of the deck, staring down in the water." She shook her head. "Poor little thing. Reckon it was her way of grieving. You remember, don't you?"

He did remember. "She came through it."

"Partly because of you, best I recall. And Duke teaching her dancin' steps. She was light on her feet even then. And a pretty little thing." Aunt Tildy looked over at Jacci. "Pretty then, but a beauty now. No wonder some is getting dazzled by her. That new fella seems to be one of them." She turned her gaze back to Gabe. "He bears watching, I'm thinking."

"I'd like to watch him go down the stage plank and forget to come back," Gabe muttered.

Aunt Tildy patted his hand again. "You was always her protector. Did any of you-uns figure out what went on with her mama? Poor woman."

"If Ma or Captain did, they never told me. That night she came aboard, she told me she fell on the knife."

Aunt Tildy gave him a look. "That is about as likely as the sun coming up in the west of a morning. You know somebody stuck that knife in her side, sure as anything."

"I know."

She sighed. "I'm reckonin' it don't much matter after all these years down the river. Nothin' to do about it now. Long as it doesn't bother our girl there." She looked at Jacci a moment before she stood up. "Guess I'd better be puttin' up what cookies weren't gobbled up."

"I'll help you with the dishes," Gabe said.

"No use of that. I ain't so old that I can't manage a few cups and saucers." She nodded over at the other table. "I'm thinkin' you could squeeze another chair in there were you to want to. No need you sittin' here at this table crumbling up my cookies all by your lonesome."

Aunt Tildy was right. It wasn't like him to sit off in a corner and stew about things. He scooted his chair over to the other table even if he couldn't push it in between Jacci's and Cameron's the way he wanted to.

Duke moved his chair to let Gabe sit on the other side of Jacci. "Glad you decided to join us, Gabe. We were beginning to think you were keeping your distance because you weren't sure we entranced the audience this night."

"You always entrance the crowd, Duke. You and Jacci." Gabe smiled at her.

"My beautiful Princess captures the eye for certain." Duke beamed at Jacci.

"You went up on your lines again in your scene, Gramps." Cameron Drake let out a bored sigh as he looked across the table at Duke.

The room went quiet. In their family of performers, they never criticized one another after a show, especially not for forgetting a line. Every actor forgot a line now and again. Of course, Duke was going up on his scripted lines more and more, and sometimes blanking out so much that he couldn't recover. But his part was little more than a walk-on, where his flub was easily covered by Jacci, who shared the scene with him and Cameron.

Beside Gabe, Jacci set her cup down, pulled in a breath, and seemed ready to set Cameron straight. Duke reached over to touch Jacci's arm and then gave Gabe a look that let him know he didn't need them rescuing him from Cameron's jibe. Jacci let out her breath and sat back. Gabe did the same.

"Did I?" Duke said. "That make you forget yours, young Drake?"

"I never forget my lines, although some of the lines in this excuse for a play are certainly forgettable."

Gabe's face flashed hot. Their shows weren't works of art, but they were crowd pleasers. Cameron Drake was being anything but a crowd pleaser in this room, as several of the cast glared at him. Gabe could feel his mother staring at him, not Cameron, and so he tamped down his anger. He could almost hear her whisper in his ear to not insult Duke more by thinking he couldn't handle the upstart actor.

In fact, Duke hardly seemed bothered. "Ahh, then I guess if I forgot one it hardly mattered." He took a sip of coffee before he leveled his gaze on Cameron. "But there is only one person I let call me Gramps and that person is not you."

"Oh, come on. Up on the New York stages the actors always call the old guys in the cast Gramps. It's a term of affection."

"We're not on a New York stage now," Jacci said.

"You can say that again," Cameron muttered.

Jacci acted as though she didn't hear him. "We're on a showboat. Here we call people the names they want to be called."

"Is that why they call you Princess? Because you want them to?" Cameron smiled at her. "Although I'm not saying the name doesn't fit."

Gabe stiffened. One more word and he was going to have to

knock the man out of his chair. Jacci didn't seem any happier with his remarks. At least that much was good.

"No one calls me Princess except my grandfather." The cold look she gave him said more than words.

Cameron pointed toward one of the show bills on the table. "It's always Princess in the printouts. Why's that? Are you in hiding or something?"

That was it. If Gabe didn't stand up and tell the man off, he was going to explode. He was pushing back from the table when Ma stepped behind him and put her hand firmly on his shoulder to keep him in his chair.

"That's quite enough, Cameron." She stared straight at the man. "We know you're relatively new to our group, but we do expect every member of the cast to be respectful to all. Duke and Jacci are part of our family and have been for a long time. You now are part of that showboat family at least for this season or until you choose to leave."

"Hold on." Cameron held up his hands. "I didn't mean to upset anybody. You southerners are thin-skinned."

"Not at all." Ma's voice stayed calm. Gabe had learned at a very young age that when his mother sounded like that, he better keep his mouth shut and do whatever she said. "But I do think you owe all of us an apology."

"For saying the play lacked dramatic flair? I simply spoke the truth."

"For that and more."

"Ah, then, if you insist. I can do a bit of acting for you." He stood up and made a bow. "I am extremely sorry if my words were ill chosen and offended any of you gentle souls."

Ma's hand stiffened on Gabe's shoulder. He wanted to ask her if he could just sock the man and get it over with. But she pulled in a little breath and let it out easy. "Very well, Mr. Drake. I suggest you turn in for the evening after that performance. Perhaps by morning we will be prepared for more of your scenes."

"I feel rather like a schoolboy who has been dismissed." Cameron looked around with a smile as if he expected others to be smiling with him.

But the others in the room weren't ready to side with him against Marelda Kingston. They knew who doled out the pay. That left Cameron like a comedian dying onstage with no one laughing at his jokes.

Duke twisted his mouth to hide a grin and stood up. "Come on, Cameron. Let an old man accompany you on a stroll around the deck before we both turn in. We'll all have a new act to do tomorrow."

Cameron didn't seem to know what to do, but when Duke put his arm around his shoulders, he went out with him.

For a moment, nobody spoke after the two left the room. Then Aunt Tildy said, "You think somebody ought to follow them to make sure Duke doesn't pitch him in the river?"

Ma laughed. "If we hear a splash, I'll send Gabe out to throw Cameron a rope."

"I'm thinking Gabe might just let him flounder a spell." Aunt Tildy raised her eyebrows.

"I'd haul him out, Aunt Tildy. We need a leading man," Gabe said.

That made the others laugh and the talk started among them easy again. His mother patted him on the shoulder, a way of letting him know she thought he'd said the right thing before she went to sit with the Loranda family.

This was the Lorandas' third season with the Kingstons. They had an acrobatic act and did double duty in the band. Joseph could play any instrument, and son Joey was almost as good. Reva was a wizard with costumes, and daughter Winnie could coax some fancy notes from her flute that set the perfect mood for some scenes. At seventeen, Winnie was pretty and shapely enough that she got wolf whistles from some of the rowdier men in the crowd whenever she was onstage.

Unfortunately, Gabe thought she had a crush on him. Not exactly the one he wished was thinking of him in a romantic way. He looked over at Jacci, who was still frowning a little.

"Don't let Cameron bother you," he said. "He just likes to have center stage."

"I guess that's what makes him such a good actor." Jacci shrugged. "You know what they say about creative people."

"No. What?"

She smiled a little. "We're all eccentric. Why else would we want to live on a boat?"

"True enough."

She pushed back from the table. "I don't think Duke will pitch Cameron over the side. Not sure he could, but he looked tired. I better go check on him before he turns in."

"You want me to go with you?"

She shook her head. "Stay and enjoy the talk. I know how you love this time with the cast."

"But I like you being here too."

She smiled again then. "You want everybody to be one big, happy family."

"Sure. What's wrong with that?" Gabe wanted to take her hand, but he wasn't sure she would want him to.

"Not a thing, but even families have their problems." A worried look slipped across her face. She covered it up with another smile. "I'll see you in the morning."

He did grab her hand then before she could turn away. "If he bothers you, you let me know. Who we hire we can fire."

"What about needing that leading man?"

"Actors are a dime a dozen. We probably could pick up a new guy in the next town. Some rube who has always dreamed of being onstage."

That made her laugh. "Duke and probably Aunt Marelda too would say we better stick with the known problems instead of hunting up unknown ones."

"According to how irritating the known ones are. Anybody can be replaced."

"Not you, Gabe. Or Aunt Marelda. Or Captain Dan." She looked around. "Where is he tonight?"

"He was talking to some of the locals the last I saw him. Him and Cap Sallie. I think they are over on the *Little Ruby* talking river lore."

"He'll be full of stories tomorrow then." She smiled as she pulled her hand free. "Really, Gabe, I'm fine."

And that quick she was gone before he could tell her she was one of the irreplaceable people on the *Floating Palace* and even more so in his life.

chapter
14

THE MOON SPREAD a silvery glow over the river and gave Jacci light to make her way through the boat. Not that she really needed it. Even on the darkest of nights she had no trouble making it to her room. The layout of the third *Floating Palace* was the same as the earlier *Palace* showboats, only bigger.

When they first walked through this new *Palace* and stood on the stage to look out at the many seats in the theater area, Captain Dan had asked Aunt Marelda if she thought they could ever expect a full house.

"Too late to go smaller now, Captain." She had laughed as she patted his arm. "As long as we give them what they want, we'll have standing room only."

She'd been right. As Gabe sometimes liked to say, his mother was always right. The dramatic plays, the comedy routines, the circus acts mixed in with some vaudeville were what the people wanted to see. The calliope drew them in. Even after so many years on the showboat, Jacci's heart still beat a little faster each time she heard the steam-powered music start up. The tunes sounded for miles out across the river bottoms and up into the hills to let the people know a showboat was coming.

Tonight Aunt Marelda had been right again to keep Gabe from blowing up at Cameron. A showboat's season went better when they kept the peace on board. Sometimes that took work and knowing when to speak and when to sit down and keep your mouth shut. Cameron hadn't figured that out yet. He seemed to take pleasure in stirring up things, as if he needed a cure for his boredom on the river.

For certain, he had stirred up Jacci tonight. And not in a good way.

"Are you in hiding?" His question echoed through her head. She doubted he had meant it seriously, but perhaps he had hit on the truth anyway. Was she in hiding? Had her mother died making sure she could hide? And if so, why?

She wanted to go demand Duke answer her questions. She was old enough to know the truth about whatever had happened that night on the *Mary Ellen.* But when she got to his room and cracked open the door to look inside, she heard him snoring. The dear man had been extra tired lately. She had tried to get him to go to a doctor while they were wintering off the boat, but he laughed away her concerns by reminding her of his age. "A man can't pile on the years without slowing down a bit."

She gently shut the door. She wouldn't wake him to demand answers. Those questions had gone unanswered for years. Another night would hardly matter. In fact, it might be better to first explore the uneasy feelings Cameron's words had awakened in her. Besides, who knew if Duke could remember the answers now, even if he had once known them?

With a sigh, she went back out on the deck. Her thoughts were too scrambled for her to fall asleep. Perhaps a few minutes watching the river gently slip past them and seeing the stars scattered across the sky would calm her worries.

They were tied up to some willows for the night, so she didn't go to the railing on the second deck where she liked to watch the river when they were on the move. Instead, she climbed up to the top deck with the square pilothouse seeming to balance right in the middle. In the morning when they would start on down the river, either Captain Dan or Gabe would be in the little house, hands on the wheel, eyes forward, watching for sawyers and other dangers in the water.

Both of them knew the rivers like the backs of their hands and steered through the curves and twists while avoiding the known hazards. But the rivers were ever changing with new dangers to watch for like those sawyers, trees brought down in storms that could float just below the surface and pop up without warning to jab a hole in the hull.

Not that a showboat's hull dipped very far below the surface of the water. Jacci had heard some refer to showboats as nothing more than dolled-up rafts. This one was certainly a sight to behold, with the name in big letters along the side and again around the top of the pilothouse. Railings laced around the second deck and up here on the hurricane deck like picket fences around a yard to add eye appeal, plus keep the careless from tumbling off the boat.

A showboat's design was only limited by the showman's imagination, and Captain Dan and Aunt Marelda had imagined a boat to match her name, *Floating Palace.* But the showboat had no boilers or paddle wheels to give it power to speed its way down the rivers or chug it back upstream. That was why they needed a towboat like the *Little Ruby* to push them along.

She once asked Captain Dan why they called it a towboat instead of a push boat. He had laughed and shoved up his cap to scratch his head. "You've asked a stumper there, kid. Don't know that anybody has an answer to that one."

More questions without answers.

She looked back at the *Little Ruby.* Since the stern-wheeler wasn't as tall as this new showboat, Captain Sallie, who piloted it, couldn't see past the showboat. He had to trust the captain in the pilothouse on the showboat to properly guide them both as he provided the locomotion to move the *Palace* along.

"Not what I did in my younger days," Captain Sallie often grumbled. "No sir. Back then, I was the one finding the deep channels and steering away from trouble. This follow-the-leader ain't any kind of piloting, but steamboats are dying out on the river. That clackety old railroad is shuttling folks and products around these days." He would yank his fingers down through his shaggy beard, probably the only combing it ever got, and laugh a little before he went on. "Guess I'm doing nothing but shuttling folks around too."

He always finished with a lament. "Why anybody would want to travel any way other than the river is a mystery to me."

She liked Captain Sallie. He'd been towing or pushing their showboat around for a few years now. She stared over at the towboat where the moonlight bounced off the smokestacks. No smoke was pouring out of them now the way it would in the morning after Mac, the engineer, fired up the boilers. The sound of a man's laugh drifted over to her. Captain Dan and the other men were clustered on the main deck's bow watching the river while they swapped tales and river news.

Most of the rooms on the *Ruby* were dark. The crew not listening in on the river talk would already be abed. At dawn, they had to be ready to move the showboat on down the river. A couple of windows did show lantern light in the rooms occupied by single men from the showboat cast and band. No women slept on the *Ruby*. Aunt Marelda took steps to ensure nothing she considered unseemly behavior went on. Duke was the only single man with a room on the *Palace*.

One of those lights on the other boat might be Cameron in his room on the *Ruby*. Just as well. She had no energy for a war of words with him. He seemed to take pride in topping anything she said. The man could be infuriating, but then, he had a way of being charming at times. He wasn't happy on the showboat. He must have been desperate for a job when he agreed to join the cast. Obviously, acting on a showboat hadn't turned out to be glamorous enough for him.

When Jacci told him she thought the *Palace* was very glamorous and that she couldn't see that much difference between their shows and those she had seen in land theaters, he had given her a pitying look. He assured her she would change her mind if she ever went to the big cities where famous actors and actresses occupied the stages. That was where Cameron wanted to be, but he claimed a new actor needed a benefactor to help him get a start in those shows.

"It takes money," he said. "And lots of it to be a success."

Money wasn't something that had ever worried Jacci. For most of the year, she and Duke were comfortable on the *Palace* with their meals and housing supplied plus their pay. During the season, they were either riding to new landings or giving shows, with little time or temptation to spend their earnings.

Kelly did show up broke now and again, but he had too much pride to ask Jacci for a handout. Either that or Duke made sure it didn't happen. While Duke wouldn't admit to it, Jacci thought he sometimes slipped Kelly enough money to live on until his luck changed.

In ways Cameron reminded Jacci of Kelly. Instead of gambling at a game table the way Kelly was wont to do, Cameron was a man ready to gamble on his future. Now he was stuck here on this showboat where no gambling could take place. Where upright behavior was expected. No drinking allowed. If any of the women smoked, they hid it. Marelda didn't write the rules out to post on the greenroom wall, but everyone knew them. Perhaps everyone but Cameron. From the look on Marelda's face tonight, if he didn't, he would soon.

When she heard steps behind her, she didn't look around.

She didn't need to look. Gabe would have come after her to make sure she was all right. She smiled. He never forgot about her. He had started watching over her when he was barely into his teens and she was a scared little kid after her mother died. He always knew how to make her feel better.

But it wasn't Gabe.

"I saw you up here from the towboat. So I came back over to do some stargazing with the prettiest showgirl on the river." Cameron slipped his arm around her waist.

Jacci stiffened at his familiarity. It wasn't that she hadn't felt his arm around her before. They embraced in the drama's final scene every show. But that was acting when she was a girl named Penelope and he was a man named Sterling. The script called for him to hug her close to his chest in their happy ending.

That was fine when she was being someone different and not herself. She had no thought to do the same now, but she felt trapped. The railing kept her from stepping forward to move away from his touch without it being obvious that was her intent.

"Not many stars visible tonight with the nearly full moon," she said as she twisted away from his arm. Obvious or not, she couldn't allow him to be so forward. "I best go see about Duke."

He grabbed her hand. "Come, my beautiful Jacinth. Your grandfather is fine. He was not nearly as upset as you and our redheaded director. Plus, even if he were, he would have forgotten it by now, the way he forgets everything else."

She scowled at him and freed her hand. "Do you rehearse being obnoxious or does it come naturally for you?"

He laughed as if she'd said something that pleased him tremendously. "My tender little sweetheart." He touched her cheek lightly. "You really don't have to act that much to play the part of the ingénue, do you?"

She blew out a breath and took another step away from him. "No, I suppose not."

"The very type of character they love here on the river. The beautiful innocent who must always be rescued by the virile hero who saves the day. I could write a play like this in my sleep."

"Then perhaps you should. I'm sure Gabe would be glad to take it into consideration."

"I doubt I could make it simple enough for the likes of him and the country bumpkins in our audiences."

"I daresay I'm one of them. I like our shows."

"Even the individual performances after the drama? Where the captain does those cheesy magic tricks and the Lala-whatever family bounces all over the stage, rides unicycles, and balances swords on their noses? Along with who knows what else. Not to mention the ventriloquist and his tired jokes."

"Yes, all of them." She lifted her chin and stared at him.

"Your loyalty is touching. Unbelievable but touching." He looked amused before he went on. "However, your singing is a highlight and dear Winnie's flute expertise isn't bad." He raised his eyebrows at Jacci. "If I'm not wrong, and I rarely am, that young lady would like to take your place in the drama. There appears to be more than tumbling tricks on her agenda."

"Has she caught your eye?" Jacci asked.

"I can appreciate beauty when I see it, although she doesn't have the princess shine." He smiled at her. "Like you."

"The moonlight must be blinding you." She tried to shrug off his words.

"I can see very clearly," he said. "I see a young woman afraid of the future. Someone who should follow me to New York and make her place on the stage there. You could be the next Jenny Lind." He paused a moment. "If you weren't hiding out here on this showboat."

"I daresay Jenny Lind never sang 'The Boy I Love Is in the Gallery.'"

He shook his head and mimicked her singing. "'There he is waving his handkerchief at me, as merry as a robin that sings on a tree.'" He laughed. "I tell you, Jacci, your talents are wasted on such as that."

"The people like it."

"So they do. Enough handkerchiefs start waving that at least it gets some air stirring in the theater."

"That can be a good thing."

"True. It can get heated onstage, but unfortunately they don't wave those hankies during our scene." He winked at her. "Plus, if such were your aim, you could take your pick of eager young suitors and marry an engaging rube. Then, instead of hiding out on a showboat, you could fade from sight on some backwoods hog farm."

"What a fabulous idea." Jacci gave him a level look. "I would fit right in with the country life. And as you say, it would surely be a better hiding place, were I needing to hide, than being onstage in front of hundreds of people most every night from March to November."

"I suppose that's true. You aren't a girl anybody would forget easily. In fact, our voice thrower, Perry Wilson, says you remind him of someone, but I can't remember if he said who. Or perhaps it was his dummy Corky talking. You never know with him."

"Oh? I've heard everyone has a double somewhere."

"I've yet to see mine, if that is so."

"I guess some people are one of a kind," she said dryly.

"I'll take that as a compliment even if my actor's ear is catching a bit of sarcasm in the line you're delivering."

"I'm sorry. That wasn't nice of me." Jacci reached to touch his arm, but quickly pulled her hand back before he could try to claim it. "Actually, it is very good to be one of a kind."

"Like you think Duke is and our man Gabe too?"

"I suppose so. For sure they are both very important to me."

He stepped closer and whispered, "I could be important to you too."

She pretended not to hear. "Duke might be having problems remembering things now, but he was a lifesaver for me after my mother died." Cameron would never realize how literally she meant that. Not that she intended to share that truth with him.

"Was your mother a showgirl too?"

"No, far from it. I don't think she ever sat in a showboat audience."

"Are you saying she watched from backstage?"

Jacci smiled. "Something like that."

She had never given up the feeling her mother saw her dancing with Duke on the night she died. She liked to imagine her pausing a moment to peer down at Jacci before moving on up to heaven. Even now, while the feeling was not as strong as it had been that night so long ago, she still sometimes felt her mother watching over her.

"Not the best way to watch a show," Cameron said.

"I suppose not. But while my mother didn't get the acting bug from Duke, she did get the love of the river. She worked on a steamboat before we came to the *Floating Palace* years ago. I really don't remember any time I wasn't on the river."

"Are you saying you don't know where you're from? Kentucky? Indiana? Somewhere south?"

"I've never thought about being from somewhere." She peered over at him and turned the question back to him. "Where are you from?"

"Chicago. My father was a company clerk. An unhappy company clerk who said he sometimes had nightmares about adding up columns of numbers. He wanted to make me into an unhappy company clerk too. I caught a train to New York when I was sixteen. Haven't been back since." He sounded proud of that.

"Your poor mother," Jacci murmured.

"Yes, poor. She died the year before I left. From boredom, I think." His face softened. "She had a beautiful voice. She would read to me and she loved to sing. She made me want more. Unintentionally to be sure, but it still grew until I had to try my wings."

"She sounds like a lovely woman. I'm sorry you lost her when you were so young."

"Sad, for sure, but turned out to be perfect timing for my escape." He brushed aside her sympathies. "But what about you? Were you born on a steamboat?"

"No. I was born near a little town in Kentucky called Dove Creek and lived there awhile before Mama got work on a steamboat again. She had worked on one before I was born. But I only remember the river."

"So, you have no roots."

She shrugged and looked back at the river flowing past. "I guess not. Only floating ones."

"Then it should be more than easy for you to head to New York and drift around there from stage to stage. I could introduce you to the acting circle."

"I'm happy with this stage, and you should be too." She turned back to him, but still heard the music of the river behind her. "At least for a season. We're always one big family during our showboat season."

"And I'm messing that up with my truth telling." He put his hands behind his back and took his turn staring at the river. "Doesn't the Good Book say we shouldn't lie?"

"Thou shalt not lie," Jacci said. "But it also says something about doing unto others as you would have them do unto you."

"I'm always ready to hear the truth."

When she started to say something, he held up his hand. "But no more sermons. I do know what you're saying and you are right. We do have to survive the summer and on into the fall unless we jump ship."

"Are you thinking of doing that?"

"I suppose not. I needed the job when I took it, and I must admit I still do. A man needs a little jingle in his pockets in order to put forward his best appearance." He sighed. "Actually, I did have every intention of coming over here to apologize profusely to you if my words upset you earlier. I do want the princess of the river to think of me kindly."

"It's the queen you have to worry about. Aunt Marelda doesn't put up with nonsense and she doesn't like conflict among those on her boat."

"Then it is good I came to practice being contrite with you before I next see her."

"If I were to guess, I'd say that would be very early tomorrow once we get underway to our next landing." Jacci took a last look at the moonlight kissing the river before she turned for the stairs. "Good night, Mr. Drake."

"Goodnight, Princess Jacinth."

"I told you only Duke calls me Princess."

His laugh followed her across the top deck. It wasn't until she was going down the steps that she realized he had never really said he was sorry about anything. The man pulled lines out of the air as if he were always on a stage, acting a part. Could it be that he was the one hiding even more than she?

chapter

15

EARLY THE NEXT MORNING, Gabe's mother found him as the towboat crew was untying the *Palace* and getting the boilers fired up on the *Ruby*. She handed him a biscuit and sausage and a cup of coffee.

"I gather this means no sit-down morning for me," he said.

"You can sit down on the stool in the pilothouse. Captain forgot to get to bed at a reasonable time, so I told him to sleep in and let you take us on to the next stop. It's Westport. Not far down the river. Your father says there's some excitement down around there, according to the river talk. One of the candidates for president is stumping along here, and Captain thinks if we catch up with where he is, the people that come out to see him might also be in the mood to come aboard for the show. The man might even talk up our show to his supporters if we let him have the stage for his speech where he'd have a captive audience."

"You think that's a good idea?" Gabe took a bite of the biscuit. From the look of the smoke rising from the *Ruby*'s smokestacks, they would be ready to push off soon. Chains were clanking and ropes slashing across the decks. The actors would be burying their heads under their pillows to try to block out the noise disturbing their sleep.

She shrugged. "Why not? His followers' money will be as good as anybody's."

"Is he Democrat or Republican?"

"Neither, the best your father could discern. Seems he's after the Progressive Party nomination. They haven't had their convention to pick a candidate yet."

"Who is it?" Gabe finished off the sausage and biscuit and wished she'd brought two.

"You know your father. He's no good with names unless it has captain in front of it. But I did see the newspaper the ventriloquist brought aboard last night."

"I guess he wants something to read to his dummies." Gabe made a face as he wiped his hands off on his pants.

"The man is a little strange, but our crowds like his act."

"We've got a boatload of strange with this bunch."

"Could be we're the strange ones and they're the ordinary ones." Ma smiled and took his cup after he chugged down the coffee.

"Kingstons strange? Not a chance, but even if we were, those that come aboard our showboat have to match their strange to ours and not be bringing in new weirdness."

"Cameron isn't exactly strange."

"Then what do you call him? Arrogant? Insufferable?"

She laughed. "Well, he could learn a few manners. He needs to give up that artistic temperament until he's back on those stages he's pining after in the big towns." She dipped her head and stared up at Gabe through her eyelashes. "And you need to find a way to tamp down your jealousy."

He wanted to tell her she didn't know what she was talking about, but then she almost always did know exactly what he was thinking. Had since forever. "Yes, ma'am."

"I'm serious, Gabe."

"I said yes, ma'am." A little irritation sneaked into his voice. He sighed. "Sorry, Ma."

She put her hand on his cheek. "She won't fall for him. She's got too much sense for that."

"Maybe. He's got looks and can be charming in between being a bum." He turned his face away from his mother. He didn't want her reading any more of his thoughts.

But again, she already knew them. "She loves you."

"Yeah, like a brother."

"Not a bad kind of love." His mother's smile was a little sad as she pulled her hand away. "Give her time. She might start seeing you in a different light the way you did her when she turned into a young lady."

He looked straight at his mother then. This was one time she didn't know everything. He had loved Jacci, and not ever as a sister, since that day when she was dressed like a little boy hitting the tambourine against her leg as they marched together in that first parade while her mother lay dying on the showboat. Of course, she hadn't known that. She'd thought her mother would get better.

He, on the other hand, had feared the worst from the first after he saw all the blood. Maybe that was one of the reasons his heart had so softened toward Jacci when he was really too young to know what love was. Jacci had been so brave.

"Time doesn't fix everything," he said now to his mother.

"True, but sometimes it's all we have to make things better. Except prayer. You know I've done that for you and for her too forever and will continue for the rest of forever. Maybe you should try the same."

"Right, Ma." He didn't want to hear a lecture on his prayer life. Besides, his heart sent up plenty of prayers when it came to Jacci, whether those prayers had words or not. Didn't the Bible say the Lord knew a man's heart? "Look, Captain Sallie will be sounding his bell ready to go. I better be up at the wheel. Wouldn't want him to push us into a tree."

He started toward the steps to the hurricane deck. He looked over his shoulder at his mother. She was watching him, probably saying a prayer right then. He didn't know why that was poking him so. Maybe because it seemed so hopeless.

He called back to her. "You didn't tell me the name of this fellow that Captain wants to let do a stump speech on our stage. Still not sure that's a good idea. Best to stay away from politics."

"Giles. Griffith Giles. He's a Kentuckian. A senator, I think."

"As a Progressive?"

"What I read said he was changing parties to try to get that nomination."

"I think you should advise the captain to collect their quarters and let them come to the show and forget the speech. We don't want folks fighting over politics in our new auditorium." He gave her a look. "You remember what happened on *Palace 1* that time those miners started fighting over some girl and the whole crowd joined in the melee."

"Don't remind me." Ma shuddered. "You could be right about this. No need alienating those not feeling progressive right now. I'll talk to your father."

With a smile, Gabe ran up the steps to the pilothouse. It was a rare day for his mother to admit he was right when he was speaking against something she or his father wanted to do.

His smile slipped away when he remembered coming up these steps the night before to see Cameron and Jacci standing close together by the railing. He'd expected Jacci to be up top after the scene in the galley. He hadn't expected her to be with Cameron.

He told himself she hadn't arranged a meeting with the man on the hurricane deck. Cameron could have been the one to follow her. That didn't mean she wanted him there. But then, she had reached across the space between them to put her hand on Cameron's arm. That was when Gabe had slipped back down the steps out of sight.

A cowardly thing to do, he decided now. But what if she was getting ready to let the man embrace her the way she did in the play? To let him kiss her? Gabe couldn't have stood seeing that. Hard enough to watch when it was Penelope and Sterling in the play. He couldn't watch Jacci and Cameron doing the same when it might not be an act.

Jacci waited until after Duke had his coffee and was on what he called his morning constitutional around the deck. She glanced toward the steps up to the top deck. She'd seen Gabe talking with Marelda and then running toward the steps to the pilothouse. Watching the river with him when he was at the wheel was her favorite way to spend a morning.

But today she wanted answers more. Gabe would be busy anyway with this stretch of the river. A lot of bends to wrap the long showboat and towboat around.

She planned to join Duke on his last turn around the deck and stop him where some chairs sat along the starboard side. That should give them some privacy. Most of the cast members liked to sleep while the showboat rolled down the river.

She hadn't seen Cameron this morning, which was more than fine with her. His talk about her hiding had stirred up old memories about when her mother died. Whether she had them right, she didn't know. She'd been so young. It could be the wisps of memory still floating around in her mind were nothing more than something she'd dreamed during that time when she had hidden here and there on the showboat to keep anyone from seeing her tears.

Duke could ease her mind about that by telling her more about her mother and what had happened the night they came aboard the *Palace*. She clenched her right fist. The memory of the gun jerking in her hand when she shot that man stayed burned in her mind. She hadn't dreamed or imagined that. The man attacked her mother. Jacci had shot him. Maybe killed him.

Even now, if she didn't block the memory, she could see his face as he grabbed his middle and fell. Why had he wanted to take her from her mother? That would be her first question.

But Duke stopped short of his last round to head to the galley where Captain Dan was having a late breakfast. When she caught the scent of Aunt Tildy's fried doughnuts, she could hardly blame him. Plus, he'd want to know whatever river news the captain had heard at the last stop. News could sometimes fly down the river faster than their boat.

Nothing for it but to follow him to snag one of those doughnuts and wait until she could catch him alone. Captain Dan had the center seat at the middle table. His deeply lined face always looked a little red from the burn of the river wind. When she first saw him those many years ago, she'd been afraid of him. Though he really wasn't a big man, not as tall as Duke even, he'd seemed big to her then with his broad shoulders and muscular arms. The hair sticking out below his captain's hat used to be the same red as Gabe's but was now snow white.

He had what Duke called sense of presence. That was why he was always so good with his magic acts. He made rabbits appear and disappear. He made Aunt Marelda float in the air, or at least he convinced those watching he did. He had a way of making a person believe whatever he wanted them to.

Everyone said Gabe was the captain made over. Jacci supposed he was in looks. Still, she had never felt in awe of Gabe the way she sometimes did Captain Dan. Maybe that was because Gabe didn't do magic tricks. But in his way, he had that sense of presence too and knew how to grab the attention of an audience with his words. He could make them laugh or tear up if the scene was sad. He knew how to bring on the applause. Marelda said he had a gift for giving people showboat fever.

Jacci smiled thinking about Gabe up in the pilothouse, his gaze sweeping the river ahead for unexpected dangers. If she had gone up to keep him company, he might have let her take the wheel on some straight stretches. But she needed to talk to Duke and figure out why Cameron's words about her hiding bothered her so.

She couldn't ask Duke about that in the dining area. Not with others around. Over in the corner, Perry Wilson had the dummy he called Corky propped in a chair, as though the doll was listening to the conversation and any minute might join in. The other dummy, Cindy, lay on the table in front of him as he adjusted her costume. At the end of the captain's table, Mr. Loranda was oiling his trombone slide.

"Come sit with us, Miss Jacci." Mr. Loranda looked up from his horn to smile at her. "Always good to have a lady among our company. You won't be seeing my ladies out this early. They guard their beauty sleep." He gave his head a little shake almost as an apology when she pulled out the chair across from him. "They aren't early birds like you."

The black of the man's hair wasn't broken with even one gray hair. Duke said the man had to be putting boot black on it. After all, his daughter, Winnie, was seventeen and his son, Joey, fourteen. Two teenage children would give any man a few gray hairs.

That had made Jacci laugh and ask him if she was the reason for all his gray hairs.

"Let's just say I was much relieved when you turned twenty."

Now she glanced over at Duke, who smiled a welcome at her. He still looked tired, and she was almost glad she hadn't caught him alone to ask her questions.

"Our Jacci likes knowing the river with her eyes." Captain

Dan smiled at her too. "I think she wants to wrest the wheel away from me sometimes."

"I've heard of women riverboat captains." Jacci smiled back at him.

Aunt Tildy brought a new tray of doughnuts for the table and a cup of coffee for Jacci.

"You've outdone yourself with these." Jacci picked up a doughnut and took a bite. "You must have stayed up all night."

"Got up some before the sun. Had a hankering for something sweet." Aunt Tildy sat down beside Jacci.

"I keep eating these, I'll have to let the seams out in my costume." Jacci took another bite. "These are heavenly."

Aunt Tildy nodded toward the ventriloquist at the other table. "Looks like Mr. Perry's already having to do that for his dolls. I don't reckon they've been eatin' any sweets."

Perry looked up at her. "I'll have to eat their share. Just adding a ruffle to Cindy and a new spotted tie to Corky. Give them a little more flounce while they're sitting on my knee."

"Your act is a crowd pleaser," Duke said. "I tried to learn how to do that once some years ago but couldn't get the dummies to talk for me."

"Not everybody has the gift," Perry said. "It came natural for me. I used to talk for the squirrels in the trees when I was a boy."

"Long as you don't do no more mouse squeakin'." Aunt Tildy pointed her finger at him.

"You don't have to worry about that. I'm not a fan of onion tears."

Captain Dan laughed. "Not a good idea to try to get anything over on Aunt Tildy. She's been on the showboat so long, she's seen it all."

"How long is that, Aunt Tildy?" Mr. Loranda asked.

She chewed on her lip a minute before she said, "Not sure I can name the number. Seems about forever. However long, Duke has been here longer. You remember, Duke?"

Jacci wanted to speak up for him, afraid he'd be upset if he couldn't remember. But he nodded. "Forever sounds about right, Tildy—1879, best I recall. You came aboard the next year after Marelda was ready to pitch the cookstove on that first showboat over the side into the river."

"True enough," Captain Dan said. "She claimed it was demon possessed. She never knew if it was going to burn the biscuits or leave them half done while smoking up the place."

"Meals were an adventure then." Duke nodded his agreement.

"I thought Aunt Marelda did everything well," Jacci spoke up.

"She is a wonder," Duke said.

"As long as it doesn't involve sticking wood in a cookstove," Captain said.

"Wasn't never no call to be thinkin' about demons. There weren't a thing wrong with that stove 'cept the stovepipe needed a good cleaning." Aunt Tildy shook her head at them. "Marelda knowed that. She just had more'n she could do keeping up with her boys and doing shows to watch that stove too. Its oven did have a way of being contrary."

Perry Wilson looked up from his dummy. "Did Miss Jacci come aboard with you, Duke?"

The question hung in the air a moment before Duke answered, "No."

Perry seemed a little surprised at Duke's curt answer as he looked at Jacci. "So, you are a more recent addition to the cast then. Or have I asked something I shouldn't have? Such as a lady's age?"

"Our Jacci is too young to worry about that." Aunt Tildy put her hand on Jacci's arm. "She came to live with her granddad when she was just a little tyke. Five, I'm thinkin' she was. But took to being a showman right away, didn't she, Duke?"

That seemed to ease back the unhappy memories the man's question must have awakened for them. Jacci wished Perry and

Mr. Loranda would get up and leave the dining area. Without them there, she could ask for answers from Duke, Captain Dan, and Aunt Tildy. Perhaps she was wrong to think only Duke knew what happened that night.

"She did that." An easy smile spread back across Duke's face.

Perry was still staring at Jacci so intently that she shifted in her chair. "You know, Miss Jacci, I keep feeling I've seen you somewhere before."

"Maybe you've seen one of our shows in the past," Jacci said. "Or one of our show bills."

"I have seen the show bills, but I don't remember your picture ever being on one." The man narrowed his eyes on her and shook his head a little. "No, that can't be it. But now that I give it more consideration, I think it's only that I've seen someone who looks like you. Very much like you."

"Oh. Someone you know?"

"I'm not sure. I haven't exactly figured that out yet. The memory is tickling at my brain but not coming clear. Could have been someone in the news or perhaps on a different show-boat."

Duke spoke up. "Lots of people have similar looks." His voice was light, but Jacci heard a tense undercurrent in his words.

"That's true," Captain Dan said. "Speaking of someone in the news makes me remember the rumors I heard last night. They tell me that down at our next stop, one of the men hoping to be a presidential contender this year is doing some stumping. If he brings in a crowd there, that could overflow to our show this evening. We could entice them in by letting him say a few words between acts."

"Are you a supporter?" Duke asked.

"I'm a supporter of a full gallery."

"What if the people boo him?"

"Won't be the first time we've heard boos, now will it, Duke?"

Captain Dan reached for another doughnut. "I don't care what the folks do so long as they pay their tickets and don't decide to throw tomatoes at us."

"Or this politician either," Aunt Tildy said. "If they do, you's the one to clean it up, Captain."

Captain Dan laughed. "I've got Gabe for that."

"Poor Gabe," Duke said. "Did you get the name of this political candidate?"

"He's not a candidate yet. Just wants to be. Seems like the name was Giles. Something Giles."

"Griffith Giles." Perry Wilson looked up from his dummy's costume. "The paper I bought at the last town had a piece about him. Wants to start a Progressive Party to challenge the Republicans and Democrats. Thinks he can win over the farmers around here."

"Griffith Giles," Duke echoed with a frown. "That name sounds familiar for some reason."

"I've never heard of him." Mr. Loranda slid his trombone's slide back and forth. "But with how we're always moving on down the river, news never seems to matter all that much."

"Tonight it might matter to our profit. The man is a Kentucky state senator, I remember now. Popular enough around here, they claimed, which is good for us if he brings a crowd to South Odom. Has a rich wife. A beauty, according to one of the men last night." Captain finished off his doughnut and picked up his coffee. "She comes from a prominent family from somewhere in the central part of the state. They said her name." The captain frowned a little as he thought about it. "Maybe Elizabeth. No, that doesn't sound quite right, but something like that."

Duke pushed back his chair and got up so suddenly he knocked over his coffee cup. He didn't seem to notice as Jacci grabbed a towel to mop up the spill. His face was pale.

"Are you all right, Duke?" she asked.

He stared past her as if seeing something none of the rest of them could. "Lisbeth."

The sound was more a breath of air than a whisper and Jacci doubted if anyone else heard it. But the name found a home in her memory.

chapter
16

JACCI WAS SILENT as she followed Duke out of the kitchen. With each step, his pace slowed as if his feet were growing heavier.

"Are you all right, Duke?" Jacci slipped her arm around his waist.

"Tired. Just very tired." He leaned on her and kept walking.

Once in the small sitting room that adjoined their bedrooms, she helped him to a chair. "Should I go get Aunt Marelda?"

"No. No. Just give me a minute."

She studied him a moment, not sure she should push him for answers, but she had to know. "Who is this Lisbeth?"

The question rose from somewhere deep inside her.

Duke didn't meet her gaze as he sank back in the chair. "I can't, Princess." He sounded out of breath and his hands shook on the arms of the chair. "Not now. I need to think."

He shut his eyes. She stood in front of him, ashamed to be demanding answers when he looked so tired and ill. At the same time, she needed to know why remembering the name Lisbeth had brought him to the point of collapse.

"You have to tell me why you're so distressed. If it has to do with my mother, then don't you think it's time I know? I'm twenty years old. No longer a child." She kept her voice calm but insistent.

His eyes stayed closed as he let out a shaky breath. "Irena should have been the one to tell you."

"Irena. My mother," Jacci said softly. "But she can't tell me."

"No." He opened his eyes then to look straight at her. "She did love you so. She died protecting you."

"But why? Why did I need protecting?" Jacci frowned and threw her hands out. "Don't you think I should know that?"

"I'm not sure I can come up with a true answer for you about that. Irena didn't trust me with the whole story, but I've never doubted that whatever she did, it was with the aim of protecting you. To give you a better life."

"It can't be better to have seen my mother stabbed and then slowly die." Those memories stayed clear in her mind.

"Irena didn't want to die. She wanted to stay with you."

Jacci remembered her mother touching her chest over her heart and promising that her love would be there forever. "I know." She sank down on the floor beside Duke and put her head on his knee the way she used to when she was younger. "And I know you love me too."

He stroked her hair. "I do. So very much. More than I would have ever thought possible before your mother asked me to care for you. She made me promise to keep you with me. To not let Kelly take you. It was the last thing she asked of me before she died."

"Why?" Jacci looked up at him. "Kelly is my father."

"Yes, in a way. Something the same as I was a father to your mother. Only when it suited us and didn't interfere with what we wanted to do. For me it was finding the next play on a stage. For Kelly, it is chasing the next big win."

"Mama loved him." She believed that.

"She did, but she also knew him." He was silent a moment before he went on. "I've sometimes wondered if I would have been man enough to give up acting for you if you hadn't taken to the showboat life. Your mother wanted to believe I could be that man. She did not think Kelly could give up his vices to be your father."

"He loves me." She had always wanted to believe that was true too.

"I don't doubt that. It could be he even cared for Irena, although I don't think he ever intended to allow such feelings to develop. At the beginning, he was simply playing a part, much as I've done most of my life."

Jacci sat back to stare at Duke. "What do you mean? Being a father isn't about playing a part on a stage."

"No. No, it isn't." He leaned forward and put his hand on her cheek. His fingers trembled against her skin.

She met his gaze then and saw truth he hadn't spoken. She stared at him and didn't know what to ask. Not only that, she was no longer sure she wanted answers.

His eyes grew sad as if he knew her thoughts. "Perhaps it is time for you to know the truth. At least as much of the truth as I can tell you. As I said, I don't know the whole story, and some of it I have only guessed and was not actually told. That's why I never wanted to answer your questions about your mother. You should have asked Kelly."

"I did ask him. He always found a way to drift away from any serious conversations."

"Indeed. In ways, he is every bit as much an actor as I am. Perhaps we are all actors in our show of life." Duke attempted a smile as he dropped his hand from her face and leaned back again. "Get me a glass of water, and I'll tell you how the play of your early life went. At least the few acts and characters I know."

Jacci got to her feet. Suddenly she wished she hadn't followed Duke into the galley and heard him whisper the name Lisbeth. Instead, she wished she was on the top deck watching the river unfold in front of the showboat. Gabe might start singing and she could join in. She would feel safe there with him.

But hadn't she always felt just as safe with Duke? Why was this feeling of dread growing in her at the thought of knowing the truth she had so thought she wanted? She pulled in a deep breath as she filled a glass out of the water pitcher they kept in their rooms. Perhaps the truth was what she had been hiding from all these years. If so, she could hide no longer.

He took the glass, his hand still trembling, and sipped the water before he set the glass on the table beside him. "Pull a chair over here in front of me."

When she did, he took her hands. "Do you remember when I used to tell you stories before you went to sleep? Fanciful tales of princesses and fairy-tale lands?"

"I loved those stories, Grampus Duke."

He smiled. "You haven't called me that for years. Irena laughed when she heard you call me Grampus. I think that may have been the last time I heard her laugh. And she called me Father for the first time ever. I nearly waited too late to earn the title, and then only due to the providence of the *Palace* tying up beside the *Mary Ellen*. The Lord had a hand in that. I'm certain of it."

"I don't know what would have happened to me if Mama hadn't found you."

"You could have been adopted into a farm family and ended up a landlubber."

"Or ended up in an orphanage." Jacci shook her head. "Or with another man wanting to take me." She paused a minute and then made herself ask. "But why?"

Duke turned loose of her hands and leaned back again with a heavy breath. "I'm not sure I can tell you the right reasons why. If there are right reasons. I just know Irena feared for you."

"You surely know something."

"Yes."

"About this Lisbeth? I remember hearing her name before Mama died. Seems somebody, maybe you, told me she was a friend of Mama's."

"I may have told you that. It's true, in a way."

"You keep saying in a way. What do you mean? Things either are or aren't. She either was a friend or she wasn't."

"You're old enough to know everything isn't always black or white. Much gray settles into our world like a muddy stream flowing into the green of the river. Mixtures of right and wrong."

"But Aunt Marelda—" Duke held up his hand to stop her.

"Marelda has seen her share of gray too, but she does have a clear vision of right and wrong. That's a gift. To know what is right to do. That was not quite as clear to Irena about you."

"Me?"

He rubbed his forehead. "Don't pester me with questions, Princess. Let me tell you the best way I can."

"All right." She sat back and bit the inside of her lip while her dread of what he was going to tell her grew.

"You want to know who Lisbeth is. I never met her, but I know who she is. Irena's mother, your grandmother, was a dressmaker. She made many gowns for Lisbeth's mother and for Lisbeth. They lived in a manor house on a very large farm with horses and servants. I suppose Lisbeth still does, although I have no way of being sure of that other than what was said moments ago about her."

He pulled in another breath and looked toward the window out at the sky before he went on. "Irena and Lisbeth became friends, again in a way, while your grandmother made measurements for dresses and then adjustments when the dresses were fitted, I suppose. I say in a way, because it is hard for a girl like Lisbeth with everything at her fingertips and a girl like Irena to be truly equal friends."

He took another sip of his water and continued. "Your grandmother told me about the worries she had for Irena being exposed to so much affluence. Not that she and Irena lived in poverty, but their life had little cushion should hardships come. I did share my earnings with Estelle when I could. Unfortunately, an actor very often lives hand to mouth. At least that was true until I found work on showboats and eventually came home here to the *Palace*."

"I wish I had known her," Jacci said.

"So do I. She was a wonderful woman so full of love and patience with a man like me who wasn't what I should have been for her." He bent his head and was silent a moment. "But I'm telling you about Irena and Lisbeth, not Estelle."

"What about them?"

"When the two girls got older, things changed as they must for two from such dissimilar backgrounds, especially after Estelle became ill with a lung issue and no longer had the energy to do the dressmaking jobs. When Estelle's condition worsened, Irena didn't send me word. Estelle asked her not to, but I might have been hard to reach anyway. I was on a showboat down in Louisiana then. That was before I joined with the Kingstons. I should have found a way to keep in touch. I did know Estelle wasn't well, but I truly thought she would get better. She was always such a strong person."

"But she didn't."

"No. After Estelle died, Irena had to sell their house to pay debts they'd accumulated during Estelle's illness and for her burial costs. Then she found a maid's job on a steamboat." He shook his head with a sad little laugh. "Estelle would have been distraught to know her daughter went on the river after she had tried so hard to give Irena a different life. But Irena liked the steamboat life, even though the work was hard and not always appreciated by the dandies and their ladies who traveled on the river."

"I wouldn't call the people that come to our shows dandies," Jacci said.

"Things are a little different on a showboat. We play to the country folk along the rivers. The working people."

"That might be different if this Griffith Giles brings his party aboard for the show tonight."

Duke's face stiffened. "We can hope he doesn't have a taste for showboat dramas or, even better, has gone on up the river to some of the bigger towns."

"Why?"

"I'll get to that. I need to tell this as it happened. One act at a time."

He was quiet for so long that Jacci thought he might have forgotten which act he was in for the story. "So Mama started working on the steamboats before I was born. Is that where she met Kelly?"

"In a way." One side of Duke's mouth went up in a sideways smile when she frowned at those words. "Sorry, Princess. But I didn't write the play."

"All right. Go on."

"You are right that your mother was already working on a steamboat before you came along. Not the *Mary Ellen*. A different one. Not sure now of the name. So many things have gotten jumbled up in my memory lately. It's not good for an actor's memory to slide away." He blew out a breath. "But I think I have remembered with some clarity what happened with Irena and Lisbeth." He gave Jacci a piercing look. "With you."

"What?" She leaned toward him.

He danced his fingertips up and down on the chair arm a moment before he started talking again. "You have lived a sheltered life here on the *Palace.* Here you are, twenty and without the first official suitor."

"I'm not worried about getting married."

"Another result of your absorption into this showboat life. You haven't had the opportunity to meet young men you might wish to share your life with."

"I see young men every night. I do shows with young men."

"True enough, but you haven't seemed to want any of them to pursue you unless now you're considering young Drake. He does seem attracted to you, but I fear he might be a worse husband to you than I was to Estelle."

When she frowned and started to protest, he waved away her words. "But I digress. That is a worry for another day. My point is that here in this world of make-believe, you haven't been exposed to the realities of a young woman's life. A young woman like Lisbeth."

"I thought you didn't know her."

"I did not, but I know about her and the expectations families have for rich young heiresses. Her father planned to use her beauty—and I know without seeing her that she was and perhaps still is beautiful—to advance his own ambitions by marrying her to someone of importance. At least in his eyes." Duke shook his head slightly before he said more. "The thing is that many young women in this day and age have minds of their own and often follow different paths than their parents lay out for them."

"A woman should have the say in who she marries," Jacci said.

"I don't disagree with that at all, but Lisbeth did not have a forward-thinking father and had little choice about her future, as it turned out. She fell in love with a man below her social level. A horseman hired by Lisbeth's father. They succumbed to the joys of love with no thought of the consequences. The father, unaware of this, but very aware of the girl's attraction to this man he considered an unsuitable suitor, found a way to send him away. But unfortunately, evidence of their love had already been planted in Lisbeth. She was with child."

"Are you saying . . . ?" Jacci stared at him, suddenly wishing this was no more than a plot of a play he'd seen instead of the truth she had thought she wanted.

Duke held up his hand, palm toward her. "One act at a time. You can imagine Lisbeth's dilemma. The suitor her father had arranged for her was demanding a wedding date. Lisbeth feared her father's wrath. So she was silent as she hoped and prayed for the return of her lover. She must have hoped her father would allow their marriage when he found out about the coming child. Alas, at times good fortune does not smile down on young lovers."

He was silent for a moment as if he didn't want to share what happened next before he went on. "The boilers exploded on the steamboat her young man had passage on as he was returning from whatever task Lisbeth's father had arranged for him. Many on the boat did not survive, including Lisbeth's love."

"This is a terrible story."

"And gets even more terrible, I fear. Lisbeth planned an escape when she heard news of the steamboat disaster. How she achieved that, I have no idea. Nor do I know how she found Irena, but she did and convinced her to hide her in her maid's room. I can't imagine that even possible in a maid's quarters, but somehow they must have accomplished the deed for several weeks, perhaps longer. I saw Irena once during that time, but she told me nothing then about sheltering Lisbeth or the plot they were concocting to protect you."

"So, Lisbeth is my mother." She whispered the words. No wonder that name had stayed alive inside her head.

"No." Duke spoke so sharply Jacci jerked back from him. He softened his voice and went on. "Irena may not have carried you in her womb, but she was your mother in every way that mattered."

"And Kelly?"

"I don't know how Kelly found a part in this play. That's something you'll have to find out from him, but he did marry Irena. They found a house in that Dove Creek area."

"Where Mama is buried."

"She remembered the church there. Said it overlooked the river. I think the time she lived there might have been the happiest of her life."

"Why did she leave then?"

"I don't know that either. When I next saw her on the steamboat *Mary Ellen*, she said it had to do with needing money. But I wondered then if it had more to do with Kelly."

"Kelly never stayed with us," Jacci said.

"But he came in and out of your lives. Perhaps Irena thought that might happen more if she were on the river the same as he." Duke rubbed his eyes. "And perhaps she simply inherited my river-wandering ways. So much of this can be surely laid to my blame."

She leaned closer to him then. "I feel no blame for you. Only gratitude that you're my grandfather."

"But the same as your mother, as Irena, that is only in my heart and not in bloodlines."

"Hearts are more important than blood." She gripped his hands in hers. "You are my Grampus however the Lord worked it out."

A tear edged out of his eye and down his cheek. "I've done my best for you, Princess, but I'm getting old."

"I've always felt safe with you."

The look on his face changed from tenderness to worry. "Don't take part in the show tonight if Griffith Giles comes aboard. Stay here in our rooms. You can say you're ill."

"Hide away from sight?" She spoke more to herself than to Duke. He had explained much, but not why that man had tried to take her from her mother. "Why?"

"I don't know. I've never known, but it must go back to your natural mother. To keeping her shame secret."

"What would that man have done to me if he had been able to get me from Mama?"

Duke looked at her a moment before answering. "I can't answer that either, but I don't want to find out. If Giles is hoping to be a presidential candidate, he won't want any rumors sullying his family life."

"It was all so long ago. Surely none of it matters now."

"We can hope not."

"Does Aunt Marelda know any of this?"

"I don't think so. She never asked questions I couldn't answer. She only knew you were in need of help and love. In the same way that she took me into this showboat family after too many failed scenes in my life, she embraced you as a daughter."

"Should I let this all stay a secret? Not tell anyone?" Jacci said.

He studied her again before he spoke. "It's your play to finish with however many acts to come. You must find the ending. Irena would say with the Lord's help. She was at peace at her ending, confident that the Lord had forgiven her for whatever wrongs she'd done. She went on to the other side, sorrowful for leaving you but trusting the Lord to take care of her. And of you. I pray I will go with the same ease."

"No, Grampus." She squeezed his hands. "Not yet. I need you still."

He smiled. "I do hope I have a few more acts left." The smile disappeared. "But I don't want to be in them if you aren't too."

"You will always have a part in my plays." She got up and hugged him. "But why don't you lie down awhile before the show?"

"I don't think either of us should go onstage tonight."

"But they'd have to cancel the show."

"Only the drama. Or somebody else could be Penelope.

Marelda could. Or Winnie. She wants a bigger part." He stood up and put his hands on her shoulders. "At least consider it."

"This Senator Giles might not even be at the next landing."

"A blessing if he isn't."

She kissed Duke's cheek. "Thank you for telling me what you know. Let me think about what is best while you get some rest."

She didn't tell him she would stay hidden in her room. Surely she'd be in no danger on the stage or in the greenroom. Not after so many years. She was only known as Princess in the shows, and she looked much different than she had when that man attempted to steal her.

Besides, the Kingstons didn't cancel shows. Ever.

chapter
17

THE SHOW MUST GO ON. Wasn't that what she had been taught since forever? At least since she had been part of this showboat family. Sickness? A showman soldiered through. Sprained ankle? A dancer kept dancing. Sore throat? A singer drank lemon tea and found a way to squeak out the high notes.

Somebody wanting to kidnap her? That seemed no more than a ridiculous thought. After all the years with absolutely no trouble, she had to wonder if it had all been some sort of tragic mistake. While she had been unsettled, even frightened those first months on the showboat, that feeling faded. No, not just faded. Disappeared like river mist burned off by the sun. While some wisps of the fear lingered in her nightmares, she had no trouble waving them away when she awoke.

Duke was always ready to teach her a new dance or some silly song that might make the audiences laugh. When they laughed, so did she. She played with the children along the river at each stop. She learned to swim, and on the hottest days of July, the river was their playground, with Gabe always close if she needed help. The showboat was a happy place that got her past the sorrow of losing her mother.

Her mother who turned out not to be her mother. At least not the mother she was born to, but she was her mama. While sometimes she couldn't pull up her mother's face in her memory, she had never forgotten her love.

She used to ask Duke to describe her mother in hopes that would bring a clear image to life in her memory instead of the fuzzy recollections she had.

"She wasn't a showstopper like you, but she was pretty enough. Brown hair she kept in a twist, and brown eyes."

"I have black hair and dark blue eyes." She was always disappointed when what Duke said about her mother didn't match her own looks. "Don't I look like her at all?"

"Not on the outside, but you do on the inside where it matters most. She was generous and loving. You are the same."

She supposed she knew now why she didn't look like her mother. Or maybe she did look like her. Her birth mother. Or her father. She didn't even know his name. At least she had a name for her mother. Lisbeth. Duke said she was beautiful, but that might only be on the outside if she had given away her baby. Given away Jacci.

She should be thankful for her good appearance. She was. Being attractive was an advantage for an actress in leading roles, but she was more than a pretty face. She wanted people to know that and like her for who she was inside.

The way Gabe did. He had started liking her when she was just a kid. He probably never even thought about how she looked. She was just his sister. Not really a sister, as he continually told her, but almost the same after the years they had been on this showboat together. He was the best friend she could have.

Jacci looked across the greenroom at Winnie Loranda as her family got their instruments ready to do the music for the drama before their acrobatic act. Winnie could make flute music that had Jacci up on her toes ready to dance. This was the third year her family had been part of the cast, but in spite of all that time together, Winnie never accepted Jacci's overtures of friendship.

This year was the worst yet. Winnie made it plain the first week on the showboat when they were learning their parts that the less she was around Jacci, the better. Her brother, Joey, was fine. Always ready to play a game of checkers or try to teach Jacci a tumbling trick, even though they both knew it was hopeless. Jacci could dance. She wasn't an acrobat.

Duke said Winnie was probably attracted to the new handsome leading man.

"That's fine with me," Jacci had said. "I'd wish them the best."

"But you're the one he's hugging every night."

"Not me. Penelope."

Duke had laughed. "I guess to Winnie, Penelope looks a lot like you."

Jacci had paid more attention since then, but she wasn't sure Duke was right. Most of the time Winnie was talking with Gabe, not Cameron. Always about the show whenever Jacci was near enough to hear what they were saying. She could have been hoping for a bigger part in the drama than playing her flute. Perhaps Cameron was right and she did want to do Jacci's role in the drama.

Had Jacci listened to Duke and refused to go onstage this night, Winnie might have gladly stood in for her. She'd heard all the lines many times from her front-row seat as part of the band. She could take Jacci's place while Jacci couldn't play a note on a flute, ride a unicycle, or do a handstand.

But she hadn't listened to Duke. Surely there wasn't a reason to do so, even if Marelda had come into the greenroom and announced a full house with the senator and his entourage in attendance.

She beamed as she shared the news. "Captain is turning people away. We've already filled the standing room too."

"Does that mean a bonus for us?" Cameron asked as he slicked down his hair in front of one of the mirrors.

Aunt Marelda narrowed her eyes on him. "It means you'll get paid, Mr. Drake."

"I expected that in any case."

Duke looked across the room at Jacci and stopped knotting his tie. When Jacci shook her head the slightest bit, he dropped down in a chair and slipped the tie free from his neck. "I'm not going on tonight," he announced. "Someone else can play my part."

Gabe broke the silence that fell over the room. "What about your act with Jacci? The Duke and the Princess."

"No one will miss it." Duke stood up and removed his coat.

"It's on the program," Gabe said.

"Not tonight." After another look at Jacci, Duke turned and left the room. Marelda followed him.

"He hasn't felt well today," Jacci announced to the room in general.

"I don't think Duke has ever missed a show," Gabe said.

"No reason for concern." Cameron turned from the mirror. "Perry's dummy could play his part. And if the princess needs someone to sing and dance with her, I am more than capable."

"No." Gabe's voice was sharp.

Jacci pulled on the skirt for the first scene over top of the final scene's dress. Her hands were shaking so that she couldn't get it buttoned.

Mrs. Loranda came over to fasten it for her. She patted Jacci's shoulder. "I wouldn't worry, dear. I'm sure your grandfather will be fine. A show every night can be taxing."

She had blond hair the same as Winnie, piled into a bun on top of her head. She was already dressed in the red-and-white-striped costume for their acrobatic act following the drama.

She and Winnie wore bloomers fastened at the ankles, with silky red-and-white panels draped down from their waists to flow out around them during their act. Mrs. Loranda was the tightrope walker. Jacci had seen her do it without a care in practice, but during the show, she always wobbled a bit to make the audience gasp.

"I could play my flute while you recite some Shakespeare, Gabe." Winnie spoke up. "Maybe from *Romeo and Juliet?*"

"Oh, that girl." Mrs. Loranda shook her head a little as she looked across the room at Winnie, who had stepped over next to Gabe. "She knows who she wishes was her Romeo. Whether his red hair fits the role or not."

"Gabe?" Jacci couldn't keep the surprise out of her voice.

"You hadn't noticed?" Mrs. Loranda gave her an odd look. "Young Mr. Kingston is a very likable young man. While Mr. Loranda and I wouldn't be at all upset were he to take notice of our Winnie, I don't think it will happen."

"Oh? Why not?" Jacci watched Winnie still talking to Gabe, but quietly now where no one but he could hear. "She's a very pretty girl."

"It takes more than one to make a couple. I fear Winnie's Romeo does not look upon her as Juliet."

"*Romeo and Juliet* has a terrible last act anyway."

"True." She smiled. "Better to end up a Penelope and Sterling with a happy-ever-after ending. Perhaps that will happen for you."

"Not with Sterling," Jacci said.

That made Mrs. Loranda laugh. "No one wants to pair up on this showboat. That's just as well. Romances on board can cause some messes among a cast."

"I suppose so."

"I know so." The woman looked around the room. "It's hard enough to get along all summer in the close quarters of a showboat without the added trials and tribulations of romance, welcomed or not. But I am surprised you're not taken with our handsome leading man. I've known many a young actress to fall for the actor who romances her in every performance."

"I guess I haven't met the right leading man."

"Or perhaps you don't recognize the right man when you see him." Her mouth twisted in a sideways smile. "But looks as if one of those leading men is coming your way. Almost time for the play to start."

Cameron was crossing the room toward them. Jacci glanced from him back to Winnie and Gabe. She'd never thought about Winnie being attracted to Gabe. She'd simply assumed the girl would be swept off her feet by Cameron's good looks. Not that Gabe wasn't nice looking, but more in a boyish way with his freckles and red hair in spite of being well past boy age.

A funny feeling stirred in Jacci. One she didn't especially like.

"You look like you just swallowed a sour pickle," Cameron said. "You'd better find your smile again before Marelda starts pounding on that piano to get the show underway."

"I don't smile in every scene," Jacci said.

"You're certainly not smiling now. Is it something our feckless director did?" Cameron glanced over at Gabe.

"Feckless?" Jacci frowned at him. "Whatever do you mean by that?"

"Oh, did I say feckless? I surely intended to say freckled." He linked her arm in his. "Come, find that smile for the audience. For me."

"I'm worried about Duke, but I'll manage the smiles when the script calls for them." She eased her arm from his and turned to put the finishing touches on her makeup. In the mirror she saw Gabe step away from Winnie to come over toward her. Winnie's face tightened before she turned and shoved a stool out of her way.

"Are you all right, Jacci?" Gabe stared at her in the mirror.

"It's Duke that isn't all right." Jacci looked around at him.

"Yeah. You know what's wrong? Is he sick?"

"He's tired. And worried about the big crowd. About Senator Giles."

"Does he know him?"

"Not really. Just about him." The concern in Gabe's light-blue eyes made her wish she could tell him everything Duke had told her, but they only had a few minutes before the show. "He didn't want me to go onstage either."

"Why?"

"It's a long story. No time for it all now, but it goes back to my mother and whatever happened then."

"Your mother?" He looked puzzled, then worried. "You don't have to do the show if you don't want to."

Jacci smiled. "Aunt Marelda would never forgive me, and Captain Dan might put me off the boat if we had to give everybody their money back."

"The money doesn't matter. You matter, and Ma and the captain would never put you off the boat."

She touched his arm. "It will be fine. Really. All that was so long ago."

"But somebody tried to steal you then, you said. And whoever it was killed your mother."

She met his eyes then. "Yes, but Duke doesn't know why. Nobody knows why."

"The man who attacked your mother knows why."

"It's been fifteen years. How could anyone even know I was that little girl?"

He ran his hand through his hair. Something he did when he wasn't sure about something. Then his mother began playing the opening number, the signal for him to go out on the stage and introduce the drama.

"Go. That's your cue." She smoothed down his hair and gave him a little push toward the door out to the stage.

"Right." He walked backward as if he didn't want to lose sight of her.

Marelda was playing through the song again.

"The show must go on," she called to him.

Finally, he turned and ran toward the stage.

She followed him out. Not onto the stage, but beside the curtain out of sight as she peered at the crowd. Lots of heads, but the light was dim in spite of the lanterns along the walls. She had no idea what seats the captain might have given the senator and his party. Toward the front, she would guess.

She swept her gaze over the faces, watching Gabe as he did his talk. He made a joke of some sort and got his laugh as he did every night. He had a way with people. A showman's charisma, Duke called it.

A couple of crewmen from the *Little Ruby* went along the walls to lower the lantern light even more. Jacci wished she could grab one of the lanterns and illuminate each face, row by row.

Was her mother, her birth mother, out there? Jacci remembered the night her mother died and how sure she'd been that her mother was watching the play. This was a different kind of expectation. If Lisbeth was sitting out in one of those seats, how could she even know Jacci?

Something drew Jacci's eyes to the piano just to the left of the stage. And there was Duke. He wasn't watching Gabe. Instead, he, the same as Jacci, was searching through the crowd. Perhaps looking for Lisbeth too. What would he do if he did pick her out? But he said he'd never met her. Just knew her name. And that she had married Griffith Giles, senator and prospective candidate for president. It might be presumed that if a lady was sitting next to Giles, that would be his wife. Lisbeth.

Then the curtain was closing and Gabe was coming offstage. Marelda began the music to signal the play's opening scene.

Jacci's heart bounded up in her throat. She was always a

little nervous at the start of every show, but this was different. What if Duke was right and being onstage in full sight of Griffith Giles was a danger? But she couldn't back out now and let Marelda and Captain Dan down, not to mention the rest of the cast. Besides, who knew what the crowd might do if the curtain crashed closed without the show they were expecting?

The show must go on. She looked heavenward, touched her chest over her heart, and silently asked the mother who loved her to watch over her.

chapter
18

GABE DIDN'T WANT to do a song with Winnie Loranda. He'd already told her that wasn't going to happen, but Winnie knew how to get her way. She went to his mother, who said it not only should happen, it would. If Duke and Jacci didn't do their song routine in the acts following the play, there was absolutely no reason Winnie and Gabe couldn't come up with something to fill the spot.

Ma told him that in no uncertain terms when he went to take over the piano after she played the crashing start to the last act of the drama. The band supplied the music for the play until Gabe filled in at the piano for the climactic final scene. His mother had to get things ready for the captain's magic show.

"We haven't got an act," Gabe protested. "Have never had an act." He wanted to add "would never have an act," but his mother was not likely to accept that.

"Nonsense. I've heard her. She can sing. You can sing along with her or while she plays the tune on that flute. People like hearing the flute."

"I can't sing to flute music."

"Then I'll accompany the flute on the piano." She waved away his arguments. "Just sing that song from last year's show. 'Moonlight Waltzing' was the title, I think. You know the one I mean. You sang it a hundred times last season."

"Not with Winnie."

"Well, no. That was with Jacci."

"Then if you want me to do that song, don't you think I should sing it with Jacci?"

A frown settled between his mother's eyebrows. "Duke asked me not to let her do a song. Any song."

"Why?"

Ma's frown deepened. "I'm not sure, but he was adamant. Something about that senator, I think, but I can't imagine what."

"Jacci thinks it has something to do with when her mother died." Gabe felt a sudden urge to go grab Jacci off the stage, to simply close down the show mid-scene. But that might be the worst thing he could do. Jacci was right. It had been fifteen years. Nobody would connect her to the little girl she'd been then. Not unless he pulled a crazy stunt like that.

"That's been so long ago," Ma said, but she looked a little worried.

"Maybe she shouldn't be out there on the stage at all." Gabe leaned down to speak directly into his mother's ear. They had to be very quiet to keep their murmurs from interrupting the play.

"Too late for that now. She'll be fine. She doesn't look a thing like her mother. So how could anybody even connect our Jacci with that child then? Plus she'll be further hidden in the character of Penelope. Most people don't notice the actor beneath the part."

"And we've never used her name," Gabe said. "I've always wondered about that."

"Duke asked us not to use her name in the program way back when. I thought it was just because he called her Princess and

ANN H. GABHART

it worked with him being Duke, but maybe there was more. I don't know, but whether there is or not, I promised Duke she wouldn't do anything after her part in the play tonight. So you can fill in for her." Her face tightened into the look that meant she wouldn't change her mind. "Besides, Winnie very much wants this opportunity to show she can do more than tumble and ride a unicycle."

"You know what she wants." Gabe gave his mother a hard look.

"I'm not asking you to marry her. Just sing a song with her." Ma narrowed her eyes on Gabe. "I don't want to hear another word. She says she can sing the first verse. You sing the last. And then waltz her off the stage."

"Duke is right calling you Queen Marelda," Gabe said.

"I'm not your queen." Ma poked her finger into his chest. "But I am your mother."

"Ma, I'm twenty-eight years old."

"And still my son. Now get over there to the piano. Time to play that last song. Jacci is fine and Winnie deserves a little consideration from you. Her family has been part of our show-boat family for three years."

Gabe shut his eyes and bit his lip to keep from saying more. The queen had spoken. It was useless to argue with her. But Winnie was going to get the wrong idea when he sang that verse about waltzing the night away with her. The very wrong idea. He would simply have to tell the girl once and for all that he was never, ever going to return her affections. It didn't matter what might happen between Jacci and Cameron.

That didn't bear thinking about. He kept his eyes away from the stage while he played the last romantic tune. Sterling would be embracing Penelope, promising to be with her forever. If Gabe could go back to the beginning of their season, he'd recast that character. He knew no reason, absolutely none, why the hero of the piece couldn't have curly red hair.

169

He hit a sour note that Mr. Loranda covered up with his trombone. Gabe pulled in a deep breath. He was at the piano for Captain's magic act and then the Lorandas' tumbling and high-wire act. Jacci would be back in the greenroom. No one could bother her there. And once he somehow got through what was sure to be a disaster with Winnie, he would make sure Jacci didn't come back onstage to talk to those in the audience who came down front to chat before they left. Then, he would find out what about Griffith Giles had Duke so upset.

Meanwhile, he would somehow get through this song with Winnie and hope she didn't think he meant every romantic word. If the girl ended up in tears when the romance didn't last after they waltzed off the stage, Queen Marelda could handle it.

He banged out the next song with more enthusiasm than necessary, but the crowd didn't seem to notice. They were a good group. Laughing at the right times. Booing the villain. Crowds loved booing the villain. From their aahs and oohs, they were properly amazed by the captain's magic tricks. Playing to a full house always made for the best shows. At least almost always. Tonight he couldn't forget Duke's look as he said he wasn't going on and then how he stared over at Jacci as though he might never see her again before he left the greenroom.

After the play, Jacci peeked through the curtains on the side of the stage while Captain and Marelda did their magic act. She found the cluster of men in the center of the seats who didn't look like their regular crowd. Just enough light spread from the stage that she could see several of them wore suits and cravats. Two women sat among them with brimmed hats that shaded their faces, making it even harder to see what they looked like.

For one insane moment, she considered walking out into the audience up to that row. But what would she say if she did? *Are you my mother?* The very thought of the question seemed to be a betrayal of the memory of the mother who had loved her.

Jacci turned away from the audience to find Duke. Marelda had told her she couldn't do another act without Duke. Not that Jacci hadn't gone onstage alone to sing many times when they needed a fill-in act. But she didn't argue with Marelda. At the same time, she wasn't about to stay and watch Gabe sing that waltzing song with Winnie. Jacci and Gabe had done that song who knew how many times last season. But if Marelda wanted Winnie to do it instead of Jacci, well, as Duke always said, what Queen Marelda said was what must happen.

With a sigh, Jacci tamped down her irritation. It wouldn't hurt her to give up the stage to Winnie, who had been begging for a bigger part in the show than her acrobatic act and playing her flute. And it looked as if she wanted even more than that. Perhaps to be a part of the Kingston family.

Jacci had no reason to be surprised by that. Gabe was a great guy. Of course Winnie would be attracted to him, and it was understandable if Gabe was attracted to her. She was cute, full of energy, and a perfect match for a showman in spite of being so young.

That was no reason for Jacci's insides to clench as though the boat was scraping the trees alongside the river. If Gabe and Winnie did end up together, she would be happy for them. Of course she would.

That thought had nothing at all to do with her fists jammed down among the folds in her skirt. No doubt, that had everything to do with Lisbeth sitting out in their audience. And Duke being afraid for her to go onstage.

She found him in the shadows beside the stage as though keeping guard. She put her arm around his waist. Why hadn't she noticed how much weight he'd lost?

"Let's go to the galley." She leaned close to his ear so he could hear her words over the music. "Since I'm not going back onstage, I can help Aunt Tildy."

Even in the dim light, she could see relief replacing the worry on Duke's face. "She'll appreciate that," he said.

She wanted to step around to see Gabe pounding out the tune on the piano, but she didn't. Instead, she turned with Duke to go through the door beside the stage. Jacci waited until they were under the stars out on the deck before she asked, "Did you see her?"

He didn't pretend to not know what she meant. "I saw the group that came in. Two ladies were with them. I couldn't see them well enough."

"But you were watching before the lanterns were turned down."

"True, but you forget that age has dimmed these eyes. I did see one I thought could be the senator's wife. She wore a fancy hat and kept her head tilted down most of the time. When she did look up, she waved a fan in front of her face. Did you look for her?"

"I did. But then I decided I didn't care if Lisbeth was here or not. That it didn't matter. If she was out there in the crowd, it had nothing to do with me, but merely because her husband wanted to advance his political ambitions by using the crowd we attracted."

"True. But I'm still glad you didn't go on to sing a song."

"Aunt Marelda refused to let me. She replaced our act with one by Winnie and Gabe." She worked to keep her voice easy. "That 'Moonlight Waltzing' song that Gabe and I did last season."

"I see." From the sound of Duke's voice, he did see. "You don't have to worry about Gabe and Winnie."

She pretended not to know what he meant. "I'm not at all worried. I'm sure they will be crowd pleasers."

He let it go. "Gabe does have a way with the folks who come to our shows."

Aunt Tildy looked up when they went into the eating area. "What are you two doin' here? They close the stage down? Or did that Perry Wilson take it over with them dolls of his?"

Jacci laughed. "Nothing of the sort. Aunt Marelda just decided Duke and I needed to let some others have some stage time."

The old woman gave Jacci a look that showed she didn't believe that. "Tell me the truth, girl. Which one of you is sickly? I've got some tonics if you need them."

"Not sick." Jacci looked at Duke, but he seemed glad to let her explain. "A little worried about some of the crowd."

"They ain't that shootin' kind we had back a few years ago, are they? You remember that crazy fella what wanted to shoot you during one of them plays, Duke, thinking you was really hurting our Jacci here in whatever part you was playin' that season." She stirred some sugar into a pitcher of tea and laughed. "That was some night, best I recall."

Duke laughed with her. "I had my hands up ready to surrender for sure that night, Aunt Tildy, but no, this is nothing like that." He looked around as though to check if anybody else was in the room. "This has to do with when Jacci and her mother came aboard. You remember that, don't you?"

Aunt Tildy's face changed. "Oh, my soul, I do. Sad times." She patted Jacci's arm. "You was such a dear little thing to lose your mama like that. And her so very young."

"Do you know what happened, Aunt Tildy?" Jacci asked. "Did Mama tell you why that man attacked her?"

"No, sweet child, she didn't. But she was some worried about you. Wanted all of us to know to protect you." She stopped stirring and looked at Jacci and then Duke. "Has trouble finally caught up to us about all that?"

"Hard to know for sure," Duke said.

Aunt Tildy's eyes sharpened on him. "Seems you do know somethin' to get you in a worrying state."

"We don't really know anything. No real reason to be concerned. It's been so long." Jacci sighed. "It's just that this senator came on board tonight because Captain told him he could talk about his campaign for president. Griffith Giles. He has a wife named Lisbeth, and Mama had a friend named Lisbeth. And, well, lots of other things about what happened then, but I can't see why any of it would matter now."

"It must have mattered then," Duke said. "Enough for Irena to die."

And enough for Jacci to shoot that man. The image of him falling flashed into her mind. She hadn't touched a gun since then, but she still could feel how the gun jumped in her hand when she pulled the trigger.

She couldn't think about that now. She couldn't think about any of it. Not even Lisbeth sitting out there watching the rest of the show. Better to push it away and think about helping Aunt Tildy get food ready for the cast after the show.

"Nobody is going to bother me now, Grampus Duke." She used her little-girl name for him on purpose to keep him from being cross. "We'll be on down the river tomorrow. Senator Giles and his wife will be on to wherever they are going next. I don't know why I was a danger to them then. If I was. But I'm not now. I'm just a showboat actress named Princess. The name you gave me."

He made a sound that wasn't quite *humph* but very close.

She went over to where he'd dropped down in his usual place at one of the tables and kissed his cheek. "Let's act out the rest of the show tonight as if nothing in the world is wrong except you didn't feel well enough to go onstage."

Aunt Tildy's head came up. "You didn't go on, Duke?"

"A man can feel bad now and again and skip a show."

"Never in the sixteen years I've been knowin' you." She stared at him. "This has to be worser than you're tellin' me."

"We don't know that." Jacci looked from Duke to Aunt Tildy. "And even if it is, tonight we're going to act like it's not. You surely don't think we have anything to worry about from the people on the boat."

"I don't know." Aunt Tildy frowned. "There's that funny guy who carries them dummies around like as how they're about to do some talkin' 'stead of him."

Jacci laughed. "If Perry's Corky and Cindy are all we have to worry about, I think we'll be fine."

Aunt Tildy didn't laugh. Instead, she came out from behind the counter where she put the food. "I don't know about that. But I'm hearin' the poundin' of those Lorandas jumping around. They shake this whole boat. Anyhow, that gives us time to do somethin' better than frettin' by askin' the Lord to take this worry and sink it to the bottom of one of his oceans. That's some deeper than this river here."

She took Jacci's hand and then Duke's. Then without closing her eyes, she looked up at the ceiling. Jacci had no doubt she wasn't seeing the wooden pieces over her head but was peering straight into heaven.

"Dear heavenly Lord and mighty Savior. We are but three poor river travelers down here on your good earth. This girl here." Aunt Tildy squeezed Jacci's hand tighter. "Our child and your child has seen some evil happenings in her life. Protect her from such as them and all of us from dangers seen and unseen. We can feel the love you throw down on us like as how we feel the sun on our faces. Thank you, Lord, for the blessings and for the troublesome times too when we learn to lean on you. In your holy name we pray. Amen."

"Thank you, Aunt Tildy." Jacci always felt better after one of Aunt Tildy's prayers.

Even Duke looked a little less worried. "You're right about the boat bouncing, Aunt Tildy." He smiled. "I've never noticed that back in the greenroom. It's a wonder your dishes aren't dancing in the cabinet."

Jacci felt the vibrations of the floor too as she remembered what the next act would be. The one that was usually her and Duke, but now was Gabe and Winnie. She wouldn't think about that. Better to think about dancing dishes and slapping some ham between bread. The cast would want more than cake and coffee.

chapter

19

ONCE ALL THE ACTS were done and Gabe got through the waltz with Winnie, he stood at the edge of the curtains to watch Griffith Giles come onstage. The captain assured Gabe the senator promised to keep his speech short before Gabe finished off the night with happy talk that didn't mean anything but generally sent the folks away in a good mood.

Gabe had no idea what the people were going to think about being a captive audience for a political speech. But his father was as hard to sway from what he decided as his mother. Sometimes Gabe wondered if he shouldn't just build his own showboat and find some new rivers to tour. Not that he really wanted to do that. He liked being part of the family show. Besides, if he did try to branch out on his own, he couldn't be sure Jacci would go with him. He wouldn't leave Jacci.

The senator had a politician's gift for glib talk. He got the crowd laughing with an old joke and then launched into what he would do when he was president. From what Gabe had read in the papers, there wasn't much chance of that actually happening. Even if Giles won the Progressive pick as a candidate, he had no chance in a national election. The Republicans had already selected William McKinley as their candidate in their convention the first of June. The Democratic Party was more divided, but this Progressive Party Giles was stumping for hadn't been in the newspapers hardly at all. A politician had to get print.

He was a big man, barrel shaped from shoulders to thighs in the long suit coat he wore. He had to be sweating. A showboat's stage could be the hottest place on earth, with all the lanterns and the heat of the packed auditorium. Gabe wondered if the man wore a hairpiece. It was hard to tell.

He was dressed fine in the gray-striped coat, a starched shirt, and cravat. Way too fine for a showboat crowd, but maybe not for a political campaign. Gabe was on the river so much, going along through this state and then another, that he'd never been absolutely sure which politicians to claim represented him. Of course, the president represented the whole nation. The trouble was that even if he did want to cast a vote, election days generally found them on a river somewhere miles from Cincinnati, which was the closest to a land address they had.

Gabe watched Giles throw out easy words, promises to get the country back on track after the last rough years of the economic downturn. Open up better markets for farm products. That had to play well here in farming country. He got some cheers and only a few boos from way in the back where the boo birds always settled down to roost. Some people would boo if somebody was handing out their favorite cookies. In bags.

At least the man was smart enough not to talk so long that he would fray the patience of the crowd. As he bowed off the stage, the people with him did some raucous cheering that drowned out the boo birds. Only a scattering of applause came from the rest of the crowd. A definite lack of enthusiasm. Gabe hoped that was because of the speech and not the show.

He went out, gave his final five-minute appreciation speech, while Joey and Roy ran along the walls to turn up the lanterns.

"So glad you all came out to our show. Hope you enjoyed every minute and that next summer you'll come on down to the river when you hear Miss Marelda playing the *Kingston Floating Palace* calliope. But before I go, here's one more smile to carry home with you. But you'll have to listen good to catch the funnies."

He hesitated and then, with a smile he didn't feel, rattled off his joke. "'I'm up against it,' said the wallpaper. 'Hard luck,' replied the horseshoe over the door. 'Cut it out,' cried the scissors."

He paused to make a scissoring motion with his fingers and to let the people catch up with the silliness. He didn't want to talk faster than they could listen. "'Well, I've been walked on lately too,' remarked the carpet. 'I'll get someone to look into this,' said the mirror. 'Needn't,' said the desk. 'I haven't any kick. Everything is all write for me.'"

Again he stopped to pretend to write in the air in hopes they would get the joke of "write" for "right." He took a breath and went on. "'Oh, shut up,'" shouted the window shutters. Whereupon the gas became very angry and, after he flared up, got hot under the collar, and because he refused to throw any light on the matter, went out."

About half the audience kept up with what was supposed to be funny in all that, while the other half looked at him as if they wouldn't be able to find their way off the boat. But that was all right. Captain already had their quarters and dimes and he'd see they got back to the riverbank.

"And that, dear people, is our show for tonight. The cast will be up front here at the stage ready to do some talking and smiling should any of you be in a friendly mood. Naught but friendly is allowed. Good night and God bless."

Another spattering of applause sounded as people started

standing up. With the lanterns turned up now, he could see people he knew from years past. Others were new faces. He had no trouble picking out the senator's entourage. About ten of them. Some were local politicians. He recognized a judge he'd met here one other time.

Only two women appeared to be with them. One looked to be a lady's companion to the other. She was gathering up their wraps and reticules while the lady, dressed as if going to a big-city play, stood with her back to the stage. She wore an elaborate dark-rose hat decorated with feathers and pearls. Even without seeing her face, he knew she was beautiful from the way she held herself as she waited for the other woman to finish fussing with their things. She definitely didn't fit in with their usual crowd. She looked more like a patron of the arts in New York City. Somewhere far from West Chester.

The judge he remembered pushed his way through the crowd toward Gabe.

"Hello, Judge. So glad you came out for the show tonight." Gabe couldn't remember his name but figured calling him judge would be safe.

"Wouldn't miss it, Gabe. Always a boatload of fun." He grinned, pleased with his pun. "Looks like you might finally have something going with that little gal you were singing to tonight."

"Oh, that was just part of the show."

"You best take advantage so you won't end up an old bachelor with no good woman to take care of you when you get past your dandy age." The man laughed and punched Gabe's shoulder.

"I'll keep that in mind." Gabe laughed too. He knew how to play the parts people expected.

"But what I come over here for is to tell you Senator Giles wants a word with you. What the senator wants, we make sure to get for him. You know, you grease my hand, I'll grease yours.

He makes it to president like he's wanting, we'll be in high cotton down here in our neck of the woods."

Gabe started to ask why the man didn't come over himself if he wanted to talk, but Judge Somebody liked being the senator's message boy. Besides, could be the man was right. It didn't hurt to have a friend in the legislature. He looked around to see if he could spot the captain, but his father was nowhere in sight. He'd be out on the deck making sure people got down the stage plank safely and without doing any damage to his new showboat.

Cameron had the senator cornered and appeared to be pouring on the charm. With a bare nod of his head, the senator stepped away from Cameron when he saw Gabe coming his way. Cameron frowned at his sudden dismissal, but another of the senator's men took him in hand to smooth over the senator's abrupt departure.

"There you are. Gabe, isn't it?" The senator held out his hand.

"That's right." Gabe shook it. The man was older than he'd thought him to be while watching him speak. He definitely did wear a toupee. Too dark brown for his age.

"Great show. Be sure to thank your father for me if I don't see him before I leave. I appreciate him letting me share a few words with your audience."

"I'll do that, but he'll be around somewhere out on deck."

"I can't blame him for wanting to be out of this crowd. Hot as Hades down here by the stage." He yanked out a handkerchief and wiped his brow.

"The lights heat things up and then today was one scorcher of a day for June."

"True enough." The man kept smiling as he peered around. "Where's that girl that played Penelope? I want to talk to her. Tell her what a fine performance she gave."

"I'm sure she's around somewhere. It's easy to miss somebody in the crowd," Gabe said.

"I'd count it a favor if you'd find her and bring her over."

"I'll tell her you liked the play." Gabe sidestepped his request.

The man's eyes didn't seem to match his wide smile. "I think it means more when you tell a performer that in person."

Gabe lifted up on his tiptoes and pretended to look around for Jacci. If he had seen her, he wouldn't have told this man, but he didn't see her. He shook his head. "I'm sorry, Senator. But I think she must have already gone back to her room. She felt a little under the weather today."

"I see. What's her name? Princess is all the program shows."

"Princess it is." Gabe tried to change the subject. "I hope Mrs. Giles liked the show too."

"Oh, you know women. They like anything with a little drama." Giles looked toward the two women waiting in the aisle next to their seats. "Especially the missus. Do you know her?" His eyes seemed to sharpen on Gabe when he looked back at him.

"No sir. I haven't had the pleasure."

"Perhaps your mother or father knows her?"

"If so, they've never mentioned it. I don't think she's ever been to one of our shows. She looks to be the kind of lady who might feel more comfortable at a private showing."

The senator laughed. "The little woman isn't too fond of rubbing shoulders with the common man. Or woman. But I think she'd be as interested as me in speaking with the young woman who played Penelope."

"I'm so sorry, but the actors and actresses aren't required to meet the people after the show. Especially when they aren't feeling well."

"I see." The man stopped looking as friendly. He must have expected Gabe to run fetch Jacci and bring her out to meet him.

Without moving to do his bidding, Gabe met his look, careful to keep smiling.

After a few long seconds, Giles blew out a breath and rocked back on his heels. "I'm sorry not to get to talk to her personally, but I understand about a lady's vapors. So I suppose it will have to do for you to pass along my good words to her. Be sure to tell her how much we enjoyed her performance and how we do hope to see her again soon. Both myself and my wife, Lisbeth." His smile was completely gone now. "Lisbeth Bridwell Giles. You check with your parents and see if they don't remember her. I wouldn't be surprised if you find out they do."

"Tell you what, Senator. My mother is heading over this way. Why don't you ask her yourself?" Gabe's mother always knew when Gabe was losing patience with somebody after the show. When she stepped up beside them, Gabe said, "Senator, my mother, Marelda Kingston."

Ma gave him her brightest smile. "So good of you to grace us with your presence tonight, Senator Giles."

"The pleasure is all mine, madam." The man took Ma's hand and lifted it toward his face as though to kiss it.

Gabe's mother gently extricated her hand before that could happen.

Gabe spoke up. "Senator Giles thinks you might know his wife, Lisbeth."

"Yes." Giles nodded. "She was a Bridwell from Boyle County. She still spends much of her time there at the manor house. That is, when she's not with me in Washington."

Ma wrinkled her brow in thought. "I don't think I've had the pleasure, sir." She must have noted the senator's frown because she went on. "But we do meet so many people up and down the river that I might have forgotten."

"I'm sure that's true, but I don't think you would have forgotten Lisbeth had you met her." Giles kept pushing. "Or even heard others speak of her."

Gabe could tell his mother was beginning to lose her patience the same as he had, but she kept her voice sweet. "I'm sure you're right, Senator, but now if you'll excuse us, we have others to see." Ma put on a winning smile. "Thank you again for being here, but duty calls." She took Gabe's arm and started to turn away.

Giles grabbed her shoulder to stop her. "Madam, I suggest you finish your duty here with me first."

Ma stopped stonestill and stared at the man's hand on her shoulder and then back at the senator with an icy glare. When Gabe started to speak up, she sent some of that icy stare toward him to freeze his words before they could leave his mouth. Gabe had no trouble interpreting that look. She intended to handle this without his assistance.

"I suggest you take your hand off my shoulder, Senator Giles."

He pulled his hand back and blustered out something that could have been an apology from a more sincere man. "I simply asked you as nicely as I could if you knew my wife."

"And I said I did not."

His smile appeared to be pasted on. "Then we must change that. I'm sure you will like her."

Something about the way he said that made Gabe wonder if the senator liked his wife. He looked out at the two ladies waiting for their party to be ready to leave. "Lisbeth, come here."

For a second, Gabe thought the lady with the fine hat was going to ignore his command, but then she turned toward them very slowly. She lifted her chin and looked across the room at her husband before she hid most of her face behind a flutter of a black fan.

Gabe felt as if the wind had been knocked out of him as Ma's fingers tightened on his arm, obviously seeing the same thing he did. The woman looked enough like Jacci to be her sister. Or her mother.

Chapter

20

MA RECOVERED FIRST. She let go of Gabe's arm to hurry toward the senator's wife. Gabe tried not to stare at the woman as he and Giles trailed her.

"Mrs. Giles, it's so nice to meet you." If Ma was flustered by how much the senator's wife looked like Jacci, she didn't show it. "Your husband thought we might have met before, but I'm sure I would have remembered if we had."

The lady lowered the fan. Her voice was soft, but at the same time sounded reluctant to be in conversation with them. "How nice of you to say so, but I regret to admit this is the first time I've been aboard your showboat. Or any showboat. But I have heard others speak very favorably of the dramas you put on. So nice to finally have experienced that firsthand."

The lady's maid moved closer to Mrs. Giles, as though ready to intervene for her should the need arise. The lady did look pale as she waved air toward her face with the fan. The movement didn't quite hide the tremble of her hands.

Senator Giles spoke up. "Lisbeth, dear, I was just telling Mrs. Kingston and her son how much we enjoyed the performance of the young lady who played Penelope. Princess, they call her."

"Yes. All the actors and actresses were excellent." She didn't look at her husband but continued to smile at Ma. "Thank you so much for taking time to come speak with me. Where will you be performing next?"

"We stop at a little landing not far down the river. Point William," Ma said. "We're always surprised at how the crowds show up even when the village is so small the way it is there, but they hear our calliope and come streaming in from the countryside."

"Point William is always a good stop for us," Gabe put in simply because he felt he needed to say something instead of standing there like a wordless idiot.

His wide-eyed stare might be what was making the woman nervous, or maybe it was seeing Jacci play Penelope. Something was definitely causing the air around them to feel like a tie rope about to snap in a flood. When that happened, all one could do was ride out the torrent.

He turned to Senator Giles and caught a look on his face he couldn't quite read as he watched his wife. Not anger. More amusement to see her so unsettled. The man slid a smile on his face as easily as a turtle sliding off a log into the river.

"Thank you again for coming out, Senator, and introducing us to your lovely wife." Gabe nodded toward the lady, and this time he slipped his hand under his mother's elbow to encourage their leave-taking.

The lady bent her head in acknowledgment before she looked straight at her husband. "Ellie and I are ready to go back to the hotel."

"Are you sure there's no one else you want to speak to here?" The man was definitely prodding her with his words.

"Very sure." Again she lifted her chin and the resemblance to Jacci was even more striking close at hand.

"Good night." Ma smiled at the lady and her maid before she slid a quick glance past the senator. Then without delay, she turned back toward the stage where most of the people were leaving to head home.

Gabe started to say something, but Ma gave her head a bare shake to stop him.

He glanced over his shoulder. The senator had been joined by several of his companions along with, oddly enough, Perry Wilson. Perry wasn't even carrying one of his dummies. That was certainly a rarity. Maybe he, like Cameron, was hoping for some special favors, although Gabe couldn't imagine what either of them hoped to get from the senator.

He caught sight of the lady's skirts as she and her maid went out of the theater. If he hurried, he might sneak out to the deck another way to talk to her without her husband around, but what would he say? *You look just like the girl I love.*

As if his mother guessed his thoughts, she tightened her arm against her side to trap his hand. "It could be a coincidence," she said softly almost as if she were talking to herself.

"But Duke—"

"Not now." She interrupted him. "Just keep smiling."

She slipped away from him then to greet some of the crowd still hanging around the stage. Gabe did the same, even though his heart wasn't in it. Usually he loved the interaction with the audience who came to the shows, but the senator had spoiled that for him tonight. He couldn't stop thinking about how the man looked at his wife as if pleased by her discomfort. Not only that, he had also seemed to be laying out traps for Ma with his insistent questions.

He wasn't the only one setting traps. When Gabe finally worked his way through the last of those waiting to speak to him and headed to the greenroom, Winnie appeared out of the shadows to grasp his arm.

"I thought you would never get here." She stepped close to him. Too close.

"You know we always talk to the people after the show."

"I did my share of that, but who I really want to talk to is you. That song was so perfect." She took his hand and slid her other hand up around his neck. "I think we should do some more of that waltzing, don't you?"

"I don't hear any music."

"We can make our own." She was so close he could feel her breath on his cheek.

He pulled away from her. "No, I don't think we can, Winnie. That act was a onetime deal. I'm sure Duke will be feeling better by showtime tomorrow night to do his song with Jacci."

With her lips pressed together in a thin line, she stared at Gabe a moment before she almost spat out her next words. "Princess Jacci. Why is it always about her?"

He tamped down on his irritation one more time tonight. People were doing their best to rile his redheaded temper. He pulled in a breath and summoned up his patience. After all, Winnie was still so young. Maybe only a few years younger than Jacci, but Jacci had been robbed of a lot of kid years by her mother's death.

"It's not about anybody," he said. "It's about the show. Those are the acts listed on the playbill."

"I could do her part just as good as she can. Better even. Cameron says Jacci doesn't know how to relax when he embraces her." She leaned closer to Gabe again. "He says he can give me lessons on love scenes, but I'd rather you did."

"You be careful around Cameron." Gabe narrowed his eyes on her.

"Why?" A smile curled up her lips. "Jealous?"

"I don't want to see you get hurt." That was the worst thing he could have said when he was trying to push her away. That sounded as if he cared, and he did care. Just not the way she hoped he would.

"That's so sweet, Gabe, but in case you haven't noticed, I've grown up. I'm not a little girl anymore."

"Right, Winnie. Look, we'll have to sort all this out later." He pushed her away from him as gently as he could. "I need to go check on Duke."

"It's not Duke you want to check on. It's Jacci, isn't it?" Her face tightened in anger. "But you need to think again. She's the one after Cameron. She'll be the one he teaches how to do a real love scene."

He pulled up the last shred of his patience and tried to smooth it out to cover the flare of temper that was threatening to break through. His parents would never forgive him if he did something to make the Lorandas quit the show. They were a big part of the band, and a show needed music.

"That could be." He shrugged and moved away from her before she could grab him again.

The bad part was that indeed it could be exactly as she said. He kept picturing Jacci and Cameron on the top deck close together in the moonlight. He gave himself a mental shake. Right now, he needed to push aside the worry about whether he could ever steal Jacci's heart. Instead, he could play the brother role with her to find out what was going on with Duke and if she knew why she looked so much like Lisbeth Giles.

He headed toward the galley. Duke and Jacci might be there the same as any other night. Besides, he needed coffee. He looked back at Winnie, still standing where he'd left her.

He tried to make peace. "Come on. I think Aunt Tildy made that apple cake you like."

"I'm not hungry. Maybe I'll go hunt up Cameron. He will have time to talk to me."

Gabe looked at her a moment and felt sorry when he saw her lips trembling. He wasn't sure if she was about to cry or so mad she wanted to punch him. Either way, he couldn't do much to change things.

"I'll tell Aunt Tildy to save you a piece in case you get hungry later. After you see Cameron." He regretted those last words when she whirled away and leaped off the stage without bothering with the steps. But then she was an acrobat.

He sighed and headed on toward the greenroom, empty now. Later, after they ate whatever Aunt Tildy had for them, the cast would come back and straighten their costumes and props. Perry's two dummies were on a chair, arms and legs akimbo. Gabe had to fight the urge to go sit them up. He had seen Perry treat them like real people so much that it seemed wrong for them to be in a disheveled heap. Perry must still be out there talking to the senator. That seemed strange too.

But then tonight everything was feeling strange. He was ready to slide back out on the river and leave this night behind. Move on to the next landing without pushy senators and nervous wives. He also wouldn't mind stepping away from demanding mothers and clingy girls not old enough to know the difference between a song in a show and a song of the heart.

That might be a little harder to do, since he had to live with his mother and finish out the season with the Lorandas.

In the dining area, the scene was almost like any other night after a show. Winnie didn't follow him in. Cameron wasn't there either. That was a worry after what Winnie had said about love scenes. Almost enough to make him go hunt her up again. He might have, but Mrs. Loranda must have noticed the same thing Gabe did. She said something to her husband, who left his cake uneaten and went out with a frown on his face.

Jacci smiled and laughed as she helped Aunt Tildy put out the food and pour drinks. If she was concerned about anything, she wasn't showing it. Duke, at his usual table, assured everyone he was fine and would be more than ready to go on next show. Gabe's mother settled in the chair beside Duke, no doubt hoping for a private moment to talk to him.

Perry Wilson showed up late, still without either of his dummies. Joey Loranda asked him where his kids were.

Perry laughed like his Corky dummy and flexed his hand before he shrugged. "Put them to bed early. Kids need their sleep." He looked around at Joey. "Could be you should go turn in."

"Hey, I'm not a kid," Joey said.

"Yeah, kid. Tell that to the queen." Perry looked over at Ma. "Not you, Marelda. I'm sure you've heard more tales than you can remember during your time on showboats."

"I've heard my share," Ma said.

Perry laughed and turned back to the counter to grab a sandwich off the plate Jacci had just filled up. He stared at it and then at Jacci.

"Something wrong with the sandwich, Perry?" she asked.

"No, no." He took a bite without moving away from the counter. He chewed a minute before he asked, "Did you get to meet Senator Giles tonight, Jacci?"

Jacci froze with the coffeepot in her hand. Gabe glared at Perry. What was he up to? Gabe was about to say something to set the man straight when Jacci spoke first.

"No, I didn't. Since Duke and I weren't doing our act, we came on to the kitchen to help Aunt Tildy." She poured the coffee and handed Perry the cup. "Did you get to meet him? I heard he gave a speech."

"Regular political double talk." Perry took the cup and found a place at the table. "But he's an interesting man. And nobody to mess with."

"Oh." Gabe went to lean against the counter. "What makes you think that?"

"I don't just think it. I know it. I've met him before." Perry sipped his coffee. "I've met his wife before too. Lisbeth. Did you talk to her, Jacci?"

"I didn't go out in the crowd. I told you I was down here with Aunt Tildy." Jacci sounded uninterested as she wiped up a little spill of coffee. But she was acting.

"We had a great crowd. Laughed and cheered at all the right times." Gabe tried to turn the conversation.

"A packed house is always good," Ma added.

But Perry was undeterred as he kept eyeing Jacci. "You remember how I told you that you reminded me of someone. Strangely enough, that turns out to be Mrs. Giles. She is a beauty."

Jacci stared straight at Perry. "Then I suppose I'm fortunate to resemble her."

"A striking resemblance for sure. You should have gone out to meet her." Perry looked from Jacci to Gabe. "You noticed it, didn't you, Gabe? I saw you and Marelda talking to her."

"She had dark hair like Jacci's," Gabe said. "At least what I could see under that elaborate hat."

"It's more than just her dark hair," Perry said. "A lot more."

The room was oddly quiet as people quit eating and chatting to listen. Gabe pushed away from the counter to let Perry know he was out of line, but Aunt Tildy stopped dishing up cake to push in between Gabe and Perry.

She planted her fists on her hips and glared at the man. "What are you trying to say, Perry Wilson?"

Perry put his coffee cup down with a rattle and sat back in his chair. He looked at a loss for words.

Aunt Tildy didn't give him time to recover as she went on. "You needin' one of those dummy dolls of yours to do your explainin' for you?"

Perry held up his hands as if to fend off her words. "I don't think I have anything to explain. I was simply making an observation."

"Well, go observe somewhere else." Aunt Tildy glared at him another minute before she began picking up plates and cups. The way they clattered when she dropped them in the sink, Gabe figured they'd need to go dish shopping at the next stop.

Ma looked over at Gabe, obviously expecting him to get

things back on an even keel. So he said, "Let's stick with talking about the show, people."

"It's all right." Jacci touched Gabe's arm as she stepped past him to give Perry a piece of cake. "I'm happy that Perry thinks I look like a woman he's calling a beauty. Thank you for that. I hope you will introduce me to her, Perry, if she comes to another show."

Perry looked even more surprised by her words than he had Aunt Tildy's. He mumbled something and began eating the cake. Attention turned away from him when an obviously unhappy Winnie came in behind her father to plop down in a chair beside her mother. Everyone started talking again.

A few minutes later, Jacci whispered something to Aunt Tildy and slipped out of the room. Ma looked at Gabe again, but she didn't have to tell him to follow Jacci. He was already on the way to the door.

chapter
21

Jacci breathed in the air off the river, relieved to be away from Perry Wilson's stare. What difference did it make to him if she looked like the queen of England? Or a senator's wife. At the same time, his words made her wish she had waited for the lamps to be turned up after the show so she could actually see this woman named Lisbeth. This woman who had given her life. Not mothered her, but carried her in her womb.

She walked quickly away from the galley and climbed up to the hurricane deck. She hesitated on the top steps, hoping Cameron would not be there ahead of her. He hadn't been in the dining area. She glanced over at the towboat, but everything was dark there. If the riverboat captains were talking the night away, they were doing it by moonlight.

Cameron wouldn't be in that group. Who knew where he was? She didn't really care, as long as he didn't search her out the way he had last night. She needed some time alone.

The water shimmered in the silvery light of the moon as the river flowed gently past the showboat. The moon was waning, but it still shed enough light to hide all but the brightest stars.

Jacci looked up at the North Star, the one Captain Dan once told her she could always use as a guide. At the time, she had been too young to understand about navigation, but she had been desperate for a guide to help her get through the hard days without her mother.

So she had chosen that star when she longed for her mother's touch and wanted to pull up the memory of her love. Every clear night, she would lie on the top deck staring at the star and imagine her mother looking down at her from heaven until somebody found her and made her go to bed. Sometimes it was Duke. Sometimes Marelda. But most of the time it was Gabe.

She always liked it best when Gabe came to find her, because he would lie down on the deck beside her and stare up at the stars too. He showed her the constellations. When she said she liked the Little Dipper better than the Big Dipper, he laughed and asked her why. Because she could drink out of it, she had told him and made him laugh more.

Now it could be he was showing those constellations to Winnie. She pushed that thought aside. She would not be jealous. She had no reason to be jealous. None. Besides, she had enough worries without adding that.

When she heard the footsteps on the narrow stairs leading up to the top deck, she almost ran to hide behind the pilothouse. But then she recognized the steps. Not Cameron. Not Duke. Gabe. So, she stood still in the moonlight next to the railing. Perhaps she didn't want to be alone after all.

He stepped up beside her and watched the river a moment before he spoke. "I love nights like this when the water laps against the boat and you can hear the whip-poor-wills. We're close to some woods here."

"I heard an owl a while ago." She shifted a little until her shoulder touched his upper arm. She seemed to need that touch tonight.

"Do you remember when we used to listen up here and try to name everything we heard?"

"I do. That was fun." Jacci smiled.

"I was always surprised at how many different things we could hear." He didn't move away from her touch. "But you always heard some things I never could."

"Oh, you mean the stars." Jacci stared up at the North Star. "I did think I could hear them sparkle."

"I sometimes pretended to hear it with you, but I never really did."

"I know. You weren't listening with the right ears."

"What were the right ears?"

"The ones that wanted to hear my mother in that sparkle." She couldn't have admitted that to anyone but Gabe.

"Do you hear the sparkle tonight?"

She knew he was looking at her instead of the stars, but she continued to gaze at the skies. "I want to. I do so want to."

They were both silent then for a few moments. She could hear Gabe's breath and was glad he didn't mind the silence. Another whip-poor-will's call floated across the river to them.

"I've heard them, but I've never seen a whip-poor-will," she said. "Have you?"

"No. Captain says even he hasn't. He says they look just like the tree bark and are almost impossible to spot. A good way to avoid those owls."

"They hide out," Jacci whispered.

"I guess that's one way to think about their camouflage."

Again they were quiet a moment before Jacci said, "Did you see her?"

"Yes."

She was glad he didn't pretend to not know who she meant. "Do I look like her? The way Perry said."

"Yes."

She gripped the railing a little tighter, not sure what to say next or whether she should say anything.

This time Gabe broke the silence between them. "Did you know you would?"

"No. But I knew I could."

"Do you want to tell me why?"

"She's my mother."

"Your mother?" Gabe didn't know what he had expected her to say, but it wasn't that.

"Not my real mother. Irena was the mother that counted." Jacci looked up at the stars again a moment before she sighed and turned back to Gabe. "But it seems this woman named Lisbeth did give birth to me. Or so Duke told me today."

"I don't understand."

"I'm not sure I do either. Who even knows if Duke is remembering right, but he says Lisbeth gave me to my mother when I was born. That they did it to protect me." Jacci stared down at her hands clutching the rail. "From being illegitimate."

"Are you saying that this Lisbeth had an affair with Kelly, but they didn't marry?"

"No. Kelly isn't my father."

She raised her head and lifted her chin, and Gabe remembered the senator's wife doing the same. Before Gabe could come up with the right words to say, she went on. "I don't know who my father is. Just that it isn't Kelly."

She wasn't crying. She sounded too sad for tears. Gabe put his arm around her and pulled her close to his side. Not the embrace he wanted to do, but a brother's embrace. "Duke didn't know either?"

"He said not, although he did know he died in a steamboat accident." She let out a heavy sigh. "I don't know who I am any longer." She didn't move away from his arm, but at the same time, she stayed stiff against him.

"You are still the same person."

She twisted her head to look up at him. "Do you think you would feel like the same person if you found out your mother and father weren't your mother and father?"

"I don't know. I would hope so, but I don't know."

She looked back out toward the river. "I feel as though I'm drifting away from everything I've always known and loved. That I'll never know where I really belong again."

He tightened his arm around her. "You belong with me." He said it exactly the way he meant it, but in case that wasn't what she wanted to hear, he added, "With us. You always have. And whether your mother gave birth to you or not, you can't doubt that she loved you."

"I know. She died to protect me. But from what, Gabe?"

"Do you think Kelly knows?"

She puffed out another breath that carried a sound of disgust. "Kelly! I haven't even seen him for over a year. What good is a father, even a pretend father, if you never see him? If he never tells you the truth?"

"Maybe he would tell you the truth now. Now that you know this about Lisbeth."

"Maybe. I'm sorry, Gabe." She moved away from him. "I shouldn't be crying on your shoulder."

His side felt cold. "My shoulder is always available, but I haven't seen any tears."

"It's foolish to cry when a person doesn't know what there is to cry about. Or to fear."

"Fear?"

"If I'm hiding, I must have something to fear."

"I suppose you did once, but not now. Not with us around you. I'll make sure no one hurts you."

She smiled then and reached to touch his cheek. "Dear

Gabe. You've always tried to protect me." She dropped her hand away. "But what if I've brought trouble to you? To your family? Maybe Duke and I should just leave the *Palace* and find a little place in the country to hide out."

"No." The word came out with more force than he aimed. But he couldn't let her leave them. Leave him. He pulled in a breath and managed to make his voice calmer. "We need you here." Why couldn't he just say the truth that he needed her here? But he was afraid she wasn't ready to hear that from him. Maybe from Cameron, but not him.

"Winnie could play my part." She moved another step away from him with a look he didn't quite recognize.

"That's crazy. She does fine in her act with her family, but that's all."

"People love hearing her flute."

"Well, yes. The Lorandas know their music along with the tumbling tricks."

"And you did that song with her tonight. Mrs. Loranda said you danced together as though you'd been doing it forever." She gave him another funny look.

"The act was all right, I guess. Nobody booed anyway." He shrugged and shifted a little closer to her. He had to fight the urge to grab her and keep her from backing away from him.

"So, you'd be fine. I know she could do my part in the drama. She told me she and Cameron had practiced it during the day a couple of times. Just in case. Cameron says everybody needs an understudy."

Gabe would like to understudy him. Right off the boat. But the one he didn't want off the boat was standing there in the moonlight beside him. She was so beautiful that when he feasted his eyes on her the way he was doing now, he could scarcely breathe.

He tamped down his feelings. Seemed that was all he was

doing tonight. Trying to keep from feeling anger and irritation. And now love.

"You can't leave the boat, Jacci. You might need help with Duke if he starts having more problems with his memory. Besides, it would kill him to leave the river."

"You're right. It would, but maybe I should leave anyway."

"You're not making sense." Gabe did reach over to take her hands then.

"But what if I'm putting you all in danger? Now that they know where I am."

"They?"

"Don't you think whatever happened back then to my mother had to do with Lisbeth? I remember Duke asking my mother if it was all because of me." Her face tightened in distress. "I don't remember much about then, but I do remember that. And Mama." She glanced back toward the sky.

"Why do you think it was because of you?" Gabe was trying to understand.

"I don't know." Her voice wasn't much over a whisper. "Maybe Lisbeth was afraid her husband was going to find out about me. Maybe she sent that man after me. To make me disappear."

"She didn't look like someone who would do anything like that. Now the senator, he might be a different matter."

"So, it could be he was afraid a scandal about his wife having a baby out of wedlock would ruin his political chances back then. And now, you say he wants to run for president. His opponents might be trying to dig up bad things about him. About his family. If I look so much like her and here I am on a showboat for all the world to see, who knows what those supporting him might do to keep him from being ensnared in that kind of scandal."

"Hardly anybody has even heard of this Progressive Party he's trying to get to pick him as a candidate. The man doesn't have a prayer."

"Prayer." She bent her head. "Do you pray, Gabe?"

Her quick switch of subjects surprised him. "Not as much as Ma thinks I should."

"But don't you think that's something you have to decide to do for yourself? Not because your mother wants you to."

"I guess." Gabe frowned. "But what has you thinking about prayer?"

"Sometimes it seems praying is all a person can do." She pulled her hands from his and gazed up at the stars again. "I prayed for Mama. I was so sure the Lord would answer my prayers, but he didn't. Not the way I wanted him to, anyway. But Mama told me before she died that the Lord had answered a prayer we didn't know we needed to pray by having your showboat with Duke on board tie up beside our steamboat that night."

"I'm glad we were there."

She looked at him again then. "I'm glad too. So very glad. I don't know what I would have done without you after my mother died."

"I haven't gone anywhere. You can still count on me."

"Things change." She looked down.

"Not that." With a finger under her chin, he tilted her face back up so he could look into her eyes. "Look, Jacci, tomorrow we'll be on down the river. The senator will be on to wherever he wants to give his next speech. He may give his poor wife a hard time over whatever it is he knows about you and her, but we'll be gone away from them. Everything will be fine."

"Do you promise?" Tears glistened on her cheeks in the moonlight.

"I promise." He couldn't keep from pulling her into a hug then. Nothing about it felt the least bit like a brother hug. If only he knew how the hug felt to her.

chapter
22

THAT NIGHT JACCI'S DREAMS seemed to mock her. First, she dreamed she was looking into a mirror, but the glass stayed blank, with no reflection of her face. The dream was so vivid that when she jerked awake, she almost lit a lamp to go peer into a mirror to prove that couldn't be.

But that was foolish to even consider. She touched her face. Nothing had changed about how she looked. She didn't need a mirror to prove she was the same person she'd always been. Not knowing who her mother and father actually were didn't change that. She was Jacinth Reed. Jacci Reed. Her mother was Irena Chesser Reed. Her father was Kelly Reed, the gambler. And her grandfather was Tyrone Chesser, better known as Duke.

The fact that she carried none of their blood in her veins didn't change that. A family was more than blood. Love was what made a family. She had Aunt Marelda and Captain Dan. They were family. She had Gabe.

She stared up at the wood ceiling over her bed. She thought again of Gabe's embrace up on the hurricane deck. It wasn't that he had never hugged her before. He had. Many times. A quick hug when she was a kid and skinned her knees. A hug to celebrate if a show went well. An arm around her shoulders when they shared a laugh. A pretend embrace when they were acting in a drama or doing a song together.

But she had never felt the way she did a few hours ago when he put his arms around her and pulled her close. He was simply comforting her. She was the one imagining something different. No, not imagining. Feeling something different. She had wanted to lay her head against his shoulder and just stay there. Forever.

She threw off her cover and flipped over in bed, not sure she should even think what she was thinking. Gabe was the same as her brother. Hadn't she just now assured herself that she was part of the Kingston family? But he wasn't actually her brother. He'd told her that himself plenty of times. *"I'm not really your brother."*

Still, she'd always thought of him as a brother. Or maybe not. How could she even know what a sister was supposed to feel for a brother? She didn't have a brother. Or a mother or father. She was afloat in unknown waters.

Could she really be falling in love with Gabe? She loved him. Had loved him since she was five. But falling in love was different. She knew what that was supposed to be like. She'd acted the part in plenty of dramas. Falling for the leading man. She pretended to fall in love with Cameron every night. That wasn't real love. Could what she had felt there in the moonlight in Gabe's arms be the feeling that needed no acting?

"Stop being ridiculous," she whispered aloud.

And now she was talking to herself. Gabe had only been doing his best to comfort her the way he had so many times. The way a brother would. She simply needed the touch more after Duke's truth telling yesterday. Come daylight, things would settle back into the usual routine.

Gabe was right. They would be heading on down the river to a new landing, a new night to perform. The senator and his wife would be yesterday's crowd with a new crowd coming aboard for their show. Gabe would be her brother again, and if he had eyes for Winnie, then she would be glad for him.

But when she drifted back to sleep, new dreams came to mock her as she stood unseen on the upper deck watching Gabe and Winnie dance in the moonlight.

She was glad when the deckhands untying the boat to get underway down the river pulled her from her unhappy dreams. By the time she got up and dressed, the boat was out in the middle of the river with the *Little Ruby* pushing it downstream. Smoke puffed up out of the towboat's smokestacks, but it wasn't taking too much steam to keep the boats on the move with a good breeze pushing them along too.

Clouds had moved in overnight to cover up the sun and promised rain before the day was through. But rain never kept the people away when they heard the calliope. She hoped they could find a place to tie up that wouldn't be awash in mud should the storms come.

She and Marelda and some of the crew would have to clean the clumps of mud off the auditorium floor if the landing was muddy. Having a showboat wasn't all singing and dancing the way most who came to the shows assumed. But Jacci loved it. The same as Duke, she'd hate being relegated to a house that never rode the rivers.

Maybe Gabe was right and she was letting her imagination get the better of her when she worried about bringing danger to the showboat. Years had passed with no dangers that Jacci knew anything about. Plus, they were on the move again. The people on board were her family and friends. And Gabe promised to protect her.

She wouldn't think about what had happened to the last person who had protected her. Things were different now than they had been when that man had tried to take her from her mother. Yes, mother. Irena was her mother. Just thinking that made her feel better as she looked up toward where the North Star was. She wouldn't be able to see it in the daytime even if clouds weren't covering the sky, but she knew it was there.

A few raindrops plopped down to make circles in the water. Jacci had thought about going up to the top deck. The rain wasn't what stopped her. The feelings she'd explored while trying to sleep were what kept her feet on the main deck. Besides, Winnie might have gotten up early too. She might be the one Gabe was letting take the wheel in this straight stretch.

That was unlikely. Winnie liked to sleep the morning away. But then, several unlikely things had been happening lately.

Jacci wished she had at least looked at Lisbeth the night before. Putting a face to a name was no reason for fear. Now, to hear Perry Wilson tell it, to come up with that face, all she had to do was look in a mirror. That thought brought back the memory of her dream.

She went around to the port side of the boat and found one of her favorite places to watch their progress down the river. Here in this place she was sheltered from the rain. The fat drops were coming faster now and making dimples all across the river.

They passed a couple of boys on a raft, fishing as they floated along safely away from the *Little Ruby*, but they would be bouncing in the wake of the stern-wheeler for a while. The boys waved. They looked happy to have some bounces in their ride.

That's all this was for Jacci. A rough patch in the river of her life. While she might not enjoy the bumpy wash the way the boys on the raft seemed ready to do, she could ride it out. She might even get brave enough to look in a mirror later, but for now she'd watch the rain fall on the river and not mind the wind blowing some of the drops in on her.

"Oh dear! She's going to get wet." Perry Wilson walked

toward her, his Cindy dummy riding on his arm. He used his doll's high voice.

"Good morning, Perry." Jacci didn't join in with his pretending.

"I don't think she wants to tell me good morning." He continued talking for Cindy. "Do you think she's still mad at you?"

"I'm not upset at you, Perry. But I'm not going to talk to you through your dummy."

He shrugged and gave up the pretense. "I don't know why not. Sometimes it's easier to talk through an interpreter."

"I think we can talk one-on-one."

"You do look like Lisbeth Giles."

"I know. You told me."

"And you really don't know her?" He stared at her.

"I really don't know her." Jacci turned to look out at the river again. "I like watching the rain, don't you?"

"I prefer smooth waters, to be honest." He stepped up beside her next to the rail but held his doll behind him to keep it from getting wet. "But you enjoy watching from here, don't you? I see you here all the time."

"Sometimes this is the best place. Here or up top. I've always loved watching the river. I don't remember living anywhere except on a boat in season."

"So you've lived on the showboat all your life?"

"Most of it. With Duke." She glanced over at him. "How about you, Perry? Always a showman? With the dummies?"

"Not always on a showboat, but a showman. It can be a hard life, trying to please the common man."

"The common and the uncommon," Jacci said. "But whoever they are, they love your act."

"It's not too hard to entertain these country folks. They think somebody standing on his head is funny."

"Or talking through a doll." Jacci smiled over at him. "I

suppose we had some more sophisticated people watching last night."

"Giles was only there to take advantage of the crowd to do some campaign stumping, and his wife was only there because she had to be."

"Why did she have to be?"

"To show a unified family front. Voters like that. The idea of their politicians being happily married and, in Giles's case, happily married to a beautiful woman." He sounded as though he was ridiculing the idea.

"That seems a good thing, don't you think?"

"If it were true. In the case of Senator and Mrs. Giles, I think it is very far from the case. More acting went on between them than up onstage."

"Do you know them that well?"

"I have eyes. I see things."

A gust of wind whipped more rain in on them. Perry stepped back and took on his Cindy voice again. "Oh no. You're going to get my hair wet." He changed back to his regular voice. "Guess I'd better get her in out of the rain. Wouldn't want her makeup to run."

"That would definitely not be good." This time Jacci played along with the ventriloquist. "See you at the show, Cindy." She even smiled at the dummy, which made Perry look happy. He was an odd little man.

He took a couple of steps away and stopped to look back at Jacci. "Look out. Here's comes that Loranda girl. She was in a sour mood last night when her father made her come in the dining room, and from the frown on her face, things aren't going any better for her this morning."

"Maybe Cindy can cheer her up with a few words," Jacci said.

Perry went into his Cindy voice without a blink. "Hide me, Perry. She'll try to pitch me in the river."

Winnie stopped and stared at them a moment, as if deciding whether to turn around and go the other direction.

Jacci called to her. "Good morning, Winnie. Kind of a gray day, isn't it?" She refused to let her conflicted feelings about Gabe keep her from being nice to Winnie, even if the girl didn't seem to care if they were friends or not.

Winnie came on toward them. Perry grinned as he made his Cindy doll nod at Jacci. Then he waved the doll's hand at Winnie. "Breakfast is calling." He made a quick escape.

"That man is weird." Winnie stared after him. "Always talking through those dummies as if we don't know it's him doing the talking."

"He gets into his act." Jacci shrugged.

"A person should know the difference between make-believe and reality." Winnie's frown got darker.

"I guess so. Especially on a showboat. I hear you and Gabe did great on that song last night."

"Yeah, well, it's not like it was a hard song to sing or anything." She turned away from Jacci and stepped closer to the railing. She grabbed it so hard it wobbled a little.

"Careful," Jacci said. "Captain wouldn't be happy if we broke the railing on his new boat."

"What do I care if he's happy or not? Or if anybody is happy." She gave the railing another shake, before she let it go and pushed her hand through her hair that had exploded into curls. "Stupid weather. I don't like it when it rains. Makes my hair frizz up."

Jacci tried to think of something nice to say to put a little cheer back in the morning. "You've got pretty hair." The girl really did have great blond curls.

Winnie gave her a narrowed-eyes look. "Stop trying to be nice to me."

"All right," Jacci said slowly.

The girl was definitely in a bad humor, but Jacci had enough to straighten out in her own thoughts without borrowing whatever trouble Winnie was toting around. She turned back to stare out at the river.

She expected the girl to head on to wherever she was going when she spotted Jacci and Perry, but she didn't. Instead, Winnie stayed where she was beside Jacci. After a minute, she said, "You're always here at the railing staring out at something. What are you looking for?"

"Nothing really. Just whatever there is to see, I guess."

"Looks like nothing but water, trees, and rocks to me."

"You don't like the river?" The rain, coming down a little harder, made a wet veil to look through.

"What's to like or not like?" Winnie grabbed the railing again and went up on her toes. "It's a good way to get places to do shows, I guess."

"That's one thing for sure." Jacci thought about trying to say how she liked wind on her face and watching the side creeks spill out into the river. How she liked seeing the birds and fish and other animals along the riverbanks. The people along the river were fun to see too, those on land and those in boats passing by. But she didn't think Winnie would understand any of that. Some things couldn't be explained in words.

Gabe would understand. For a second she remembered his arms around her again, but then her dream of Gabe and Winnie dancing on the hurricane deck came to mind.

"But you don't have to stand out here in the rain to watch every mile of the way," Winnie said.

"I guess not, but I sort of like watching the rain too."

"Weird. Everybody is weird around here." Winnie stepped back from the railing.

"Maybe you have to be a little weird to like being on a showboat."

"That's what Cameron says."

Jacci had to smile at that. "Does that mean he thinks he's weird too?"

"No, not at all. He hates being on a showboat. He wants to be on a stage in New York or somewhere. And before you ask if I think I'm weird too, my parents are the ones loving showboats."

"The Weird World of Showboating," Jacci said. "That sounds like a great title for a new showboat play."

When the boat shifted direction to head around a turn in the river, rain dashed in on them. Winnie let out a shriek and they both jumped back.

Jacci laughed as she shook the water off her arms. "Guess that's telling us it's time to find somewhere dry. Besides, if we want to get breakfast, we'd better hustle before Aunt Tildy closes up the kitchen."

"I don't eat breakfast. I'm going back to bed." She started on around the deck, then stopped to ask. "Is this the best spot to stand and watch the river?"

"I like it."

"I think it would be better on top in the pilothouse."

"Both places have their appeal. More rain on you up there. Even whoever is at the wheel. Captain doesn't like a window in front of him. Says the glass keeps him from seeing what's ahead."

"Captain's not up there. Gabe is," Winnie said. "But he said he had to pay attention to the river and couldn't talk."

"Probably because of the rain," Jacci offered. But that didn't seem right. The rain hadn't really started that much when Winnie came around the main deck, and the river here was easy riding.

"Yeah or something." Winnie gave her another hard look before she took off back the way she had come.

Or something. Jacci didn't know whether to be sorry for Winnie or glad that if a romance was developing between Gabe and her, it wasn't drifting along too well. That really shouldn't make her as happy as it did. Not if she thought of Gabe as a brother.

"I'm not really your brother." His words echoed in her head and she was glad to hear them.

Chapter
23

Rain stayed with them as they went down the river. As they approached Point William shortly after noon, Jacci held an umbrella over Marelda up on the top deck while she played the calliope. Raindrops sizzled on the instrument.

Steam piped over from the *Little Ruby* gave the calliope power and made playing it a challenge with the heat it produced. Marelda wore asbestos gloves to protect her hands as she pushed down the levers for the notes that sounded something like a piano with a cold mixed with a steamboat whistle. Marelda had tried to teach Jacci to play the calliope, but while Jacci had no trouble carrying a tune when she was singing, she lacked talent for playing any instrument except the cymbals or a tambourine.

Jacci liked watching Marelda play and didn't mind how the loud steam-powered music wrapped its deafening sound around them before it lifted into the air and drifted to be heard miles away. Wherever people heard the calliope music, they hurried to finish up their work to head down to the show. Gabe could also play the calliope, but he couldn't pull the music out of it that Marelda could. She was one of the best on the river.

While a showboat needed ornate trimming and its fancy name in big easy-to-read letters, the calliope was the showman's trump card at announcing a showboat was coming.

In spite of the rain, people streamed down to watch the *Palace* pull in and tie up. Some of them Jacci recognized from years past at this stop. Children of the kids she and Gabe used to play with now jumped up and down on the riverbank with excitement to see the showboat.

Something about the familiarity of the scene and the smiling faces helped her shrug off the worries of the night before. While what she had always been so sure of in her life had taken a seismic shift, the show they would be doing a little later was the same.

Then when the rain slowed to a steady drizzle, grabbing her tambourine was the same. Duke beside her with his trumpet was the same. She smiled over at him and decided maybe she would start calling him Grampus again. Forget about saying Duke and claim him as the grandfather she loved.

While she couldn't do anything about the decisions people had made when she was born, she could certainly make happy decisions now. Decisions that bolstered her idea of the person she was. She could almost feel her mama's touch, as if letting her know she was thinking right.

Anytime her other mother came to her mind, she'd just block out thoughts of this woman named Lisbeth and get on with her life. She had more important things to figure out, such as her new way of looking at Gabe.

He was up in the front of the parade drumming out the cadence of the march. Winnie with her flute walked beside him. Jacci hung back beside Duke. She'd done this march into little towns all up and down the Ohio, sometimes the Kentucky and the Green and on to the Mississippi. She'd sung, danced, and acted at more places than she could remember. She'd always been safe with the Kingstons. With Gabe.

As if he knew she was thinking about him, he smiled over his shoulder at her, and that strange new feeling wiggled awake inside her. Maybe feeling so at sea the last few days made her think of Gabe as a safe harbor. He knew the showboat Jacci. The Jacci she had always been with a known mother and father. He wouldn't turn his back on her because she now had a different mother and an unknown father. Their years together on the river would be more important than that.

Even if he had fallen in love with Winnie, he wouldn't stop being her friend. Her treasured friend. She would tamp down on these new feelings awakening in her. She had simply needed someone to lean on. Gabe had been her first choice, but she could make a different choice. She could lean on the Lord the way Aunt Tildy said she should. The way her mother would tell her to if she were with her now. The Lord knew everything about her and he was unchanging in his love.

After the parade, she hurried to change into dry clothes to lend Aunt Tildy a hand with their afternoon meal. Once they had eaten, some of the cast settled in chairs on the shady side of the main deck to enjoy the fresh-washed cooler air. Others went to their rooms for a nap before the show. A few, like Perry, went into the village along with Captain Dan, who had lists of needed supplies.

Sometimes Gabe went with him, but today Gabe and Joey were by the railing trying to catch some fish. So far they hadn't gotten a bite. Winnie was a shadow behind them as she pestered Joey to let her have his fishing pole. Jacci tried to block out her voice as she read the same paragraph three times in *Oliver Twist*. Her own thoughts were tumbling around, making the words a jumble in her mind.

When the sun peeked out between showers to light up the river, she gave up on the story. "Oh look. A rainbow," she said.

Just the sight of the rainbow brightening as it made a bridge over the water lifted Jacci's spirits.

Marelda looked up from the costume she was mending. "I don't know if there's anything prettier than a rainbow over the river. Seems to be a promise of a better day to come."

Jacci wanted to embrace that promise after the worry of her dreams the night before.

Cameron glanced up and then back down at the magazine he was leafing through. "A better year is what I need."

"We're having a good season. Much better than last year. I think things are improving for the people along the rivers," Marelda said.

Something about Marelda's voice sounded a warning Jacci recognized. She hoped Cameron would have the sense to be quiet.

Mrs. Loranda, who had been writing a letter, pointed her pen at Cameron. "Dear Cameron, you should relax and enjoy the peace of the river. I promise you'll miss this if you go back to your city stages after our run this season."

"I doubt that." He sounded bored. "This isn't my kind of life. But you watch. I'll make it on those other stages. Just as soon as I find someone to sponsor me while I get my foot in the door."

"A sponsor?" She dipped her pen in the ink bottle but didn't go back to writing. "You mean someone to pay your keep while you push those doors open? Perhaps a wife to support your dreams?" She glanced at Winnie and then grinned at Jacci.

"She'd have to be rich." Cameron didn't seem to notice her pointed looks.

"And not have those pesky babies." Marelda smiled. "The captain decided a showboat was the only way a couple of troupers like us could keep a family afloat."

"Afloat. You are that," Cameron said.

"So we are. Definitely that, but we wouldn't want to be anywhere else." Marelda rethreaded her needle to start stitching on the costume again.

"It's such a blessing to do something your whole family can do. Some of your boys have left the show, but you're fortunate to still have Gabe with you." Mrs. Loranda smiled at Gabe and then at Winnie as if glad a connection was forming between them.

"We miss the other boys, but they wanted a life off the river. We're blessed that Gabe didn't feel that way, but in truth, on a showboat everyone begins to feel like family. Like Duke, and then Jacci is the same as a daughter to us."

"Don't forget Aunt Tildy. She's been the cook forever," Jacci put in.

"And you and your family, Reva. We've gotten to watch Joey and Winnie grow up the last few years." Marelda smiled at Mrs. Loranda.

"Just one big family." Cameron put on a fake cheerful voice.

Marelda's smile disappeared as she gave him a hard look. "The best way on a showboat."

"I think our Cameron has no desire to be part of our family." Mrs. Loranda laughed and leaned forward to look directly at Cameron. "Perhaps you will meet someone at one of our shows who will be that rich wife or sponsor." She dipped her pen in the inkpot and started writing her letter again.

"Not much chance of that with the country bumpkins who come to see our shows."

"Oh, you never know," Mrs. Loranda said without looking up. "We had a senator in the audience last night whose well-to-do wife is a patron of the arts."

"Who told you that?" Cameron seemed interested at last.

"Perry talked to the senator. He said you did as well," Mrs. Loranda said.

Marelda spoke up again. "Did you obtain his favor then? His sponsorship?"

"He's all about politics. And I didn't get to talk to his wife. He did say that he would keep me in mind. That sometimes he needed help with this or that project."

"Acting projects?" Duke, who had appeared to be dozing, suddenly sat up in his chair.

"He didn't go into details. I assumed help with his campaign. Speech coaching perhaps, although he did fair at capturing the audience with his talk."

"You did sign on with us for the whole season," Marelda reminded him.

"Of that, I am sadly aware, madam," Cameron said.

Before Marelda could say anything, Gabe called over from where he was fishing. "Don't worry, Ma. We wouldn't want to stand in the way of Cameron's chance for fame and fortune. We'd find another leading man."

"I guess you think you could do it, Gabe," Cameron said.

"I know the part, should that become necessary. As I said, we wouldn't want to be the reason you missed your big break."

"And I know the part of Penelope." Winnie did a little twirl on the deck behind Gabe and Joey.

"Do you think you could be any noisier, Sis?" Joey groused. "You're scaring away the fish."

With a sideways grin, Cameron looked at Jacci. "I think we're being replaced as Sterling and Penelope. Oh well. After you do the same show fifty times, it gets old anyway."

"We're expecting many more than fifty performances before the season is over." Marelda used her same no-nonsense voice. "Unless of course you get that great opportunity, Cameron, and then I suppose Gabe is right. We wouldn't want to stand in your way. But Jacci is our Penelope." She sent a look over at Winnie.

"She's just talking," Mrs. Loranda said. "We know what we hired on to do. But you can't fault a girl's ambition."

"Certainly not. Perhaps Gabe can write her into the show.

If not this year, next season if your family comes on board with us again."

"I'm sure she would love that," Mrs. Loranda said.

It was obvious what else she would love, as Winnie leaned close to Gabe and whispered something. Jacci looked back at the rainbow that had faded away except for a bit of color close to the treetops across the river. But the sun kept shining. She didn't bother opening her book again. She yawned and stood up. "Time for a rest before the show."

But instead of going to her room, she climbed up to the hurricane deck to drop down next to the railing. The dampness from the rain soaked through her skirt, but she didn't care as the sun wrapped warm arms around her. All along the riverbank, birds sang their after-the-rain songs.

She remembered Marelda saying the rainbow was a promise that tomorrow would be better. Gabe had told Jacci that so often after her mother died. He'd find her wherever she was hiding so no one would see her tears and tell her tomorrow would be better. Sometimes that "better" was only because of him.

That night the seats in the auditorium were full again. The people at Point William loved their shows. Jacci thought they would clap and cheer no matter what they did onstage. But a friendly audience was a gift to showmen. At least tonight she didn't have to worry about having a mother she didn't know watching her.

Cameron might grumble about doing the showboat drama over and over, but he played his part without a misstep. He was good enough to be on a bigger stage and she hoped he got his break. But she wasn't about to get carried away with his dreams. She was happy on this showboat stage.

As usual, she helped Aunt Tildy in the galley after the show.

Everybody talked and laughed, enjoying the good feeling of a show well done. Aunt Tildy's raisin roll added to the good.

After Jacci's trouble sleeping the night before, she kept yawning until Aunt Tildy ordered her to her room. Jacci's ears were tired of the noisy room anyway. Sometimes when everyone was talking at the same time, it was as deafening as the calliope.

Clouds had moved back in to make the night very dark. She considered climbing up to the top deck, but the stars would all be hidden. The soft sound of water lapping against the boat's hull brought on another yawn. Best if she caught up on her sleep.

She passed the stage plank still out to the bank. Gabe or the captain would pull it up after everyone was settled for the night.

Something rustled behind her. Her heart lifted at the thought that Gabe might have followed her out. But no, he'd call to her if that was so or move up beside her without lurking in the shadows. Then again, it could be he wasn't intending to talk to Jacci but was meeting Winnie.

The rustle came again. The sound of skirts and then a step. Jacci's heart began beating a little harder and every sound was heightened. A deck plank creaked behind her. Jacci looked over her shoulder. Nobody was there. At least no one she could see.

But somebody was there. She felt their presence in the dark. "Who's back there?"

She had no answer from the grainy blackness of the night, but the very silence pulsed with threat. Her imagination was surely running away with her. But at the same time, she couldn't keep from whirling around and running for her room. She could feel foolish once she had the door slammed behind her and a lamp lit.

Someone reached out of the shadows and grabbed her. Before she could scream a hand was tight over her mouth. A man's hand.

Chapter
24

She tried to jerk free, but the man's hold tightened. He grunted when she kicked his legs, but didn't loosen his grip over her mouth or around her chest.

The rustle of a woman's skirts came up to them. "Shh, Jacinth." She stepped close to whisper in her ear. "Be still and listen. We will not harm you."

Jacinth. The woman knew her name. She stopped struggling. That might make the man relax his hold enough for her to break loose.

"I am sorry to have Samuel capture you like this," the woman whispered. "But we cannot trust those on your boat. We must keep our meeting strictly secret. Just between you and your mother."

Jacci went perfectly still then. The man spoke in a low voice. "If you promise not to scream, I will take my hand from your mouth."

She nodded. She wouldn't have to keep the promise. Not to a man who had attacked her from the shadows.

He pulled his hand an inch from her mouth. "No screams. It is for your own good. Your own protection."

"It is," the woman insisted. "I am your mother's maid."

"My mother is dead." Jacci's breath bounced back to her off the man's hand.

"That is so. A deep sorrow to the mother I speak of. That mother does very much wish to see you. Will you come with us? We will have you safely back before the dawn."

"Duke will miss me."

"Your grandfather, yes. Except my lady wrote a note to explain. We left it in your room. We planned to wait for you there where we could convince you we mean you no harm. That would have been safer, but you came too soon." The woman glanced behind her. "It could be very dangerous for you if we are seen. Please, come with us. My lady, Lisbeth, does so desire to speak with you."

"I owe her nothing."

"Only every breath you take. Believe me when I say she has much love for you."

The man did relax his hold, although he still held his hand near her mouth. Jacci might be able to twist away from him and scream for help, but she didn't. Instead, she nodded again.

The woman kissed her cheek. "Thank you, child. But now we must go as silent as cats stalking a mouse. We cannot let anyone hear us."

The woman moved in the front, her steps a bit tentative on the unfamiliar decking. The man stayed behind Jacci. She sensed he was prepared to grab her should she move a step out of the way, but she didn't. She matched her steps with the woman's and had the feeling they were acting out a new drama, one with a script she hadn't read. To know how the story ended, she had to go with them.

The woman stumbled as she stepped onto the stage plank and Jacci reached out to keep her from falling.

"Are you all right, Ellie?" The man sounded worried.

"I am fine, Samuel. Remember silence is needed. We must not put our girl in danger."

Jacci wasn't sure where they expected danger to come from, but the very urgency of the woman's whispers had Jacci's breath catching in her throat. With her eyes adjusting to the dark night, she could make out her captors a little better. Their faces seemed to almost float above the dark clothing they wore. The man's hat was pulled low over his forehead, and the woman's face was shaded by her dark bonnet. In contrast, Jacci's light blue skirt could be easily seen by anybody on the deck.

She looked back at the showboat. If anyone was watching, they would surely call out unless they thought she was someone from the village lingering about the showboat. And however would she get back aboard if the captain pulled up the stage plank?

She shook away the worry. She had committed to go with the two, for good or bad. She tried not to wonder if they had told her the truth. At the same time, she had a sinking feeling that it wouldn't matter if the stage plank was up or down. She might never see the *Kingston Floating Palace* again.

The thought was so strong she almost turned to run back toward the boat, but instead she kept following the woman to whatever the next act would reveal.

They had hidden a small carriage with one horse on the rise above the river. Jacci climbed in beside the woman, while the man untied the horse and climbed onto the driver's seat. Neither of them seemed worried she would try to get away from them now.

The woman the man had called Ellie touched Jacci's arm with a trembling hand as the carriage lurched forward. She let out a long breath. "I am not made for such as this."

The man spoke without looking around. "Your lady shouldn't have asked it of you."

"Now, Samuel, the deed is done. And she will generously compensate you."

"If he doesn't find out and fire me, or worse, trump up some charge against me to land me in jail." The man's voice was a growl. "Not to mention how the young lady with us could decide to charge the both of us with kidnapping."

"No, no. We did not force her to come with us. She agreed to do so." The woman patted Jacci's arm again, the trembles gone now. "And I thank you for that, my dear. I am very sorry we had to approach you in such a way, but my lady has reason to believe someone on your boat is a danger."

"To me?" Jacci said.

"Perhaps, although we cannot be sure of that. But definitely to my lady, should he find out about this meeting she has so desired."

"He will find out. He always does." The man named Samuel sounded resigned to the ill fate he expected for all of them.

"Who is he?" Jacci asked.

"No one you need to worry about this night. He is far from here on a train headed away," the woman said.

"But someone I need to fear on another night?"

"My lady will explain it all." The woman sounded worried that she might have already said too much. "We do not have far to go. My lady is at a friend's house just outside the village. She was very pleased to hear you were stopping at Point William."

"How did she know that?"

"She asked when we were at your show yesterday. So she had Samuel and me come aboard for the show tonight. I enjoyed it once again, and it was nice seeing it with Samuel. We both think you are very talented. As does my lady. She beams when she speaks of you."

Jacci wasn't frightened anymore, although she wondered why not, as she rode through the dead of night to an unknown destination. But the woman beside her seemed to be trustworthy. She almost laughed at that thought. She was ready to trust two people who had grabbed her and spirited her away to who knew where. Even if such trust might be ill given, she was not sorry she was in this carriage going to meet the woman who had given birth to her.

Ellie chattered on about the play. "Are you romantically attracted to the handsome man in your play? He appeared to be very charming."

"He is a good actor," Jacci said.

The man laughed. "Is that to say he lacks charm off the stage?"

"He can be charming when it suits his purposes."

"And is that purpose to charm you, my dear?" Ellie asked.

"At times."

"And so, are you in love with him? I've heard that often happens between an actor and an actress playing such parts in a play."

"No."

"Ah, that was spoken with great assuredness. That makes me think someone else has already taken possession of your heart. Does it not seem the same to you, Samuel?" When *humph* was his only answer, Ellie laughed. "My Samuel can be a man of few words, but the words he does say are always the right ones. We hope to marry soon."

"Oh?"

"I hear much in that one word, my dear. You think we are old for marrying. It is true that I am not so young."

"Young enough," Samuel said.

"Oh yes, young enough for love." While Ellie's voice was soft, no doubt sounded in her words.

"How do you know when you are in love?" Jacci couldn't believe she was asking this stranger about love. But then, perhaps a stranger was the best one to ask.

"Samuel, how should we answer our girl?" Ellie said.

"When a man is fool enough to do what he knows he shouldn't because the one he loves asks him to do it." He glanced over his shoulder at Ellie.

That made Ellie laugh again. "Come, Samuel. Can you not think of a more romantic proof of love?"

"Pretty words mean nothing. Actions are the proof."

"So they are. But pretty words can be nice as well." Ellie shifted in the seat beside Jacci to look at her. "So I will give you some of those, my dear. When your heart is full to overflowing with thoughts of the one you love. When you yearn to be with him. When he is the first one you think of in the morning and the last one at night and perhaps even then he walks through your dreams. Is this how you feel about the man you think you might love?"

"I don't know." Jacci wasn't sure how to answer. "He's always been my best friend. I've known him since I was five. But now things feel different."

"Different can be nice. Perhaps a bit upsetting or confusing at first. But a friend can be the best for when you are ready for a love to last forever."

"But what if he doesn't have that different feeling?"

"So, you worry that is the case?" Ellie didn't wait for Jacci to answer. "Perhaps you could ask the Lord to send you a sign. A way to know if your friend wishes to be more to you as you wish to be to him."

"Women!" Samuel almost snorted the word. "Always tiptoeing around things. Just ask the man."

"But what if I ask and he doesn't?" Jacci said. "If it spoils our friendship?"

"Then the friendship was not as strong as you thought, and you wait for the one the Lord intends for you." Samuel sounded even more irritated as he went on. "The way your lady should have done, Ellie."

"Now you know it wasn't that simple for my lady. Or for

that matter, any highborn woman. Such young women are expected to make matches that increase the wealth or position of their family." Ellie sighed. "Sometimes it is a good thing to not have two coppers to rub together. At least a woman is free to choose the man with whom she desires to share her bit of bread and meat."

"I don't think my mother, who certainly lacked any riches, had that freedom. The mother who loved me," Jacci said.

"Never doubt that my lady loved you every bit as much. Sometimes great sacrifices must be made for love."

Samuel turned the carriage into a lane. "Let your lady do the explaining, Ellie."

"That is best. And here we are." When the carriage came to a halt, she went on. "My lady awaits inside. The man and wife who live here have gone away for the night."

When Ellie didn't move to climb out of the carriage, Jacci asked, "Aren't you going in?"

"It is best if you go in alone. Samuel and I will stay out here and watch."

"You mean in case someone followed us?"

"Yes."

"What would you do if they did?"

"Don't concern yourself." Samuel was beside the carriage to help Jacci down. "No one followed us. So, it is not likely we will face any trouble."

"We prayed we would not," Ellie said.

Jacci looked from her to Samuel. She knew not all prayers were answered as one wanted. But she was here. Whatever happened, she was at their mercy. She gave her hand to Samuel and stepped out of the carriage. The next scene in this drama would happen inside the house.

A dim light showed through one of the windows. Lisbeth would be waiting for Jacci in the circle of that light.

"I have no reason to be frightened of this woman," Jacci

whispered under her breath as she approached the door at the end of the walkway Samuel pointed out.

She could just see the light gray rocks spaced a few feet apart in the darkness. She wondered if Ellie and Samuel had prayed for this kind of black night to cover their actions. Perhaps Lisbeth had prayed the same. If she believed in prayer at all.

Jacci shook her head to get rid of that thought. She was here. It was time to listen, not judge. *Judge not that ye be not judged.* While that was a good verse to remember, her mind kept coming up with *buts.* But this woman deserted her. But she never tried to contact her. But . . .

Too many thoughts ran through her mind, all the way back to her mother. Her mama. Would she want Jacci to meet Lisbeth? She had never told Jacci about her. But Jacci was so young. Perhaps she intended to tell her when she was older. Perhaps she intended Duke to tell Jacci the truth of her beginnings, and he had delayed the telling so long that he decided she would be happier never to know. The two of them had enjoyed a settled, happy life on the *Palace.*

Jacci stood up straight, took a deep breath, and let it out slowly the way she always did when she was ready to go onstage. Then she reached for the doorknob and turned it without knocking.

Chapter
25

JACCI STEPPED INTO THE HOUSE. She didn't close the door behind her.

"Hello, Jacinth." The woman stood up and held out a hand, but she didn't move toward Jacci. She waited in the flickering light of the lamp on the table beside her chair.

Shadows crept in from the edges of the room. The lamp was turned down low, as if the woman didn't want to be fully seen. But enough light lifted up to the woman's face to see that Gabe was right. Looking at her was like looking in a mirror dimmed by age.

"Please shut the door and come sit with me." She still had her hand stretched out toward Jacci.

She was very slender, slimmer than Jacci, and with the appearance of fragility. Perhaps that was why Ellie sounded so protective of her.

Jacci took another step into the room and pulled the door closed behind her. She couldn't run from this meeting. She didn't want to run from this. Instead, she felt as though she had been moving toward meeting this woman named Lisbeth ever since she first asked her mother who Lisbeth was.

Her mother, Kelly, Duke, none of them had wanted to answer her question. They hadn't lied, but they hadn't told her the complete truth. Not until Duke had the day before, when it seemed the truth could no longer be hidden in vagueness.

Jacci went to the chair the woman indicated and sat down. The woman settled back into her chair as well, her gaze never leaving Jacci's face.

"Should I call you Mrs. Giles?" Jacci asked.

"No." The woman grimaced slightly as if the very thought of that was painful. "Lisbeth will do. And are you called Jacinth or Princess as I was told on the showboat?"

"Only my grandfather calls me Princess. Everyone else calls me Jacci."

She smiled a little. "I knew Kelly shortened your name to Jacci, but I wasn't sure if Irena did as well."

"She did." Irritation poked Jacci when Lisbeth spoke her mother's name. She tried to push it aside. She was here to see what this woman had to say. Anger served no purpose when what she wanted was the truth.

"Kelly named you. Did he ever tell you that?" She didn't wait for an answer before she went on. "You were already a couple of weeks old. Irena wanted me to name you and I wanted her to name you. So, Kelly, as he was sometimes wont to do, took matters into his own hands." A little smile lifted her lips. "He first suggested Violet, but Irena refused that name. I left it up to her. I thought that only right."

"Why? Because you didn't want me?" Jacci hated the edge in her voice.

Lisbeth pulled in a sharp breath and sat back in her chair as if Jacci had struck her.

"I'm sorry. That was cruel of me," Jacci said.

"No, no. You have a right to be angry. A mother shouldn't

give away her child." She pulled in a deep breath, as though to get her emotions under control before she leaned toward Jacci. "But what I did, what we did, we did for you. Irena, Kelly, and I. Please, believe that."

"But why did you have to do it at all?"

Lisbeth leaned back and looked past Jacci as if seeing something in the shadows Jacci couldn't. After a moment, her gaze came back to Jacci. "I don't know how much you know. Or if you know anything other than what Ellie may have said to convince you to come with her."

"Duke told me what he knew yesterday, but his memory is fading. I'm not sure if everything he said was right."

"Duke?"

"My grandfather."

"Do you mean Irena's father?" She looked puzzled. "I never met him, but I thought his name was Tyrone."

"It is, but they call him Duke on the showboat because of the times he played a duke in the dramas."

"And is that why you are called Princess in the showboat flyers?"

"Duke asked that my name never be put in print or announced in the shows."

"I see." She looked thoughtful. "He must have feared for you."

"My mother died protecting me." A memory of her mother's blood all over her nightdress flashed through Jacci's mind.

"Yes." Lisbeth looked very sad. "When I learned of that, I was devastated and so very sorry. I never thought it would come to violence."

"What did you think?"

"That no one would ever have reason to doubt you were Irena's natural-born child. I stayed hidden away once my condition began to be obvious. Our plan seemed so perfect. Kelly first suggested it." Another ghost of a smile slipped across her face. "Your mother had to be convinced. She was not sure about even pretending marriage to a gambler."

"It wasn't all a pretense." Jacci needed to hold on to a shred of an honest connection between her mother and Kelly. "Mama loved Kelly."

"She did fall in love with him after we began the sham. Much to her detriment, I fear. Although I do think Kelly loved her as much as he is able to love anyone besides himself. Except you. He does truly love you."

"I haven't seen him for months."

"That is Kelly. He gets caught up in his chase for the next big game. I don't think it's even the money. Merely having the winning hand." She sighed.

"Are you related to him?"

"No."

"I don't understand. If Kelly isn't related to you and he isn't my father, why would he agree to say I was his child?" Jacci frowned. "And if it's not Kelly, who is my father? Not your husband now?"

"Certainly not Griffith Giles. Who would not be my husband had your father lived. Our story is long and sad." Her voice trembled as if even now the telling of it was difficult.

"Don't you think I have a right to know that story?"

"That is why you are here." A smile touched her lips, but she didn't seem able to hold on to it. "I don't know that I can tell it all in the time we have, but I will share what may matter most to you."

Jacci waited without speaking while the woman stared at the shadows dancing in the light of the lamp, as though searching for the right words. Just as Jacci was ready to break the silence that seemed to press down on them, Lisbeth looked back at her and began speaking.

"I fell in love with a horse trainer named Jason Charles when I was younger than you are now. He was so very handsome and genuinely good. But not a man my father would have ever approved as a match for me. My father had already made a deal with Griffith Giles for my hand."

"A deal?"

"That is the proper word to describe their machinations. Griffith wanted the money my father could funnel into his political aspirations. He was running for state senator. He even hoped to be governor someday. When that fell through, he set his sights on Washington and won the Senate seat in Congress some years ago. My father didn't live to see that, but if he had, he would have claimed the credit for Griffith's win. I was merely a pawn in their plan. An attractive wife for campaign reasons and my father's money." Her words were laced with bitterness.

"Why didn't you refuse to marry him?" Jacci asked.

"It sounds so easy when you speak the words." Lisbeth's voice was almost too soft to hear as she stared down at her hands tightly clutched in her lap.

The room was so quiet the ticking of a clock somewhere behind Jacci sounded too loud. She wondered about the time but didn't turn to see the clock. Whatever hour of the night it was, she couldn't leave until the scene was played out.

After a moment, Lisbeth raised her head and began talking again as if she had never paused in the telling. "At the time, I thought it would be just as easy. My father's plans would come to naught when Jason and I married. We planned to run away when the time was right. We waited too long, or perhaps you might say we didn't wait long enough in other more intimate ways. My father must have found out about our romance and sent Jason to New Orleans to buy a horse. A way to keep us apart. I did not know I was with child until after he left. When I was sure, I managed to send word to him. So at least he knew about you. He was returning to me, but my Jason perished along with many others when the steamboat boilers exploded and the boat sank."

"Duke told me he died." A wave of sadness swept through Jacci for this man she'd never known, but whose blood ran through her veins.

"I was distraught. If not for you, I might have stopped eating and hoped for my life to end. But even though I had not yet even felt the quickening of life in my womb, I loved you every bit as much as I loved Jason." She stared at Jacci. "Can you believe that?"

"I want to," Jacci said.

"I did so very much. But I knew my father would never accept you as his grandchild. Worse, I feared he would try to force me to do something to keep you from being born. To eliminate that possibility, I concocted a story about visiting my mother's friends in the East and went to Irena. We had been friends as children, brought together when her mother came to fit the dresses she made for my mother and me."

"Duke said you were a friend of Mama's."

"She was more than a friend. She was a lifesaver. My only hope. I hid out in her maid's room on the steamboat where she was working." Lisbeth shook her head a little. "I sometimes think back to then and wonder how we managed. The room was so very small, and I had to stay silent during the day to keep from being caught. She gave me her bed and slept on the floor. Oftentimes she would sit next to me and put her hand on my belly to feel your movements. Your kicks were so strong we both were sure you would be a boy."

Another smile slipped across her face. This one lingered longer. She leaned forward in her chair a little as she went on. "I don't know if you can understand what I'm going to say. I'm not sure I ever understood it myself. But somehow you became her baby too. I think she felt the pains I felt and shared the joy of motherhood."

"How could you have joy at such a time?"

"Joy is not necessarily happiness. I was sad. So very sad that

I lost Jason. And I was frightened about what the future held. I couldn't bear to think of what lay ahead for me. I was surviving day by day. But you growing inside me, all I had left of Jason, seemed reason for joy, even if I would be ostracized for the sin of conceiving a child out of the legal bonds of marriage. I did love him so."

"What was he like?"

"He wasn't the most handsome of men, but he had such strength, such goodness. He would have faced down my father. For him, I could have given up everything I knew. All the servants and fancy dresses and manor houses. With him, I could have been content in a house such as this." She looked around at the small room they were in and then back at Jacci. "With you."

She must have guessed the unasked question in Jacci's mind. "But I could not do it without him. I would have had no way to supply my needs. Or yours."

"Mama had no way other than her maid's job."

"I did send her money. That is one reason I went back to do as my father wanted and marry Griffith. So that I could send money."

"Why didn't you marry Kelly instead of asking Mama to?"

"We would have all starved had we needed to depend wholly on Kelly." Lisbeth actually laughed softly. "He's a lovable man. There is no doubt of that, but as Irena said from the beginning, one cannot depend on a gambler."

Jacci frowned. "I still don't understand."

Lisbeth held up her hand to stop Jacci from saying more. "It is a convoluted story. I don't know where to start to explain."

"With Kelly. If he is not related to you and didn't know my mother, why did he agree to be my father?"

"In my mind, that was the Lord's doing. As I said, I was merely living day to day. A black curtain seemed to hang between me and my future. Irena started out the same way, but as the weeks passed, she began to push me to develop a plan for when you were born.

"I had suggested she start padding her dress to look expectant, but she feared they would make her leave the steamboat if she was thought to be with child out of wedlock." Lisbeth sighed and looked down at her hands again. "It was wrong of me to ask so much of Irena, but as I said, by that time she felt almost as if you were hers. So we prayed. With desperation. For one thing, as stoic as I was trying to be, we both were not sure how we could disguise the noise of me birthing you."

As if she couldn't even face speaking about that, she gestured over toward a table that held some cups and a teapot under a cozy. "Ellie made us some tea if you would like some."

Jacci started to refuse, but instead said, "If you want some."

"I think it might be helpful. Would you mind pouring?"

Jacci stood to do as she asked.

"Leave mine less than full. My hands are a bit unsteady."

When Jacci handed her the half-filled cup, the cup rattled on the saucer. She set it on the table beside her, then lifted the cup to her mouth for a sip before she said, "Such has been my life. So less than full."

Chapter
26

Jacci fought against the sympathy rising inside her as she sat back down and took a drink of her tea. The woman had made her own choices.

"I need to finish the telling of my story so that Samuel can get you back to your boat before you are missed." She took another sip of tea. "Where was I?"

"Praying. You and my mother."

"Yes." Lisbeth cradled the cup in her hands. "The Lord sent us Kelly." Another smile slipped across her face. "Your mother couldn't believe that a gambler could be the answer to our prayers, but the Lord can work in mysterious ways at times."

"He didn't answer my prayers for Mama."

Her face was sad again. "It is true that not all our prayers are answered as we wish. Mine weren't either or we would never have had to have this talk. I would have watched you grow up instead of loving you from afar. But what happened happened. Do you want to know about Kelly?" She peered over her cup at Jacci.

"Yes." She needed to listen and not dredge up old sorrows.

"All right. While I was hiding out on the steamboat with your mother, I would sometimes get so closed in that I had to sneak out to the deck for a bit of air. I always waited until the early hours just before dawn when no one would be around, but one day Kelly was there."

"Did you know him?"

"I did. He and Jason had grown up together, and he had been to the farm to visit Jason a few times. Anyway, I was so frightened he might know me and our subterfuge would be discovered that I whirled to go the other direction." Lisbeth shook her head. "Whirling when one is expectant is not the best idea. I got light-headed and lost my balance. Naturally, Kelly rushed to help me. By that time I was weeping."

"And he recognized you?"

"He did. It turned out that he had been on the same steamboat as Jason, who had told him everything before Jason was killed in the explosion. Kelly had already gone to my farm to offer his sympathies. Of course, he was told I was in the East visiting my mother's friends. So, he thought they would help me. When I confessed the truth to him of the desperate situation Irena and I were in, he said he would come up with a plan."

"Did you think he really would?"

"I wasn't sure, but when one is at wit's end, one is apt to clutch at straws. Kelly was that straw for me." Lisbeth took another drink of her tea before setting the cup on the saucer. "The next night he came to Irena's room. How he found it, I can't say and never asked. But it was his idea to marry Irena and to claim you as his own."

"Your answer to prayer."

"Yes, and yours. A prayer you were too small to know, but the Bible says the Lord forms us within the womb and already loves us there. I believe he made a way for you that would not sentence you to a life of blame as an illegitimate child. While that would never have been any fault of yours, such children do suffer for their parents' sin."

"But I did suffer the loss of my mother." Jacci hesitated and then added. "Both my mothers."

Pleasure at Jacci claiming her as mother seemed to war with Lisbeth's sadness. The sadness won out. "Irena was the same as a sister to me. We grew so close in those months we awaited your birth and those precious few after you were born before I returned to my father's house. Kelly found us the place at Dove Creek and rented it. With my money, of course. Irena had good years there. I didn't take the chance of corresponding with her, but I did send money to Kelly. Or at least I did so the first few years, but once Griffith found out about you, I feared sending anything that could lead him to you. I prayed Kelly would help Irena or that she would find work in Dove Creek. She was talented with her needle like her mother. I never knew why she would go back to work on the river."

Lisbeth paused, then shook her head. "That's not true. I do know. She wanted more opportunities to see Kelly. As you say, she loved him. I fear that led to her death."

"Why? Do you think Kelly betrayed her?" Jacci shrank from that thought, but she needed to know.

"Oh no. One of our servants guessed my condition and decided to profit from the knowledge. If only she had asked for money from me instead of Griffith. I would have found a way to give her whatever she wanted to keep my secret and make sure you were safe." She was silent a moment as if she needed to compose herself. "No, Kelly has many faults, but he would have never betrayed you. No matter how much he needed a stake."

Relief swept through Jacci, but she had another question in need of an answer. "Is the man who killed my mother still alive?" The memory of the man's face after she shot him hovered in her thoughts. Would Lisbeth know about that?

"Your mother shot him, didn't she?"

Jacci let the question slide by her as though no answer was needed. Not a lie, but not exactly the truth either. Something the same as Kelly and Duke had done when she asked about Lisbeth.

Lisbeth didn't seem to notice as she went on. "I don't know if he's alive or not, but he didn't die from his wounds then. But if he had, it would have been no more than he deserved. Griffith swore to me later he had instructed his man not to hurt anyone."

Jacci felt a strange relief that she hadn't killed the man. She wasn't sure why. As Lisbeth said, he deserved to die. "What was he supposed to do with me?"

"Griffith would never tell me the truth about that. But I think he planned to have you taken to an orphanage where your identity would be forever hidden. I was furious with him. You were safe with Irena and no one would ever know you were my child. But Griffith didn't trust Irena not to someday bring out the truth. He feared his constituents knowing I'd had a child out of wedlock would spoil his political chances. It was always about winning the next election."

Her eyes flashed with anger before she went on. "We came to an agreement then. I would continue to pretend to be his loving wife while he used my money to further his political career." She made a face as if the words left a bad taste in her mouth. "In return, he would leave you alone. You were no danger to him."

"You should leave him." Jacci's heart hurt for this woman who appeared to have lost so many chances for happiness.

The corners of her lips lifted slightly in a sad smile. "I left him years ago in every way but name, if indeed we ever had any kind of marital connection. This campaign will soon be over. He cannot win the nomination, and even if he did, he could not win the election. He will settle back into his senator role in Washington, and I will rarely have to see him."

"But why did Ellie say I was in danger? Has your agreement changed?"

"No, but perhaps other things have. While people didn't see us together, they did see us in the same place where our resemblance was easy to note. Irena said from the very beginning that you looked like me."

"Some in the cast who met you did remark on how much we looked alike."

"I feared they would. Had I known you would be in that drama, I would have feigned illness and not appeared with Griffith."

"Duke wanted me not to go onstage, but it seemed cowardly not to perform."

"You are so like Irena. Ready to tackle any obstacle." Lisbeth pulled a handkerchief from her sleeve and touched her eyes. "You could not have had a better mother."

"I know."

"Naturally, I knew you might favor me, but I had never let that be a concern. After all, strangers can have similar features. Same eye color, dark hair." She leaned forward a little as though to see Jacci better before she went on. "Of course, your father had hair as dark as mine, perhaps even darker, so no wonder your hair is midnight black. You look to have some waves as Jason did." Lisbeth tightened a comb that held her hair back from her face. "My hair lacks any curl."

Jacci touched her own hair. In the carriage ride without a hat to shield her hair from the wind, some strands had pulled loose from the ribbon that tied it back at the nape of her neck. She smoothed down the stray locks, feeling the waves Lisbeth mentioned, and felt a flicker of pleasure to know she had something from her birth father.

"And your chin makes me think of Jason." Lisbeth narrowed her eyes as she studied Jacci. "Even with those differences, our likeness is striking. But once Griffith is done with this sham of a campaign, I will go back into seclusion on my farm. I have no interest in being part of the society world. I'm content with my horses and my garden. No one will see us together again."

"If it's true I have nothing to fear from your husband, what did Ellie mean when she said someone on the showboat might mean me harm?"

"Samuel heard talk in a tavern that someone was asking about me and about you and whether they might profit from selling that information to Griffith's competitors in this political campaign." She picked up her cup and then put it down without taking a drink. "Or how much it might be worth to Griffith to see that you were never seen in public again."

"Who was it?" Jacci's heart did a stutter beat.

"Samuel didn't see the person. Just heard the someone-told-someone-told-someone sort of gossip. They knew Samuel worked for me."

Jacci didn't know what to say.

When Lisbeth stood up, so did Jacci. She was a bit taller than Lisbeth as they faced each other without touching.

"I don't truly believe you have any worries about such idle talk. None of Griffith's competitors are concerned enough about his chances to try anything underhanded that might end up hurting their own campaigns. But I did want you to be aware of potential danger so you could take whatever precautions necessary. If you would like, I can finance a place for you to stay until the campaign is over."

Jacci shook her head. "I can't take Duke off the river. Not now. He would be lost."

"He would want you to be safe."

"But you believe there is no real danger."

"I do think that true. However, I cannot be sure. Hiding away from curious eyes would be a safer, more sure thing."

"No."

Lisbeth smiled slightly. "I hear Irena in that word."

"She was my mother."

"Yes, she was."

"But so were you." Jacci held her arms out to her then.

Tears streamed down Lisbeth's cheeks as she stepped into Jacci's hug. They held each other a moment before Lisbeth kissed Jacci's cheek and whispered, "Thank you."

The clock Jacci had heard earlier chimed two times. Lisbeth stepped away from her. "But now we must get you back to your grandfather. Would you be afraid to ride with Samuel? You can make better time on a horse and that would perhaps draw less attention than a carriage at this hour of the night."

"I am not afraid."

"Of course not. As I said, you are Irena's daughter." She gave Jacci another quick hug before she went to the door.

Samuel had the horse ready. Ellie waited beside him. She hugged Jacci without hesitation and whispered, "You will be safe with my Samuel. Thank you for giving my lady this gift."

"Do you know how to ride, miss?" Samuel said.

"I've never ridden a horse."

"At all?" He sounded surprised.

"I ride boats on rivers."

"I see." He sounded concerned. "Perhaps the carriage would be best then."

Lisbeth stepped over to him. "She can straddle the horse in front of you, Samuel."

"But, madam, she wears a skirt."

"Her skirt is full and it is dark. No one will see her ankles," Lisbeth said. "Now, off with you before the sky begins to lighten."

Without any further protests, he showed Jacci where to hold the saddle as he coupled his hands to make a step for her foot. He easily vaulted her up onto the horse. As if the animal knew someone different was on its back, it whinnied and tossed its head. Samuel spoke a few words to the horse and then stepped into the stirrup to swing into the saddle behind her.

Before Samuel could make the horse move, Lisbeth stepped close to them to slip Jacci a folded paper. "My address. If you ever need anything, you only have to ask."

Then she moved back, and Samuel, with an arm on each side of Jacci, flicked the reins.

As they started away, Lisbeth's words chased after them. "I love you."

Jacci looked back to see the two dark figures embracing.

"Best face forward, miss," Samuel said in her ear. "Hold on to the mare's mane. She won't mind. And sit back against me. Think of me as your father."

Jacci wrapped her fingers around the mare's mane and felt less afraid of falling. "You will make a good father," she said.

He made a sound that could have been a laugh. "Ellie might not be young enough for that, but you can be assured I will be a good husband to her if we survive the foolishness of this night."

"I'm sorry to put you in danger."

"You have no reason for regret. It was not you who arranged this escapade, miss."

No reason for regret. Was that true? Weren't there always reasons for regret? Jacci rested her back against the man's chest. But she did not regret this night with the woman who gave her birth. With her mother. Not her mama, but her mother.

She couldn't think about it yet. Not until she was back on the showboat. Until then she would think only of the sound of the mare's hooves and the strong arms of the man behind her making sure she didn't fall. A damp feel against her face and the smell of the river let her know when they were close to the showboat.

"I don't know how I'll get back on the boat with the stage plank pulled up," Jacci said.

"Do not worry. In the note we left your grandfather, we asked him to watch for your return. He will be waiting."

"I'm not sure he can lower the plank by himself."

Samuel sighed. "In that case I will wade or swim to the boat to help him. Have no fear. I will see that you get aboard."

He stopped the horse in the trees above the river landing. "Best to leave the mare here." He slid off the mare and then helped Jacci to the ground before he tied up the mare.

Jacci's legs felt odd for a couple of steps. She smiled, thinking it wasn't unlike coming ashore after days on the boat. She needed to get her land legs under her. Samuel didn't seem to have that problem as he took her arm and walked with her toward the showboat.

The stage plank was already lowered and waiting. As soon as he saw that, Samuel stopped. "I will watch from here to be sure you get safely aboard. Wave if all is well, but if there is danger, call and I will come to your aid." He touched her shoulder then. "May the Lord watch over you."

"I pray the same for you," she said before she hurried down the bank to the landing. She felt very alone and too visible, even though the night was as dark as ever.

She almost ran up the stage plank onto the boat where two figures stepped away from the shadows toward her. Duke and Gabe.

Gabe grabbed her shoulders. "Are you all right, Jacci?"

"I am fine." She blinked to keep back the tears of relief that wanted to spill out of her eyes. She raised her hand to wave Samuel on his way.

"Who are you waving to?" Gabe no longer sounded concerned, but angry instead. "And where have you been?"

She pulled away from him. Before she could say anything, Duke stepped up beside her.

"Not now, Gabe. She is safe. That is all that matters." Duke put a hand on Jacci's cheek, and once again she felt the tremble of his hand touching her. "Go, Princess."

She spun away from them and ran toward her room. Behind her, she heard them lifting the stage plank.

Chapter
27

AFTER THEY PULLED UP the stage plank, Gabe started to follow Jacci, but Duke stepped in front of him. "It's late," he said.

Gabe wanted to push the man out of his way, but he couldn't do that. Not to Duke. "I need to know what's going on."

"Not tonight. Tomorrow."

"It's tomorrow now."

Duke put his hand on Gabe's shoulder. "Let her rest. She will tell you, tell us both what she wants us to know."

"I have to know everything."

"Can we ever know everything about another?" Duke said.

Gabe pulled in a breath and let it out slowly. He couldn't fight Duke. He stared out at the river a moment before he said, "I love her."

"I know you do." Duke tightened his hand on his shoulder.

"And not as a brother." Irritation crept into his voice as he looked back at Duke.

"That I know as well." Gabe could hear the smile in Duke's

voice as he went on. "But she is the one you must let know that. Not me."

"If you know, why doesn't she?"

"Perhaps because you act more like a brother than a swain."

"Swain? What kind of word is that?" He jerked away from Duke, not even trying to hide his irritation now.

"A very good one, but if you like lover better, then that works as well. She cannot know you feel differently about her if you don't act differently toward her."

"I've told her a million times that I am not her brother." Gabe's shoulders slumped as he stared down at the deck. "I've loved her since forever. As that swain."

"Then perhaps it is time you tell her that in words instead of waiting for her to guess."

Gabe looked up at him. The night was softening toward morning, and he could see the kindness on Duke's face. "But what if she doesn't want me to love her that way? What if she only wants to be my sister?"

"Then your heart will be broken, but you will survive."

"But will I want to?"

Duke laughed a little. "That I cannot answer for you, but it could be an answer you won't need."

"Do you think I have hope?"

"I cannot speak for Jacci, but as you say, you are not her brother. She is not your sister. It could be that how she loves you is not the love for a brother she has always assumed it to be. What does she really know of brothers or swains?"

"But what about Cameron?"

"Cameron is not a rival."

"Who is then?"

"Perhaps the past. A flood of truth has overwhelmed Jacci in the last two days. Much of what she believed about herself has been washed away. She will have to learn to trust again."

"I've never lied to her."

"Nor have I, but I have evaded the truth. Such evasion is the companion of lies." Duke stared at him a moment before he went on. "She may think you have done the same as well."

"But I haven't. I don't know any truth to tell her."

"Except that you love her."

"I will tell her. And protect her if that is what she needs."

"Both of us will do that, but now it is time to sleep the few hours we have before the new day begins."

"I don't think I can."

"Then as Queen Marelda would tell us, we can pray."

"Do you really believe she is in danger?"

Duke blew out a breath. "I don't know. But we can't forget that Irena died protecting her."

"So many years ago," Gabe said, but he hadn't forgotten. Some things a person couldn't forget.

"But there are those who saw Lisbeth. Who saw Jacci." Duke paused a moment. "There is Griffith Giles, a man of means and little conscience who would not want the embarrassment of a scandal."

"Then surely he will be glad to see us move on down the river."

"I think, I hope that is true." Duke turned away from him. "Good night, Gabe. Thank you for your help with the stage plank."

Gabe stood rooted to the deck as he watched him walk away. Duke hadn't asked for help with the stage plank. Gabe had heard the creak of the pulleys and come out of his rooms to see what was happening. Duke had not fully explained, only saying that Jacci had gone off the boat and would need a way to come back aboard.

When Gabe had insisted on knowing more, Duke revealed that she had gone to meet the senator's wife. Her mother. He would explain nothing more, saying Jacci would have to be the one to answer his questions. And then he had sent Jacci on her way without giving Gabe the chance to find out anything. Not even who she had waved to from the deck. Gabe had seen the tall figure moving away in the darkness. A man. But what man?

The questions raced circles in his head as he paced back and forth on the deck. The clouds had thinned enough that a few stars appeared. Gabe stopped at the rail and looked up. "Lord, help me to help her. And please, let her trust me enough to tell me what is happening. And most of all, let her be glad I love her."

He didn't feel as if he should pray for the Lord to make her love him. That didn't seem right. But he wanted to. And hadn't his mother always told him the Lord was ready to listen to any prayer? But she had also taught him that some answers were no or not yet instead of the yeses he wanted. So perhaps it was better not to offer up the prayer. He couldn't bear the thought of no. That could be why he had never revealed his heart to Jacci. Fear.

But the prayer was offered whether he spoke the words or not. He bent his head and whispered, "Thy will."

Then as if he had already received an answer he did not want, he headed to his room. On the way he passed Duke and Jacci's door. His feet slowed and stopped. After a long moment, he moved on.

He thought he wouldn't be able to sleep, but when he lay down, the worries seemed to slide off him. As Duke had said, they could be glad Jacci was safe aboard the showboat. Daylight would come soon enough, and with it, the answers he needed. He had prayed. Now he had to trust.

In her room, Jacci lay on her bed staring at the ceiling as Lisbeth's words played over and over in her head. She heard Duke when he came in and went into his room. She thought about getting up to talk to him, but he needed his sleep. Besides, he had already told her what he knew. There would be time to share what Lisbeth said come morning.

She listened for Gabe's footsteps following Duke, but only heard the creak of the boat as it shifted in the water. What would she tell him even if she did go out to try to catch him? That her hair curled like her father's? She ran her fingers through those waves and almost smiled. Would Gabe understand how that bit of truth warmed her heart? She needed him to understand. To not be angry the way he'd sounded when she came back up the stage plank.

Duke was right. Answers must wait for the morning. She flipped over to face the wall, but even after she pulled a curtain down over thoughts of Lisbeth, other worries stirred awake in her mind. Had she always loved Gabe? Of course she had, but what had awakened inside her when she saw Gabe and Winnie together was different. Not jealousy so much as a hollow feeling of loss, as though she'd held treasure in her hands and hadn't realized it until she threw it away.

She should have recognized the treasure of love after acting in so many romantic scenes on their showboat stage. She shifted in bed to stare once more at the ceiling. She could play parts in a drama. Would she have to do the same if Gabe was in love with Winnie?

Wasn't that what her mother had done? Played a part. And what Lisbeth was still doing. Even Duke and Kelly. Was everybody just playing a part in the drama of life?

She blew out a long breath, turned toward the wall again, and pulled her pillow over her head. When she woke, early morning light was spilling through her window and the boat was moving.

For a moment, she lay still to see if sleep would slide over her again, but instead all the crazy thoughts that had kept her awake earlier came back to poke at her. She had no more answers now than she had then. Pushing it all aside, she got up and looked out her small window.

The clouds had floated away to another part of the world to let the sun, barely above the horizon, spread golden light across the river. A perfect time to be out on the deck. She could sleep this afternoon once they were at their new landing. But now she wanted to feel the air on her face and let the loveliness of the river surround her. Perhaps that would clear her muddled thoughts.

As the sun rose higher in the sky, its bright warmth streaked through her window to cheer her and make Lisbeth's warnings in the shadowy night fade in importance. She washed her face and pulled on an everyday skirt and detached shirtwaist.

As she ran a comb through her hair, she thought of the father who had never seen her. A good man, Lisbeth had said. She smiled as she caught her dark hair back and gathered it at the nape of her neck with a ribbon. Later she would write down everything Lisbeth had said about her father. Those words would be all she would ever have of him.

She slid her feet into her show slippers that didn't have to be laced up. She wanted to get outside while the river water was still glittering in the early morning light. Plus, Gabe might be in the pilothouse, even if he had given up some sleeping time to help Duke with the stage plank.

She wanted to talk to Gabe. Not to do as Samuel said and admit how she felt about him. No, not that. That could wait. But she needed to tell him about Lisbeth and see what he thought about her warning that someone on the showboat might mean her harm.

That couldn't be true. Idle talk at a tavern surely meant nothing. They were on down the river from those places. Lisbeth had appeared confident her husband would abide by his word to leave Jacci alone, and she had no reason to suspect anybody in their showboat family of wishing her ill. She needed to rid her mind of those thoughts before it could spoil the rest of their season.

But a niggling worry lingered. She needed Gabe to tell her everything would be all right. He would know if something was amiss.

She climbed up to the top deck, but Captain Dan was at the wheel, guiding the boat down the river.

"Looking for that Gabe, I'm guessing," he said when she went over to the pilothouse.

"Yes, but glad to say good morning to you."

"The same to you, my girl. But that Gabe must be sleeping in this morning. His ma said he was out in the night watching over the boat and told me not to rouse him. The boy does put in the time," the captain said. "I reckon he deserves a little ease."

"Maybe I'll catch him at breakfast." She started back toward the steps to the lower deck.

"He's a popular fellow this morning. That Loranda girl popped her head up here a while ago. I didn't think that girl ever got up with the sun." He chuckled. "She seemed some disappointed to see me at the wheel instead of Gabe. I'm thinking the lass has a crush on our boy."

"That could be." Jacci held on to her smile. Maybe this was a sign, even though she hadn't done as Ellie said and prayed for one. Now, her prayer might need to be for a way to forever hide her feelings instead of revealing them.

Back on the main deck she walked around to where she could better see the sun on the port side. She should go help Aunt Tildy with breakfast, but she needed a few more minutes to prepare her heart in case Winnie and Gabe were there. Together.

She stopped in the same place where she'd talked to Winnie and Perry the morning before in the rain. When she put her hands on the railing, it felt even looser than it had yesterday. She would have to tell Gabe. Captain Dan would be upset if a section of the railing fell into the river to spoil the decorative look of their new showboat.

Everything seemed to come back to Gabe. Tell Gabe this. Tell Gabe that. But first she needed to take a few minutes to let the beauty of the morning calm her thoughts.

The sky was that clear blue after a rain. The water looked fresh too as the showboat pushed by *Little Ruby* glided through it. The paddle wheel would be churning up the river behind the boats, but ahead the water seemed to beckon them on to their next stop. A slight breeze lifted little riffles that sparkled as they caught the sunlight.

Jacci thought of Lisbeth's offer to find her and Duke a place off the river where she wouldn't have to worry about any dangers. The very thought of leaving the river clenched her heart, and not only because of her grandfather. She loved the river as much as Duke. As much as Kelly did, if for different reasons.

She would have to thank Kelly the next time she saw him. Thank him for continuing to drop into her life even after the desperate plan he'd come up with for Lisbeth didn't matter anymore. She had been safe with Duke. She was still safe with Duke. And the Kingstons. With Gabe, even if he was in love with Winnie.

If that was true, she'd find a new role to play. No, not a new role. She'd be the sister she'd always thought she was.

She wouldn't think about it. She would just think about the river and the trees and rocks along the banks. A few crows flew up out of the woods and loudly cawed their complaint about the morning. Two ducks took flight from the river in front of them as if hurrying to get out of the way of the showboat. Two other ducks floated near the edge of the water, not concerned at all about the boat's intrusion. A fish jumped, its scales flashing in the sun before it dropped back into the river with a loud splash. That was one Gabe would like to catch.

Gabe again. Was her every thought going to circle back to Gabe? She pulled in a big breath of the fresh morning air and lifted her face to feel the sunshine.

Silently she offered up a prayer. *I thank thee for the blessings of the morning. Give me courage to face the day no matter the challenges. The same courage my mother had, both my mothers had, each day as they tried to protect me in their own ways. And thank you for Grampus and Gabe, who are always ready to do the same.*

That was why Gabe had sounded angry when she came back on board in the wee hours of the morning. He had been worried about her. He would understand when she told him about Lisbeth.

At a noise behind her, she started to turn, when something slammed into her back. Hard. The blow took her breath and knocked her against the loose railing. She grabbed for a post, but her fingers merely brushed it as she and the railing went over the side. She barely had time to pull in a breath before she hit the water.

Chapter
28

THE WATER CLOSED IN over her head as she went down and down. She kicked off her shoes and pushed back toward the surface, but the folds of her skirt tangled between her legs. Sinking again, she fought against panic as she tore at the buttons on the skirt's waistband. At last the skirt slid free as she kicked toward the surface.

She gasped in some air before the river sucked her under again. Even with her eyes closed she could tell things were suddenly darker. When she once more tried to propel herself to the surface, she hit something solid. Panic threatened to disorient her. Seconds were passing. She needed air. She opened her eyes. The water was a dark, murky green. She couldn't see sunlight. The showboat was over the top of her.

Think. She had to be toward the front of the showboat, but the steamboat was coming. The churning water from the paddle wheel would send her to the bottom of the river. To her death. Colors were exploding in her head. She had to get air before her mind went black.

Maybe it would be easier to let the water swallow her. The

people she loved flashed through her mind. Then her mother's face was in front of her, clearer than it had been for years. At first Jacci thought she was reaching for her to welcome her to the other side of life. But then words were in her mind.

It is not your time. Fight.

Whether they were her mother's words or her own, she didn't know. But she did know she couldn't give up. She could swim. Had swum in the river every summer when she was a kid. With Gabe always close by to be sure she didn't sink.

Gabe. She couldn't die before she told Gabe she loved him.

With a last ferocious burst of energy, she pushed through the water out from under the showboat and got her head above water. She gulped in air and tried to yell for help. No sound came out. Instead, she was spewing out river water.

No one knew she was in the river. No one except whoever pushed her.

She went under again. Everything about her was so heavy. She could barely keep her arms moving. It would be so easy to just keep drifting down, but Gabe's face was there in her thoughts again. With another burst of energy, she broke the surface of the river. She treaded water and watched the boats steering toward the middle of the river away from her. She tried to yell again but coughed up water instead.

Then the wake of the paddle wheel bounced against her, knocking her under again. She came up and grabbed another breath of air before she gave herself over to the push of the water toward the bank. Only a little farther. She could almost see Gabe on the bank, telling her she could make it if she would just keep kicking her legs.

How many times had he encouraged her like that? *"You can learn the song. You can memorize your parts. You can swim."*

Her mother could swim. Kelly said she begged him to teach her, that she said anyone who lived on a boat should know how to swim. But Kelly hadn't taught Jacci. That was Gabe.

So many summer days in the river when she was a kid. Never with even a thought of drowning.

She bounced into a fallen tree partially submerged near the bank and grabbed hold of one of the branches. She coughed and tried to throw up at the same time as she clung to the tree until the wake from the steamboat stopped bouncing against her. She grabbed another of the branches and worked her way closer to the edge of the river until at last her toes touched mud.

Somehow she made it the last few feet out of the water and onto the bank, where she fell to her hands and knees and heaved out more river water. She tried to stand up, but her head seemed to be floating away. Everything turned gray except one pinhole spot of sunlight. Fearing she was sliding back toward the river, she clutched at the ground and scraped her hands across some rocks as everything went black.

She awoke to birds singing. For a few seconds, she wondered if she was in heaven until a rock jabbed into her thigh to let her know she was still on the riverbank. Every muscle in her body hurt. She lifted her face out of the dirt and rolled over. The birds overhead went silent.

With effort, she scooted up to sit beside the nearest tree where she coughed until she threw up again. At last she was able to pull in a breath and lean back against the tree trunk.

She was alive. She shut her eyes and dwelled on that thought. A slight breeze touched her face like a caress. She opened her eyes and looked out at the river flowing past. So good to be alive.

Slowly she flexed her ankles and bent her knees. She clenched her fingers and lifted her arms. She hurt, but everything still moved the way it was supposed to. What now?

She had no idea how much time had passed. Minutes? Hours? Perhaps a day? The sun was still shining, but the light on the river looked different. Not morning light. Not midday bright. Afternoon shadows lay across the water. So, probably not minutes or a day, but hours.

Who knew how far down the river the *Palace* and *Little Ruby* would be by now? Far from her. Would anybody miss her or would they think she was still in bed? Captain Dan knew she was up, but he must not have seen or heard her fall.

Fall. Somebody had shoved her. Lisbeth had been right. Somebody on board the showboat meant her harm. Deadly harm. But who?

She couldn't think of that right now. She breathed in and out carefully, fearful of setting off another coughing fit. Then she pushed on the bottoms of her ears to try to clear the water from them. She was glad when she heard the birds start singing again. Such a beautiful sound.

The willow limbs swayed in the breeze and the river licked against the bank not far below her. She wiggled her toes. No shoes. One stocking. Her pantaloons were muddy. She pulled up the cotton fabric where it was plastered against her leg. At least the ribbon tie had been strong enough to keep them from being torn off her, and she still had her corset firmly buttoned beneath what was left of her shirtwaist.

She ran her fingers through her hair to push it back from her face. All at once a laugh bubbled up in her. She considered it. Hysterics about the spot she was in or joy because she was alive to consider how she must look? She decided to claim joy. Hysterics would be of no use at all.

When she smiled, her cheek felt stiff. Another laugh threatened to lean more toward hysterics when she touched her face to feel a layer of mud. An actress once told her river mud was great for the skin. But nearly drowning before collapsing on a muddy riverbank wasn't the best way to apply such a beauty treatment.

She found a damp tattered piece of her shirt that wasn't covered with the same mud to rub off her cheek. Not that a dirty face mattered when she was in such a shambles with no shoes, and worse, no skirt. Any rescuer who might come along would get an eyeful.

Rescuer. That was what she needed no matter how she looked. She sat very still and listened to see if she could hear any sounds that might mean someone was nearby. The birds still sang overhead. A few crows flew past, with the one trailing, cawing for all it was worth, as though to get the others to wait for him.

Why hadn't the boat come back for her? Surely they knew by now she was missing. Would Duke and Gabe think she had slipped off the showboat this morning before they started on down the river? But Captain Dan had seen her after the showboat was underway.

A chill shook her even though the sunlight filtering down through the leaves was warm. She leaned forward and twisted to peer up at the sun easing toward the west.

The showboat would probably be at the next landing by now. She tried to think of which one that was, but her mind was in a fog. Wherever it was, they might be parading into town. She always took part in the parade. Marelda made everybody do that, even some of *Little Ruby*'s crew, who couldn't play a note on any instrument. But they added to the numbers as they pretended to play horns. Gabe or Duke would have to miss her in the parade. Have to.

That would be miles down the river. Even if they guessed she had gone overboard, they wouldn't know where. It was a big river. A big, lonely river. She shook away that thought. The river wasn't lonely. It was a busy river. Another boat would come along. Or a raft. Or a fisherman.

As if she had summoned it, a small steamboat came around the bend. Jacci scrambled to stand up. Her head started spinning and her legs trembled. She grabbed the tree trunk to keep from falling. She kept an arm around the tree and waved, but willow branches floated in the air in front of her. The boat hugged the other side of the river and chugged on past.

When tears jumped up into her eyes, she swiped them away. Another boat would come by. The next one might see her. She could step down closer to the river. That thought made the tremble in her legs race through the rest of her. She tried to shake the shivers away. She wasn't afraid of the river. It wasn't going to reach up and pull her under again.

Even so, she stayed by the tree and looked up the bank behind her. She didn't have shoes, but she could climb the steep bank and look for a road or path that might lead to people. Somebody who would take her back to the showboat. Rescuers always turned up in the nick of time in the dramas they performed on the showboat. That could happen in real life too, even if it took a while for the rescue scene to be played out on a real-life stage.

But hadn't she somehow made it out of the river? That had to be a scene hard to believe. She pulled in a thankful breath. Then she made herself turn loose of the tree and start up the bank. If need be, she could grab more trees to keep from sliding back toward the river.

She couldn't just sit and hope for someone on the river to see her. Most likely, even if they did see her waving, they'd simply wave back the way she herself had done hundreds of times from their showboat. Never once had she thought anyone might need rescuing. Maybe no one ever had, but now she did.

Gabe was always her rescuer, the one who made things right. If only he were here.

Chapter
29

THE SHOWBOAT WAS ALREADY on the move when Gabe had wakened that morning. He had lain in bed a little longer as he tried to think through everything. His father would be in the pilothouse guiding the boat down the river. Most of the cast would still be trying to sleep. Likely even Jacci too, after whatever had kept her out practically all night, although she was usually up with the sun.

He refused to dwell on where she'd gone or why. He would fight against being angry that she had left the showboat without telling him. He would try to keep praying that whatever was wrong would be fixed, the way Ma would tell him he should. He would try.

He had intended to find Jacci first thing and get her to tell him what was going on. But his mother was waiting when he got up with orders to work on one of their backdrops for the play.

"The braces on the back are loose. It's going to fall over in the middle of the play, and there wouldn't be much way we could work that into the scene," she had said.

So once he grabbed breakfast, he headed for the stage to fix that. Besides, Aunt Tildy hadn't seen Jacci. That was a pretty good indication Jacci was sleeping in.

"She ain't been in here. Could be she ain't feelin' so pert. That happens to a female from time to time. 'Specially when things has been mixed up for her. Poor girl pro'bly don't know which end is up what with ever'body talkin' 'bout that senator's wife lookin' like her." Aunt Tildy clucked her tongue. "I sometimes wish that Perry would just take his dolls and find him another place to make them pretend to talk. That man's a strange one."

"You surely know by now that all showmen are strange ones, Aunt Tildy." Gabe smiled.

"Some more'n others." Aunt Tildy poked her finger into his chest. "You and me, we're fine. It's them others you got to watch." She laughed.

"I'll keep that in mind," Gabe said. "But if you see Jacci, tell her to hunt me up. I'll be working on some of the scenery back of the stage."

"I 'spect I won't have to tell her. She'll be lookin' for you the same as you is lookin' for her. You two is close as two peas in a pod."

But Jacci hadn't come to find him. He was just finishing the repair on the backdrop when his mother started playing the calliope. That meant they were near the next stop. He jumped off the stage and leaned back against it as he listened. Even here in the auditorium, the music made the wooden rim around the stage vibrate.

The way Jacci made Gabe's heart pound. She had to be up by now if she wasn't sick. He went out on deck to help tie up the showboat. People were at the landing to watch the boats come in. Just seeing them started up a little excitement in Gabe, even after tying up at too many landings to count through the years they'd been on the river.

Jacci always felt the same excitement. He looked around for her, but she wasn't out on the deck. She must be hiding away from him the way she used to hide away from everyone when she was a little girl and missing her mother. Maybe Duke telling Jacci that this woman named Lisbeth was actually her mother had sent Jacci down some of those same sorrowful paths. But she didn't have to hide away from him.

When he went to get his drum for the parade, others were already there to collect their instruments from the band area. Mrs. Loranda picked up a cornet and Mr. Loranda hooked the accordion over his shoulders. That was always a favorite in the parade. Gabe's mother was handing out horns to some of the crew and telling them in her no-nonsense voice to not bang them against anything.

"We need some props," she muttered when Gabe went over to her. She picked up the tambourines Jacci usually carried. "Here, give these to Jacci."

"I don't think she's here yet." He looked around. "In fact, I haven't seen her today. I've been backstage fixing that scenery."

A little frown wrinkled Ma's brow. "That's odd. I haven't seen her either. Maybe she's helping Aunt Tildy."

"She wasn't when I grabbed breakfast this morning. I think she must have slept in."

"That doesn't sound like our girl."

"Something's going on with her," Gabe said. "Did Duke tell you about it?"

"No, but he hasn't been himself since the other night when he wouldn't do the show." Ma glanced around and lowered her voice. "Is it about that senator's wife looking like Jacci?"

"Yes. But we can't talk about it here. Too many ears." Gabe saw Winnie coming toward them and couldn't keep from groaning.

"Be nice, Gabe. She's so young. She just doesn't know better."

"She's not that young," Gabe muttered.

"Well, just tell her you're in love with Jacci," his mother said. Gabe whipped his gaze back to her.

"Don't look so shocked," she said. "I know you. You've loved Jacci since you were thirteen."

"Does everybody on this boat know that except Jacci?"

His mother laughed softly and patted his arm. "That could be. I guess it's up to you to make that change. As for Winnie, I'll have a talk with her mother."

"When you do, you best tell her to watch Winnie. She's been hanging around Cameron since I wouldn't cooperate with her ideas for us. And I don't trust Cameron to know she's too young to know better, as you say."

"Don't worry. I will. And I'll talk to Cameron too. That man is pushing his luck with me." Her frown came back. "I'll intercept Winnie, and there's Duke. Go ask him where Jacci is."

She moved in front of Winnie, and Gabe wasted no time heading over to Duke, who looked the worse for wear after their long night.

"Where's Jacci?" Gabe asked.

Duke looked around. "I thought she'd be here. I haven't seen her since she came aboard last night. She was already gone from her room when I woke this morning."

"I thought she was sleeping in."

"She might have for a while." Duke looked worried. "I didn't get out of my room until almost eleven, but she wasn't there then. I thought you would have talked to her by now."

"I haven't seen her."

"She's probably helping Aunt Tildy," Duke said.

"She wasn't earlier, but I haven't been back to the kitchen since this morning." An uneasy feeling was poking Gabe. "You don't think she got up early and left the boat again."

"No." Duke looked sure of that. "She wouldn't have left without telling me. She wouldn't want me to worry."

"She left last night."

"I'm not sure she had a choice. Someone else wrote the note I found in our rooms. They said they had taken Jacci. Actually they said Jacinth."

"I need to talk to her." The uneasy feeling was turning into concern. Worried concern. He took a breath to calm himself and then turned toward the others in the room. "Has anybody seen Jacci today?"

Captain looked up from adjusting the straps on his drums. "I saw her this morning. Early. She came up to the pilothouse. I think she was looking for you, Gabe. It was right after Winnie poked her head up to check out who was at the wheel." He looked over at Winnie. "Did you see Jacci, Winnie?"

"I didn't see anybody. When I realized how early it was, I went back to bed." She turned away from Ma and picked up her flute. "Just ask my mother, if you don't believe me."

Cameron spoke up. "She was supposed to meet with me at noon to go over some script changes I wanted to make. She never showed up." He shrugged. "I guess she forgot." He sighed as he stared at the trumpet Marelda handed him. "This is ridiculous. I'm an actor. Not a marching monkey. You shouldn't expect me to parade into that excuse for a town and pretend to blow this instrument."

"It's part of the job you signed on for," Ma said flatly.

Cameron rolled his eyes and took the horn. "But where is Jacci? If she's sick and can't go on, we need to know what to do tonight."

"Nobody has said she's sick," Ma said.

"Nobody has said she isn't." Cameron looked around. "Surely somebody has seen her today."

"I was up at nine or so," Perry said. "Went and got coffee. Didn't see her then."

Everybody else shook their heads too.

"She's got to be here somewhere," Captain said.

Perry spoke up again. "Oh, by the way, Captain, there's a broken section of railing on the port side."

"Broken? Where?" Captain sounded ready to go repair it.

"Not now, dear. Parade first." Ma gave him a look. "We need your drum. Gabe can find Jacci and catch up with us." She clapped her hands. "Everybody out on the deck. It's parade time." She flashed a big smile toward Cameron, who didn't smile back.

Gabe wasn't concerned about what Cameron did or didn't want to do. The little pokes of worry were stabbing jabs now. Duke looked every bit as worried. Gabe touched his shoulder. "I'll find her. She's got to be on the boat somewhere if Captain saw her this morning after we were on the move. Go parade with Ma. She needs your trumpet playing."

Gabe went to the kitchen, but Aunt Tildy hadn't seen Jacci all day. He went to her room. The door was open. Her bed had been slept in. The pillows and blankets were in a tumble. He climbed up to the hurricane deck. No one was there.

The sun beat down on his head as he watched their parade head to the town with kids running along beside them. Older people lined the way and then followed them. His father was setting the cadence for the march with the drum the way Gabe usually did. He looked for Jacci in case she'd joined with them at the last moment. But she wasn't there.

Where could she be? Had she sat down somewhere and fallen asleep? Maybe in the auditorium. He was hurrying that way when he spotted the broken railing Perry had mentioned. Not just broken. A whole section gone.

Gabe would have to figure out a way to fix it. He ran his hand along the jagged broken edge of the railing. A piece of material was caught there. He pulled it free and stared at the rose-colored material. Jacci had a skirt that very color.

Gabe's blood ran cold as he stared down at the water and could practically see her falling into it. He stared back up the river as questions swirled through his head. If she went overboard, why didn't somebody see or hear her? When had it happened? And most important, where?

The section of river they'd come down wasn't that wide. Jacci could swim. She could have made it to the bank. He clutched the material in his hand and closed his eyes. He had to believe she could have made it to the riverbank.

chapter

30

JACCI HAD TO STOP TO REST against a tree several times as she climbed the steep bank away from the river. She didn't sit down because she wasn't sure she could get back up. Her legs felt as if she'd danced all day and night and now every step was an effort. Rocks bruised the bottoms of her feet that weren't tough the way they'd been when she was younger and went barefoot all summer.

When she finally made it to the top of the bank, she nearly cried. Thick stands of trees ran along the river as far as she could see. No pasture fields with cows or sheep. No houses. No roads. Not even a path into the trees. Nothing that promised any kind of help.

She leaned against a big oak. Overhead a squirrel chattered at her, as if warning her away from its tree. Jacci looked up at it, all at once so angry she wanted to be strong enough to shake the squirrel off its branch.

She took a breath that made her start coughing again. At least she didn't throw up this time. That had to be a good sign. She held on to the tree trunk as the coughs shook her. The squirrel stopped chattering, and Jacci almost smiled thinking it might believe she was fussing back at it.

"Pull yourself together," she said out loud when she stopped coughing. "Be glad you can see these trees instead of being at the bottom of the river."

But what now? She did know which direction to go toward the showboat's next landing. Downriver. It would be miles. She tried to remember where their next regular stop was after Point William. They did the same landings every summer.

Nothing came to mind. She couldn't come up with a place. But she was more than sure she couldn't walk that far before nightfall. That didn't mean she wouldn't find a farmhouse before night. She stared at the forbidding shadows under the trees. If she wandered in there, she could get lost and no one would ever find her.

Duke had to have missed her by now. He would tell Gabe. They would look for her. When they didn't find her on the showboat, they might see the broken railing and guess she'd fallen overboard. Not fallen. Been pushed. Somebody on board the *Palace* wanted her dead.

That truth brought on more trembles that had nothing to do with how exhausted she was. She couldn't think about that. Not now. She had to focus on getting back to the showboat. Then there would be time enough to figure out who had intended her harm.

Gabe would look for her. But he wouldn't know where to look unless whoever pushed her admitted it. Not much chance of that. So, if he did come back for her, he'd be on the river and not up on the bank searching through these trees. He'd look along the river. Even if he doubted she had survived, he wouldn't leave her body to float unclaimed.

She shook away the image of her body face down on the surface of the river, or worse, caught on the bottom to never be seen. That hadn't happened. She could be seen if she were somewhere they could see her. Where somebody on the river could see her.

She gave the squirrel back his tree and started toward the river again. She struggled more going down the steep grade than coming up. She moved sideways along the bank, grabbing trees when her feet slipped. She didn't want to end up in the same place she'd been in the midst of the thick willows. Better to find a place open to the water.

The rock ledge jutting out of the bank and spilling more rocks down toward the river was just what she needed. Jacci walked right to the edge, no longer fearing the river would reach out and pull her under. At least she'd gotten that much sense back. She sat down on a flat rock and put her feet in the water to soothe the bruises and scrapes they'd endured.

It felt good to sit there in the sun and just wait for whatever might happen next. She was tired. Very tired. She wanted to lie down on the rocky bank and shut her eyes. With a shake of her head, she sat up straighter. She had to watch for somebody, anybody who might come along the river.

Please, Lord. Send someone. Let it be Gabe.

She pulled her feet out of the water and scooted back up the bank where she could lean against the ledge. Idly, she wondered if a snake might be resting in its shade. She didn't think she could jump away even if it decided to crawl up in her lap. She might just stroke its head and be glad for the company. The sunshine felt so good. In spite of the climb up and down the bank, she felt chilled.

A bird started singing. A mockingbird, from the variety of its songs. A breeze brushed across the river and made the water softly lick the bank edge. A hawk gave a shrill cry as it flew over the river. A few buzzards circled in the wind currents high above. She waved her hands to prove she wasn't their next meal. They paid no notice as they floated on out of sight.

She tried to judge how much time had passed. She counted

to sixty three times, but then lost count on the fourth time. Her eyelids felt heavy. She ordered herself to stay awake. She had to watch. But the sun was warm and she was so very tired.

Surely she could close her eyes to rest them from the glare of the sun glancing off the river for just a few seconds. She didn't even realize when she fell asleep.

Gabe's mind was racing. He had to do something. Now. Every minute, every second might count.

He shook his head. That was crazy. She wouldn't still be in the water. She had to have fallen off the showboat hours ago. Why hadn't he gone to find her this morning instead of waiting for her to come to him?

He pushed the thought aside. It did no good to think of what he should have done. He had to think about what he needed to do now. She could be somewhere along the bank waiting for them to come back for her. Waiting for him.

The sound of the drums and horns drifted back to him. The parade probably still hadn't reached the village where they would stop and play another song before the captain talked about their show. They wouldn't be back for an hour at least. He couldn't wait that long. He wouldn't wait that long.

He could get Captain Sallie to fire up the *Little Ruby* to head back upriver. The man always stayed with the boats while the others went parading. Fear gripped Gabe's heart that he might not find her waiting on the riverbank. She could have hit her head when she fell. She hadn't yelled. Surely somebody would have heard her if she yelled, even if they didn't see her.

Captain Sallie and the engineer, Mac, were taking their ease in some chairs on the deck of the *Little Ruby* when Gabe ran aboard and rushed out his words. "It's Jacci. She went overboard this morning. We've got to go find her."

"Overboard?" Captain Sallie frowned and ran his fingers through his beard. "This morning?"

"That was hours ago." Mac pushed his hat back off his forehead to stare up at Gabe. He was even older than Captain Sallie. "You pulling some kind of joke on us, son?"

"No." Gabe tamped down on his impatience. "We didn't miss her until now. There's a broken rail where she must have fallen. I found a piece of her skirt." He held out the scrap of material he still held. His hand shook.

The two men looked at each other again, and Gabe could read their thoughts even though they didn't say anything as they stood up. Gabe said, "She can swim."

"That she can. Like a fish. Get some steam up, Mac, while we loose *Ruby*." Captain Sallie gripped Gabe's arm for a second. "We'll find her if somebody hasn't already seen her and picked her up."

As they steamed back up the river, Captain Sallie pulled down his whistle twice. Gabe's father might recognize it as a signal of distress, but Gabe couldn't worry about what they would think. He could explain it all after he had Jacci safe back on the showboat.

For the first few miles, they went full speed, watching for any other boats that might have come along after them. The river was practically deserted along this stretch. They did pass a couple of rafts, but when they called out to them, the men on board hadn't seen anything.

Gabe stood on the top deck and tried to watch in every direction as Captain Sallie slowed *Ruby* to a crawl. If only he knew where Jacci had fallen into the river. Perry noticed the broken railing this morning, so it had to be early. Maybe not long after his father had seen her. Why didn't Captain hear the splash when she hit the water? What would make her hit the railing hard enough to break it and fall? Why had he waited so long to look for her?

He shook away the questions. Dwelling on them didn't help. He couldn't change any of that.

"See any sign of her?" Captain Sallie called from the pilothouse.

Gabe shook his head. "Not yet."

"Want to keep going? Maybe we missed her."

He hadn't missed her. Not if she was waiting by the river. But then she might have walked up the bank to find help.

"How far to where we tied up last night?" Gabe asked.

"Maybe another hour." The captain stepped out of the pilothouse and looked at the sky. "But it will be heading toward dark soon."

"We have to find her before then," Gabe said.

"If she's to be found." His voice was sad. "She might not have made it, Gabe."

Gabe spun around to stare at the captain. "Don't say that."

"It's not what I'm wanting. You have to know that. But even if she did make it out of the river, she might not be where you can see her. She wouldn't just sit there." Captain Sallie peered at first one side of the river, then the other. "The banks are steep here, but could be a house up in the trees. Or a fisherman might have come by. Our girl might even now be on the way back to the showboat."

If only he could know that for sure. "Keep on around the bend up ahead, Captain. I can't quit until I know she's not waiting for us to come back for her."

"I'll signal Mac for more steam." He stepped back into the pilothouse.

A flash of color of something tangled in bushes along the bank caught Gabe's eye. Rose color. The same color as the scrap of cloth he had shoved in his pocket. His heart jumped up in his throat. It couldn't be her. It couldn't.

"Hold her steady, Captain," he yelled as he ran for the steps down to the main deck. He threw off his hat, jerked off his shoes, and dived in.

He swam like a madman toward the bushes. When his feet hit bottom, he waded to the edge of the river to pull the material free. A skirt. Jacci's skirt.

He held it to his face as despair turned the day dark. She must not have made it. The river had claimed her.

But he wouldn't let the river keep her. He would find her. He threw the skirt aside and dove under the water. The water was murky. He couldn't see anything. He came up for air and went under again. He wouldn't give up.

The next time he came up, the boat had drifted away from him. He didn't care. He went under again. Terrified he would see her body. Worried he wouldn't. Nothing was there.

When he surfaced, he was farther from the boat. Captain Sallie pitched a rope with a float toward him. "Grab the float, Gabe. I can't go back and tell Captain Dan I lost you too."

Lost too. Gabe treaded water and stared at the float sliding away from him. He felt lost already. Slowly he began swimming toward the boat.

Chapter
31

Mac pulled Gabe back on the boat while Captain Sallie held Little Ruby steady. Gabe collapsed on the deck, pulling in heavy breaths. He couldn't bear to think about Jacci sinking in the river, unable to breathe.

Mac sat down beside him. "Weren't no reason for you to try to kill yourself looking for her under the water. She won't be here."

"That was her skirt." Gabe stared up at the sky that was too blue. He couldn't lose Jacci on a day like this. Storm clouds should be covering the sun. His sun was gone forever.

"That don't mean nothing. Think, son. The skirt would have washed downstream."

Think. He did need to think.

"Then her body would have too," he said.

"It ain't like you to give up so easy." Mac pulled his hat down tighter on his head. "Me, I fall in, I'm a goner, but the girl could swim. I used to watch you kids playing in the water some years back. Swimming ain't one of those things you forget how to do."

"But that was her skirt."

"Skirt snirt." Mac turned his head and spat toward the river. "She coulda lost the fetched thing. Mebbe on purpose. It woulda messed up her swimming."

A spot of hope tickled awake in Gabe's heart. "You really think so, Mac?"

"Well, I ain't got no guarantees. The good Lord don't give such as them out. 'Cept to that Hezekiah feller in the Bible what he give extra years." Mac shook his head.

Gabe stared at him. He'd known the man for years without ever hearing him say the first thing about the Bible. "Hezekiah?"

"Never mind that old geezer," Mac said. "We ain't got time for a Bible lesson. Time for me to shove another log in the fire so's we can head on around the next bend. You can give up if'n you want, but I'm not giving up on the girl till we've looked the whole way."

"Mac!" Captain Sallie yelled down from the pilothouse. "I'm losing steam."

"Right, Cap. I'll take care of that." Mac looked at Gabe as he got up. "You ain't gonna slide back off into the river, are you?"

Gabe sat up. "Not unless I see a reason to."

"Now you're thinking." He headed for the boiler room. He glanced back over his shoulder. "Reckon if you're just sitting there like a bump on a log, you might think on asking the Lord for some help. Your ma would tell you to do that afore you go to jumping in the river."

Gabe watched the man disappear down the steps to the lower deck. He was right. Ma would tell him to pray, but was it too late for prayers?

As he stood up, from somewhere the story of King Hezekiah came to mind. Maybe the Lord had sent it. The prophet told Hezekiah he was going to die. He gave the king three days, best Gabe could remember. The king turned his face to the wall and wept and prayed for more time. The Lord gave him fifteen more years.

"Lord, please." Gabe looked up at the sky as that tickle of hope grew. "More years for Jacci too."

Mac was right. He couldn't give up until he was sure. Even if they didn't find her around the next bend, the Lord could have sent somebody to help her. She might already be back on the showboat, wondering where he was.

The boilers rumbled under his feet as he headed for the top deck, still dripping river water. No need to bother putting on his shoes. Not yet.

The paddle wheel began turning faster. When he got up top, he told Captain Sallie to blow *Little Ruby*'s whistle. "Let her know we're coming."

With those words and then two blasts of the steamboat whistle, his hope grew. Mac was right. She could swim. She was strong. She could be around the bend.

The steamboat whistle woke Jacci. She knew that whistle. *Little Ruby.* She tried to get up so fast that the rocks slid out from under her feet and she fell and slipped toward the water. She sat there and stared out at the river. No boats were there. She must have been dreaming.

She lay back and stared at the sky. She didn't know how long she'd been asleep. The sun had gone out of sight over the bank behind her. If she had to spend the night here, she could. She'd find a softer place than these rocks, and when the sun came up in the morning, she'd wrap her feet with the remains of her shirtwaist and make her way down the river until she found somebody to help her.

She wouldn't let how she looked stop her. Her chemise and pantalets covered her. Mostly. Modesty was surely her least worry. Her growling stomach might be a bigger concern, and the energy to keep moving. At least she had water. Not filtered by the calliope as it was on the *Palace*, but she wouldn't die of thirst. She might find some blackberries if she climbed up to the top of the bank again. By morning, she would have surely recovered some strength.

She heard something. A boat was coming. A steamboat. She sat up and stared out at the river, hoping against hope she wasn't imagining it. But no, she spotted puffs of smoke rising into the sky. She hadn't dreamed up smoke.

She scrambled to her feet and stared toward the bend where she'd seen the smoke. If it was a steamboat, she had to do something to make sure they not only saw her but knew she needed help. She yanked off the tattered remains of her shirtwaist. If she waved it, they would have to know she was signaling them. They had to see her.

When the boat rounded the bend and kept coming, she almost cried. It was the *Little Ruby*. They had come looking for her. She started to wave her shirt, but the boat was still a good distance from her and moving slowly. They wouldn't see her yet.

A man stood on the top deck. Gabe. She couldn't see his face, but she didn't need to. She knew it was Gabe. She couldn't wait any longer. She started waving her make-do flag and yelling his name.

She climbed up on the rocky ledge and kept waving. They had to see her. They had to.

The steamboat whistle blew again. A long blast that sounded joyful to Jacci's ears. Gabe disappeared from sight. The next minute he was on the main deck.

He waved both arms and looked as though he was bouncing up and down as the steamboat kept churning up the river, a little faster now. She could feel his eyes on her across the distance. She moved back to the edge of the river, but she couldn't jump in. She didn't have strength to swim out toward them. Instead, she stood, no longer waving, and waited.

When the boat moved on past her, she nearly despaired. He had seen her. He'd waved at her.

Patience. The word whispered through her head. She didn't know if it was from her mother or from the Lord. Wherever the word came from, it calmed her. Gabe would come for her.

Gabe could hardly keep from diving into the river the minute he spotted Jacci on the riverbank. But he had to wait until the distance was the shortest between them. Then he made himself wait even longer so that the current would help him get to her.

Captain Sallie knew the river. He would know where he could get closest to the bank. The riverside was steep here and rocky. Limbs from fallen trees stuck up out of the water. Gabe considered going back to the pilothouse to ask the captain what was possible, but he couldn't take his eyes off Jacci.

She had stopped waving as the boat moved past her. But she knew they had seen her. She would know they wouldn't leave her.

Gabe's insides felt as if a hundred bees were stinging him. He told himself to count to twenty after they moved past Jacci. He got to seventeen before he thought his heart would explode if he didn't go to her. He dived in. He'd leave it up to Captain Sallie to get close to where Jacci was standing. Where he would be standing with her in minutes. Somehow they would get back on board.

He should have waited those extra seconds. The current carried him past her and he had to fight the river to swim back to her. But when his feet touched bottom, she was there, her feet in the water, holding her hands out to pull him toward land. Toward her.

"I knew you'd come." Her voice sounded rough.

He couldn't talk at all. Not because he was out of breath

from swimming. His heart was up in his throat choking out his words. She stood there in front of him, still breathing. Even smiling. Her hair was in tangles. In nothing but her undergarments streaked with mud, she looked so very vulnerable. He gently touched a red scrape on her cheek.

"You are the most beautiful sight I have ever seen," he managed at last. He smoothed a strand of hair away from her face with trembling fingers.

Her eyes widened before she covered his hand with hers and held it against her cheek. "I thought I was going to die and never see you again."

He reached for her, and she stepped into his arms as if she'd been waiting all her life for the invitation. She lifted her face toward his and without hesitation he claimed her lips. He felt as if he were drowning now. Drowning in love.

When at last he lifted his face away from hers, she leaned slightly back and stared into his eyes. "That didn't feel like a brother's kiss."

"I've told you a million times that I'm not your brother."

"I know," she said. "But I'm not sure I ever completely believed you until now."

"Believe this." He stared down at her without loosening his arms around her. "I love you, Jacci Reed. I've loved you since you were five. I've just been waiting for you to grow up to tell you that."

"I've been grown up for a while."

"But you grew up so beautiful, I got scared. And when you kept saying that about me being your brother, I got more scared."

"I didn't think anything scared you." Jacci smiled as she stroked his cheek.

"Then you just don't know. I've been terrified ever since I figured out you must have fallen overboard without anybody hearing you."

"Somebody heard me." Her smile disappeared as her face stiffened. "I didn't fall."

"What do you mean?"

"I was pushed."

"Pushed?" His insides clenched at her words. "Who would do that?"

"I don't know. I didn't see them, just felt them shove me hard against the railing." Jacci shook her head slightly. "Maybe they didn't think it would break."

"Whether they did or not, they knew you fell and didn't raise an alarm." Rage at that thought burned through him. "They didn't do anything to save you."

"No." She tensed in his arms. "Lisbeth told me somebody on the showboat meant me harm. I didn't want to believe her."

"Lisbeth?"

"I need to tell you about her. About last night. About everything." She sighed and rested her head against his chest. "But right now, I'm just so tired."

Chapter
32

GABE'S HEART THUMPED under Jacci's ear as his arms encircled her again. She was safe in his embrace. So very safe. She wanted to stay there forever.

His heart was beating too fast. He was angry. Not at her. But at whoever had pushed her into the river. Funny that she had hardly thought about that at all. Her every thought had been on finding a way back to the showboat. Hoping to be rescued. Hoping for Gabe to come.

But now safe in his arms, she had to face the fact that Lisbeth was right. Somebody did want to hurt her. Not just hurt her. Whatever the original intent had been, whoever had shoved her against the railing had been willing to let her die.

When she shuddered, Gabe held her tighter. "They won't get away with this."

"Maybe I shouldn't go back to the boat. Lisbeth offered to find a place for me to hide for a while. Maybe that's what I should do." She cringed at the idea. Her mother had tried to hide her and she'd died. Lisbeth, in another way, had hidden her too. Lisbeth was still hiding. Jacci didn't want to live like that. But she did want to live. To keep feeling this man's arms around her.

"That can't happen. Not unless I hide with you." He kissed the top of her head. "I plan to never let you out of my sight again."

That sounded good, even if Jacci knew it wasn't possible. Another fear poked at her. Would she ruin his life as she had her mothers' lives? She shook her head against him. "You're like Duke. You need the river."

"I need you more."

"I can't live always afraid of what lies in the shadows."

"Shadows fall on land the same as on the river." Gabe's voice was soft, but sure. "We will find a way to make the shadows safe." He put his fingers under her chin and raised her head up to look at him.

"How?" she asked.

"I don't know, but we will. Somehow."

"I've always believed you could do anything." She smiled a little. "Don't all little sisters believe that about their big brothers?"

"I am not your brother." He blew out an exasperated breath. "I have never been your brother. I will never be your brother. I have something else in mind."

"I know." She nearly laughed. "But I was afraid being a sister was all I could be. I thought you were falling in love with Winnie."

"I sing one song with the girl and everybody gets the wrong idea." He shook his head. "You're my forever dance partner."

He dropped his head down to cover her lips with his again. Sweet heaven.

The blast of the steamboat whistle made them both jump. Gabe looked over his shoulder at the river. "I think Captain Sallie is trying to tell us something."

The boat was still a good way from the bank.

Jacci's cheeks felt warm. "What must he think of me standing here half undressed, kissing you in broad daylight?"

"There are extenuating circumstances. A rescue can't be
scripted like a play. The costumes are what they are, and when
the scene calls for a kiss, it doesn't matter who is in the audience." He brushed her forehead with his lips. "But the captain
is right. Daylight is losing that broad look, and we need to get
back down the river before everybody goes crazy with worry."

"Everybody but one."

"That one might be worrying the most." He frowned. "As
he should."

When he turned away from her to call out to Captain Sallie, Jacci shivered as the shadows engulfed her. Hugging Gabe
had gotten her wet again, but that wasn't what chilled her.
She missed his arms around her. How could she have known
him so long and not recognized how desperately she loved
him?

"Close as I can get, Gabe." Captain Sallie stood on the top
deck. "Fear I'd ground *Ruby* if I try any closer. I can hold her
here if you can swim out. Or I can head on up to West Chester
and send someone down for you."

"Night would be on us before that," Gabe called back. He
looked around at Jacci. "It's not that far to swim. They'll pitch
us a float."

She stepped up beside him and stared at the river. Another
chill shook through her. She couldn't go back in the water.
Not yet.

She shivered and he put his arm around her. "You can hold
to my waist. You remember how you did that back when I was
teaching you to swim?"

"I do." She moistened her lips. "But that was before the river
tried to swallow me."

His voice was gentle. "That won't happen this time. I'll be
right there with you. I won't let you sink."

When she didn't say anything, he went on. "But if you want to wait, we'll wait."

She looked back at the steamboat where Captain Sallie was still staring across the water at them. Mac was on the main deck watching them too. "Do you think the captain will have a shirt I can borrow?"

Gabe smiled. "I'm sure he does. And a blanket too. They might even be almost clean."

She pulled in a breath and let it out slowly. "Then what are we waiting for? I need some of Aunt Tildy's hot cocoa."

Gabe held her hand as they waded into the river. Jacci forced her breathing in and out slowly. She would not panic. The boat was only a few yards away. Yesterday she wouldn't have thought twice about swimming that far. But now her arms felt stiff and her legs trembled. Today she had almost drowned. But Gabe was with her. He wouldn't let the river have her.

Telling herself she wouldn't panic was easy, but each step into deeper water made it harder to take the next step. She had defeated the river that morning, but this time the river might win. She tried not to pull against Gabe's hold, but when her feet started slipping in the mud on the sloping river bottom, she jerked away from him and slid under the water.

Strong arms reached and pulled her up. He held her against him a moment before he looked down at her. "Jacci, you can do this."

"I'm afraid."

"I know, but I'm here with you. Grab on to my shirt and let me swim for us." His eyes burned into hers. "We can do this. Together."

She found her footing and pushed a little away from him. He held on to her arm as she wiped the hair out of her face with her other hand. The water eased past her as she stared out at the *Little Ruby*. She couldn't let the river win. She couldn't let whoever had pushed her in win.

"I can swim." She moved away from Gabe and gave herself over to the river. Her arms felt weak, but they pulled her through the water toward the boat. Gabe swam not far away from her, matching his strokes to hers.

Then Mac threw a float in front of her. She slipped her shoulders through it. Seconds later she was on the deck.

"If you ain't a sight for sore eyes." Mac had the biggest grin she'd ever seen on his whiskered face.

She was laughing and crying at the same time as she yanked the float off. Mac threw it back in to help Gabe up on deck.

Then Captain Sallie hollered for more power and Mac took off for the boiler room. Gabe tried to swipe the water off her face with his wet shirttail. "That's not much help," he said. "Wait."

He jumped up to run toward the crews' rooms. Water dripped off him with every stride. In minutes he was back with a man's shirt and a blanket.

Jacci pulled on the shirt. "This smells pretty good to be Captain Sallie's."

"Don't know whose it is. First room I came to." Gabe wrapped the blanket around her.

"Smells like whatever Cameron uses on his hair," Jacci said. "Must have been his room."

That made Gabe frown. "Not sure I like you wearing his shirt. Maybe I should go hunt for Captain Sallie's room."

"I'm keeping it. I don't care whose it is." Jacci pulled the blanket closer around her. "Besides, you can't be worried about Cameron and me."

"And you can't be worried about Winnie and me."

She leaned against him then. "I guess I have other things to worry about right now."

"But me loving you and only you is not one of them." He put his arms around her, blanket and all.

"How about both of us missing the show tonight? It should be starting about now and you aren't there to do your part."

"Captain can do it or Ma."

"Do you think Aunt Marelda is taking my place in the play with Cameron?" Jacci shook her head at that thought. "I can't imagine her letting Cameron hug her in that last scene."

"She could probably pull it off, but Winnie said she knew the part. She was ready to step into your role when Cameron worried about what would happen if you were sick."

"That would work," Jacci said.

"Maybe. Or they could have canceled the drama."

"Aunt Marelda cancel a show?" Jacci shook her head. "Not likely."

"She might, with her favorite niece missing and her formerly favorite son stealing the towboat to take off upriver without the first explanation."

"You shouldn't have done that."

"They were still in the village when I found the broken railing and a scrap of your skirt caught on it."

"You could have scribbled a note for your mother."

"No time for that. I had to save you." He tightened his arms around her.

"But you didn't even know where I might have gone overboard."

"So I wasn't thinking straight. Maybe it was better this way. Ma not knowing what happened. That way she can go on and collect the quarters and have the show thinking you had somehow been left behind at the last landing and I was going back for you."

"But Captain Dan saw me after we were underway."

"Don't try to make sense of everything. Nothing about any of this makes sense."

"You're right." Nothing did make sense. Not even how good it was to lean against Gabe and feel how strong he was. Then again maybe that was the only thing that did make sense.

Gabe pointed up at the sky. "Look. The first star of the evening. Remember how we used to make wishes on that star?"

She smiled. "And then had to see another star before we saw that one again in order for it to come true."

"Want to make a wish now?"

"My wish came true already." Jacci gazed up at the star. "When I saw *Little Ruby* coming around that river bend and you standing on the hurricane deck."

"And mine when I saw you waving at me, but that was more an answer to prayer than a wish."

"Yes." She sent up a silent prayer of thanks now. She was breathing air. She was back on a boat. Gabe had his arm around her.

"Are you praying now, Jacci?"

"A thankful prayer. That I'm standing here beside a man who is not my brother."

He laughed. "I can pray that same hallelujah prayer."

Silence wrapped around them as they both gazed up. Another star appeared and then another, as though flashing into view just for them. One was the North Star. She touched her chest over her heart and thought of how she saw her mother's face when she was ready to give up under the water. Another thankful prayer rose up toward that star.

After a moment, she looked back at Gabe. "But now what, Gabe?"

"Now we go raid Captain Sallie's extra rations."

"He eats in Aunt Tildy's galley."

"True, but he'll have a stash of something here. Then you can tell me everything before we get back to the showboat."

"All right."

She could tell him all she knew, but that wouldn't be everything. She didn't know everything. And nothing she did know gave her any idea of who had shoved her off the *Palace*. That was what she needed most to know.

Chapter

33

GABE WANTED TO STAY WITH JACCI, hear everything she had to say, but night was falling. Captain Sallie needed help getting *Little Ruby* back down the river. Gabe lit the lanterns around the main deck. The boat had one spotlight, but as long as there was some moonlight, Captain Sallie depended on his river savvy more than what he called a blinding light.

"A man can't see what's ahead on the river with that fool light in his eyes." He stared out toward the water. "Fact is, I could pilot this stretch of the river with my eyes shut if nobody got in my way."

"Best use your whistle to tell them you're coming." The blast of the whistle followed Gabe down to the boiler deck to see if Mac needed help.

"What's with the whistles?" Mac asked.

"To warn any rafts or boats on the river we're coming. Even with the moonlight, the river's a pool of dark."

"Good thinking. We don't want to have to fish anybody else out of the water," Mac said. "Our girl holding up?"

"We found the captain's candy stash. She's doing all right."

"I expect that was mine 'stead of Captain's. I'm the one with the sweet tooth and I reckon it shows." He smiled as he patted his broad middle. "But I'm glad for her to have it. Poor thing, after what she's been through."

Gabe moved past Mac to the boilers. "Take a rest. I'll feed the fire." He shoved a hefty chunk of wood into the fire.

"That ought to keep the steam up for a while." Mac went back to his stool beside the signal bells he and Captain Sallie used to communicate. "Miss Jacci tell you how come her to go overboard? Don't seem like something that would happen on the calm waters we had this morning."

"Somebody pushed her." Gabe brushed off his hands as he followed him away from the boilers.

Mac jerked back as though Gabe's words hit him. "Pushed her? Of a purpose?"

"So it appears, since he didn't raise an alarm to stop the boats."

"What's this world coming to?" Mac rubbed his whiskered chin. "Who coulda done such a thing?"

"I don't know, but I intend to find out." Gabe turned to head back to the main deck. Back to Jacci. "I'll come and put some more wood in later."

"You tell your pa that we'll have to take on more wood before we start on downriver tomorrow."

"All right. How long do you think before we get there?" He looked around at Mac.

"Appears as how we're making good time. Last I looked, no fog was rising to slow us down. So, I'm thinkin' two hours."

Two hours. Plenty of time to hear whatever Jacci needed to tell him. But when he went back to the galley, she was curled up in the blanket on the floor, asleep. He watched her, his heart swelling with so much love it seemed to almost run out of room in his chest. With soft steps, he crossed the room to lie down beside her.

Her eyes flew open, but when she saw him in the lamplight, she sighed and went back to sleep. He needed to know what she had to tell him, but he didn't wake her. They would have time. *Dear Lord, let us have years and years of time together.*

Jacci half woke each time the steamboat whistle blew. The vibrations of the floor under her were different from the feel of moving down the river on the showboat. The steamboat was the one with power. Somehow the rumble of the *Little Ruby* was soothing and put her back to sleep. She knew when Gabe lay down beside her, but she couldn't keep her eyes open.

The steamboat whistle sounded again, and this time when she stirred, she was alone. She sat up and looked around. Enough light filtered into the room from the deck to see Gabe wasn't there. The whistle blasted again. Captain Sallie must be making sure people on the river knew he was coming.

Maybe they were almost back to the showboat. And she hadn't told Gabe anything. But she didn't know anything that gave her the first idea of who had pushed her into the river. Jacci got up. She ran her fingers through her damp hair. She wished for a comb. Maybe she should hunt up Cameron's room. He would have a comb. She wondered how he had dressed for the show without being able to come to his room on *Little Ruby*. She could almost hear Marelda telling him to make do. That was what she was doing. Making do. She pulled the blanket closer around her.

Where was Gabe?

She sat down in the chair next to the table. There was another chocolate bar in the box in front of her. She'd already eaten one, but she needed something different. An apple. Or a sandwich. Or Gabe.

She looked toward the doorway. Yes, mostly Gabe.

He would be helping Captain Sallie or Mac. That was Gabe.

Always doing whatever had to be done. Finding her. Rescuing her.

Had he really said he loved her? Yes, that hadn't been a dream. She hadn't said the same back to him, but he had to know when she kissed him. She touched her lips. She had almost died without knowing the joy of a real kiss, so unlike the pretend embraces in the dramas they presented on the showboat. So very different.

As if she wished him there, Gabe's shape filled the doorway. "You're awake." He came in and set the lantern he carried on the table.

"I missed you when I woke."

"I was feeding the fire. Mac's getting old to handle those big logs. We sort of took off without any of the crew." He came and sat in the chair next to her. "Are you all right?"

"I am. Now." She reached for his hand. "Thank you for not finding someone else to love before I grew up."

"I could have. To keep you from calling me a confirmed bachelor." He smiled and turned his hand over in hers. "But I would have been that lonesome old bachelor if you had never decided to look on me with favor."

"When I saw you with Winnie, I realized that what I thought was love for a brother was much more than that." Her heart beat a little faster with those words.

"I can't believe you thought I would fall in love with Winnie."

"She's pretty, and her mother told me she was in love with you."

"She's a kid. She doesn't know what she wants."

"She might be a better match for you than me. At least you know her parents." Jacci's throat felt tight, but she made herself keep talking. "She doesn't have a past shadowed by illegitimacy."

"You think I care about any of that?" He frowned and gave

her hand a little shake. "I know you. I don't need to know anything else."

"I wish I could feel that way too. Just let the past slide away like last year's leaves that fall in the river. Let new leaves, new memories fill that place inside me, but I can't. I want to know." She stared at Gabe in the shifting lantern light. "Can you understand that?"

"I don't know if I can completely. My life has been an open book. Even how I've loved you forever. Everybody on the *Palace* knew that but you. Nothing secret in my past."

"Plenty of secrets in mine. All these years I've known there were things about Mama, about me, that Duke refused to talk about. Kelly too. They both wriggled around my questions. Not lying. Just not telling all the truth." She pulled in a breath and let it out. "I think Mama would have told me. I think."

"Does that matter to you?"

"Yes." She hesitated, then went on. "Yes, I think it does. You know, now, even after so many years and my memories of her sometimes almost lost in the fog of the past, I still miss her so much." Jacci stared at the flickering flame in the lantern. "I did see her face, clear as if I'd just had to say goodbye to her yesterday, when I thought I was going to drown."

He tightened his grip on her hand but didn't say anything.

"I thought she was coming to take me to heaven with her." Jacci shut her eyes and could still see her mother's face as she had when she was ready to give up.

"But you didn't go with her." Gabe leaned closer to her.

"No." Jacci smiled and opened her eyes. "That wasn't it. She told me it wasn't my time. That I had to fight. It seemed so real to me. As if she were actually there in the water beside me and almost pulling me back to the surface. That couldn't have really been, could it?"

"I don't know. Aunt Tildy might tell you the Lord sent her to help you."

"But what do you believe, Gabe?" She wasn't sure why, but she needed to know what he thought. If he believed.

He looked at her without saying anything, as though searching for the right words. She waited with a prayer that had no words in her heart.

After a moment, he said, "I believe the Lord answered my prayers to keep you safe, even though I didn't know the danger you were in. I believe he could have sent an angel to help you. I believe I will never stop thanking him for helping you find that way to the surface, however it happened, and then helping me find you."

Tears filled Jacci's eyes. "I'm glad you believe. I believe too. I always have, even when I was angry with God because Mama died after I prayed she wouldn't."

He leaned closer to her and gently rubbed away the tears that had spilled out of her eyes. "Not every prayer is answered as we wish, but here we both are together now, just as I believe the Lord intended. Can you believe that?"

"I can." She turned her head to kiss his hand. Then she sat up straighter, pulling away from his touch. "Do you want to know about Lisbeth and what happened last night?" She shook her head. "Last night. Seems that was weeks ago now."

"I want to know everything." He frowned a little. "But why didn't you tell somebody where you were going?"

"I didn't know where I was going. Lisbeth's lady's maid and another of her servants grabbed me when I was going to my room. They didn't intend to harm me. Frightened me for sure, but after they explained, I agreed to go with them. They said they left a note with Duke. I assume they spoke the truth, since he was there waiting to be sure I had a way back on the *Palace.* Thank you for being there too. Forgive me for not telling you about Lisbeth then, but Duke was right. I needed time to think it all through."

"I'm sorry I was mad, but I was crazy with worry."

"I know. I was going to tell you everything this morning. I went to the top deck to find you, but Captain Dan was at the wheel. And then . . ." She let her gaze drift to the flicker of lantern flame, not wanting to think about the dark water swallowing her.

"And then somebody made sure you didn't tell anybody anything."

She sighed. "I don't understand. Lisbeth told me the senator had promised to leave me alone, but then she said somebody on the boat might mean me harm. That doesn't make sense."

"Just tell me what she said."

Jacci pulled in a breath as she tried to organize her thoughts. After a moment, she started at the beginning and told him about Lisbeth and the plan she made with Kelly and her mother.

Gabe listened without interrupting her.

When at last she had it all told, she said, "So you see, my whole life has been a lie. I have no idea who I really am. The woman I thought was my mother didn't give birth to me. The woman who did carry me and give me life is afraid to claim me as a daughter, and the man who fathered me died before I was born."

"But this Lisbeth, she said she loved you."

"What kind of love is that? To give me away."

Gabe took her hands. "Perhaps the hardest kind."

Jacci stared down at their hands. "I don't know what to think."

"Maybe you shouldn't think."

She frowned at him. "What do you mean? How can I not think about what happened?"

"Maybe you can't keep from thinking about it. The problem is you can't always figure out why other people do what they do."

"But—"

"Wait." He tightened his hold on her hands. "Let me finish. Instead of thinking, just remember your feelings. You had a mother who loved you so much she died protecting you. You have a grandfather who loves you more than he loves the river or acting. And trust me, that's a lot. You have me who loves you more than life itself."

She started to say something, but he turned loose of one of her hands to cover her lips with his fingertips as he went on. "Don't worry about understanding why this or that happened. It happened. And from where I'm sitting, it all sounds as if it happened because of how both your mothers and even Kelly loved you before you were even born." He stood and pulled her up to put his arms around her. "The love. That's what you need to dwell on."

She rested her head against his shoulder and tried to do what he said. Perhaps she should remember that all the lies were for her. To give her a better life.

Two short blasts of the steamboat whistle signaled they were near the landing.

"I better go see if Captain Sallie needs help," Gabe said but kept his arms around her as if he didn't want to let her go.

Jacci pushed back from him. "Go. I'll be fine."

She followed him out on the deck. Captain Sallie had the searchlight on now in order to pull in behind the showboat. She stared over at the other boat. As much as she wanted to do as Gabe said and dwell on those who loved her, the fact was, somebody on the *Palace* did not love her. Someone had shoved her overboard and left her to drown.

Chapter
34

A FEW PEOPLE WATCHED from the riverbank as Captain Sallie maneuvered the *Little Ruby* in behind the showboat. They might have been drawn to the riverfront by the steamboat's whistles or perhaps simply lingering there after the show. Jacci was probably right about Gabe's mother not canceling the performance. Especially since she had no idea why Gabe had taken off back up the river or why Jacci had gone missing.

For all she knew, Gabe might have found Jacci and talked Captain Sallie into taking them back up the river to get married. He had no idea why last night's landing would be better than tonight's for that. Any landing would suit Gabe. He smiled at the thought as he glanced over his shoulder at Jacci.

His smile vanished at the sight of her huddled in the blanket there in the shadows. She was afraid. With reason. Someone waiting on the *Palace* had tried to kill her. Had thought they had. Whoever had knocked her overboard would not be expecting to see her. Could be she should stay hidden here on the *Little Ruby* until they figured out who that was.

Gabe pitched a rope to one of the crew members ready to

help tie up the boat. He could see his mother and father staring across the decks at him. Ma had her fists planted on her hips and Captain looked ready to explode.

Captain Sallie turned off the searchlight and everything was extra dark for a few minutes. Gabe slipped back beside Jacci and pulled her into one of the rooms. "Do you want to wait here with Captain Sallie and Mac while I tell them what happened?"

She shivered and pulled the blanket tighter around her. "You think I should hide?"

"It might be safer." He put his arm around her.

"No." She pulled away from him and stood up straighter. "I'm not going to hide in the shadows like a frightened mouse."

He wanted to grab her close to him and never let her go, but instead he made himself say, "All right, but promise me you won't go out alone on the deck."

"I don't want to live in fear, Gabe."

"And I don't want to lose you. You have to be sensible. At least until we know who pushed you."

"I'll be careful." She tiptoed up and kissed Gabe's cheek. "I promise." She turned from him to look over at the showboat. "I wish it was daylight so we could see their faces. Somebody won't be expecting to see me."

She was right. He did need to watch for a shocked reaction at the sight of her.

At last the walkway plank was secured between the boats, and they came across into a storm of questions. Jacci stayed so close behind him he could feel her trembling. It was one thing to say she didn't want to live in fear. It was another to do it after what she'd been through that day.

Captain Dan stepped in front of Gabe, too angry for words. Ma, right beside him, didn't have that problem. "What in the world do you think you were doing taking the *Little Ruby* off like that without the first word to anyone?" she demanded.

"I'm sorry." He gently pulled Jacci up beside him. She had

scooted the blanket up over her head and wrapped it so tightly around her that little more than her eyes showed. "But Jacci went overboard this morning. I had to find her."

"What?" His mother's face changed from angry to confused as she stared at Jacci. "You fell in the river? This morning?"

"I, I—" Jacci stumbled over the words.

Gabe tightened his arm around her. He lowered his voice so only his parents could hear him. "Somebody pushed her."

His mother's eyes widened, and for once, she seemed to be at a loss for words.

Captain's frown darkened. "Are you sure?"

Jacci nodded slightly. She was trembling against him.

Gabe glared at his father. "Of course, she's sure."

"Ease down, Gabe." His mother held her hand palm out toward him and took control. "Captain, tell everybody the show is over and to be on about their business."

When she reached to pull Jacci away from Gabe, Jacci burst into tears and stepped into her embrace. Tears rolled down Ma's cheeks to match Jacci's. "Oh, my poor child."

Gabe's arms felt too empty. He peered past her and his mother at the people watching them. In the shadows that lay over the deck, he couldn't see a look of surprise or guilt on any of their faces. Of course, in the dim light they might not even realize it was Jacci.

"Where's Duke?" Jacci choked out between sobs.

"He was so upset, I gave him something to help him sleep. We worried his heart might fail," Gabe's mother whispered. "Captain will wake him."

"All right, everybody. Nothing more to see here," Captain ordered. "We'll have a meeting to explain everything in the morning. So off with you."

Some of the people began turning away, but Cameron stepped toward the captain. "We have the right to know what's going on. And not tomorrow. Now." Cameron used his stage voice. "You can't try to push us aside like we don't know something's wrong. What happened to Jacci?"

The others who had been heading back to the dining area to finish up their after-show food stopped.

"It doesn't have anything to do with us." Winnie pulled on Cameron's arm. "Let's go. You said I filled in fine for her in the play."

"Winnie!" Mrs. Loranda said sharply. "Of course we're all worried sick about Jacci." She peered over toward Gabe's mother and Jacci and stepped a little closer. "Is that you, dear?"

"Tell them something, Gabe." Ma turned Jacci away and without a backward glance ushered her toward the steps to their rooms.

Gabe had to make himself not follow them, but his mother was right. Nothing for it but to tell the truth as briefly as he could. "Jacci went overboard. She swam to the bank and we found her."

A murmur went through those listening.

"Is she all right?" Mrs. Loranda asked.

"She will be."

"Praise the Lord," Aunt Tildy shouted in behind the others. She was so short that Gabe hadn't seen her.

"How did she fall?" The question came from several in the group.

Before Gabe could answer, Perry spoke up. "It had to be that broken railing. I knew that was dangerous."

"Yes, dangerous." Gabe looked through the people again. He couldn't imagine any of them intentionally hurting Jacci. Perhaps wanting to kill her. But someone had pushed her and when she went overboard hadn't sounded an alarm to try to save her. "She isn't sure exactly what happened, but she nearly drowned."

"Fortunate she could swim," Cameron said.

"Yes, very fortunate." Gabe stared at him. He didn't look

guilty, but then the man was an actor. Still, why would he try to hurt Jacci? He seemed to want her to be attracted to him. But if he thought it would endear him to Senator Giles to make evidence of the senator's wife's indiscretion disappear forever, would that be motive enough?

Gabe tightened his hands into fists. He wanted to grab him and make him confess if he was the guilty one. Gabe took a breath and relaxed his hands. He might be imagining Cameron's guilt because he didn't like him.

"Come on, Cameron." Winnie grabbed his hand. "We didn't finish our cake."

"You've had enough cake." Mr. Loranda stepped between Cameron and Winnie. "Joey, Reva, we're turning in."

"Galley is closed anyhow," Aunt Tildy said. "Breakfast will come soon enough."

Winnie's father took her arm and propelled her away from Cameron. That seemed to get everybody moving toward their rooms, even though they were still murmuring.

Aunt Tildy came over to Gabe. "I'll fix her some hot cocoa and whatever else I can round up. You too. You is looking a little worse for wear. Might be some of that cake Miss Winnie was so eager for left and a couple of sandwiches."

"I could use some coffee."

"You come on with me to get it," she said. "You is tellin' the truth about our girl being all right?"

"She's tired." He followed her reluctantly as every step took him farther from Jacci, but Jacci was safe with his mother. Aunt Tildy couldn't carry a tray up the steps to their room, not with her rheumatism, and both he and Jacci did need food.

He grabbed Roy, one of the crew of the *Little Ruby*, to take something over to Captain Sallie and Mac. They'd missed the afternoon meal too.

He was glad Aunt Tildy didn't push for more answers as she loaded up two trays with food. She handed one to Roy and waited until he went out the door before she handed the other one to Gabe.

"I'm knowin' there's more to this story than you're telling, but I'm reckonin' you got your reasons for that. You tell our girl I've been prayin' for her ever since I knew she went missing."

"She needed every one of those prayers, Aunt Tildy."

She poked her finger toward Gabe and narrowed her eyes on him. "You did tell her you loved her, now didn't you?"

"I did."

That made Aunt Tildy smile. "And she told you the same."

"Not straight out. But in other ways."

"Huggin' and kissin' can be a fine way of sayin' without words what needs sayin'." She smiled as she gave him a push toward the door. "Well, get on with you before that cocoa I fixed for her gets ice cold."

Up in their rooms, Jacci was wrapped in one of his mother's soft robes. The tear streaks were gone from her face and Ma was combing her hair. Duke, on the divan beside the captain, looked as if he had aged three years in the last two days.

Gabe didn't sit down. His clothes were still damp, with a coating of mud and ash his mother wouldn't want transferred to her furniture. Besides, what he really wanted to do was sit on the floor next to Jacci where he could touch her. Instead, he leaned against the door and drank his coffee while he watched her sip the cocoa.

His mother looked over at him. She didn't shake her head, but Gabe knew the look she sent him. *Wait. Don't talk about what happened until Jacci is ready.*

"Do you remember how I loved to comb your hair when you first came to us?" Ma asked as she gently worked the comb through Jacci's tangled hair. "I had all those boys. Blessings for sure." She shot a smile at Gabe. "But I had always wanted a little girl. You were such a gift, but one who came through sadness."

"I missed Mama, but I always felt so safe with you. With Grampus too." Jacci looked at Duke and then Gabe. "And with Gabe."

"He was a good big brother to you," Ma said.

"No." A corner of Jacci's mouth went up in a half smile. "Never a brother. But a friend. Always a friend."

That made Gabe laugh, which seemed to surprise his mother.

"A brother can be a friend," Ma said.

"I don't know. I've never really had a brother. At least none I knew about." Jacci's smile disappeared. "What did Mama tell you about me? I don't think I ever asked you that. I asked Grampus, but never you." Jacci glanced over at Duke.

Duke sat up straighter and leaned toward Jacci. "I should have told you more."

"I'm not upset with you, Grampus." Jacci smiled at him. "I know you were only trying to protect me."

"I always intended to tell you someday, but it never seemed the right time," Duke said. "Did Irena tell you anything, Marelda?"

"No. She was in such pain. I did hope she would get better and someday trust me enough to share about whatever had happened."

"But she didn't get better." Jacci sighed. "Lisbeth, the wife of the senator who came to the show a couple of nights ago, is my mother. At least, the one who gave birth to me. She and Kelly and I guess Mama too came up with an elaborate plan to keep that secret. They said it was to protect me as much as Lisbeth. Being an illegitimate child is reason for shame. Not only for the mother but for the child."

"That's not the way it should be. A child has no part in what her parents did," Ma said.

"Right or wrong, you know it's true." Jacci twisted around to look up at her and then at Captain Dan.

"Is Kelly your father?" Captain Dan asked.

"Not the one who fathered me with Lisbeth." Jacci smiled a little. "But, yes, my father."

"Not a very good one, if you ask me," Captain said.

"Now, Dan." Ma gave him her warning look.

"If we're telling truths here, then what I said is just another one. The man is a gambler and just pops in and out of Jacci's life as it suits him. That's no way to be a father."

Jacci held up her hand to keep Ma from saying anything. "You're right, Captain. But I think he loves me as much as he can, and I know I've always loved him. But Duke was more my father. That's how Mama wanted it, wasn't it, Grampus?"

"She made me promise that before she died. Even though she loved Kelly." Duke smiled and shook his head. "She said a showman would be better than a gambler, but I don't think she thought it was much of an improvement."

That made them laugh.

"I've loved being part of a showboat family." Suddenly tears were spilling out of Jacci's eyes again. "But I will understand if you don't want me to really be part of your family." She bent her head to stare down at her lap.

Ma pulled her comb back. "What do you mean? Really?"

Gabe set down his coffee and was on his knees in front of Jacci before she could answer. He put his fingers under her chin and raised her head to look into her eyes. "Will you marry me and be part of my family forever, Jacci Reed?"

The room was silent, almost as if all of them were afraid to breathe. Gabe wasn't sure he could until he heard her answer.

Jacci stared at him. "I don't know what to say."

With his fingertips, he brushed tears from her cheeks. He knew why she hesitated. "Why don't you ask Ma and Captain what you should say?"

She blinked back more tears and glanced at them. "What should I say?"

"Yes," they answered in unison.

Then Ma gently stroked Jacci's head. "But it's your answer to give. Not ours. What do you want to say?"

"Oh, yes." She looked back at Gabe, her heart in her eyes. "Never anything but yes."

Gabe stood and pulled her up into his arms. He lifted her off her feet and spun her around. "When?" he asked.

She laughed. "Today. Tomorrow. Anytime."

"We could make it part of the show," Ma said.

"Ma!" Gabe shook his head at her, but Jacci just laughed.

Then the captain brought them back down to earth. "Maybe we should figure out who tried to kill Jacci before we start planning a wedding."

Chapter
35

MARELDA TRIED TO GET JACCI to stay with her the rest of the night, but Jacci looked at Duke and shook her head. He might need her. He was so pale, and when he stood, he had to catch hold of the arm of the divan to steady himself.

Gabe walked them down to their rooms. After Duke said good night, Jacci watched him disappear into his bedroom.

"He'll be all right," Gabe said. "He's had a couple of rough days. Add Ma's sleeping draught to that and no wonder he's a little wobbly." Gabe brushed his lips across her forehead. "You've had some rough days too."

"I just need some sleep," she said. "Nothing will happen tonight."

"It could. If we had a preacher on board." He smiled. "We could have a midnight wedding."

That made her laugh. "I think I need some time for my head to stop spinning first."

"I sort of like the way mine spins when I think about you being Mrs. Gabe Kingston. The sooner the better."

"No preachers on board."

"I've heard ship captains can perform marriages. Maybe showboat captains can too."

"Aunt Marelda would really have her wedding show then. But nothing more is going to happen tonight but sleep." She pushed him away from her toward the door. "Good night, Mr. Kingston."

He laughed before he got serious again. "I'm standing outside your door and not leaving until I hear the lock click."

"Nobody will bother me in here."

"Not if I sit in front of your door all night."

She shook her head at him. "Go get some sleep, Gabe. I'll turn the lock."

After he went out, she put her ear against the door, glad to hear his footsteps moving away and sorry at the same time. She didn't want him to stand there until morning, but he did make her feel safe.

The covers were thrown back on her bed the way she'd left them when she got up that morning. Could that possibly be just one day? She felt she'd lived a lifetime since then. Almost having her life end. Then being found by the one person she most wanted to rescue her. Gabe saying he loved her. Asking her to marry him.

All that happened so fast. She smiled as she thought about him spinning her around in Marelda's sitting room. They'd knocked over two vases and a chair. She smiled as the same joy sparkled inside her again.

Her smile disappeared as she sighed. She couldn't block out the worries. About Duke. About whether she needed to be afraid.

How many scenes would there be in this play? She still had a hard time thinking that someone on the showboat had intentionally pushed her overboard. Maybe they had simply been trying to scare her. But why?

She lay down, still wearing Marelda's soft robe. While she

thought she wouldn't be able to sleep with so many thoughts bouncing around in her head, the next thing she knew, light was sliding through her window and the boat was moving downstream. On to the next landing, the next show.

Her whole life had been to the rhythm of the river. Always moving on to the next place. Somehow that didn't give a person time to dwell on the past. Perhaps, for her, that was good. She couldn't change anything that had happened. She couldn't even change that someone had pushed her in the river the day before, but she could be thankful to still be breathing today. For that she could be very thankful. And for her future with Gabe that surely meant many more rivers to travel and shows to share with the people along the way.

After she dressed, she went out into their small sitting room to find Duke already up and waiting for her. He said his customary morning greeting. "There's my princess. All polished up for the day."

"And my duke the same." She went over and kissed the top of his head. His color was better this morning, although he still looked tired. "I'm sorry to have worried you so these last couple of days."

"I gather little of that was your fault, my dear." He reached out and squeezed her hand. "But don't concern yourself about me. I'm a tough old codger. You are the one we need to be sure is safe so you and Gabe can start a new showboat family."

"I need to get used to the idea of being married first."

"The way to parenthood, that two becoming one, is a treasured part of marriage. While I wasn't the best husband to your grandmother, I am aware of the joys of the marital union."

"You're making me blush." Jacci rubbed her cheeks.

"No need at all for that. You and Gabe won't need any coaching for those scenes." He lifted his eyebrows and smiled at her.

"You're being wicked. Now hush." She shook her head at him, then looked toward the door.

Duke guessed her thoughts. "Gabe was here earlier, but I told him you continued in dreamland. He left, albeit reluctantly."

She turned away from him to hide the smile that came unbidden at the thought of Gabe. "Is it too late for breakfast?" she asked. "The sun must have gone behind some clouds, so I can't tell what time it is."

"Not so late." He snapped open his pocket watch. "A quarter past ten. If you want, I can go get us a tray to eat here."

Before she could decide if staying out of sight in their rooms would be wise or cowardly, a knock sounded on the door. She hated how her throat tightened and her heart speeded up as she watched Duke rise to see who was there. She had told Gabe she didn't want to live in fear, but maybe that wasn't possible until she knew who had pushed her off the boat.

"Oh, Duke." Winnie sounded a little breathless. "Sorry. I ran up here. Marelda wanted you to know Captain Dan is having a meeting in a few minutes." She caught her breath as she peered past Duke at Jacci. "About, you know, what happened. Actually, she told Joey to come, but my mother said I should. So I could apologize for not being very nice last night. I sometimes say things I shouldn't. I really am glad you're all right, Jacci."

She talked fast as though she needed to get her rehearsed lines out before she forgot them.

"Whatever you said, I didn't even hear it, Winnie. So, it's forgotten."

"And forgiven?" She went up on her tiptoes as she waited for Jacci's answer.

"And forgiven," Jacci said.

"Whew. Mother will be relieved." She dropped back down flat-footed again. "But come on. We need to get to the dining room. That's where the captain told everybody to come."

"If you feel better staying here, they can have their meeting without us," Duke said.

Winnie spoke up. "Marelda said you needed to be there." The girl slid her gaze over to Jacci again. "You know how Marelda is. When she wants something, she expects it to happen."

Duke frowned. "I doubt if she wants Jacci to come that badly."

"Come on, Grampus." Jacci put her arm through his. "We can get something to eat while they're talking." She had to face the others sometime. Better now than later in the greenroom when everybody staring at her would make her too nervous to remember her lines.

While Duke went back to his room to get his cane and hat, Jacci followed Winnie out onto the deck. A wind was kicking up the water and dark clouds hung to the west. The boat rocked a little under their feet.

"Gabe will have to work to keep the boat steady." Winnie looked around at Jacci. "He's at the wheel or I'm sure he'd have come for you himself. The way he always does."

Jacci decided to ignore the hint of anger in the girl's voice. "He's guided boats through plenty of storms."

"Storms can upset all sorts of things."

"We can hope this one won't be that bad. People don't come out for the shows as well when it's storming."

"But the show must go on. No matter what, right?" She didn't wait for Jacci to say anything. "We nearly had a full house last night. They loved the show."

"It's good that you were able to fill in as Penelope."

"I flubbed a line or two, but Cameron covered it." Winnie shrugged. "I think I did pretty good with no rehearsal time. I can do it again tonight if you aren't up to it after your adventure yesterday."

Adventure was an interesting way to put almost drowning, but since Winnie wasn't the one in the river, Jacci supposed she could think that. Maybe she should just let Winnie do the part for the rest of the season. That might make everybody happier, including Jacci. She and Cameron had seemed to lack a convincing romantic connection in their last few performances.

"We'll see what Aunt Marelda thinks," she said.

"Is she really your aunt?" Winnie asked. "If she is, wouldn't that make Gabe your cousin?"

"She's actually been more like a mother to me than an aunt." Jacci mentally shook her head at the thought. Here she was adding another mother.

"Then that would make Gabe your brother."

"He's not my brother or my cousin. Aunt Marelda just took me under her wing after my mother died." At least one of her mothers, but then she changed that in her thoughts. The mother she'd lost when she was five was her real mother. It didn't matter if Lisbeth did declare love for her, actually did love her. She had never been in her life. But to that way of thinking, maybe Marelda was her real mother. At least she would soon be her mother-in-law.

"Oh. I guess nobody ever told me about that."

"It was a long time ago."

"Yeah. Cameron says what's happened before doesn't matter all that much. It's what is ahead that's the most important."

"Cameron is all about his future. He intends to be a star."

"That doesn't sound all that bad. Being a star." Winnie sighed. "Better than just doing flips on a riverboat."

"You're very talented, Winnie. And not just in acrobatics. I hear you were great singing the other night."

"Yeah. With Gabe. But he's not interested in an encore with me. He can't see anybody but you." She shrugged again. "Cameron says I'm lucky not to get tied down with a showboat actor."

Jacci could hear the unhappiness behind her words. She did feel sorry for Winnie, but she couldn't be sorry Gabe wasn't in love with her. "Be careful around Cameron. One thing for sure with him, he's all about himself."

"Yeah. Gabe said the same thing." A little anger flashed in

her eyes. "Both of you act like I'm just a kid who doesn't know anything. I'm seventeen. My mother was married when she was my age." She jerked open the door to the dining area and went in ahead of Jacci.

Duke, trailing along behind them, caught up with Jacci. "Oh, the trials and tribulations of youth."

"At least she didn't almost drown yesterday," Jacci muttered.

"True, Princess. Very true." Duke held the door for her. "Let us go in to see what our captain has to say."

Duke took his accustomed chair at one of the tables, but Jacci slipped back behind the counter. Aunt Tildy was ready with a hug as she whispered in her ear, "Captain will get to the bottom of this."

But he didn't get to the bottom of anything. Captain Dan talked. Everybody listened. Nobody had seen anything. Nobody heard anything. And no one confessed to giving Jacci a shove off the boat. Nobody even looked the slightest bit uneasy, as far as Jacci could tell. Then again, most of the ones listening to the captain were actors. But this wasn't like the plays they put on, where the villain always got caught and made a dramatic confession.

The villain of this piece obviously wasn't admitting anything.

Chapter

36

THUNDERSTORMS WITH HEAVY RAIN accompanied them down the river. The gloom of the day seemed to settle dark moods on everyone. Even those who ventured out of their rooms to the common areas had little to say other than grumbles about the weather.

Jacci stayed in the galley helping Aunt Tildy with the afternoon meal.

"Folks has got the grumpies today," Aunt Tildy said.

"It's the weather. Sun comes out, everybody will be smiling again."

"I ain't sure we can blame these clouds hanging over us as having the first thing to do with them clouds up in the sky." She gave Jacci a look up through her eyebrows. "I'm thinkin' it has more to do with knowin' somebody on this boat had killin' on their mind yesterday. Maybe still does."

"They could have thought I wouldn't fall off the boat. That the railing would catch me." She did want to believe that. It was too hard to wonder who among these people she had considered her showboat family all season would have had killing on their mind.

Marelda and Captain Dan had checked on her. Gabe was still in the pilothouse. Others in the cast had told her they were glad she was all right. She couldn't keep from wondering who might be putting on an act. Duke stayed in his chair in the kitchen instead of going back to the room to nap. He and Aunt Tildy were ready to protect her.

Jacci had to smile at the thought of either of them holding off someone threatening her. Then again, Duke had his cane and Aunt Tildy had her butcher knives. Plus, Jacci had the little paring knife she was using to peel apples for Aunt Tildy's pies. She shook her head. Even though her legs and arms still felt weak after her struggles in the water, some of what happened seemed almost part of a play instead of reality.

When the calliope music started, Jacci missed being the one up on the hurricane deck holding an umbrella over Marelda while she played. But the music cheered up Jacci, as it did every time she heard it. It wasn't soft and easy on the ears. Calliope music was loud and melodic in its own peculiar way. It chased through the air for miles to demand attention. She imagined people pausing in whatever work they were doing at the sound and then hurrying to finish up their chores to come to the showboat.

When the boat slowed to ease into the landing, Jacci stayed where she was in the galley instead of rushing to the main deck to watch the local people waving and shouting a welcome.

Cameron spoiled her happy thoughts when he came into the kitchen full of gripes. "Marelda says the rain is easing up, and that we have no excuse to forgo that stupid parade. I wouldn't be half surprised if a rogue flash of lightning streaks down and blasts one of the horns. Wouldn't that be something? The whole showboat cast felled in one swoop."

"Maybe you can carry the triangle instead of a horn today," Jacci said.

"An idiotic instrument. Ding. Ding." He rolled his eyes. "Besides, that thing has to be the next best thing to a lightning rod. Right along with those cymbals you sometimes carry, Jacci."

Aunt Tildy spoke up. "Jacci ain't goin' paradin' today. She's helpin' me, seein' as how my rheumatism is kickin' up. So's Duke's." She glanced over at him, and he looked up to nod before turning his attention back to the magazine he was reading. She looked back at Cameron. "We're stayin' aboard, rain or shine."

"How nice to be in the favored circle." He stepped closer to Jacci. "Are you going to be Penelope tonight?"

"I hear Winnie did a fabulous job for me."

"You don't have to tell me who told you that. Winnie has an elevated opinion of her acting ability."

"She ain't the only one," Aunt Tildy muttered under her breath.

Cameron acted as though he didn't hear her. "She told me you weren't certain that you were doing the show tonight."

"She did ask about it when we talked this morning. She seems eager for the part."

"Well, if you are letting her take your place, you need to do a walk-through rehearsal with her before the show tonight." Cameron blew out a sigh. "Just because I'm the only actual professional on this floating stage, everyone shouldn't expect me to cover for them."

"I guess we're fortunate you're part of the cast." Jacci didn't bother hiding the hint of sarcasm that leaked into her voice.

Aunt Tildy laughed, but Cameron simply took it as his due.

"I suppose I have little choice but to do the best I can with whoever plays the part." He headed for the door.

"Gabe has the right idea about that troublemaker." Aunt Tildy put her hands on her hips and stared after him. "Give him the heave-ho at the next big town and let him go about making his fortune without givin' us a headache."

"He can be charming when he wants to be," Jacci said. "He's just in a bad mood today like everybody else around here."

"I ain't in no bad mood." Aunt Tildy turned her stare on Jacci and then looked at Duke. "I'm guessing Duke over there ain't either. Are you, Duke?"

"Not when I see Princess back with us. That's not to say concern for her ongoing safety is not darkening my thoughts somewhat." Duke looked up from his magazine. "By the way, Princess, did you advise Tildy about your upcoming marriage to a redheaded prince?"

"Well, if that don't bring a little joy back into the air, I don't know what does. The boy must work fast once he decided to get his love boat moving." Aunt Tildy laughed and Cameron was forgotten.

Jacci did let Winnie play the role of Penelope again that evening. Gabe had trailed along with her while she went through a prickly rehearsal with Winnie before the show. The girl resented Jacci's every correction or suggestion. But she did a fair performance. Jacci watched from the wings, ready to whisper a line for her if Winnie seemed stuck. Jacci and Duke did a song together but left off the dancing.

But the song was good and got better when Gabe came onstage to join in on the chorus and then went down on one knee to propose to her all over again in front of the crowd. The audience seemed to hold their breaths as she kept a straight face and pretended a dramatic hesitation. Then when she did smile and say yes, some whoops sounded and they got a standing ovation. After the show, Gabe told her Marelda would want them to play that scene every night since the people loved it so much.

Later, as they gathered for the after-the-show coffee and sweets, the proposal seemed to bounce all the earlier gloominess away. Everybody was slapping Gabe's back, congratulating him and giving Jacci their best wishes. Even Winnie, after being noticeably prodded by her mother, told Jacci she was happy for her.

Cameron caught Jacci alone and gave her a very theatrical kiss on the cheek. "It seems you have exchanged your chance for the spotlight on stages that matter for a dreary life of riverboats and country bumpkin audiences."

"I love life on the river." Jacci was glad Gabe was across the room and hadn't heard Cameron, although from the frown that slipped across his face, he had seen the kiss.

"Yes, well, do try to stay on the boat and out of the river." He said it lightly, as if she had dived into the river for a pleasurable swim. "And please, please, please, if I must continue to be Sterling, please come back and be Penelope."

"I thought Winnie made a good Penelope."

Cameron made a face with a bare shake of his head. "Adequate, I suppose. But if you are truly planning to relinquish the role to her, we will need more rehearsals. Pronto."

Gabe came across the room to put his arm around Jacci.

"I have to give you kudos, Gabe," Cameron said. "That was quite a showstopper scene, proposing to your girl onstage." His smile looked a little sly as he went on. "Taking a chance like that in front of a crowd. What if she'd said no?"

"Then I guess besides being brokenhearted, I would have looked more than a little foolish." Gabe laughed. "Except on a showboat, you can always work whatever happens into a new scene. The crowd would have loved it, either way."

"True enough. Forever ad-libbing, I suppose." Cameron started to turn away.

Gabe stopped him. "Have you had any more contact with Senator Giles?"

Cameron looked back at Gabe with no hint of a smile now. "That would be more than a little difficult, with me floating down the river in the opposite direction from where he was headed, now wouldn't it?"

Gabe wasn't smiling either. "I heard you and Perry spent some time at the tavern yesterday before the show."

"Who told you that?"

"Nothing stays secret long on a showboat."

"And no reason for it to be secret. I haven't seen any rules posted against taking a break from the same faces on a showboat after the obligation of pretending to be part of a band. May heaven help me if I have to do that for very much longer." Cameron made a face. "At any rate, Perry intended to make a little extra change by entertaining the locals there with his dummy act. I went along for the novelty of it. Considered doing a dramatic reading, but determined none of the tavern patrons would have understood a word of Shakespeare."

"You might be surprised by how much the people know," Gabe said.

"I sincerely doubt it." Cameron laughed.

Gabe's body was stiff against her as Cameron walked away. "Do you think he might have pushed you?"

"Cameron?" Jacci was surprised by the idea. "Why would he do that?"

"Why would anyone?"

That question stayed with Jacci, spoiling the fun of the show and disturbing her sleep. So many unanswered questions in her life, and even when one answer surfaced, that answer seemed to do nothing but lead to more questions.

chapter

37

THE NEXT MORNING JACCI was up at the first dim light of dawn. All night she had been continually jerked from sleep by dreams of falling in the river. Awake, she hoped to pull up better thoughts and find a way to push aside those demons of the unknown that brought fears to mind.

She didn't want to be afraid of the river. She loved the river. She didn't like wondering if this or that person here on the *Palace* might mean her harm. The way the cast, who came aboard for a season, somehow became a family while they traversed the rivers had been one of the best parts of being on a showboat.

This year had somehow felt different from the beginning. Cameron, with his inflated opinion of himself and his disdain for the rest of the cast, had been a shadow over the season from the first performance. He and Gabe never established any kind of working relationship, which made rehearsing the shows awkward. Gabe was the director, but Cameron wasn't willing to take any direction from him.

Then Perry with his dummies he carried around with him as

though they were real children was more than odd. Jacci shook her head at that thought. Actors were known for eccentricities, and she could delve back through the years and come up with plenty of odd.

When she really looked into what felt wrong about this season, she had to admit thinking Gabe was falling in love with Winnie was what had kept her out of sorts. The poor girl had obviously come aboard besotted with him. Jacci supposed she should be sorry for Winnie, but the girl was young. She'd find someone else to love. Jacci just hoped she didn't transfer her feelings for Gabe over to Cameron. Perhaps Jacci should suggest Marelda talk to Mrs. Loranda.

Jacci shook her head. Didn't she have enough worries without adding Winnie to them? She went over to the window to peer out. Fog hung over the river after the rain the day before, but the boat was moving. She wanted to be up on the hurricane deck beside Gabe at the wheel, peering through the fog with him. She loved how the fog could shroud the riverbanks and wrap around the *Palace*, even though she knew the danger of boats feeling the way downriver. But she had promised not to go out on the deck alone.

She sighed. She'd made the promise, but she hated the confined feeling. She had never liked being closed up in small rooms. Kelly told her that probably came from those early years with her mother on the *Mary Ellen*. He claimed Jacci was always hiding in this or that cranny on the steamboat instead of staying in the tiny maid's room on the bottom deck.

Her last memory of being on the *Mary Ellen* popped into her mind. She saw the man attacking her mother again. She felt the gun in her hand and how it jerked when she pulled the trigger. The man's face was burned in her memory as he fell. At least Lisbeth had said Jacci didn't kill him.

A soft knock on the door pulled her away from those unhappy thoughts. She looked toward Duke's room. His snores showed he was still sleeping. Another couple of taps sounded on the door. It might be Gabe trying to find out if she was awake.

She stepped over to the door. "Who's there?"

"It's me, Winnie."

Jacci couldn't imagine what Winnie might want so early, but she unlocked the door and pulled it open. "Is something wrong, Winnie?"

"No, no," the girl said quickly. "Except for Cameron. You know how he is. He's been giving me nothing but grief about playing Penelope. He said I did good that first time and now he does nothing but gripe and say I can't do anything right." She blinked back tears. "I'm doing the best I can."

"I watched last night. I thought you did fine."

"Thank you." Winnie rubbed her hands up and down her arms. "But I need Cameron to think so. Would you come go over some of those moves again? On the stage. I know I wasn't the nicest yesterday when we were doing that, but I'll pay better attention this time."

"It's very early. The stage will be in shadows unless we light lanterns."

"Oh, it won't be that dark. Please, Jacci."

"Is Cameron going to be there too?"

"I don't think he's up yet."

"I'm surprised you are." She gave the girl a look.

"Well, I want to get that practice done before he gets up and I knew you always get up early."

"All right."

Jacci thought about waking Duke, but he needed his rest. Besides, she wouldn't be on the deck alone. She'd be with Winnie and perhaps back before he woke up. It wouldn't take that long to go through the scenes that seemed to be giving Winnie problems.

A little early morning light sifted in from the open theater doors in the back, but the shadows were deep on the stage, just as Jacci had thought they would be.

"Maybe we should light a lantern." Jacci turned toward the greenroom.

"No." Winnie's voice sounded different. Tense. Scared. "Don't move."

"What?" Jacci looked back at her and blinked. She couldn't believe her eyes. With both hands Winnie held a gun pointed at Jacci. The sight of the gun took her breath.

"I'm sorry, Jacci. I don't want to do this, but he says I have to. That they'll hang me if you tell them I pushed you." Winnie's hands started shaking. "I don't know why I pushed you the other day. I was just so mad that Gabe wanted you and not me. I didn't know the rail would break. But he said they would say I did, that I knew it was weak there. I didn't. Really, I didn't."

Jacci's heart pounded up in her ears. She forced out some words. "He? Who is he?"

She ignored Jacci's question. "I just want you to understand."

"All right." Jacci took a breath and tried to sound calm. "Since you didn't aim to knock me overboard, why didn't you stop the boat?"

"I would have. Really, I would have if you'd come up to the surface, but you didn't. I watched. He said it was too late to help you. You'd already be dead, and I couldn't change that by sounding an alarm. He said I'd hang if I told them you went overboard. That they would know I pushed you." The girl's hands were still trembling. "You understand, don't you?"

"I want to. Why don't you put down the gun and we can talk about it some more?" Jacci tried to block away the fear as she took a step toward Winnie. "Even if you didn't aim to push me in the river then, what about now? Someone will hear the gun."

"No. He says he can fix that. Make it look like an accident. He saw me push you, but he says he can make it work out all right for me if I do what he says. He gave me the gun."

"You mean Cameron?"

"Cameron?" Winnie looked confused.

Jacci scooted another step closer to the girl.

"Stay back," Winnie ordered, but her hands were shaking so much Jacci didn't know how she kept a grip on the gun.

"It doesn't matter what he's told you." Jacci stood still and spoke softly to the girl. "I know you don't want to shoot me, Winnie. Just give me the gun and we can work this out." She held out her hand toward her.

"You're right. I can't do this." Winnie's face crumpled as tears flooded her eyes. "I can't shoot you." She dropped the gun and collapsed on the stage, sobbing.

Jacci snatched up the gun. All at once, she was that little girl again pulling the trigger, watching that man fall. As if the gun burned her hand, she slung it away. It clattered on the floor between the seats.

A laugh came from the balcony. Then a different laugh came from the seats at the back of the auditorium. Strange laughs, yet oddly familiar.

Jacci stared toward the sounds. She couldn't see anyone in the shadows.

"Excellent scene, girls. Not quite as I directed, but excellent nevertheless."

The voice sounded almost like Gabe. Almost, but it wasn't him. "Who are you?" Jacci demanded.

"Your audience, of course. My dear Winnie, I fear you flubbed the scene. You were supposed to pull the trigger, you know."

The voice changed to Cameron's. Again almost, but not quite.

Winnie raised up to look out toward the voice. "I should have never listened to you."

"Famous last words."

This time Jacci knew. Perry used that voice for his dummy

Cindy. She didn't know what Perry was up to, but she wasn't staying to find out. She ran toward the greenroom.

"Mustn't leave before we play the final scene, Princess." Perry stepped out from behind the curtain and grabbed her. His laugh sounded as though it came from the other side of the stage.

Jacci tried to jerk away from him. "Turn me loose."

"I think not yet." He shoved the end of another gun against her side.

She stood still. "What do you want, Perry?" She tried to keep her voice from trembling but failed.

"Poor dear," he said. "Some scenes are hard to play. Do you realize that few women know how to swim?" He didn't wait for her to say anything. "This last scene wouldn't have been necessary if that had been true for you after our dear little Winnie played her part so perfectly the other day."

"You told her to push me?"

"Not in so many words, but it is sometimes so easy to plant ideas into other people's heads. And not that hard to weaken a railing. Just as throwing one's voice can certainly confuse the actors, or in this case, the actresses." He laughed, this time his own laugh, right against her ear. "I'm guessing you didn't know I could be such a great mimic."

"I knew it wasn't Gabe."

"Did you now? Oh, but don't you wish he really was here?"

Winnie had finally gotten to her feet. She was up on her toes and looked ready to run.

Perry kept one arm tight around Jacci and pointed the gun at Winnie. "I don't think you should leave just yet, dear Winnie."

The girl looked too scared to move.

"Why are you doing this? Did the senator pay you?" Jacci asked.

"I am sure Senator Giles will be grateful, but no, he hasn't commissioned this act. He claims to have made a promise to his unfaithful wife. A promise that came too late for my brother."

Jacci's head was spinning as she tried to make sense of Perry's words. "Your brother? I don't understand."

"I suppose not. You were very young. But I did admire my older brother so much. He was always ready to applaud my ability with voices. But then he was hired by the senator to rid him of a certain pesky problem prior to that promise the rogue made to his wife."

"Your brother was the one who killed my mother?"

"Your supposed mother, I assume. And you are the child who killed my brother."

"Lisbeth told me I didn't kill him. That he didn't die."

"Not then. But he forever suffered dreadful pain. All because of a little girl with a gun. I found him after he hung himself from the rafters of our barn. Right then, I made a promise to his departed soul that I would take ruthless revenge were the occasion to ever present itself. Some years have since passed, and I had almost given up on ever finding that child who killed my brother. But then the senator came to our play. It seemed meant to be when I realized why you looked so familiar. Me being on this showboat. You being the spitting image of your mother. Your actual mother and not the supposed one."

"Your brother was trying to kill me."

"No, no. He had no plans to hurt you. He was merely to take you from that woman and ensconce you in an orphanage in some far state where you could never be an embarrassment to our good Senator Giles, who feared you would upend his visions of political success."

"You can't get away with this." Jacci tried to sound confident. As long as he had the gun pointed away from her, she might twist away from him, but she couldn't let him shoot Winnie. She stared at the girl, trying to send her silent messages to be ready to run.

"Not a worry for you. I came up with the perfect final act. Dear little Winnie is going to shoot you. She is so very jealous of you, and then in abject despair, she will take her own life. That's a drama worthy of our dear Cameron's acting abilities, don't you agree?"

Winnie's eyes got bigger. "I would never do that."

"It matters not what you would do. It's just like in a play. All we have to do is convince the audience that it could be true. Just as I convince them my little darlings are actually speaking when I do my act." He changed to Corky's voice. "Now time to get on with it."

"Run, Winnie!" Jacci shouted as she tried to jerk free.

Perry managed to hold on to her as he fired the gun. The shot went harmlessly toward the ceiling. He turned the gun toward Jacci.

Winnie didn't run. Instead, she somersaulted toward them and kicked his arm. He dropped the gun and staggered backward. Jacci hooked her foot around one of his legs and they both fell. His head bounced against the stage floor as she landed hard on top of him. She scrambled away from him before he could recover.

Winnie grabbed the gun off the floor.

Chapter
38

THE SILENCE ON THE STAGE was deafening. Jacci scooted farther from Perry and stood up, trying to watch both him and Winnie at the same time.

Winnie pointed the gun at Perry. Her hands weren't shaking now.

"Not exactly as the scene was supposed to go." Perry sat up and rubbed his head. "I do think I saw stars." He looked at Winnie and sounded amused as he said, "Are you going to shoot me, dear little Winnie?"

"She won't shoot you as long as you stay back." Jacci eased behind Winnie.

"You sound very sure of that, Princess, but then you aren't the one holding the gun."

Jacci ignored him as she talked to Winnie. "Somebody will have heard the shot. They will be here any minute."

"Why shouldn't I shoot him?" Winnie's voice was without feeling. "If I'm already going to hang for pushing you in the river, a person can't hang but once."

"You didn't aim to kill me, and I didn't die."

"But she wished you had." Perry pushed up off the floor to stand in front of them.

"No, I don't believe that." Jacci looked from him to Winnie. "It's going to be all right."

"What if he tries to get the gun?" Winnie said.

"Then you'll have to shoot him. It would be self-defense."

"How can that be? I no longer have a gun." Perry held his hands up. "But then my brother didn't have a gun either."

"He had a knife."

"Winnie doesn't care about that." He leaned toward them. "Do you, dear?"

Jacci and Winnie backed away from him.

He laughed the way he did for Corky in his comedy acts. Somehow that made the laugh even more dreadful. "You know you don't have the nerve to pull the trigger, Winnie."

"Don't listen to him." Jacci looked around. Why wasn't someone storming into the auditorium to help them? The rushing river water must have covered the sound of the gunshot.

"Give me the gun, Winnie, and go for help." She stepped up beside Winnie.

"Yes, give Jacci the gun. She can shoot me the way she shot my brother." Perry sounded as if he were repeating lines from a script he found boring. He curled his left hand and peered down at his fingernails. "Of course, she might shoot you too. In self-defense, as she says."

Winnie looked sideways at Jacci and tightened her grip on the gun. "No."

Jacci wasn't sure which of them she was directing her refusal toward. "We can go for help together."

"And leave him here?" Winnie's voice was shaky.

"What a dilemma," Perry said. "It is true. I could find another weapon and just hole up in here and shoot whoever comes toward me. You did throw a gun out into the seats, did you not, Princess?"

Suddenly a voice called from the back of the theater. "There you are, Winnie. Ma's been looking for you. She needs your help with a costume."

Joey walked out of the shadows toward the stage. "Is that a gun you've got? What's going on? You practicing for a new drama?"

"Joey." Winnie turned her head to look at him. "Go back."

Perry rushed Winnie and grabbed the gun. He shoved the girl aside and once again pointed the gun toward Jacci. "Sometimes one has to improvise."

Jacci whirled away from him, but she couldn't outrun a bullet.

"Nooo." Winnie leaped in front of Perry.

The gun's report echoed in the empty auditorium as Winnie fell. Then Gabe was there tackling Perry and knocking him to the ground.

"Winnie!" Jacci rushed to where the girl lay on the stage. Blood was soaking her blouse.

"I don't want to die." She looked so scared. "Is that how you felt when you fell in the river?"

"Yes." The wound looked to be high on Winnie's shoulder. "But I didn't die, and you won't either." She looked at Joey as he jumped up on the stage. "Get your mother."

After a panicked look at Winnie, then at Gabe jerking Perry's arms behind him as he held him down, Joey took off in a run.

"You're going to break my arm," Perry gasped.

"Good." Gabe's voice was a growl. He looked over at Jacci. "Are you all right?"

"Yes. Thanks to Winnie." Jacci smoothed the girl's hair back away from her face. She wouldn't think about before. Only about the now when the girl had jumped between Perry and her. She looked so very young. So very scared.

"You aren't going to tell?" Winnie whispered.

"I have to tell, but I'll tell this too."

"They'll hang me." Her voice was so low that Jacci more read her lips than heard her words.

"Shh. The river has its own brand of law."

Then people were rushing in from all sides. Mrs. Loranda took Jacci's place beside her daughter. Winnie was weeping again. Marelda and Duke were there. Gabe jerked Perry to his feet and handed him over to a couple of the crew with instructions to lock him in a room on *Little Ruby*.

Gabe pulled Jacci to him in a hug and then almost immediately pushed her back to look at her face. "Are you sure you are all right?"

"I am now." She leaned against him.

He rested his cheek against her head for a moment before he pushed her back again. This time he was frowning. "Why did you leave your room? You promised not to go out on the deck alone."

"I wasn't alone. Winnie said she wanted me to help her with the part of Penelope before Cameron got up. I didn't think I had any reason to be afraid of her."

He looked surprised. "Did you need to be afraid of Winnie?"

Jacci sighed. "It's a long story and not one easy to tell." She looked over where Marelda and Mrs. Loranda were kneeling beside Winnie. "First we need to get Winnie somewhere they can take care of her."

In the Lorandas' rooms, Marelda and Aunt Tildy patched up Winnie. The bullet hadn't done any real damage as it went through the top of her shoulder. The blood spilled made it look worse than it was.

Captain Dan ordered them to lower the anchors and hold at the edge of the river. He needed time to hear what had happened before they went on to the next landing.

Propped up in her mother's bed, Winnie confessed to pushing Jacci into the river. "I'm so sorry." Winnie stared across the room at Jacci. "I didn't think you'd go through the railing. Honest, I didn't."

A moment of terrible silence followed her words before Mr. Loranda said, "You didn't yell for help."

"No. Perry told me not to." Winnie looked frantic. "He said that it would be too late to save her anyway and being quiet was my only chance not to hang."

Mr. Loranda stared at her a moment before he dropped his head into his hands without another word.

"Oh, my dear girl." Tears rolled down Mrs. Loranda's cheeks.

Mr. Loranda looked up at Captain Dan. "We will understand if you turn Winnie over to the sheriff in the next town."

Winnie started sobbing. She looked so like a pitiful child that Jacci couldn't help feeling sorry for her in spite of what she had done. Jacci crossed the room to sit on the bed beside her. When she handed her a handkerchief, Winnie simply looked at it as if she didn't know what it was. So Jacci gently wiped her cheeks.

That seemed to bring on another surprised silence. Finally the captain said, "All right, Jacci. Tell us what happened this morning."

Jacci gave Winnie's hand a squeeze before she stood up to face the others. She thought of her mother then and how she had said Jacci should never let anyone know she was the one who had shot the man that attacked them. Jacci had kept that promise except for Duke. She let her eyes touch on Duke, who sat behind the others.

She took a breath and went through it all. How it was her instead of her mother who had shot the man on the *Mary Ellen* years before. How that man was Perry's brother. How the man hadn't died but later committed suicide because of ongoing pain due to the wound. How Perry pledged revenge. How he felt that revenge was meant to be when he realized who Jacci was. How he must have manipulated Winnie to achieve his purposes. How Winnie had listened. How very young Winnie was.

Jacci glanced back at Winnie, who had stopped crying and was staring at her. "Perry confused her thinking." Jacci reached down and touched her hand again.

"Confusion shouldn't lead to murder," Marelda spoke up.

"And it didn't. She didn't shoot me. Instead, she saved my life. Twice. First, when she knocked the gun out of Perry's hand and then later when she jumped between Perry and me to stop the bullet he intended for me. She could have died doing that."

"So what are you saying?" Captain Dan asked.

Jacci looked around at the faces watching her. Marelda. Captain Dan. Mr. and Mrs. Loranda. Duke. Last, she fastened her gaze on Gabe. She was very aware of Winnie behind her. "Perhaps that two times of saving my life might make up for the first time of nearly taking it."

When no one spoke, Jacci went on. "We're on the river." She looked straight at Captain Dan. "You can decide what happens here."

Gabe spoke up before his father could answer. "Are you saying you want to forget what she did?"

"Not forget. It's hard to forget. But forgive." Jacci looked at Gabe.

"Forgiveness doesn't mean a person doesn't have to pay the consequences for what they do," Captain Dan said.

"But there can be mercy," Marelda said softly. "If Jacci is willing to offer that to Winnie, shouldn't we as well?" She looked from Jacci to Gabe.

"If Jacci can forgive, then I will try to do the same." Gabe held out his arms to Jacci, who crossed the room to rest in his embrace.

"But what about Perry?" Duke spoke up.

"Him, we'll turn over to the authorities. In the next town that has a sheriff." Captain Dan stood up. "Now let's get on down-river. We have a show to do tonight. You take the wheel, Gabe. The Lorandas and your mother and I need to talk some more."

Jacci climbed up to the pilothouse with Gabe. She needed to be close enough to touch him.

The crew pulled up the anchors. *Little Ruby* began belching smoke and the boats moved on down the river. The sun peeped out from behind the clouds to spread golden light down across the river. The air had a fresh washed scent and the wind was gentle on Jacci's face.

"What's our next landing?" Jacci asked.

"Fox Hollow." Gabe pulled her in front of him and took hold of the wheel. "I'm sure they have a church there. Want to get married this afternoon?"

"It's not that easy, is it? Don't we have to get a license or something?" She leaned back against him. He felt so solidly strong.

"I don't know. First time for this old bachelor. This marrying bit."

She laughed. That felt good too. Air in her lungs. Laughter on her tongue. "First time for me too."

"Then I guess we'll have to figure it out. But today sounds like a fine time to do that."

"Not today. Aunt Marelda would never go for that."

"No. She wants us to get married on the stage."

"You proposed onstage," Jacci reminded him.

"And you said yes onstage."

She was quiet a moment. "How far are we from Dove Creek?"

"About six stops. Maybe seven."

"Then that's where I want to get married. In that church where Mama is buried. Maybe Kelly can come." She leaned back against him, swaying a little with him when he turned the wheel. "Then we can get married again onstage the way you proposed again onstage."

"You do know Ma wants us to do that proposal scene every night the rest of the season."

"Even after we marry?"

"Probably then she'll want both. The proposal and wedding." He kissed the top of her head.

"You have to make the people happy."

"Especially when it's Ma."

"You know, she's my mother too in so many ways."

"But I'm not your brother. I have never been your brother."

"You are not my brother." Laughter bubbled up in Jacci again. "In spite of what I might have thought when I was five, you have never been my brother."

"I'm glad you are finally figuring that out."

"But you are my love. My forever love." She twisted around to kiss him.

"Watch out. You'll make me forget I'm guiding this big old showboat and run us aground. Captain would never forgive me if that happened."

She turned back toward the river and put her hands over his on the wheel. "Keep her moving down the middle of the river, Captain. Folks are waiting around the bend for the next Kingston Family Show."

"The show must go on," he said.

She looked out at the water rolling along with them. "I do love the river and how the water keeps moving. Taking you somewhere. To the next stop. The next show."

"Always moving on," Gabe said.

That was life too. A person needed to keep hold of the good while moving on to the next scene. She sent up a prayer of thanksgiving that Gabe would be the lead character with her in all her next acts.

Turn the page for a sneak peek at
another compelling historical fiction by

ANN H. GABHART

AVAILABLE NOW

Revell
a division of Baker Publishing Group
www.RevellBooks.com

Available wherever books and ebooks are sold.

Chapter

1

FEBRUARY 27, 1925

"You will never be completely well. Tuberculosis leaves its mark on your lungs."

"I know, Doctor." Rose Meadows looked at Dr. Bess Halvechs across the desk from her. "But I am so much better. I've been walking about the grounds and manage the stairs to the dining room instead of eating in my room."

"Yes." Dr. Bess's forehead wrinkled in a frown. The doctor was devoted to her patients at Rest Haven Sanitarium and worked tirelessly to help them keep breathing. "You have made progress, Rose. Excellent progress, but as you know from your time here, relapses do occur. Even if that doesn't happen, you will continually struggle with some aspects of the disease."

Rose didn't argue with the truth of the doctor's words, but she didn't have to be cured. She merely had to be well enough to leave the sanitarium and go get her daughters. "I have accepted that, but with care, I can manage."

"With care." The doctor fingered the stethoscope that hung

around her neck as though she might get up and come around the desk to check Rose's lungs right then. Dr. Bess was older than Rose, one of the first women to be accepted into a medical school. "Those are the words we must consider. With care. Do you have someone willing to give you that care?"

Rose met the doctor's eyes. "My oldest daughter will be fifteen next month. Old enough to help." Her care wasn't something she wanted to thrust on Calla, but the need to be with her two girls again burned a hole in her heart. She hadn't seen them for almost two years.

"But how will you survive, dear Rose? Do you plan to hire your daughter out to bring in money?"

"Hire her out?" Rose shrank from the thought. She couldn't imagine sending Calla off to a factory job or to be a maid. "No, no. She can help me fashion hats. And there's my husband's army pension."

"A paltry amount, I fear. Not enough for rent and food, and while you can still practice your milliner skills, you won't have the strength to work steadily as you did in the past. Do you have family who might help you?"

"No." Rose's heart sank. "As I told you, my husband died during the influenza epidemic. My parents passed on years ago."

"No sisters or brothers?"

"None living. A sister and brother died at a young age."

"So many troubles in this day." Dr. Bess clucked her tongue. "But, Rose, I cannot in good conscience release you unless you can give me some assurance that you will have a proper place to stay. You can't live on the street or in some hovel where you would be exposed to the damp and not have the proper clean air and sunshine."

"I'm well enough that my girls wouldn't be at risk if I am with them. Isn't that right?"

"Your sputum is negative, but that doesn't mean you aren't

prone to a relapse." She paused and studied Rose before she went on. "Stay with us a bit longer. Get stronger for those girls of yours."

"But I think they need me now. I got a letter from Sienna. Something about it didn't sound right."

The letter was only a few lines. *I am fine. My teacher is nice. I get enough to eat. I am learning to listen.* It read like a school assignment, with sentences dictated by the teacher. The only part that seemed truly like Sienna was the tiny sketch of a bird for the dot above the *i* in her name and a drawing of a long-tailed mouse on the bottom of the page.

Sienna had been entranced by anything in nature since her first baby giggle at the sight of a butterfly. But it didn't have to be something pretty to catch her eye. She liked spiders and once picked up a garter snake. When it bit her, she hadn't cried. Instead, she gently put down the snake and apologized for scaring it.

"Sienna is the younger one, right? How old is she?" Dr. Bess asked.

"Nine," Rose said.

Dr. Bess looked sympathetic. "At that age, she surely lacks letter-writing skills, don't you think?" She waited for Rose's nod and then went on. "Has your older daughter written to you about any problems?"

"No, but she might not if she thought it would upset me." Calla's last letter had only been a couple of paragraphs, the words stiff somehow, as though she had nothing good to write. "I just have the feeling something is wrong. Mothers have an innate sense about their children."

"Of course they do. You do." Dr. Bess stood up and came around the desk to touch Rose's shoulder. "But your children need you well. Not sick. And worry will only make you worse. Your girls are being cared for at the orphanage. They will surely be fine for another month or so."

"It's been so long already." The doctor being right didn't make it any easier to accept.

"I know, but it's best not to rush things. Let's see how you're doing in a few weeks." Dr. Bess patted her shoulder. "Now run along and find a chair outside on the sun porch. Fresh air and sunshine are the best medicine we have."

Rose did as she was told, even though every inch of her screamed to go pack her few belongings to leave. But reality kept poking her, bursting her balloon of hope. She had no car, no house, no way. When she'd left the girls at the Home for Girls, she'd thought it would be for a few weeks, no more than a couple of months, but the months had piled one on top of another.

She hadn't gotten well. She'd gotten worse in spite of the bed rest and hours in the sun. The doctor warned her it would take time, but Rose hadn't expected it to be a slow slog through mud. That was how it had felt. As if each movement was an effort she could barely make. For a while, she thought she wouldn't fight through it, that the mud of tuberculosis in her lungs would swallow her. At one time, she was so worried she'd never see Calla and Sienna again that she wrote them each a final letter about how very much she loved them. The letters were still in the envelopes in her suitcase, ready if the need arose.

But now she was finally better. Still weak. Still with a cough but no streaks of blood in her sputum. Her hands trembled so that piecing together the hats she'd made for some of her fellow patients was a struggle, but she had finished the work.

She lengthened her stride as she went down the corridor toward the door that led out onto the porch. Her breath stayed even, surely a sign she was in remission. She was so pleased she wasn't getting short of breath that she forgot to look away before she caught sight of herself in the mirror at the end of the hall. Why they left it there to mock the patients, or guests as they preferred to call them, she had no idea.

She hated that mirror. In her room a quick peek in the small wall mirror above the washstand was all that was needed to be sure her hair was combed. But this mirror blasted her whole reflection back at her. The first time she'd passed the mirror, she had looked behind her to see whose reflection it might be. As if some strange woman was beside her and her own image wasn't there.

Since then, she always quickly turned away from the mirror, but today she stopped and stared at the frail woman staring back at her. Her cheeks were hollow and dark smudges circled her eyes. Gray streaked her honey-brown hair.

Could she really persuade Dr. Bess that she was ready to leave, ready to care for her daughters?

She sent up a prayer. Could she persuade herself that she was?

ACKNOWLEDGMENTS

WRITING A BOOK IS A JOURNEY along a winding road of many words. I always want to find those very best words to bring my characters to life and help my scenes become pictures in my readers' heads. Thank you for being one of those readers. You can't know how much I appreciate your choosing to pick up one of my books to let my story come to life in your imagination.

Once I write the words, then many more steps must be taken before you can hold my book in your hands. I have a wonderful team at Revell Books to guide that process. I appreciate my editor, Rachel McRae, helping me make the story the best it can be. I thank Barb Barnes for her careful editing polish that helps me avoid stumbles along my story road. I owe much gratitude to the art department for the eye-catching covers of my books. I appreciate Michele Misiak and Karen Steele for all they do to get those books out in front of you, the readers. Many others do their jobs behind the scenes—assistants, proofreaders, copywriters, salespeople, and more. I thank you all.

My agent, Wendy Lawton, is a gift with her continual encouragement and how she shares my joy of story.

And I'm blessed with unfailing support from my wonderful husband and family.

Last of all, I humbly thank the Lord for blessing me with stories and granting me the joy of sharing them with you. Praise God from whom all blessings flow!

Ann H. Gabhart is the bestselling author of *When the Meadow Blooms, Along a Storied Trail, An Appalachian Summer, River to Redemption, These Healing Hills,* and *Angel Sister*, along with many Shaker novels. She and her husband live on a farm a mile from where she was born in rural Kentucky where she enjoys time with her family and taking her dogs, Frankie and Marley, for walks. Learn more at www.anngabhart.com.

"What a jewel of a story. Reminded me of *To Kill a Mockingbird.*"
—Lauraine Snelling,
award-winning and bestselling author

Ann H. Gabhart tells a story of hope and love in the face of desperate circumstances during the Great Depression.

Revell
a division of Baker Publishing Group
www.RevellBooks.com

Available wherever books and ebooks are sold.

One young woman must stand up
for freedom—and perhaps find her
own in the process . . .

Orphaned in the cholera epidemic in Kentucky's early nineteenth century, Adria Starr was rescued by a slave. Now at nineteen, she's determined to find the courage and strength she needs to buy his freedom.

℞ Revell
a division of Baker Publishing Group
www.RevellBooks.com

Available wherever books and ebooks are sold.

Meet
Ann H. Gabhart

Find out more about Ann's newest releases, read blog posts, and follow her on social media at

AnnHGabhart.com

Smart House
THE COMING REVOLUTION IN HOUSING

+
512
-63
88

RALPH LEE SMITH

Smart House

THE COMING REVOLUTION IN HOUSING

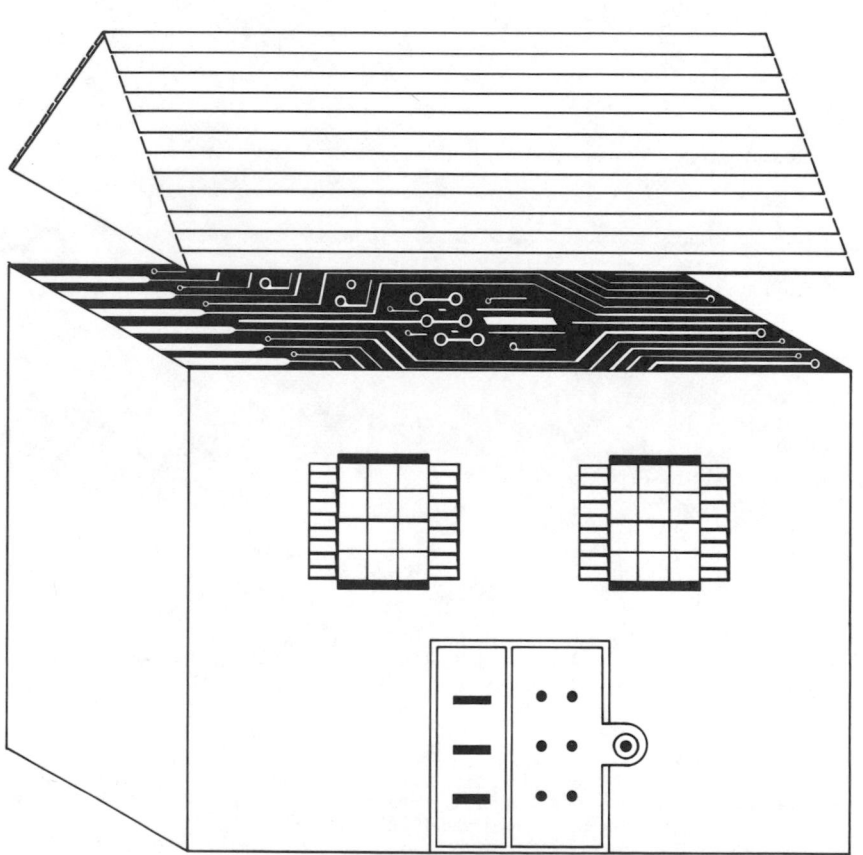

GP PUBLISHING
Columbia, Maryland

DISCARDED
WOODBURY UNIVERSITY LIBRARY
7500 GLENOAKS BOULEVARD
BURBANK, CA 91510

GP Publishing, Inc.
10650 Hickory Ridge Road
Columbia, MD 21044
(301) 964-6253

©1988 by GP Publishing, Inc.
All rights reserved
Published 1988
Printed in the United States of America
93 92 91 90 89 88   5 4 3 2 1

Library of Congress Cataloging-in-Publication Data

Smith, Ralph Lee, 1927-
  Smart house.

    1. Dwellings—Automation.   2. Dwellings—
Electronic equipment.   I. Title.
TH4812.S63   1987   643'.6   87-21262
ISBN 0-87683-918-9
ISBN 0-87683-919-7 (pbk.)

The term SMART HOUSE, together with the associated star symbol that appears in Figure 1, is a registered service mark of the Smart House Development Venture, Inc. In this book, the term Smart House, with initial letters in caps, is used to describe the intelligent home energy and communications system being developed by the Smart House Development Venture under this service mark.

The following organizations and individuals have generously given permission to reprint their copyrighted materials: *EPRI Journal*, for the quotation on pp. 11-12, from "The Smart House: Wired for the Electronic Age," by Taylor Moore (November 1986). *Potomac Electric Power Company*, for figure 18. *National Association of Home Builders National Research Center*, for the illustrations and photographs in figures 4, 7-11, 17, and 23. *NAHB National Research Center and Spyder Webb*, for the illustrations in figures 2, 3, 5-16, and 19-22. *NAHB National Research Center and Marchant and Faulkner*, for the artist's drawing in figure 1.

Contents

1
The Coming of the Smart House

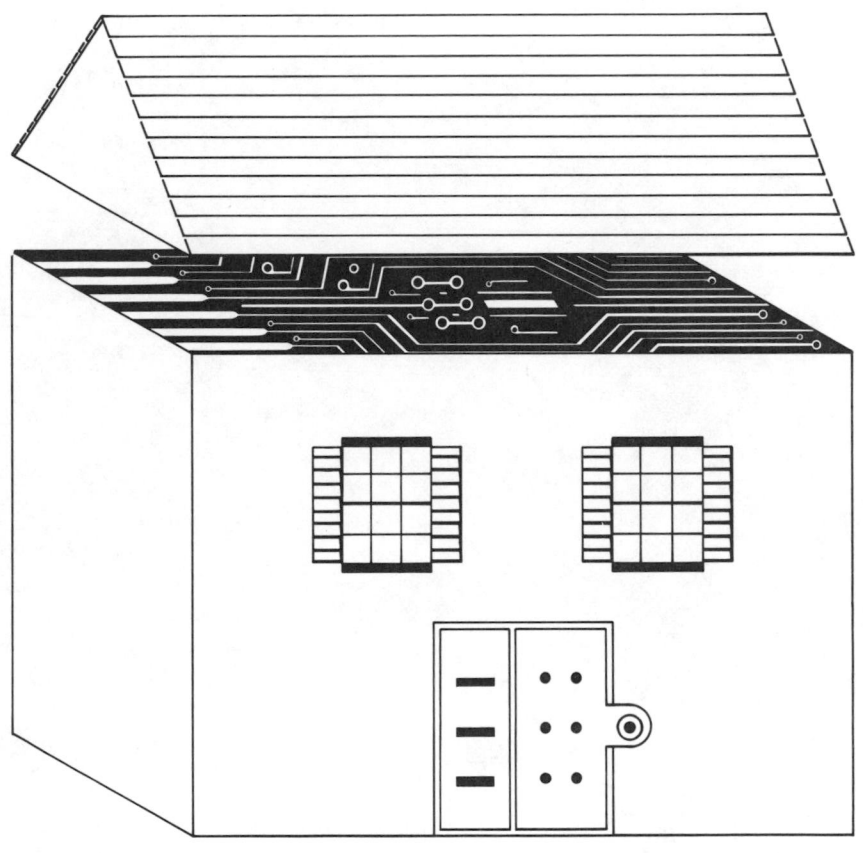

In April 1987, ground was broken for the world's first Smart House. With the building of this house (Figure 1), one of the last major frontiers of the information age was breached. In the 1990s, semiconductors, the tiny components used in computers, communications equipment, television sets, VCRs, and advanced electronics, will enter the wiring of homes. Entirely new wiring systems and new hardware will accommodate the chips.

Within ten years after this ground breaking, it is estimated that more than 8 million American and Canadian homes and light-frame buildings will contain intelligent wiring systems. Home devices and appliances will contain semiconductors— "chips"—that will enable them to communicate with the wiring network, with each other, and with the outside world. Homes will have caught up with nearly everything else in our society that employs electrical and gas energy—they will become "smart."

As with other major technological developments of the electronic age, the coming of the Smart House will have many impacts on American life, not all of which can be known or

Figure 1. Artist's drawing of the first Smart House

foreseen. Some forecasters stress the Smart House's ability to offer levels of convenience and comfort that are unavailable in homes today, although such conveniences are part of broader capabilities and a broader story.

Smart House Scenarios

Taylor Moore, writing in the *EPRI Journal*, provides the following look into the near-future, which he describes as "one of many possible scenarios that may be commonplace to new homeowners in the 1990s":

> Half an hour before you rise, the water heater turns on to reach just the right temperature in time for your shower. Bedroom and bathroom lights turn on as the radio wakeup alarm sounds. The rooms you use at that hour have been preheated. The coffee maker comes on while you're in the shower; when you finish, you're greeted by a full pot, and the television is on with your favorite news show.
>
> During the day, as it warms up outside, the air conditioner keeps the indoor air comfortable if anyone is home but avoids running during a two-hour afternoon peak period when electricity rates are the highest; the dishwasher that was loaded the night before runs itself early in the morning. A security system keeps watch while you're away but decides not to call the police when a neighborhood kid tosses the evening paper against the front door.
>
> When you return, recorded telephone messages are played back over the bedroom speakers while you change, but soothing music fills the den where you relax. A flashing light on a video screen announces that dinner in the microwave is ready. As dusk falls,

outdoor lights turn on, the garden sprinkler gives the begonias a drink, and during commercials on the evening news you watch a display on the screen of the day's energy consumption and costs.

Before you retire, the screen provides a status check of all outside doors and locks. The house turns off all nonessential appliances that were on, save for the reading lamp over the bed. Room occupancy sensors automatically light the hall and kitchen if you venture out of bed for a nocturnal glass of milk.

Figure 2 is a drawing provided by the Smart House Development Venture, Inc. The Venture, which is described in the next chapter, is serving as the coordinating group for the creation of Smart House hardware and appliances. Various capabilities of the Smart House are keyed to numbers in the drawing.

1. When an appliance is plugged in, it identifies itself to the network as an item that is eligible to receive current. This communication between the appliance or device and the network is achieved by means of a chip in the appliance that is capable of communicating with a chip in the network. Unless and until an appliance containing a chip that can communicate this information with the network is plugged in, there is no current available at the outlet. A baby sticking its finger, or a metallic object, into a Smart House outlet will not be harmed because neither the child nor the metallic object contains a communicating chip.

2. The Smart House instantly cuts off current to the hair dryer that has been accidentally dropped into the bathroom basin. The capability of cutting off power instantly wherever there is an overload, a short-circuit, or an accidental grounding, as is the case with the hair dryer, exists for every outlet in the home.

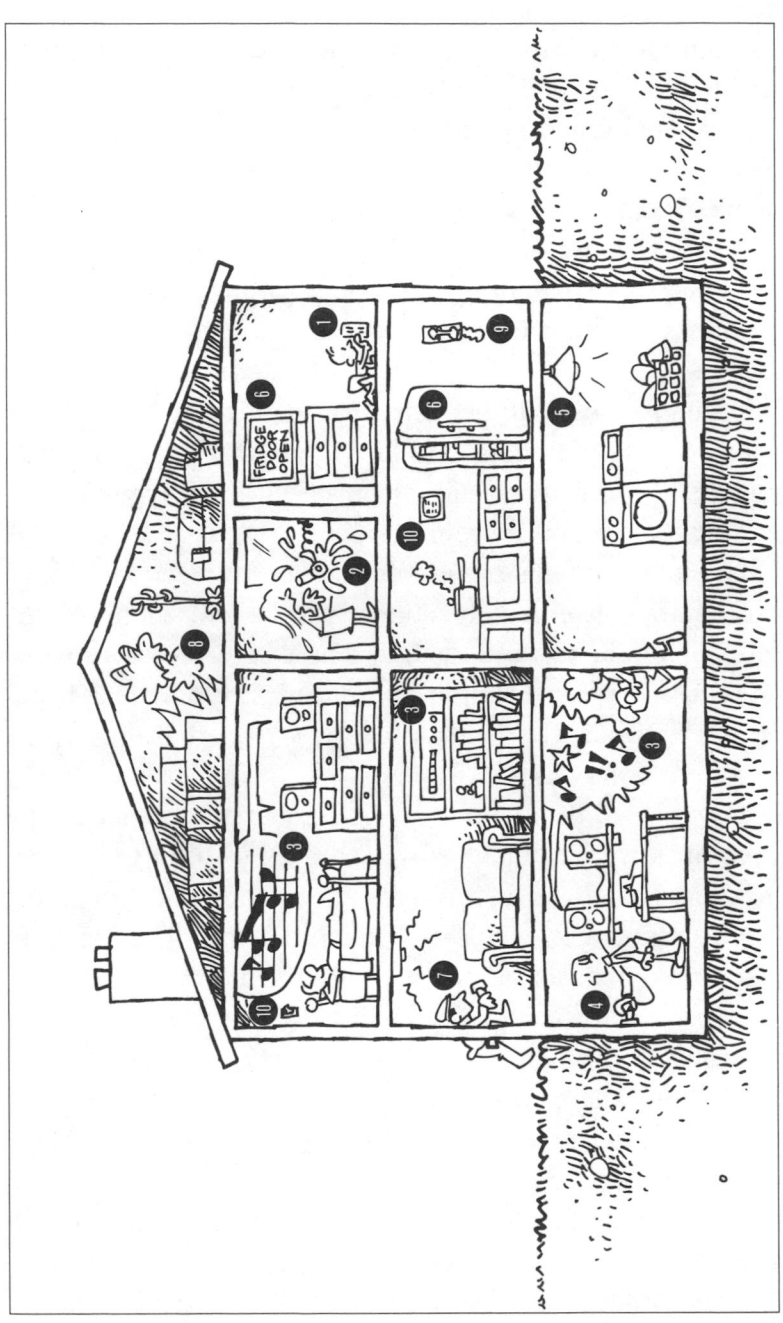

Figure 2. Smart House capabilities

3. Stereo speakers can be plugged directly into any outlet in the house without running additional wiring. In the drawing, the stereo receiver in the living room is providing music to speakers located in both the bedroom and the basement. In case of fire, anything being played on the speakers could be overridden by a spoken alarm.

4. Any Smart House device can be plugged into any outlet in the house. A person in the basement can unplug the stereo speaker and plug a telephone into the same outlet to make a call.

5. The Smart House can be instructed to turn off lights when a person leaves the room, and turn them on when the person reenters. Similar instructions can be given to regulate the temperature in unused rooms.

6. Smart House systems can employ one or more video display screens in convenient locations, which will monitor the status of appliances and devices. These screens can provide an alert when, for example, the refrigerator door has been left open, ovens or stove burners have been left on, or the front door is unlocked.

7. Sensors placed throughout the house can activate an alarm when an intruder enters. However, a dog walking through the house at night, or an inveterate midnight snacker heading for the refrigerator, would not trip the alarm. The location of sensors need not be permanently fixed. When planning a trip or vacation, homedwellers could even rent a package of sensors and plug them into any outlets.

8. Sensors anywhere in the house can also detect smoke or fire. The same or other sensors can be used to regulate heating and cooling.

9. All systems in the house can be activated or controlled remotely by telephoning instructions from any location. At an appropriate time before leaving work, a Smart House

owner could instruct the air-conditioning system to bring the house temperature to a comfortable level and could tell the oven to turn on and start cooking dinner.

10. All appliances and devices attached to the system can be given instructions from a switch or other control device anywhere in the house. A switch, or even a telephone, placed next to a bed can be used to lock all doors and windows at night, and to instruct a stereo system to wake you up and a coffee maker to start operating in the morning. Downstairs heat can be raised a half-hour before you awaken.

The arrival of Smart House is the result of two major forces—one a "push" and one a "pull." The push is provided by increasingly serious shortcomings in the wiring of today's homes. The pull is provided by the inevitable course of developments in modern electronics. Increasingly, electrical devices are becoming smart, and increasingly, they are being linked together in communication networks.

In this book, to secure a clear view of Smart House, we will begin by looking at these two converging forces, and we will review the obstacles that retarded the coming of Smart House despite both the logic and the power of these forces.

We will then explain in basic terms how the Smart House works. In the process, we will answer a few questions about new communications technologies and how they work.

Finally, we will review and comment on some likely uses and benefits that can be foreseen. This review will take account of the contribution the Smart House can make to more comfortable living. It will also consider some capabilities of the technology that have broader social value and should be given prominence in planning and development.

2
The Wire Mire

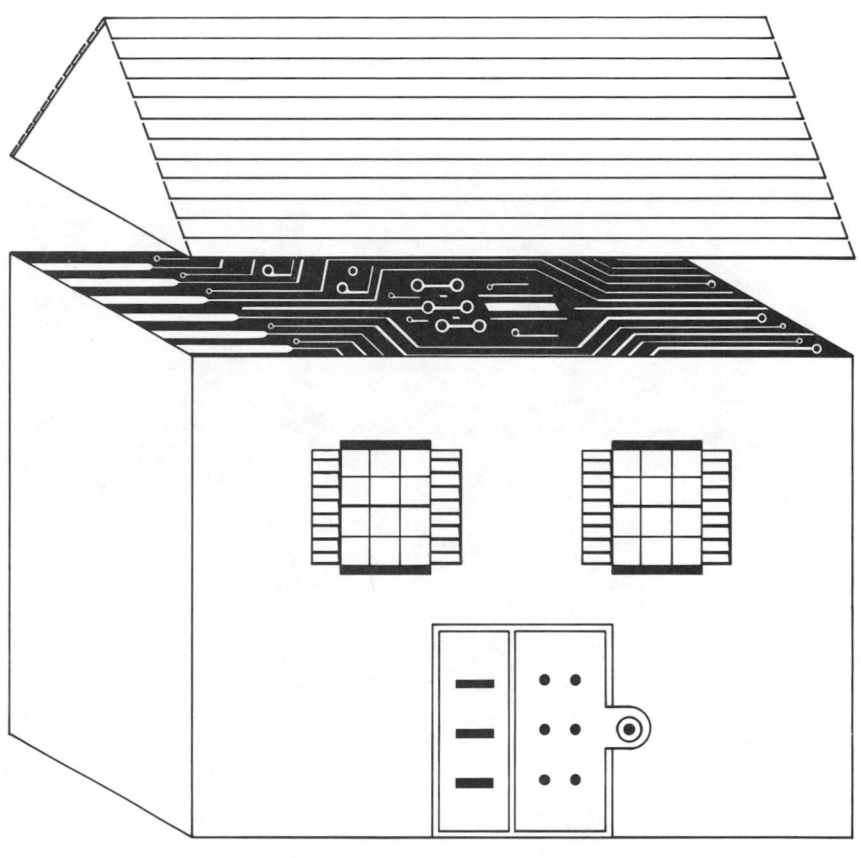

Virtually the only basic thing that has been done to the wiring of homes since Thomas Edison's day has been to proliferate the number of wiring systems that snake around the walls, and to increase the number and variety of devices that are attached to them. The result has been an ever-increasing tangle of spaghetti on both sides of the walls. Increasingly, the consequences involve more than the offending of orderly minds.

Within the past twenty years the tangle has been steadily growing. Homes which had one telephone just twenty years ago are now likely to have three or four. Some homeowners have installed security systems, requiring a whole new wiring network. Twenty years ago only a small percentage of homes had cable TV; now half of all homes have it. All of this is in addition not only to the basic house wiring, but to supplemental wiring for such items as doorbells and thermostats.

The prognosis is for continuing and unrelenting pressure on the wire mire. Consumer electronic products continue to be introduced. Meanwhile, to create a better balance of demand on their facilities, electric utilities are already experimenting with time-of-day pricing, which can be facilitated by new and better

electronics in the home. The natural gas industry is conducting research on new portable appliances that could be plugged in at various places around the home, to outlets that combine a flexible gas pipe with electronic controls.

In addition to being increasingly obsolescent, the wire mire is growing more costly to create and maintain. A building contractor must usually call in several different wiring contractors to install the various systems, at a cost in duplicated activity that goes into the price of the house. The results achieved by this additional effort and expense are nothing great. No matter what is done, outlets never seem to end up where they are needed. Rooms are rearranged, telephones are moved to other tables, stereos end up in corners where there are no outlets. Festoons of octopus extension cords blossom along the baseboards. Circuit breakers pop when two appliances on the same circuit are turned on.

That things are still done this way is not a commentary on the limits of modern science. It is a commentary on the limits of where modern science has been able to reach. With the coming of Smart House, some well-established modern technology will enter an arena where it can really be of help. The tangles of wire will be replaced by a single cable incorporating several types of wires, including a coaxial cable for TV, standard wires for electrical energy, smaller wires for telephones and other low-voltage devices, and additional wires to accommodate digital signaling. This cable will be installed in new homes when they are built.

Universal outlets that will accommodate any appliance will be installed throughout the house. When the appliance is turned on or put into use, semiconductors in the house wiring system

will communicate with semiconductors in the appliance and connect it to the appropriate circuit.

Problems of Electrical Safety

Another issue associated with today's wiring is electrical safety.

A great deal of thought, care, and effort has gone into reducing the hazards of having electrical wiring and electrical products in homes. These efforts have long been formalized in the activities of groups such as Underwriter's Laboratories and the National Electrical Code Committee of the National Fire Protection Association. The latter group maintains and updates the National Electric Code, comprising electrical safety guidelines that are widely accepted and followed.

Two important innovations of recent times have been the adoption of the third-wire ground and the introduction of devices called ground-fault circuit interrupters (GFIs).

Many people can remember when appliances such as washing machines were connected to a nearby water pipe with a wire and a clamp. After World War II this gave way to three-pronged plugs and outlets, with the third prong being a ground contact. In 1956 the National Electrical Code required such plugs and receptacles for laundry areas, breezeways, and garages, and in 1959 the coverage was extended to include exterior outlets, areas around kitchen sinks, basements, workshops, and open porches. However, a three-pronged outlet will accept a two-pronged plug with no ground. It was not until 1984 that the Code required most appliances and hand-operated tools to be grounded.

Ground-fault circuit interrupters are the second important safety innovation. GFIs are devices that shut off power to a circuit when current is being diverted from the circuit directly to the ground by some conductor such as a human body. The amount of current required to trip a GFI is much less than that required to trip a circuit breaker or blow a fuse.

When the skin is wet, the body's resistance to the conducting of electric current can drop to as little as one percent of the normal resistance of the body when dry. In 1971 the National Electrical Code was amended to require GFIs around swimming pools and in outdoor receptacles. Meanwhile, electrical appliances often used in bathrooms, such as hair dryers, shavers, curling irons, and "Water-piks," continued to proliferate in homes. In 1975 the Code was amended again to require GFIs in all receptacles in bathrooms. In 1987 the Code was amended again to require a GFI for at least one receptacle in the basement, and GFIs for receptacles in the kitchen that are within six feet of the sink and above the level of the counter top.

There are three problems associated with GFIs. One is that they should be manually tripped monthly to ensure that they are working properly. Many people do not bother. The second is that GFIs will sometimes trip themselves for no identifiable reason, to the great annoyance of homeowners. The third is the problem that is technically referred to as an unsafe failure mode. This means that if for any reason the GFI does *not* function when an emergency occurs, the victim is not protected from the continuing delivery of the current.

Despite these problems, a 1976 Department of Commerce report argued for the adoption of GFIs, stating that "requirements of ground fault protection on potentially dangerous outlets can save hundreds of lives annually." The GFI situation and the Department of Commerce's comment reflect both the importance of the electrical safety problem and the frustration of those who are doing their best to deal with it. A 1979 Consumer Products Safety Commission report estimates that 1,500 accidental electrocutions occur each year in the United States. CPSC also estimated that in 1983 there were more than 4,000 emergency room treatments for injuries, primarily burns, due to electric shock involving consumer products; an unknown addi-

tional number were treated by private physicians. Another CPSC document estimates that, in 1982, 192,000 residential fires, comprising 28 percent of the total, were caused by "electrical ignition." These fires resulted directly in 1,000 deaths and 13,000 injuries. Property loss was estimated at $923 million.

The toll is caused by two technical deficiencies of today's system. The first is that every branch and nerve of the wiring network is always activated. Electrical power is always present, up to every outlet and through the outlet into every cord of every lamp and appliance right up to the switch, even if the lamps and appliances are turned off. A child who sticks a bare metal object into an outlet will always receive a shock. The second problem is that the system usually has no way of knowing when something attached to it may not be performing properly. A malfunctioning appliance, power cord, or plug can be the cause of fire or death before a fuse will blow or a circuit breaker will trip.

Both of these problems are easily addressed if modern electronic technology is built into the wiring system. What is required is as follows:

- No current should be present at any outlet until an appliance is plugged in and turned on to receive the current. When nothing is plugged in and turned on, the outlet is dead.

- Anything that is plugged in and turned on should be able to *communicate* with the power distribution system.

- As long as the appliance is plugged in and turned on, its chip and the system chips should *remain in continuous communication*. Variance in the behavior of the appliance can then be communicated to the system, which can cut off current to that outlet.

Requirements of this type are met in many modern electronic systems. With the coming of Smart House, they will finally be met in the home.

Home Automation and Networking

Meanwhile, as we have noted, a second pressure was being brought to bear on home wiring systems—the simple but forceful pressure of electronic progress. The coming of Smart House is directly related to the increasing capability and decreasing price of semiconductors and microprocessors—that is, chips. Semiconductors provide communications and/or control capabilities. Microprocessors, which are a type of semiconductor, provide computing capability. Together they are virtually transforming the world, and in the long run there is no way that today's creaky home electrical system could escape.

Beginning in the early 1980s, semiconductors and microprocessors began to provide control and limited intelligence in a growing number of products, devices, and systems, including home entertainment products, microwave ovens, hot water systems, and heating, ventilation, and air-conditioning systems.

At the same time, semiconductors and microprocessors were increasingly employed in networks designed to link various kinds of products, devices, and systems together. In the commercial world, the trend included the introduction of so-called "intelligent buildings." In these buildings, intelligent wiring systems are installed at the time of construction, giving all networks access to communications systems and capabilities that would otherwise be beyond their reach.

It was of course understood that private homes, as well as commercial buildings, could be made smart. However, the problems were complex. In the commercial world, there were compelling bottom-line reasons for linking office machines together, and methods and protocols had been worked out to make

communications among various devices possible. But chips in home appliances typically did not communicate with each other.

By the late 1970s some firms began to interest themselves in this frontier, and a small home-automation industry began to take shape. By 1985 home control devices and systems topped $300 million in retail sales. The systems and their capabilities are very diverse, but they generally employ central controllers, along with computer screens or push-button panels, to perform such functions as turning lights on and off and controlling the operation of appliances.

Formidable difficulties nevertheless remained. Systems with certain types of capabilities could use the existing wiring in the home as a communications link. Or, as an alternative, additional capabilities could be secured by partially rewiring homes with a network that was in addition to the existing home wiring. But neither approach offered the full range of capabilities that could be achieved by pursuing an approach that included, as parts of a unified plan, a new home wiring network and appliances designed to connect to it.

Unfortunately this, the most comprehensive solution, and in the long run the only really logical one, also entailed the greatest set of obstacles to its realization. This is the tale we will tell in the next chapter.

3

Breaking Down the Barriers

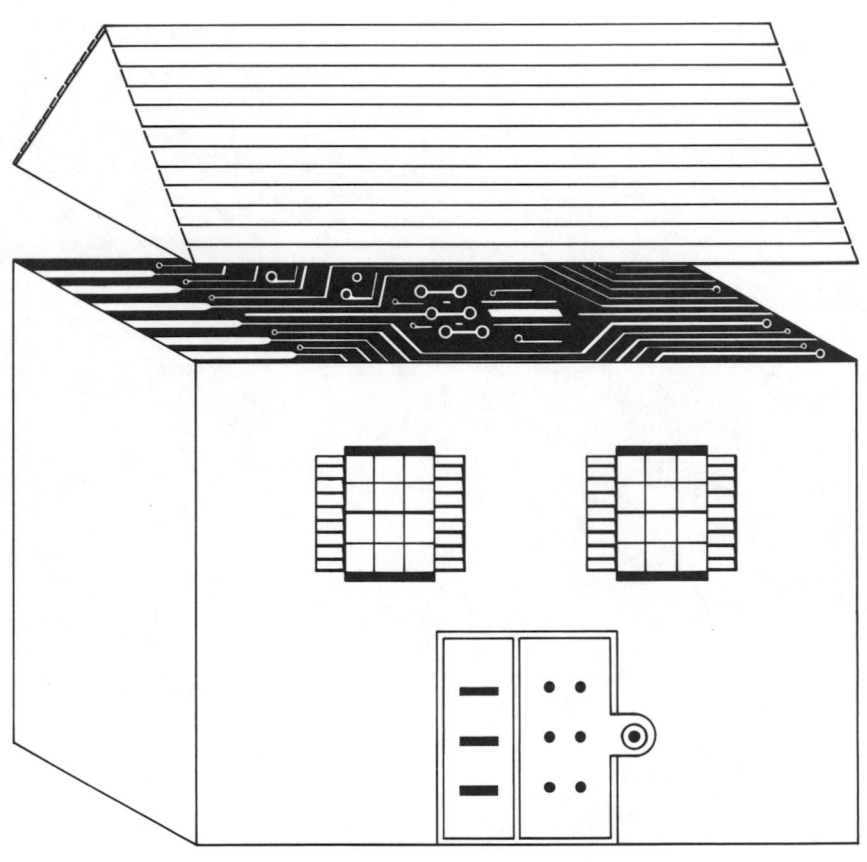

Ordinarily, an entrepreneur who is convinced that there is a niche or demand for a new product or technology, who has the assets, and who is willing to take the risks, can simply proceed to manufacture the product and put it on the market.

With Smart House, both the usefulness of the technology and its acceptability to consumers seem hardly subject to question. Yet the path from initial conception to marketing was beset with obstacles that many or most firms regarded as insurmountable.

If Smart House has such potential, why didn't a major firm go ahead to manufacture and market it a number of years ago?

The answer is that Smart House is not a single product. It comprises a very large number of products, developed and designed in accordance with a common plan that will enable them to function together with maximum capability and effectiveness. No one manufacturer—and, in fact, no two or three, however large—was in a position to design the system, produce all the network hardware, the communications hardware and the software, and a full range of appliances that could communicate with the network.

Granted that this is the case, why couldn't a number of manufacturers work together to create the Smart House? First, there was the question of who would run the show, acting as the conductor of this large and highly diversified orchestra. No volunteers for the role of conductor presented themselves.

Why not? This gets us into deep waters of American policy and tradition.

America is unique among major industrial nations in the hostility of its policies to commercial and industrial combinations. By contrast with many other countries, orchestration of multi-firm business undertakings has virtually no modern tradition in our highly individualistic commercial world. It does not reflect our approach to entrepreneurship, and there is a virtual total lack of relevant precedent, knowledge, or methodology.

There is of course a strong legal backbone beneath this aspect of American business, and that backbone is our antitrust laws. As a simple matter of fact, parties with relevant experience in horizontally or vertically organized business combinations might pay for the acquisition of knowledge and skill in this area by spending some time in jail.

The answers to the questions are therefore clear. No one firm could create Smart House. Two or more that tried to do it would probably have to spend more money on lawyers than on research, and even this might provide little protection. Companies with great interest and great faith in the Smart House concept might nevertheless think it safer not to even pick up the phone and discuss mutual efforts with other firms.

Finally, let us suppose that it was somehow possible to solve all these problems, and to design and manufacture a coordinated system consisting of the Smart House network and communicating devices and appliances. With the tremendous effort and investment made, what assurance would there then be that

builders would abandon their present arrangements and install the system in new homes?

To compound the difficulty, few industries are as decentralized as homebuilding. Builders are generally in a position to think and act for themselves, and they are well known to do just that. A long time would have to pass before sufficient consumer pressure might develop to force the hand of members of an almost totally disaggregated industry, if they were not particularly interested.

The Role of David MacFadyen

By good fortune, one of the few people in the United States who occupied a strategically situated vantage point from which all the problems might be taken on, was fascinated by the idea of an intelligent house. That person was David J. MacFadyen, President of the NAHB (National Association of Home Builders) National Research Center. MacFadyen created the Smart House Project, domiciled it at the Research Center, and saw it successfully through the many complex and novel problems that stood in its way.

In the 1970s, MacFadyen was President of Technology & Economics (T&E), a Cambridge, Massachusetts, consulting firm. T&E's major clients included NASA and the Department of Housing and Urban Development. Through his work with these clients, MacFadyen became interested in a new technology called flat cable, which could be laid directly under carpets in commercial buildings, facilitating both original wiring and changes in wiring arrangements that might be made after tenants moved in.

The National Electrical Code did not recognize flat cable as a safe type of wiring, and this effectively prevented its use. MacFadyen was convinced that flat cable was safe. After a number of years, his energy and persistence paid off. He fully satisfied

the Code writers that flat cable was safe, and provisions for its use were entered into the Code. Today it is widely used in commercial construction.

In the early 1980s, MacFadyen went to work for the NAHB National Research Center, and in 1984 he became the Center's President. By now another wiring matter was on his mind—Smart House. MacFadyen discussed the technical issues with Robert G. Edwards, a senior consultant at Oak Ridge National Laboratory. Responding to MacFadyen's questions, Edwards said that home wiring could be simplified, and could be made more safe. Since then Edwards has been a key figure in the development of Smart House technology.

The National Association of Home Builders is one of the largest trade associations in the world. Its 143,000 member-firms include 45,000 home building companies, who together account for some 90% of residential and 85% of commercial light frame construction in the United States. Other members include architects, contractors, manufacturers, and suppliers to the building trade. The Research Center is a wholly owned subsidiary of NAHB.

In the year that MacFadyen became President of the Research Center, another piece of the puzzle was falling into place. In 1984, both Congress and the Office for Productivity, Technology, and Innovation of the U.S. Department of Commerce were pondering the question of whether America's strict antitrust laws sometimes operated to place us at a disadvantage in international trade. Experts were particularly concerned with the impact of the antitrust laws in putting a damper on joint research and development, to create products that no one company could create by itself or to raise the level of technical knowledge among members of an industry.

Smart House was exactly the kind of important and constructive project that the experts had in mind, and to which existing laws posed virtually insuperable barriers.

MacFadyen spent a good deal of time with Dr. E. Bruce Merrifield, Assistant Secretary of Commerce and head of the Office for Productivity, Technology, and Innovation, and with other Department of Commerce officials as they participated in the framing of legislation to deal with the problem. In October Congress passed the National Cooperative Research Act of 1984, and President Reagan signed it into law. The law provided for an easing of antitrust restrictions that stood in the way of joint efforts among manufacturing firms to develop products that could stimulate the U.S. economy and be competitive in world markets. Under the law, a consortium can seek registration with the Department of Justice to carry out research and development efforts that are intrinsically difficult for any one firm to bring to fruition. If the consortium and its project are approved, they can go forward under guidelines in the Act that reduce their antitrust liability.

As soon as the law was passed, MacFadyen went into action. In November 1984, the NAHB National Research Center held a conference in Washington, D.C., on the Smart House idea. The response reflected great pent-up interest. Attendees included representatives of more than a hundred manufacturing firms, electric and gas utilities, trade associations, and government agencies with a relationship to the energy, communication, and home building industries. A number of major firms offered immediate support. The Smart House Project was established and became the first consortium for research and development that was formed under the new Act.

The project sought the participation of several manufacturers for every major type of hardware that would be needed for a Smart House system, and for every major appliance that would

have to be redesigned to include communicating chips. Manufacturers were pleased to accept the NAHB National Research Center as orchestrator of the effort. By 1987 more than forty leading manufacturers had joined the project, and constituted its Steering Committee. A number of these signed research and licensing agreements to develop specific products under the general guidelines established by the consortium.

Some twenty-five other firms such as electric, gas, and telephone companies, trade associations, and firms that do not manufacture Smart House–related products but have a strong interest in the functioning of Smart House, joined the Smart House Advisory Committee. Two major industrial research organizations, the Electric Power Research Institute and the Gas Research Institute, joined the project as sponsors. A list of all firms and organizations involved in Smart House appears in Chapter 9.

At the same time, MacFadyen was marshaling the support of the building industry through the National Association of Home Builders. With sponsorship of the Smart House consortium coming from the building industry's own research arm, endorsement was quick and enthusiastic. NAHB voted to provide funding to the project to see it through its initial phases. Nearly 300 builders, including many of the nation's largest, signed commitments to install Smart House networks into the homes they build, as soon as the system is available.

As is evident from the stories of the adoption of requirements for third-wire grounds and GFIs and the granting of approval for flat cable, a number of years often or usually pass before the National Fire Protection Association includes a full set of provisions for a new technology in the National Electrical Code.

With Smart House, however, it was different. In 1986, NFPA took the almost unprecedented step of approving changes in the National Electrical Code to accommodate Smart House

technology, even before the specific hardware existed. The action reflects both the established nature of the technology as it is now used in other applications, and the clear belief of the Code writers that intelligent home networks, rather than being another Band-Aid, represent a fundamental solution to serious problems. The new provisions appear in the 1987 edition of the Code.

Meanwhile, one of the project's two sponsors, the Gas Research Institute, undertook to provide financial support for the construction of a Laboratory Smart House. The Lab House is being used for hands-on research on the design of the network. In addition, research will be done on matters of particular interest to GRI. The house is located at NAHB's Research Home Park in Bowie, Maryland. As indicated at the beginning of the first chapter, it will become the first Smart House in the world.

As the project moved out of its initial stages, the NAHB National Research Center spun it off as a separately incorporated, profit-oriented entity called the Smart House Development Venture. David MacFadyen remained as Chairman of the Board and Chief Executive Officer. At the same time, in his continuing position as President of the Research Center, he was already focusing his dynamism on a broad new issue—the raising of quality standards throughout the U.S. home building industry to meet the increasing likelihood of international competition to the U.S. home builder on his own American turf.

The Smart House Development Venture is moving quickly to bring Smart House to market. About a year after completion of the Laboratory House, construction will begin on a number of prototype houses at locales throughout the United States. In these houses, advanced system integration will be tested, and operating features of the Smart House will be developed. At the same time, electric companies, gas companies, and telephone companies located in the geographical areas where the houses are built will do research to identify consumer interests and

needs, and will begin to design services that can be delivered with Smart House technology.

The research period of Smart House will end with the decade. Commercialization will be under way by 1990 with the construction of about 100 demonstration Smart Houses in the United States and Canada. They will incorporate the production model of the Smart House network, along with smart versions of standard appliances.

How will the Smart House system work? Before we explain its operation, we will first explain how houses are wired today.

4

How Homes Are Wired Today

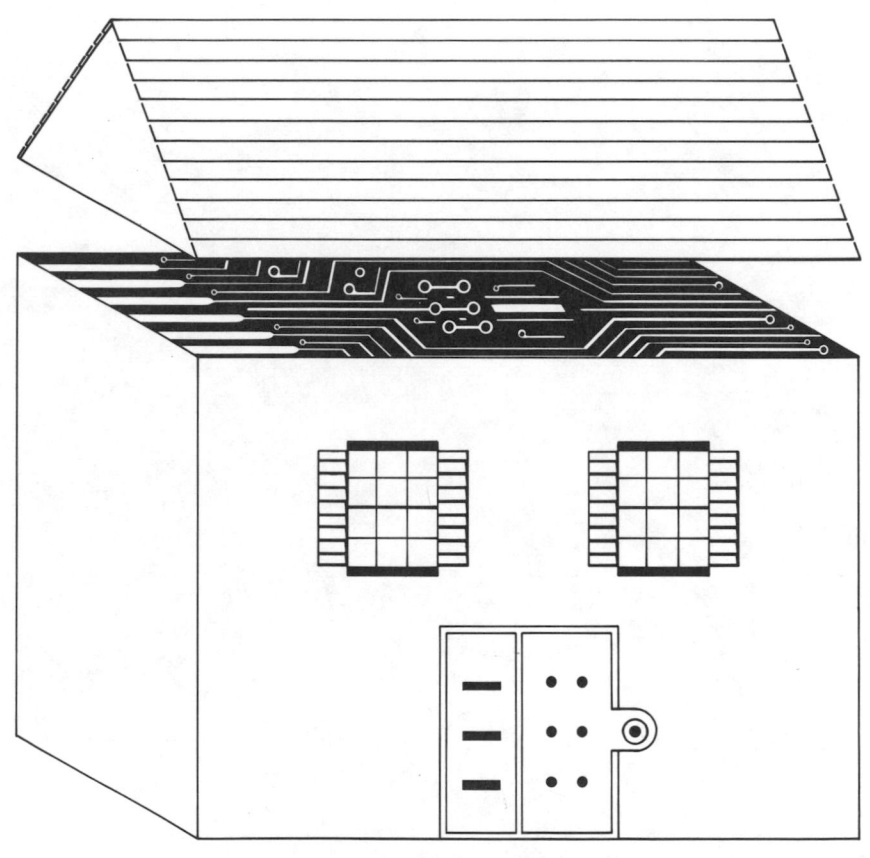

There are now a number of different wiring systems in the home that carry electrical energy. In addition, in homes using gas as an energy source, there is a separate physical piping system to convey the gas to appliances.

The "wire" that connects an individual home with the local electric utility ordinarily consists not of one wire but of three. Two of these wires each carry 120 volts of 60-cycle alternating current (a.c.). The current delivered by these two wires can be combined to deliver the 240 volts that is normally required to power certain major appliances such as dryers, stoves, ovens, water heaters, and large air-conditioning units. Each line also serves individually to deliver the 120-volt service to lights and smaller appliances.

The third wire, called the "neutral" wire, carries no current into the home. It simply performs the function of completing the circuit from the home back to the utility. When a light is switched on in the house, current flows from one of the 120-volt branches to and through the lamp and back to the utility via the neutral wire, creating a complete circuit.

When these wires enter the house, they go first to the load distribution center, as shown in Figure 3. In today's house, the load distribution center is just another name for the central fuse box or circuit breaker panel.

From here, a number of circuits pass around the house, serving outlets in various rooms. Each of these circuits is associated with a fuse or circuit breaker in the load distribution center. Major appliances requiring 240 volts are served by higher-capacity lines running directly to the appliances from higher-capacity fuses or circuit breakers in the load distribution center.

For illustrative purposes, Figure 3 shows a load distribution center with three 15-ampere circuit breakers. From each circuit breaker, current is distributed to a number of outlets, switches, appliances, and fixtures by means of branch circuits. These branch circuits are so arranged that, when any item or appliance is turned on, its power requirement is added to the total load on the circuit breaker serving that branch.

Let us first look at the branch that runs from the top circuit breaker. A lamp is plugged into one of the outlets on this branch. Someone turns it on; the bulb flashes and burns out. This familiar experience can be used to illustrate a characteristic of electrical service that is called inrush.

In the few milliseconds after a lamp is turned on, it draws a substantially larger amount of current than will be required for its ongoing operation. This is true for all electrical appliances and devices. The inrush requirement is especially great for lights and motors and smaller for appliances such as TVs and VCRs. This inrush of current is hard on appliances and devices, which explains why light bulb burnouts often or usually occur when the light is switched on.

The inrush problem has broader implications. It complicates the problem of restoring full power after an outage. When a power outage occurs, most people do not go around turning off lights

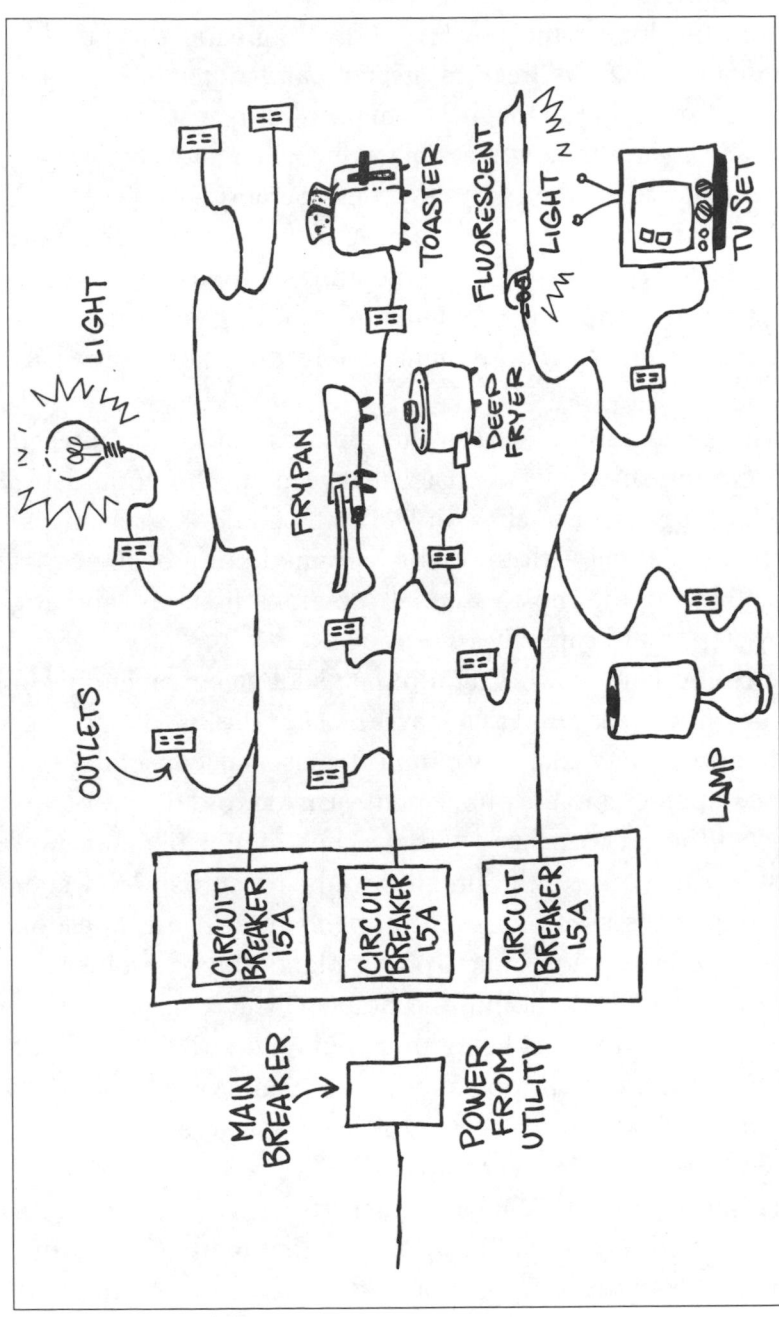

Figure 3. Today's home wiring system

and appliances that were on when the power went out. In addition, the longer the power is off, the greater the number of appliances such as freezers, heaters, and water heaters that will need power simultaneously when power is restored.

Actually, the utility might be able to furnish, relatively quickly, sufficient power for the most essential operations of the home, with full restoration of power coming in increments. But most utilities have no means of implementing such an option. They must be geared up for a full load, including a tremendous simultaneous inrush requirement, before they can restore any power.

Phased restoration of power after outages could be achieved if a communications link existed between the home and the utility. By means of such a link, power could be selectively restored in keeping with the utility's limited but growing capability, powering the most essential functions first, and moving step by step to full capacity.

The continually growing requirements for electrical energy in a largely urbanized America have placed strains on present generating capacity that have important social consequences. Power companies and the public both wish to avoid the problems and issues that are associated with the construction of new power plants. In this context, the problem of heavy inrush load after power outages is assuming a meaningful role in the question of whether construction of new power plants can be avoided.

Now let us look at the middle branch, which serves outlets in the kitchen. Dinner is being prepared, and a deep fryer and an electric frypan are in operation. Two pieces of toast are put in the toaster; the toaster lever is pushed down; and, not surprisingly, the circuit breaker pops.

This highlights basic characteristics of the wiring system. As has been noted, every light or appliance that is plugged in and operated adds to the total current load being carried by the fuse

or circuit breaker at the head of the branch. When the circuit becomes overburdened, the fuse blows or the circuit breaker trips. Power is cut off, not just to the offending light or appliance, but indiscriminately to everything on that branch.

Now let us move down to the third branch, whose coverage includes a recreation area in the basement. In one corner is dad's workbench, where he pursues his evening hobby of woodworking. There is a fluorescent light at this workbench, whose diffused light is excellent for illuminating this type of work area. However, the 60-cycle home current causes a "flicker" in this light, which sometimes bothers dad's eyes as he works. Powering the light with current at an increased cycle rate—say 400 hertz (cycles per second)—would solve the problem. So would the use of direct current (d.c.) rather than alternating current (a.c.) to power the light. But dad has no choice. He has to use the one kind of power that is available in the home.

In another corner is a TV set. It is a good one, but, in common with the set in the living room, it suffers from rather odd reception problems. Sometimes a horizontal bar rolls slowly through the picture. Sometimes—for example, when the air-conditioner goes on—a ragged static line dances on the screen. There seems to be no way to get rid of these annoyances.

Rolling bars on TV screens are often caused by the operation of electric motors elsewhere in the home. Motors can feed back, through the wiring system and into the TV set, cycle patterns that are slightly out of phase with the cycle pattern of the current that is powering the set. This all-too-common phenomenon is called electromagnetic interference; it is often referred to by the initials EMI.

Static lines are caused by radio frequency disturbances that result from the armature rotation in electric motors. This is called radio frequency interference, or RFI. These disturbances are transmitted through the air as low-powered radio signals, are

picked up by the home wiring system which operates as an antenna for receiving these transmissions, and are dumped into the TV set. As every sports fan knows, rolling bars and static lines seem to lie in wait, attacking the TV picture during the crucial play in an exciting football game.

On the other side of the room, some children are playing with their shoes off. Although they have been told not to do so, the kids have been playing with squirt guns in this room; portions of their skin, clothes, and feet are damp.

In the corner is a lamp whose cord has been scraped against the leg of a sofa, exposing a small bit of the wire. The lamp is not turned on. However, even if a lamp is not turned on, its cord forms part of the live electrical branch running from the circuit breaker right up to the lamp switch.

One of the youngsters steps on the exposed bit of wire in the lamp cord, grounds the circuit, and is shocked and burned. The occurrence did nothing to overload the circuit breaker, which had done its assigned duty of providing power before, during, and after the accident.

Statistically speaking, home electrical accidents are not a leading cause of injury or death in the United States. Unfortunately, it is equally true that as long as today's wiring system is used, it will take its relatively small but inexorable toll each and every year, despite the best that safety engineers and Code officials can do. An unusual set of circumstances such as those imagined in the preceding paragraphs, is sometimes at fault. Murphy's Law assures that unusual things always happen to someone, somewhere.

(The author can remember an instance from personal experience. When he and his brother were very small children, they got it into their heads to cut the cord of a turned-off lamp with a pair of scissors. The author's brother wielded the scissors, and was severely shocked. That he was not badly burned or killed

is perhaps due to the fact that they had not been playing with their soap bubble pipes just before putting their brilliant little plan into effect.)

The system that we have been describing is the basic energy system in the home. The piping that brings gas to home heating units, water heaters, stoves, and other gas-fired appliances constitutes another energy system. This system is separately installed, with little or no relationship to the electrical or communications networks in the home other than its link to the furnace or thermostat. Most notably, no advantage is taken of one of the more simple capabilities of modern communications systems, which is to monitor usage and provide safety checks on malfunctions.

In addition to a connection to the local utility for electrical energy, a link to the telephone network is nearly universal in today's homes, and half of all homes are also hooked up for cable TV. Each of these services involves a wiring system that is separate from the home electrical wiring system, and may be installed by parties other than those who install the electrical wiring.

Finally, another system has been entering a growing number of homes to provide security alarm service. This service must be installed by yet another contractor, at yet another increment in cost. The service would be cheaper and more people would probably have it if separate installation and wiring were not required.

With regard to the three major systems—electrical service, telephone, and cable TV—the location of their outlets often bears a decreasing relation to convenience after the home has been lived in and many things have been changed around. A fantasy has probably occurred to many a frustrated home occupant who has found an electrical outlet right where he wants to put a telephone—wouldn't it be wonderful if you could plug anything

into any outlet! This fantasy of course occurred to David Mac-Fadyen and to many others who understand that no technological barriers stand in the way of its implementation.

5

How the Smart House Works

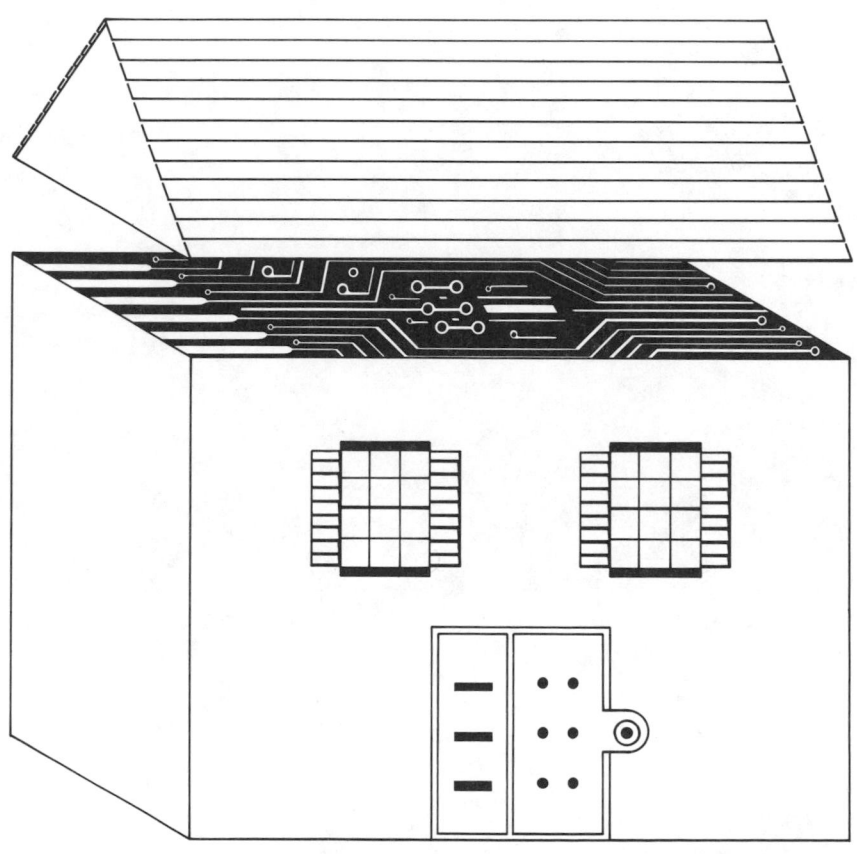

Various details of Smart House technology will be worked out in the laboratory and demonstration home programs, and the system itself will evolve with actual experience and usage. However, its basic features are known and can be described.

Five Basic Features

First, the now-separate electrical and communications systems in the home, including electrical service, telephone, cable TV, security systems, and minor additional wiring such as that for doorbells, thermostats and audio, will be united in a single system.

All outlets in the home will be served by this unified system. The fantasy of today's frustrated home occupant will be fully realized; he will be able to plug any appliance or device, such as a lamp, telephone, or even security sensor, into any outlet.

Second, for homes with gas service, Smart House wiring will accompany flexible gas piping to gas convenience outlets in any room or location desired.

Portable gas appliances can be attached to these outlets. Both appliance operation and gas distribution will be electronically monitored by the system.

Third, delivery of electric power to fixtures and appliances will be controlled and constantly monitored by a low-powered signaling link running between a chip in the fixture or appliance and a chip in the Smart House network interface. The chips and the link between them constitute the key elements of what is called the closed loop system.

In initial versions of this system, small wires will be used for the interconnections of the closed loop. In the future, fiber optics may be used. Fiber is an excellent medium for digital signaling and can accommodate very high speeds of data transmission if evolving applications of Smart House technology should ever require such speeds.

Fiber transmits electrical information by means of a light beam that is not affected by the magnetic fields that can surround ordinary electrical wires or that can be generated by appliances and devices. All possibility of interference with the closed loop signals is thereby eliminated, and precautions such as shielding that will be taken in early versions of the system to insulate the closed loop from magnetic interference can be dropped.

Fourth, the system will include an internal communications network that will link all appliances with each other, with internal control devices, and with the outside world.

As with the closed loop system, fiber may be utilized for this network in the future.

Fifth, the system will have the future capability of delivering more than one type of electrical energy. This capability is called programmed power.

Earliest versions of the system will deliver two types of power, 120/240 volts a.c., and 12 volts d.c.; the latter serves as the system's Uninterruptible Power Supply which will be described below.

It is possible or even likely that, in the future, the system will deliver at least one additional type of power. Early discussions have centered on 48 volts d.c. as a third service offering. Decisions on these future system developments await further research and experimentation in laboratory settings, and further information on consumer wishes and preferences. The author thinks it likely that 48 volts d.c. will ultimately be added to the electrical services available in the Smart House.*

Figure 4 is a cutaway house drawing showing the location of various Smart House features. The drawing will help the reader to envision the actual placement in the house of parts of the system that appear in the ensuing diagrams.

Network Interfaces

The reader's attention is particularly invited to a device in the basement and its associated caption which reads in part, "NET-WORK INTERFACES: Located here and in each room." These components contain the all-important chips and are the heart of the Smart House. They must occupy center stage in our description of what a Smart House is and how it functions.

The first step the reader should take is to expunge from his mind the image of branch-pattern wiring that he may still be carrying from having viewed Figure 3 in the preceding chapter. The branch pattern is a correct representation of today's home wiring, but an incorrect one of the Smart House. There is not even a central computer in the Smart House connected to all

---

* Delivery of a second major form of electrical power by the system will require development of a miniaturized switching power supply that will fit into the space designated for power blocks in the network interface. This switching power supply could take the 120-volt a.c. current delivered by the load distribution center and convert it to 48 volts d.c. when a device indicates that it wishes to have this latter form of power. Such a piece of equipment does not presently exist, and the R&D necessary to create it is likely to be undertaken only upon demonstration of significant consumer demand.

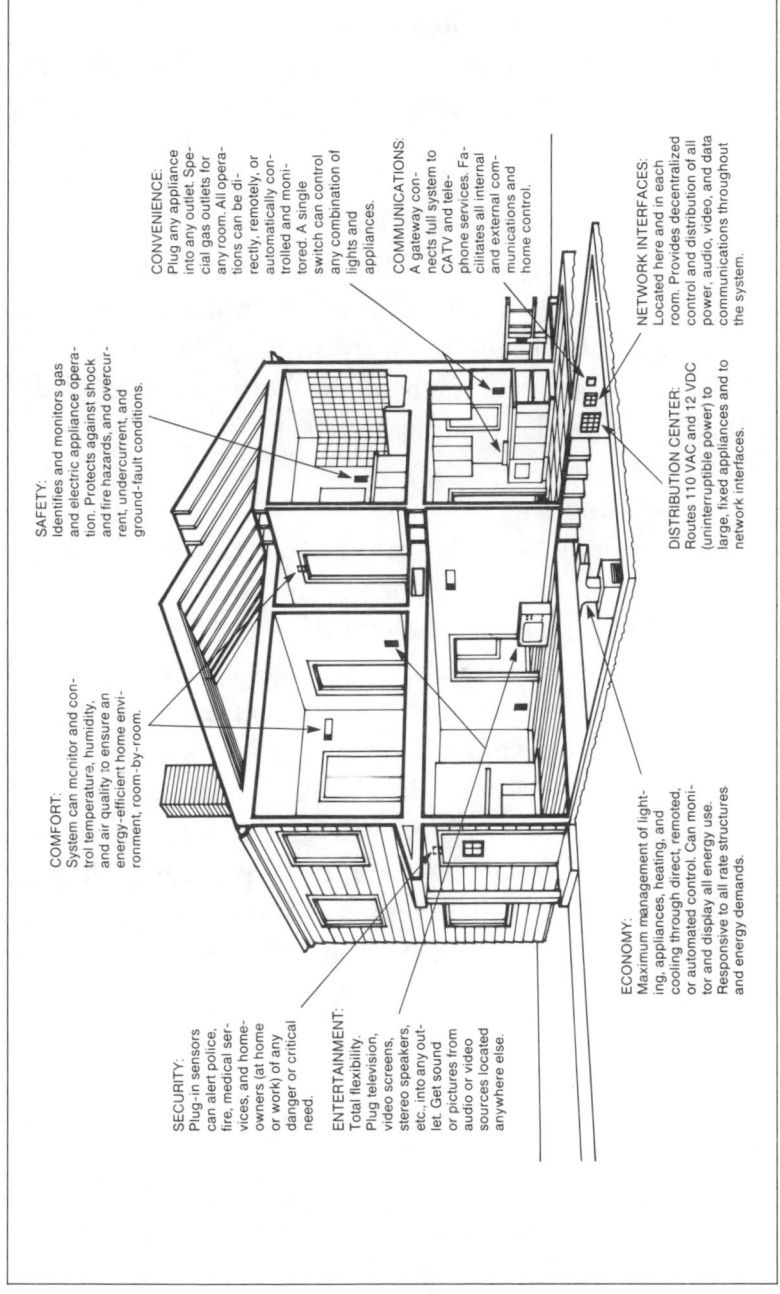

Figure 4. Smart House features

the network interfaces to function as an electronic chairman of the board.

The correct way to envision the Smart House is to see a democracy of very capable little devices, each receiving the same kinds of external input, each able to perform the same functions, and all linked together. The Smart House system is an interlinked chain of network interfaces. Figure 5 is a schematic drawing of a network interface and its connections.

At the back of the interface is a "backplane," which receives electrical power from the load distribution center. Wires from the load distribution center carry current to the backplane of each network interface around the house. The front portion of the interface consists of a number of modules, each of which contains semiconductors.

The left-hand module is called the communications module. This module is linked to the telephone and cable TV systems. As with electrical service, telephone and cable TV service is routed to each network interface.

Next to the communications module is the appliance module. This module is dedicated to internal communications among appliances and network interfaces. The appliance modules in all the network interfaces are linked together with a unified cable resembling the Smart House cable that will be described below. (In addition to wires for the internal communications system, this cable will incorporate coaxial cable for TV and wires for transmitting audio, but will not need the wiring for electrical power included in the full Smart House cable that reaches convenience outlets.) As will soon be described, lights, switches, appliances, sensors, and regional controllers all feed information into this communicating network.

Now we will proceed to the group of modules to the right of the communications and appliance modules. These are called

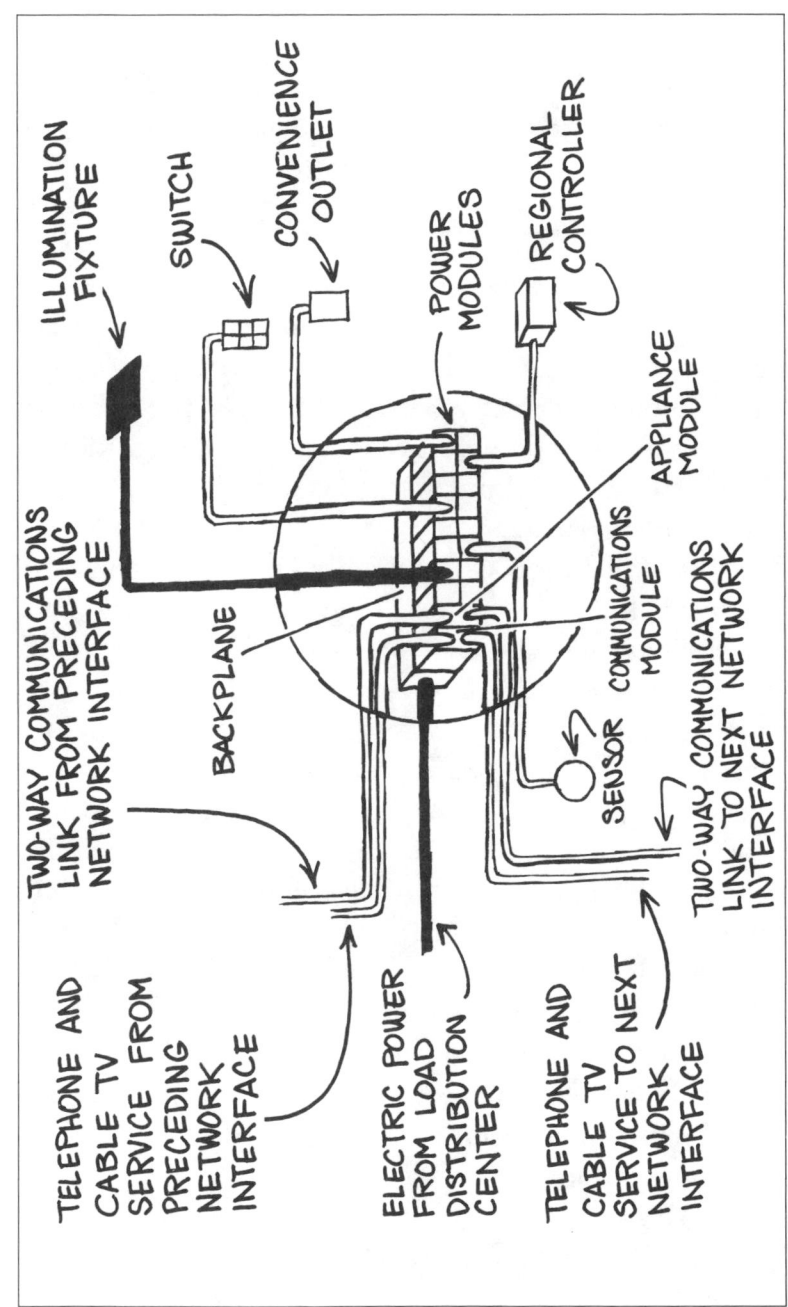

Figure 5. A network interface and its connections

power modules. Each power module contains a chip, and each serves only one outlet, appliance, or fixture.

Viewing these modules, we can see the difference between the branch pattern of today's home wiring and the wiring pattern of the Smart House. As noted above and as shown in Figure 6, each power module is connected directly to some item in the room or area. The network interface can therefore deal with each one individually. If something malfunctions, a power module in the interface can turn it off without affecting the operation of anything else. The configuration of the Smart House network is called a "star pattern."

The Regional Controller

One module is connected to a component called a "Regional Controller." This component is used by the home occupant to tell the system what he wants it to do.

This controller can take a number of forms. For instance, Figures 7 through 11 show various displays on a touch screen. Such a screen could be permanently installed at one or more designated locations in the home. Another type could be portable; it could be plugged into any Smart House outlet and would be recognized by the system for what it is. A portable controller is labeled as item No. 10 in the cutaway house illustrated in Figure 2, Chapter 1. A controller could also be cordless, like the remote controller for a TV set.

Controllers need not necessarily involve a TV display. Other types could make use of push buttons or telephone keypads. Yet others could operate through voice recognition systems or could respond to input from sensors and detectors. Some of these options will be discussed in ensuing chapters. Consumer needs and preferences will ultimately govern the types of controllers that will be available for use with the Smart House.

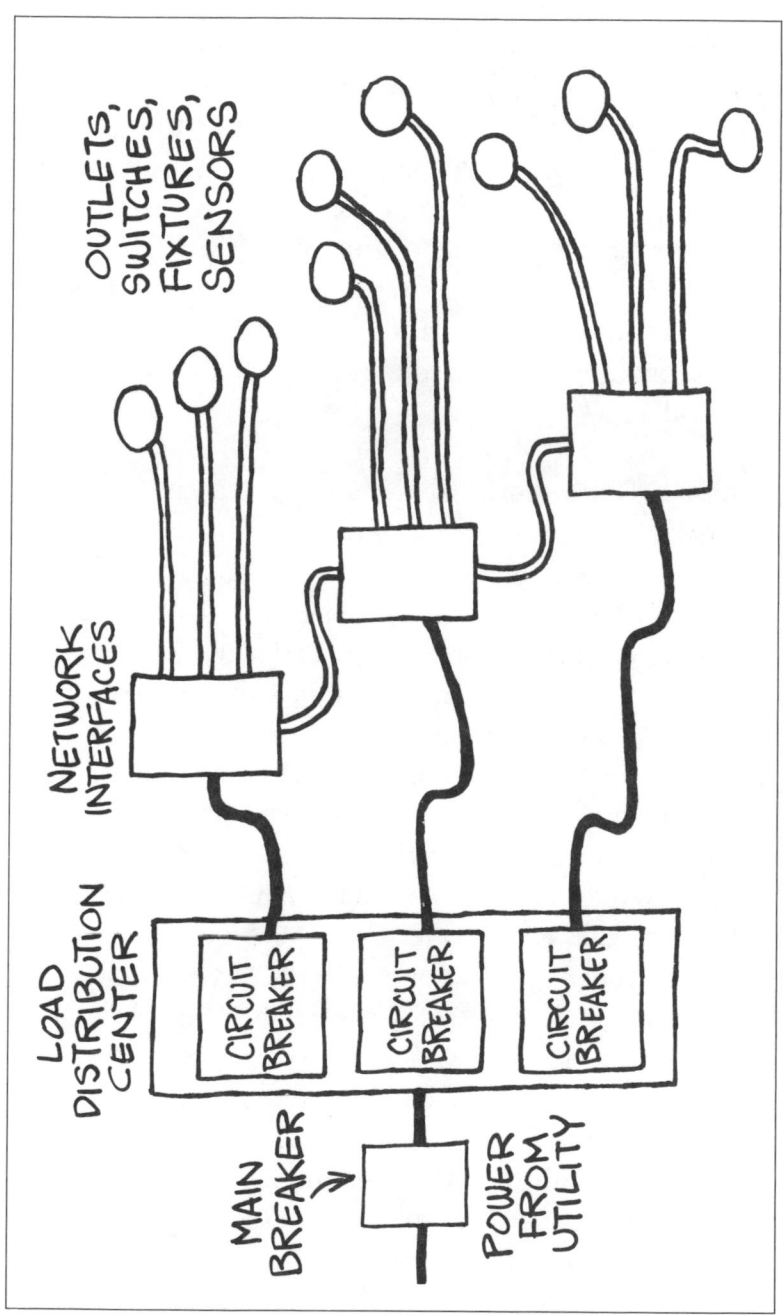

OUTLETS, SWITCHES, FIXTURES, SENSORS

NETWORK INTERFACES

LOAD DISTRIBUTION CENTER

CIRCUIT BREAKER

CIRCUIT BREAKER

CIRCUIT BREAKER

MAIN BREAKER

POWER FROM UTILITY

Figure 6. "Star" configuration of the Smart House system

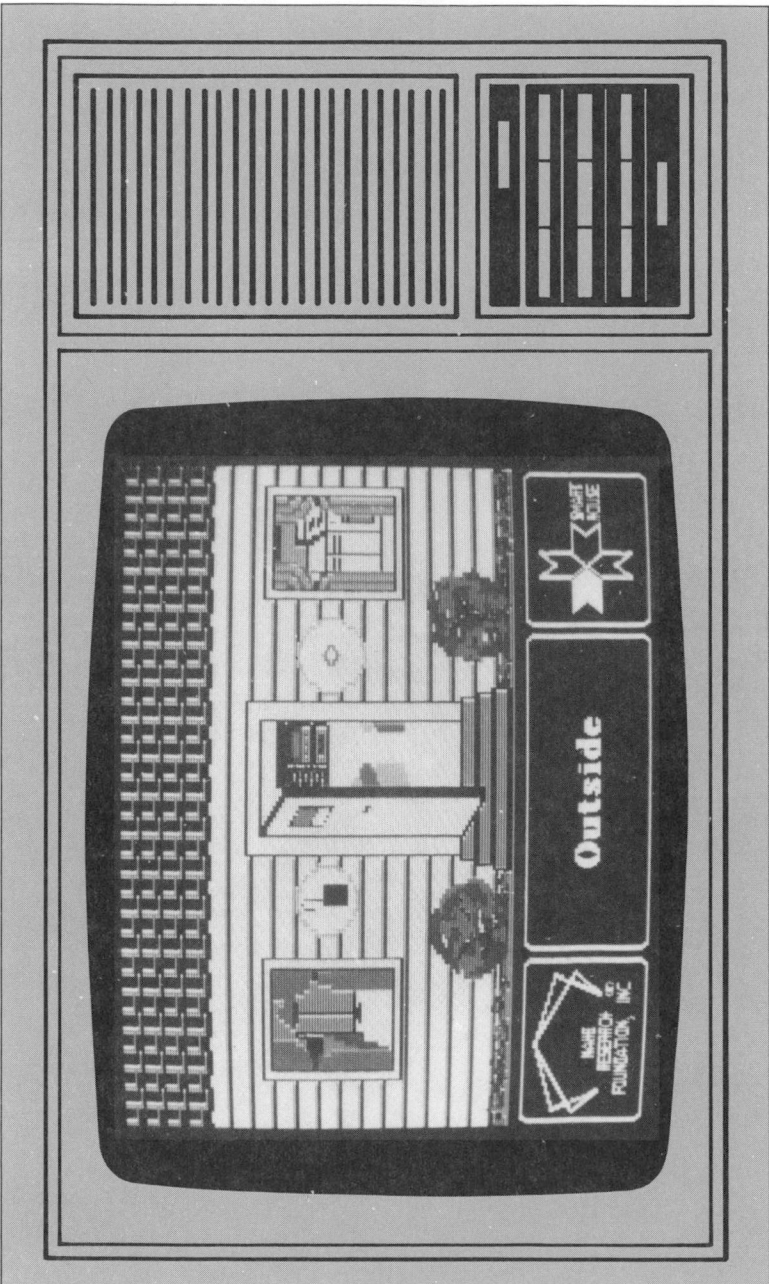

Figure 7. A typical touch-screen display on a regional controller; shown here, an outside security display

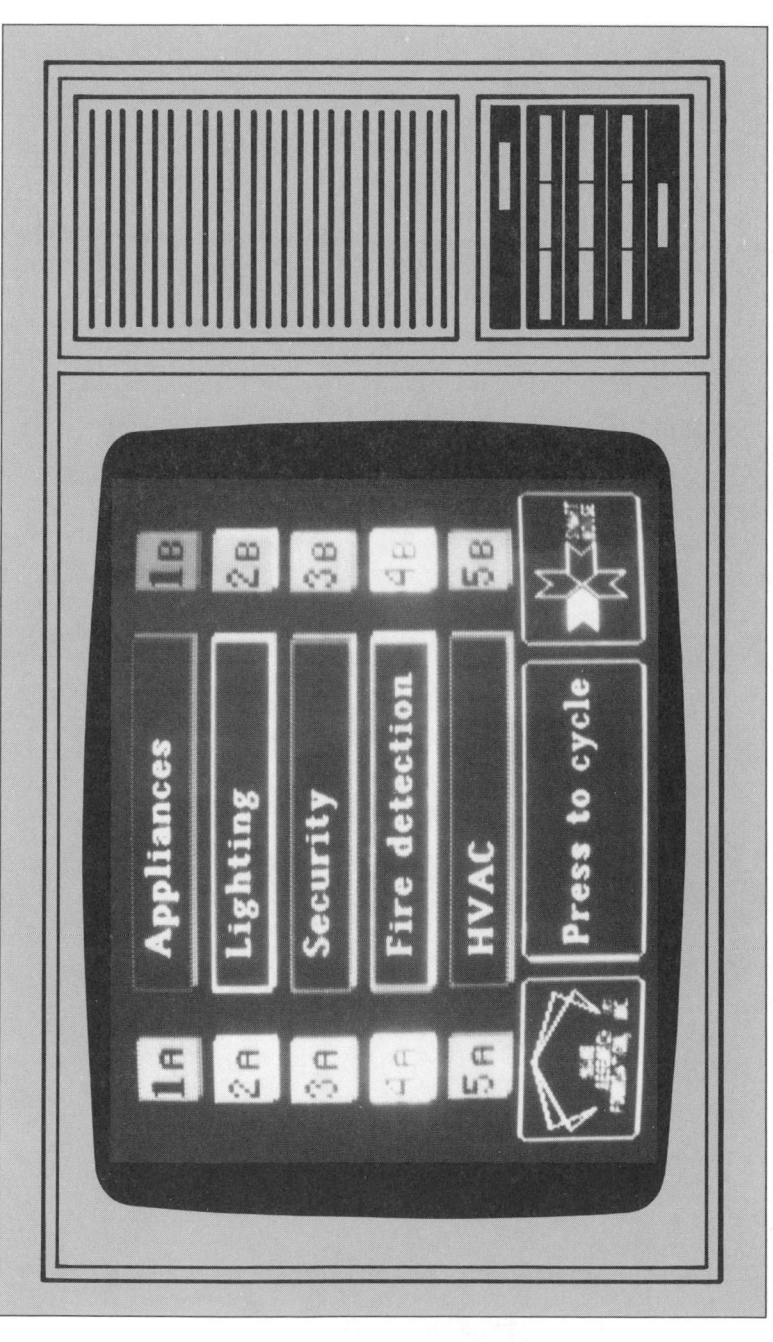

Figure 8. A sample menu

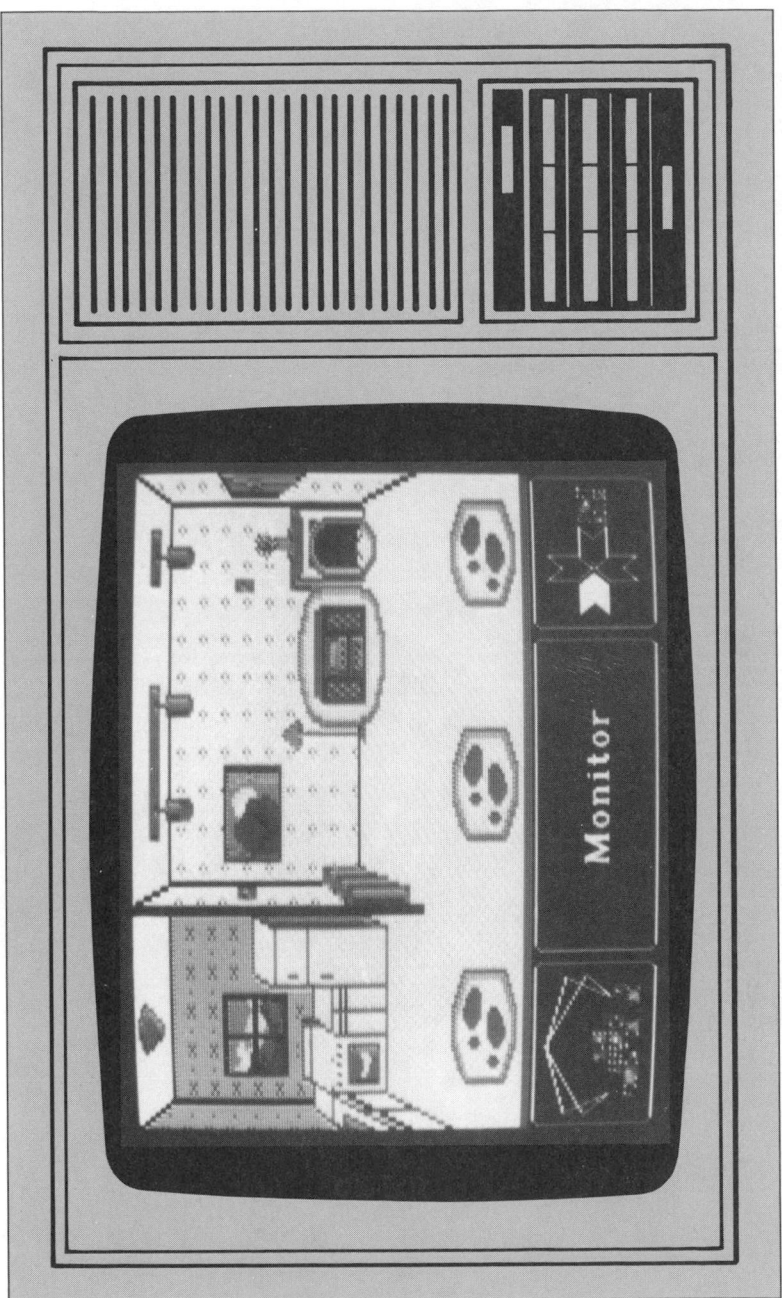

Figure 9. The kitchen and family room in "monitor" mode

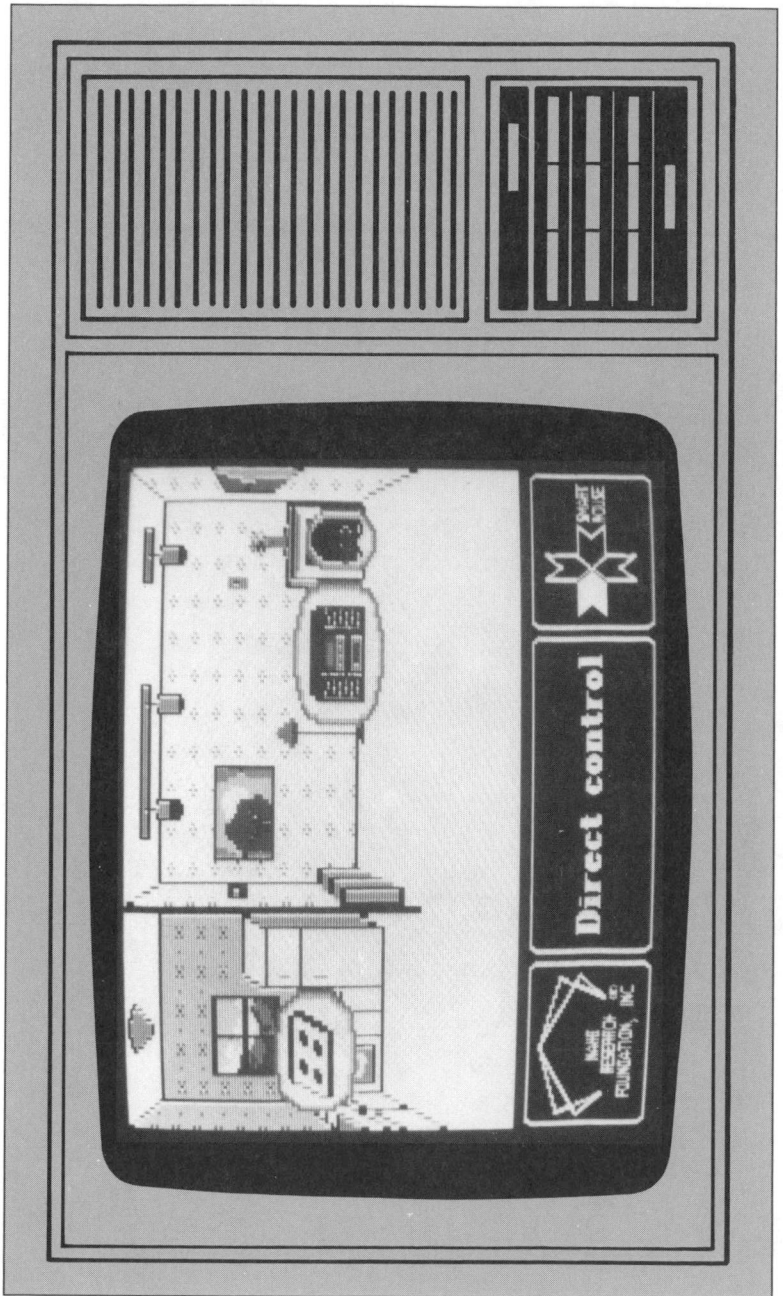

Figure 10. A display illustrating direct control of the stove and stereo

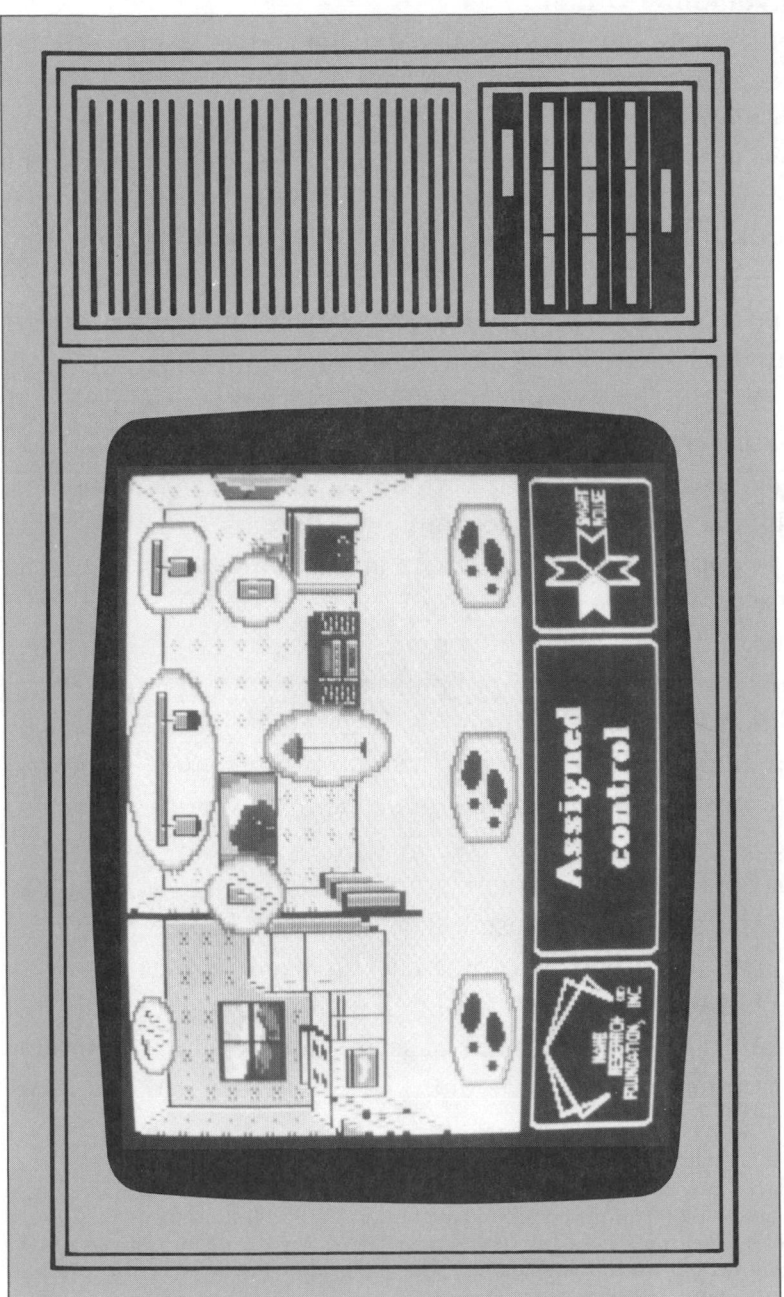

Figure 11. Homeowners may assign and reassign control of appliances to meet their needs

Convenience Outlets

Another power module in the drawing serves a convenience outlet. There would, of course, be a number of such outlets in each room or area, each served by a separate module. Here we arrive at a major crossroad of the Smart House electronic and communications highway. Through the outlet, the smart system "talks" to smart lights, appliances, and control devices.[†] The system brings its full capabilities to this meeting.

The module and convenience outlet are linked by means of the unified Smart House cable. The exact manufacturing details for this cable have not been fully settled, but in general it will contain electric wires for distribution of electricity, coaxial cables for TV, wire pairs for distribution of telephone and audio, and additional small wires to accommodate the closed loop. All wires will be appropriately shielded. An artist's rendering of the Smart House cable is shown in Figure 12.

The outlet will have more prongs than today's electrical outlet; it will resemble the multi-pin plugs of the type that have become common for many electronic products. Each Smart House light or appliance will have a plug that will fit this outlet. An artist's rendering of a Smart House outlet and plug appears in Figure 13.

Except for this plug, smart lamps and appliances will not look different from those in use today. They will, however, differ in one particular—they will contain a chip. Communications from this chip will be understood by the chips in the Smart House network. This is another way of saying that the chip in the item that is plugged in and the chip in the module at the network

---

[†] Today's "unsmart" lights and appliances can also be plugged into a Smart House system by use of an inexpensive adaptor. Appliances will function as they always have, but will not necessarily participate in the new capabilities of the system. Intelligence built into an adaptor might bring some degree of Smart House capability to older lamps and appliances.

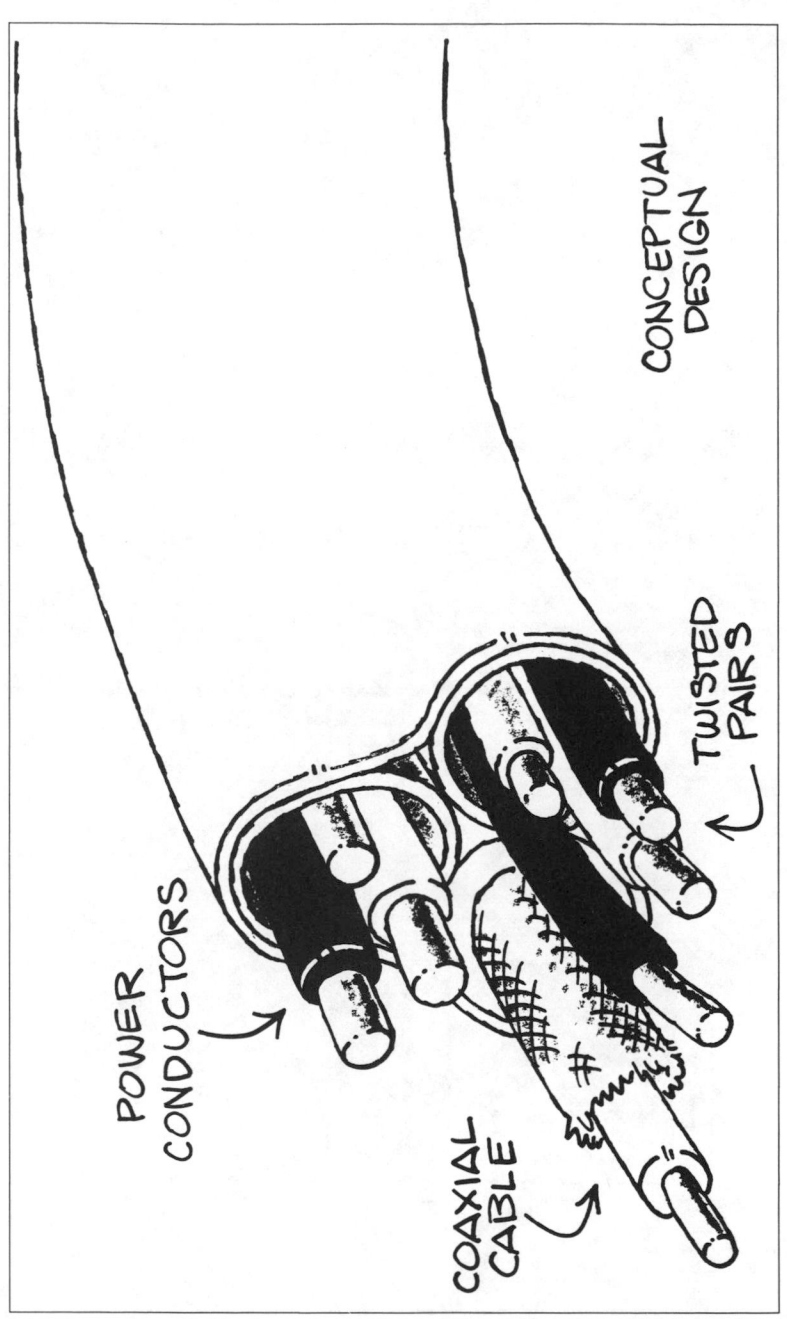

Figure 12. The Smart House cable

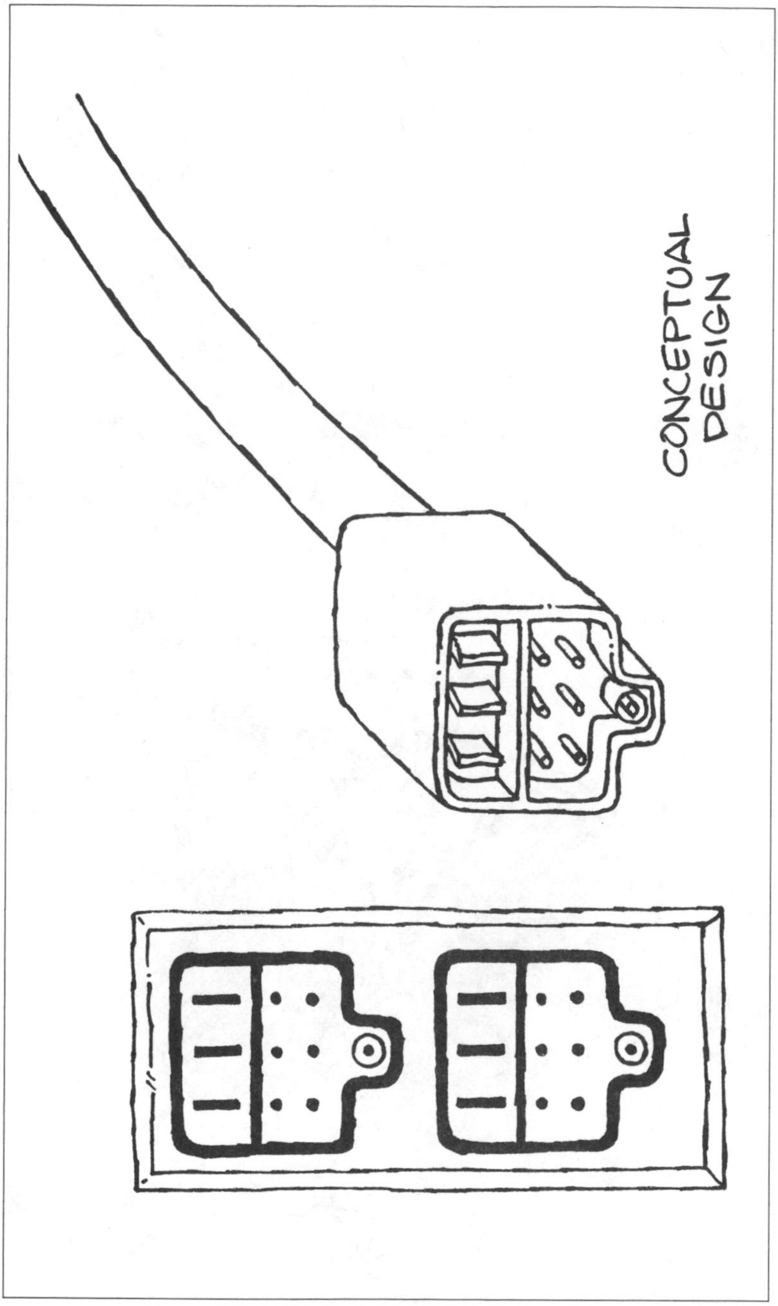

Figure 13. The Smart House outlet and plug

interface have a common electronic language and protocol by which they can share information.

The establishment of this communicating process was one of the central reasons for registration of the project under the National Cooperative Research Act of 1984. The development of numerous systems with numerous languages and protocols would have been a virtually inevitable consequence of a go-it-alone approach among manufacturers, and would have almost certainly resulted in failure of the effort to bring this form of modern electronics into the home.

A smart lamp or appliance can be plugged into the network, but until the item is turned on there is no current in the cable running between the interface and the outlet, in the outlet, or in the cord of the item that is plugged in. If the author and his brother had spent their childhood in a Smart House, their bright idea of cutting a lamp cord with a pair of scissors would have exposed them to no danger.

The Closed Loop in Action

Let us say that we have turned on a Smart House appliance. The chip in the appliance is placed in instant communication with the chip in the power module serving the outlet into which the appliance is plugged. The appliance and the system's signaling circuit are joined in a "closed loop."

The appliance identifies itself to the system as an item that is authorized to receive power—it is not, for example, a child inserting a barbeque skewer, which contains no chip and, therefore, cannot identify itself. It further identifies itself with regard to the circuit to which it should be joined, namely, the main house electrical circuit. It is not a telephone to be connected to the telephone network, or a sensor to be connected to a low-powered circuit.

Figure 14 shows the closed loop in action. Components of the closed loop include the chip in the appliance, a chip in the network interface, and the two-way link running between them. The letters UPS stand for Uninterruptible Power Supply. This is the 12-volt d.c. system, whose primary function is to power the chips in the system. We will discuss this more fully when we describe the load distribution center.

Responding to the information cited above, the chip in the network interface delivers current to the appliance. At the same time it sets up two-way communication between the chip in the appliance and the chip in the network interface, as shown in Figure 15. The two-way communication thus established continues as long as the appliance is on. If the appliance should malfunction, causing excessive current draw, a short circuit, or a ground fault condition, the chip in the interface receives this information from the chip in the appliance. The system responds by instantly cutting off power delivery as shown in Figure 16. The appliance, its cord, the outlet, and the power link between the outlet and the network interface all go dead.

Wall Switches

In Figure 5, another module is connected to a wall switch. In today's wiring, wall switches are wired to a specific outlet, appliance, or fixture, and will turn current on and off only to that item. In the Smart House such switches are wired to a power module. When a switch is turned on, it provides a signal to the power module to which it is connected. That power module then sends a signal to the power module attached to the appliance or appliances that one wishes to control. The question of which appliance or appliances will be controlled is up to the homeowner.

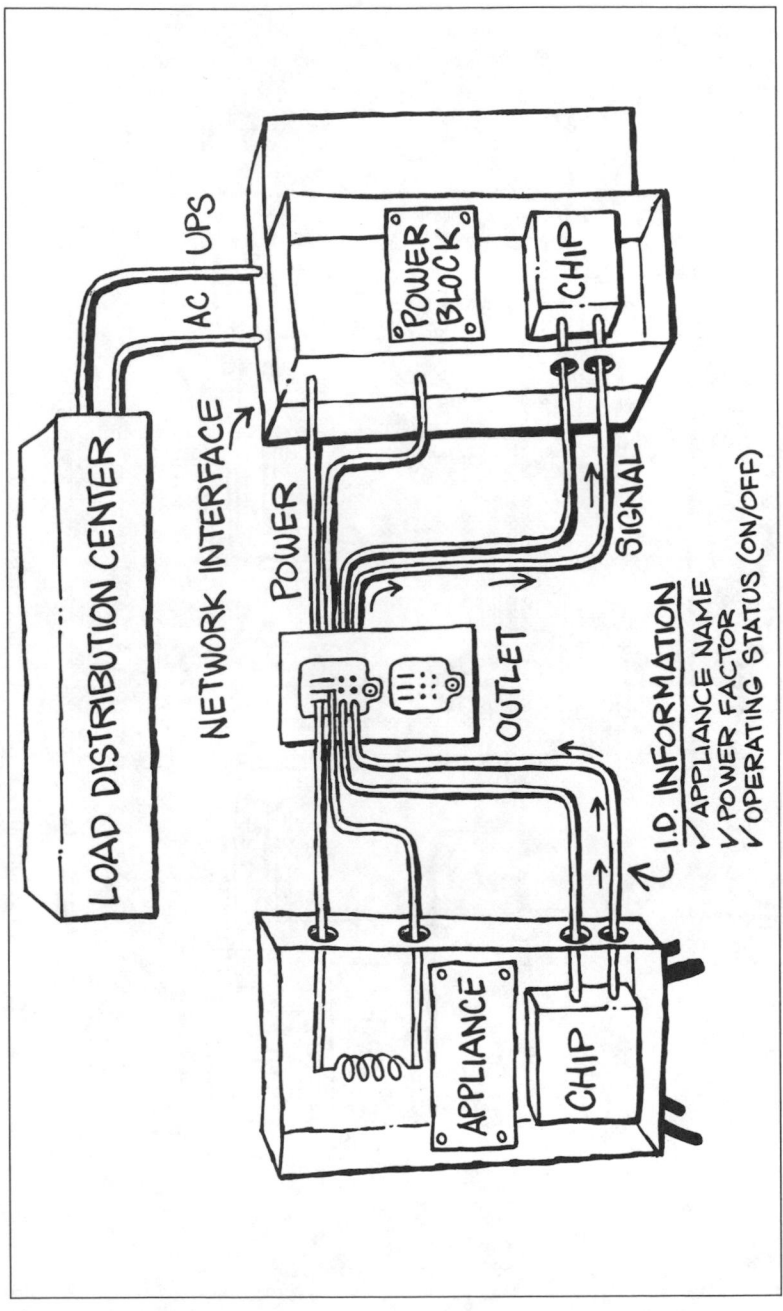

Figure 14. The closed loop in action

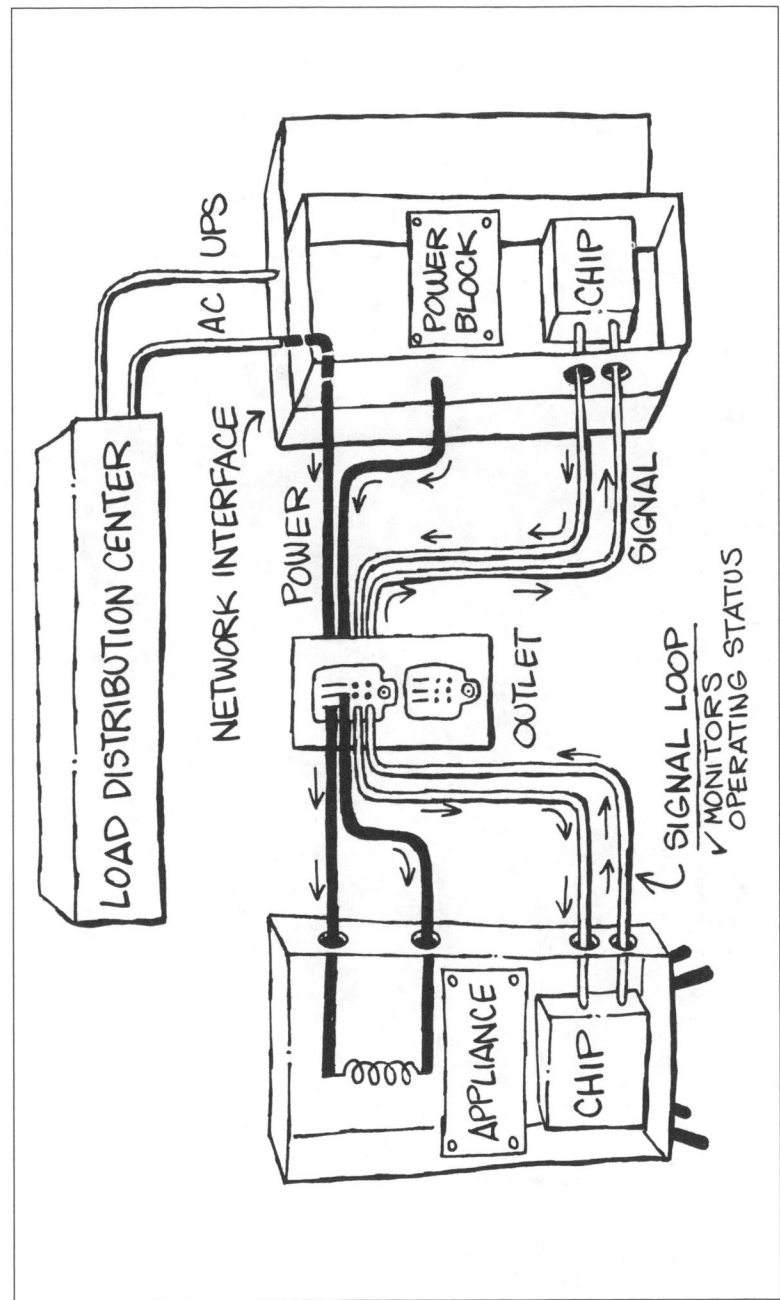

Figure 15.   Communication between an appliance and a network interface

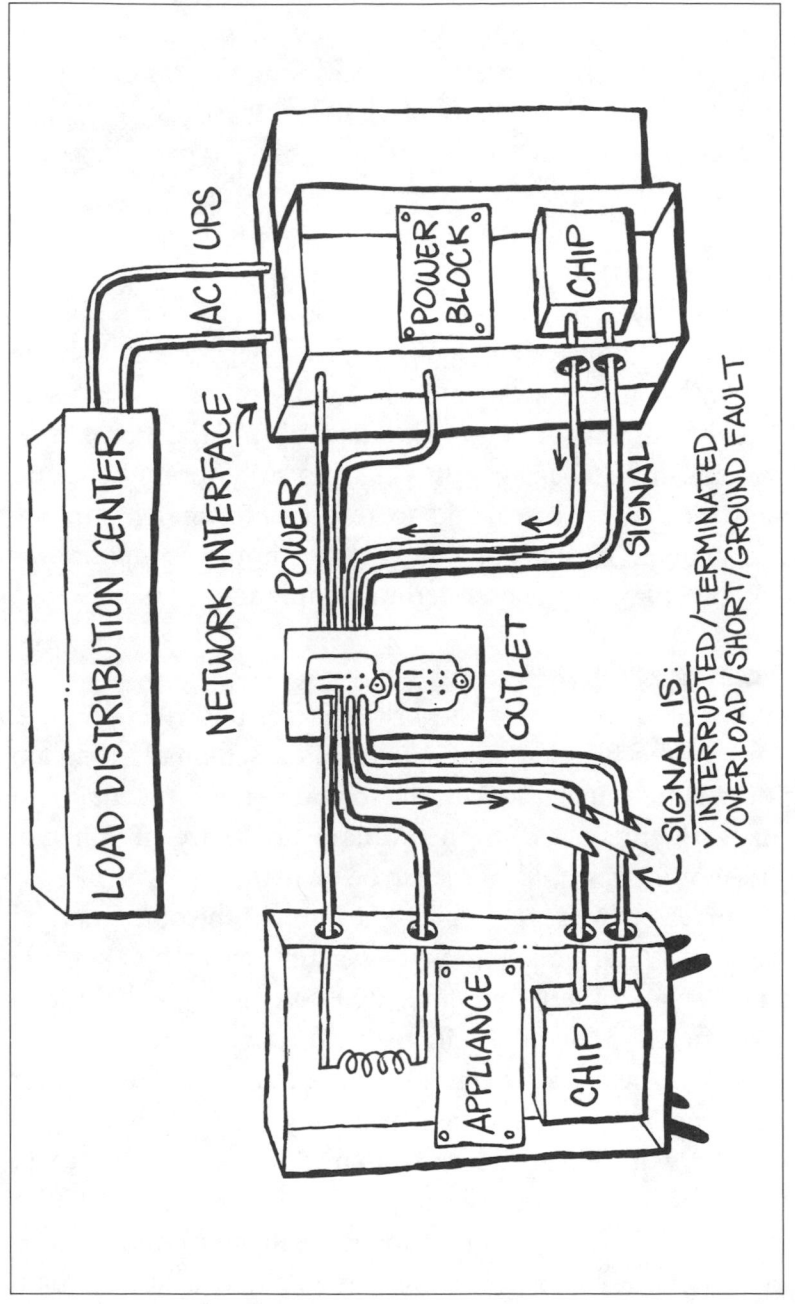

Figure 16. The system instantly cuts off power to a malfunctioning appliance

In all likelihood, wall switches will be assigned at the time of occupancy to suit the occupant's convenience as best he is able to foresee it. When experience and changing home arrangements indicate the desirability of changes, these can be made by the occupant on his touch screen or other type of regional controller.

Telephones, Lighting Fixtures, Sensors

Other items served by the network interface include telephones (which can be plugged into any outlet), permanent lighting fixtures, and sensors for fire and/or security protection. Sensors can be either directly wired to the network interface or can be plugged into outlets. Their status is constantly monitored, and the network can be instructed to respond to changes in the sensor's status in virtually any way that the home occupant may wish. Some options are described in Chapter 8.

The Total System

With the central role of the network interface described, we can now look at the full system. Figure 17 is a schematic diagram of a Smart House network, with the load distribution center and four network interfaces. In an ordinary house the number of network interfaces would of course be greater.

Standard electrical service enters the home at the point marked "AC service." After going through a main circuit breaker, the standard service of 120 volts and 240 volts is passed through Block #1 in the drawing to circuit breakers for delivery to the backplanes of network interfaces. These interfaces can deliver up to 15 amperes to each of the items they service.

Block #2 will deliver the 12 volts of direct current that will power the chips. This is designated as the Uninterruptible Power Supply (UPS) because it will be maintained and continued by storage batteries if and when there is an outage in the main

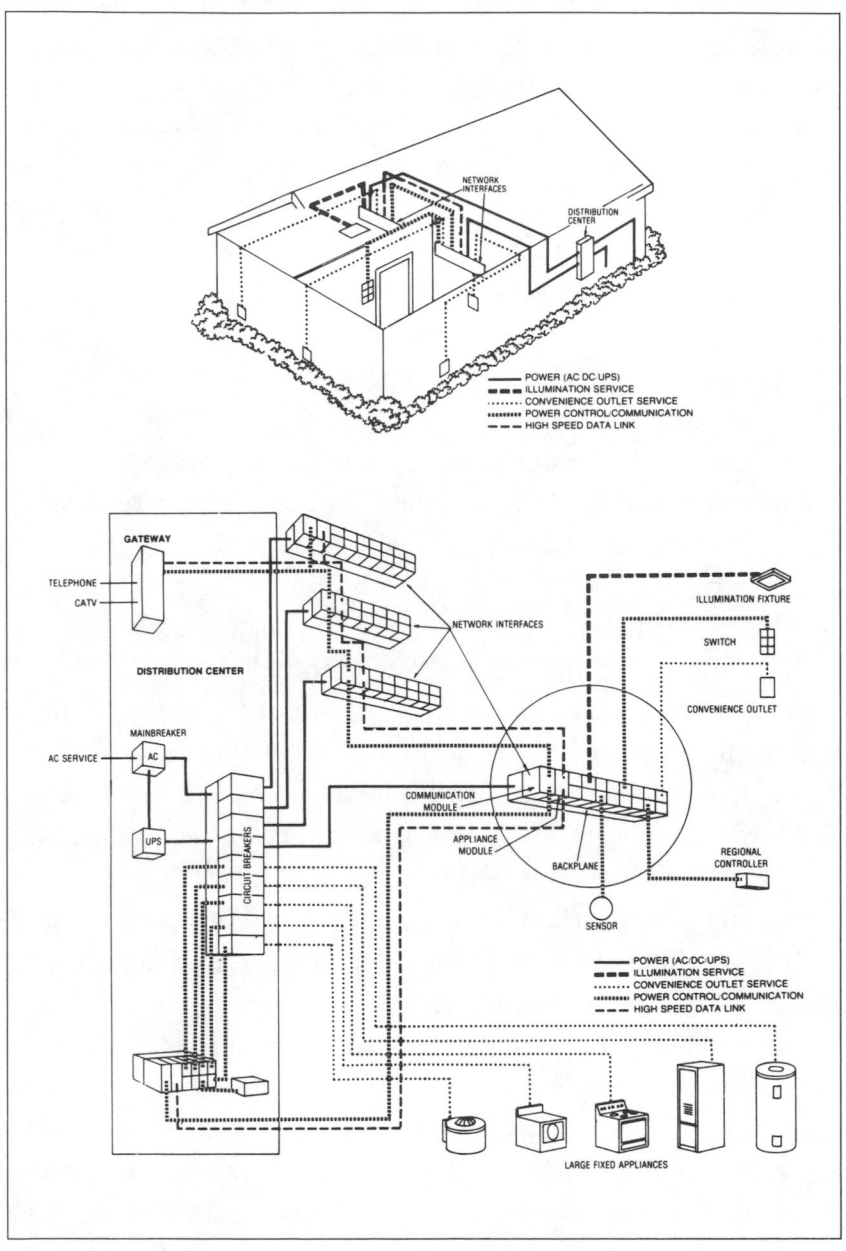

Figure 17. A Smart House network

power. In such an event the UPS will continue to power the microprocessor chips for up to 72 hours and thereby maintain their memories. In addition, it will maintain such low-powered functions as timing operations, provision of a spark for gas appliance ignition, and maintenance of the functions of sensors and detectors.

Through processing equipment not shown in this diagram, electromagnetic interference (EMI) and radio frequency interference (RFI), described in Chapter 4, will be controlled. Rolling bars and static lines should no longer dance on the TV screen during touchdown plays.

As shown at the bottom of the drawing, large fixed appliances will receive power directly from the circuit breakers by dedicated lines. However, these appliances will be controlled by the dedicated network interface shown at the lower left corner of the drawing. This interface can respond to signals from the appliance itself or from other interfaces throughout the house.

In the future, it may be that not all Smart House appliances will employ 120 or 240 volts of a.c. as they will at the outset. For many or most home applications, d.c. is a better choice. Thomas Edison is on record as saying that, in his opinion, no one would do anything so foolish as to serve homes with alternating current. His comment is often cited as an example of the myopia of even the greatest scientists. But in fact Edison was, as usual, technologically right.

Alternating current is superior to direct current for long-haul transmission because it can be managed for power loss, but direct current is frequently better for home use. When electrical service was first being introduced in the latter years of the 19th century, plans called for local conversion of alternating current arriving from distant generating facilities. However, for reasons that may have been a combination of economy and haste, the conversion

was usually not done, and ultimately a.c., the better choice for long-haul transmission, also became the home standard.

Many appliances nevertheless operate on d.c. and others would perform better if they did. TV sets work on d.c.; they require a power supply to convert the incoming a.c. into d.c. before it is passed through the set. The same is true of home computers and most other electronic devices in the home. Even a light bulb would last much longer if its filament did not have to endure the added stress of handling the 60 polarity reversals per second of alternating current.

At such time when the Smart House may offer both a.c. and d.c. to power lights and appliances, a.c. motors could be replaced by brushless d.c. motors. If a major appliance such as a washing machine were redesigned to take full advantage of the d.c. option in homes, it would have a d.c. motor that would be smaller and would require less maintenance.

In addition, the speed of the motor and even its direction of motion would be a function of the amount and polarity of the d.c. current flow that it received. This could be controlled at the network interface, and the costly and sometimes cranky transmission that is now required to put it through its paces could be eliminated. A separate timer would also not be needed; timing of cycles could be handled at the network interface.

Direct current could also have important applications in less familiar areas. For example, in the next chapter we will discuss zoned temperature control in homes. If d.c. were available in the home, the speed of blowers used to circulate both heated and cooled air could be simply and fully controlled, from the "off" position through every gradation to full speed, since their speed would be a direct function of the amount of current supplied to their d.c. motors. In so-called hydronic systems, the speed of pumps that circulate hot water through room heating devices could be also directly controlled. Valves and blowers

could thereby be added to the tools available for implementing zoned temperature control; in the absence of d.c., they are not easily accommodated.

With these kinds of considerations, we are beginning to move from a description of the system's technology, to a discussion of what the Smart House can do. In the next chapter we will begin to explore some scenarios and possibilities.

6
Heating, Ventilation, and Air-Conditioning

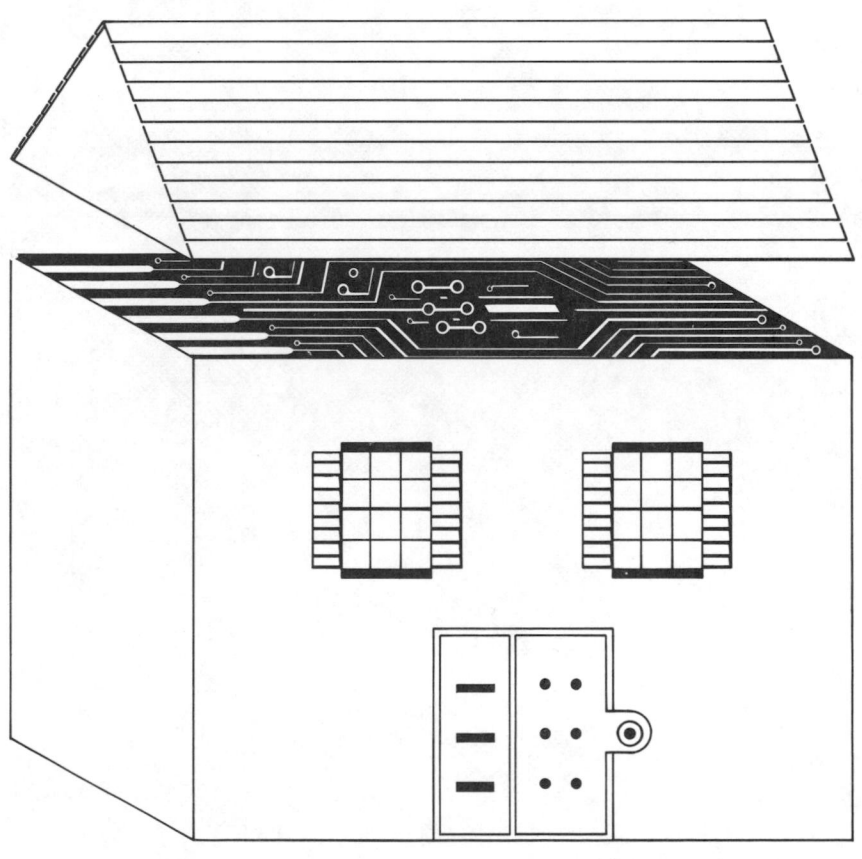

The Smart House has two characteristics that relate to its likely or possible uses. First, it belongs to the group of innovations that could be called watershed technologies. A very substantial demarcation lies between things that could be done before the introduction of such technologies and the things that can be done after their introduction. Second, the Smart House belongs to the category of innovations that have numerous diverse applications, rather than one or a few. Its impact will be broadly based and will affect many things.

Comparison with Cable TV

When considering the future of Smart House, it may be helpful to review the history of cable television, another watershed technology with which we have had a generation of developmental experience. Cable and Smart House both constitute responses to clearly recognized shortcomings of existing systems—with cable, the inability of over-the-air broadcasting to deliver a good selection of channels or good reception to many areas; with Smart House, the problems of simplicity and safety cited in Chapter 2. In both instances, established rather than

frontier technology was brought to bear on these shortcomings. With both, the technology employed has capabilities that go far beyond the solution of the immediate problems that it has been called upon to address.

As cable entered the mainstream of home technologies in the 1960s, forecasters drew up scenarios for its future that bore recognizable but only approximate relationship to what we know today. Some features of the forecasters' visions were fully realized; others were never realized at all; and, of particular interest, cable is now routinely used for some things that the forecasters did not envision. The evolution of Smart House is likely to exhibit the same pattern.

Another feature of cable's history is likely to be reflected in that of the Smart House. Cable's uses have evolved, not in a brief time span but over a number of decades. In fact, they are still evolving. Home shopping emerged as a major cable service just two years before the writing of this book. Videotex applications, which flopped when they were tried in the early 1980s, may yet succeed. Cable is a flexible facility that can accommodate many technological developments and changing consumer interests over a long period of time. Smart House has the same characteristics and is likely to experience the same pattern of growth, expansion, and change in its use.

And in fact, this process of growth and change in applications over a period of time characterizes most basic services, including electricity itself. For many decades after the introduction of electricity into the home, its principal use was for illumination; now more electricity is used in the home for running appliances than for lighting.

Zoned Temperature Control in the Home

In certain areas, Smart House makes possible the introduction of improvements in the functioning of houses that have been strongly desired by architects, engineers, and planners but could not be achieved with existing home wiring. One of these areas is the heating, ventilation, and air-conditioning of homes. These functions are collectively referred to in the building industry under the acronym HVAC, pronounced "H-vac."

It has been understood for a long time that present HVAC technology, which uniformly heats, ventilates, or cools the entire home in an on-off fashion, is costly and wasteful. Different rooms and areas of the house have different temperature requirements at various times of the day. A better approach would therefore be to divide the living area into several zones, and to provide heating, ventilation, and/or air-conditioning to each zone in accordance with actual needs at various times.

The layman whose familiarity with these matters is limited to raising and lowering the home thermostat may be surprised to learn that zoned heating and cooling for homes has been a busy frontier of activity for a number of decades. As early as the 1940s, experimental zoned control systems for the home were built and their performance tested. The results were impressive. Energy savings of 20 percent were realized by comparison with night setback of the thermostat in a conventional home heating system; savings of 33 percent were realized by comparison with a conventional system in which the thermostat was not turned back at night.

These and similar findings have already had their impact on HVAC in commercial buildings, where zoned temperature control has become common. But just as intelligent wiring lagged in homes while it was being installed in many office buildings, so zoned HVAC faltered at the threshold of the home. Few problems exist with regard to the creation of appropriate versions

of today's HVAC equipment and appliances to implement temperature zoning in the home; in fact, much of the required equipment already exists and is used in commercial applications. The problem has been the lack of a highly capable home control system to secure maximum cost-effectiveness from home zoning. The Smart House system removes this barrier.

A zoned HVAC system will be among the types of equipment that will be built into the first Laboratory Smart House, and research will be done to determine the best approaches to incorporating zoned temperature control as a standard feature of new homes.

An engineering consulting firm retained by the Smart House Development Venture produced the following scenario for heating, ventilation, and air-conditioning in the Smart House of the future.

A Winter Day in the Smart House

"It's 3:00 a.m. and not a creature is stirring except for the Smart House HVAC system. Its heat pump is raising the temperature in the thermal storage tank,* in preparation for commencement of activity by the zone circulators at 6:00 a.m.

"The lower portion of the water tank is also being heated up, for the system knows from experience that this household's demand for hot water starts in earnest at 7:00 a.m. It knows this, for it has monitored the flow from the water tank over the past week; should this pattern change, the system will change its pattern of heating up the tank. It will wait until 6:15 a.m. to turn on the electric resistance heater in the upper portion of the tank.

---

* A thermal storage tank is a large container in which hot water can be stored and circulated through the heating system on demand. Should a utility institute residential time-of-use pricing, the water in such a storage tank could be heated during hours of lowest energy cost.

"At 8:15 a.m. the last occupant leaves without telling the system when to expect someone to return, so the system determines that today is a 'usual' one, and that people will return around 6:00 p.m. Until just before then, it will take no heat from the thermal storage tank.

"At 5:30 p.m. the downstairs zone becomes alive. Each individual fan coil unit starts sucking heat out of the thermal storage tank, via the downstairs zone circulator, at a rate that is proportional to the 'need' of that room. Each room's need for heat takes into account the relative importance of that room, based on recent occupancy history. It depends also on the difference between the actual air temperature and the 'comfortable' air temperature, which in turn depends somewhat on the measured humidity and on the recent temperature history. In this case, the temperature history may imply that the walls are significantly colder than the air, so that warmer air is needed for comfort until the walls catch up.

"At 6:05 p.m. the first occupant returns to find that the downstairs zone is ready for him. The upstairs zone now becomes active, seeking to reach and maintain a temperature that is somewhat below the comfortable temperature. It excepts the guest room, though, for no one has been in it for over a week.

"At 7:30 p.m. the system brings Junior's room up to the comfortable level, for it knows that Junior tends to go there around 8:00 p.m. It will do the same for the master bedroom at 9:30 p.m. for a similar reason. Tonight, however, someone enters the master bedroom at 9:10 p.m. and stays for more than a minute, so the system brings that room up to the comfortable level as quickly as it can.

"At 10:30, the system notices that no one is left downstairs (the lights and TV are off), so it initiates nocturnal setback for

the downstairs zone. Each upstairs room will go into nocturnal setback only when all lights are out in that room."

Modifying Today's Equipment

There are four major types of home heating systems.

Hydronic systems heat water and circulate it in a closed loop through room heating devices such as baseboard heating units.

Forced-air systems use a blower to circulate air through a warm air furnace or heat pump. The air is then distributed through the house by means of a duct system.

Radiant systems heat surfaces, such as the panels in gypsum ceilings, to a temperature that is moderately above the ambient temperature of the room or space.

Baseboard electric heaters employ electrical resistance units that become hot when current is passed through them, and which heat the ambient air.

It is possible to install a central air-conditioning system with any of the above heating systems. With forced-air systems, however, it is unnecessary to install separate ductwork. The same ductwork that distributes warm air in winter can distribute cool air in summer. For air-conditioning, the air passes over a cold coil; for heating, it passes over a heater.

Smart House technology can be employed with any of the four types of heating systems, and with air-conditioning systems, to achieve zoned heating and cooling of homes. In general, with hydronic and forced-air heating systems, the function of the Smart House network will be to raise and lower the rate of firing of the heater while also operating valves and dampers to control flow of water or air to individual areas and rooms. With radiant and baseboard electric heating systems, the Smart House can control the setting of each heating unit individually to achieve different temperatures in different areas.

For zone temperature control to be fully effective with hydronic or forced-air systems, a modification will have to be made to today's furnaces, boilers, and pumps. Most of them now in use are what engineers call single-capacity devices. They have only two settings—on and off. When they are on, they operate at one level or speed.

Furnaces and boilers for use in zoned temperature control systems will have a "variable firing rate"—that is, it will be possible to increase or decrease the amount of heat that is applied to warm the circulating air or water, just as one can now adjust the flame on the burner of a gas stove. Variable firing rate furnaces and boilers are actually available now, although demand is small. Improved types at lower cost await only the stimulation of demand by developing the zoning of hydronic and forced-air systems.

The absence of a practical method or system for coordinated control has been the major obstacle to the coming of zoned home systems. Smart House can provide the hitherto-missing capability. With variable-firing furnaces and boilers, and valves and dampers with variable settings all in place, the Smart House can coordinate the operation of all the components of the system, telling each component when and how it should operate to achieve the desired results in each zone through the day and night.

In the Smart House, sensors in each room or zone will transmit information to the network interface associated with the load distribution center and the major appliances (shown in the lower left-hand corner, Figure 17). On the basis of the information received from the sensors, the network interface will instruct furnaces or cooling units regarding the level at which they should operate, and will tell valves and dampers how far open they should be, to achieve various temperatures in various zones of the house at various times during the 24-hour day.

Maximum performance, the engineers state, can be achieved if there are temperature, humidity, and occupancy sensors in every room or zone, and sensors outside the house to provide information on external conditions. The scenario presented above presumes the presence of all these types.

The HVAC system is made complete by adding a simple means of communicating the occupant's wishes and desires. As already stated, various types of user control devices will be developed and tried out in the laboratory and demonstration homes. Securing broad samplings of consumer reaction to both Smart House services and Smart House user controls is a major purpose of the laboratory and demonstration home programs.

The Smart House can make yet another contribution to heating and air-conditioning. Of the various devices cited above, heat pumps and air-conditioning systems share an important characteristic—they both employ compressors. Compressors are major consumers of electricity. Important purposes of conservation and cost reduction could be served by making it possible to regulate the timing of operation of these devices to secure maximum effectiveness at minimum cost.

The System's Flexibility

Intermediate levels of effectiveness can of course be achieved by less sophisticated configurations; for example, one could omit the occupancy sensors. These, however, are likely to be wanted for other applications, such as security, or for functions relating to the needs of older or handicapped persons, that we will discuss in ensuing chapters. In such cases they will be present anyway, and can be electronically linked to the zone temperature system.

This illustrates three characteristics of the Smart House that we will encounter frequently in describing its uses. First, when the basic system is in place, various types or groups of components can be added to it to increase its capabilities, layer on

layer. The homeowner can decide what he wishes to spend for what array of capabilities. Second, components or groups of components that are chosen are likely to have a number of different uses and applications, and their cost can be distributed among these applications. Third, because the basic Smart House network will accommodate all kinds of appliances and components, it can support new and future technologies and it can be adapted to changing times, interests, needs, and tastes.

7
Energy Management and Conservation

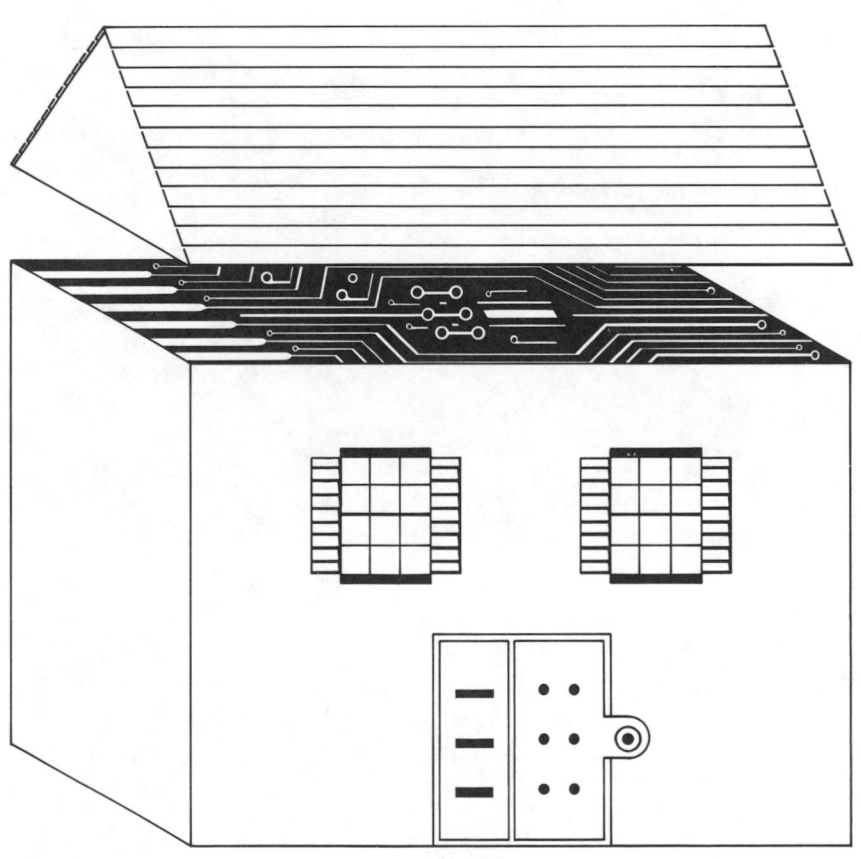

Commercial experience with zoned temperature control and experimental projects in homes both indicate that occupants of Smart Houses will have little difficulty matching the zoned-control energy savings of 20 percent that were achieved as early as the 1940s experiments cited in the previous chapter.

Zoned temperature control, in turn, is part of a larger picture. About one-third of the electrical energy generated in the United States is used in homes. The story of electrical energy use since World War II divides into two periods—the era before the Arab oil embargo of 1973, and the era that began after that date.

The Era of Cheap Electricity

Until the oil embargo, electricity was a plentiful and cheap resource. Utilities conducted substantial advertising and promotion campaigns to stimulate electrical usage. The low cost of electricity featured in magazine ads of the early 1960s pointed out, correctly, that the cost of operating a light bulb in the home had not increased since the Depression.

Accommodating increased usage was easy. When demand exceeded generating capacity, utilities built new plants, whose cost was almost painlessly folded into the rate base because the relatively modest cost of construction was coupled with constantly increasing demand.

The future looked as rosy as the present. According to everyone's vision, nuclear power would increasingly supplant fossil fuel generation as the latter decreased in abundance and increased in cost. Nuclear generation is relatively cheap, and the nation could therefore look forward to having all the low-cost energy it could use, into the indefinite future.

The New Era

As with so many aspects of our economy and society, virtually every aspect of this scene was transmuted after 1973. Power plants that ran on crude oil faced steep rises in the price of that commodity. Coal offered an alternative. However, both oil-burning and coal-burning plants, especially the latter, found themselves in a society increasingly intolerant of the combustion products poured into the atmosphere. It became increasingly necessary to accept the cost of removal of a substantial portion of certain waste products from the gases that went up the chimney. As for building new plants of either type, increasing urbanization, environmental concerns, and adverse community response made it increasingly difficult to find new plant sites anywhere.

At the same time, the great dream of nuclear power collapsed. In the late 1970s, a nuclear accident at the Three Mile Island generating facility near Harrisburg, Pennsylvania, raised public concern to levels that posed immense obstacles to the construction of new plants. Utilities themselves shared the doubts; among other things, no one has to this day found a good way to get rid of nuclear waste. No state, locality, or community wants a

nuclear dump, and all have shown willingness to fight to the bitter end in legislatures and in court to prevent one from being established in its domain.

Meanwhile, the cost of electrical power, once so steady and dependable, began to rise. Public utility commissions, who do not enjoy doing things that consumers do not like, often or usually disallowed portions of rate increases requested by utilities. But in the end, the rising cost of generating electricity asserted itself as an incontrovertible fact. Prices went up.

The scene after 1973 was therefore dominated by three factors. The cost of generating electrical power increased; the anticipated shift away from fossil fuels to generate it failed to materialize; and the building of new capacity became more and more difficult. These new circumstances fostered a broadly based concern for conservation. Among other things, utilities invested in research into such matters as energy-efficient home construction, and promoted the use of energy-conserving equipment and appliances such as high-efficiency heat pumps.

The Peaks and Valleys of Usage

The biggest area of interest from the standpoint of plant and equipment, however, is graphically portrayed in Figure 18. This graph, provided by the Potomac Electric Power Company which serves the Washington, D.C., area, shows total load demand on its system during three 24-hour days: January 28, 1986, July 8, 1986, and January 28, 1987. Similar types of graphs reflecting only differences in local climate could be produced for most electrical utility service areas in the United States.

The graph shows an uneven pattern of demand during each of the 24-hour periods. The two January days show very similar contours, with periods of peak demand in the morning and early evening. These two peaks arise from the simultaneous requirements of the subway system during rush hours and the surge

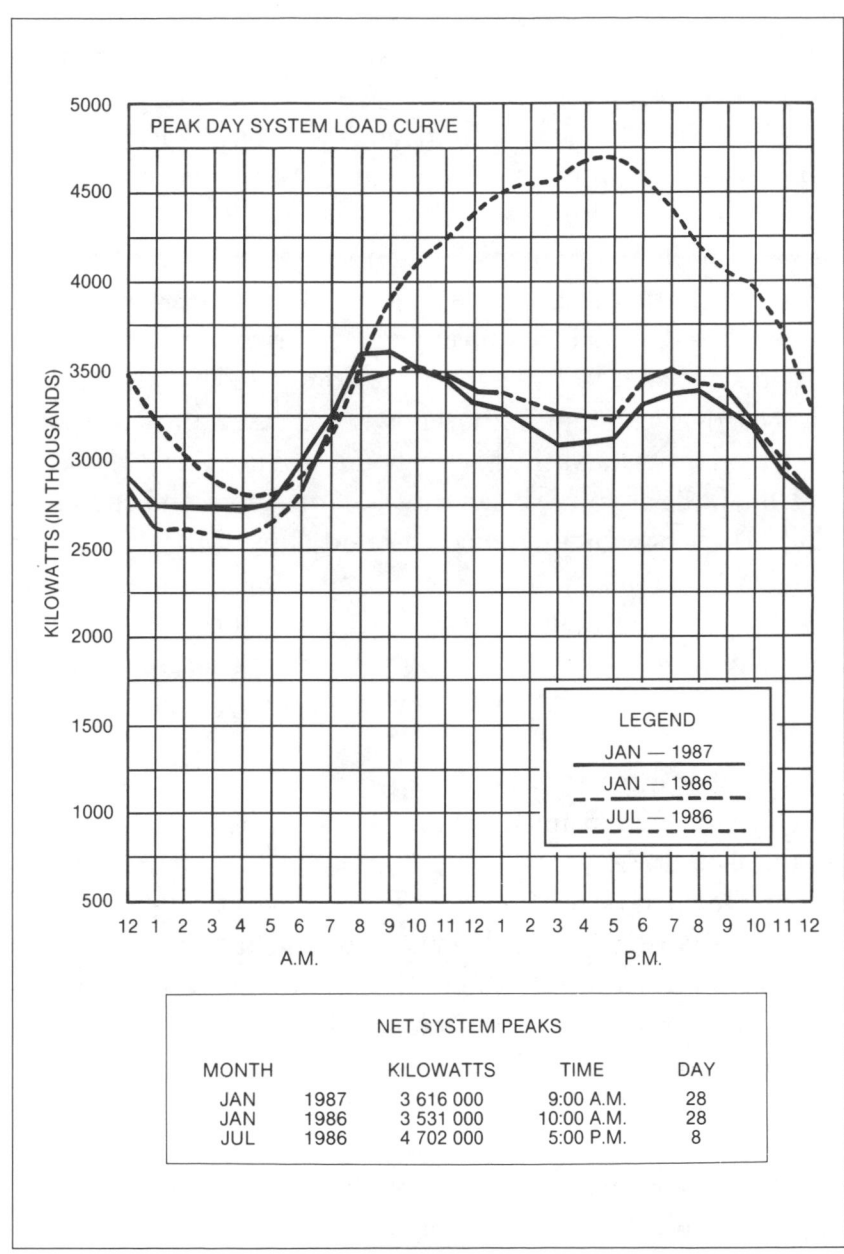

Figure 18. Potomac Electric Power Company graph showing
total load demand for several 24-hour periods

of demand in homes as members of families prepare to leave home in the morning and when they return in the late afternoon and early evening.

Now let us look at the graph line for July 8, 1986. This line looks more like Mount McKinley.

The weather report in the July 9, 1986, issue of the *Washington Post* shows that July 8 was a hot summer day, with a minimum temperature during the 24-hour period of 80 degrees F and a maximum temperature of 97. Only during the early morning hours of 4:00 to 8:00 does the usage curve approximate that of the two winter days. Starting about 8:00 a.m. the curve begins a steep climb that, by 9:00 a.m., has already carried system demand beyond the highest peaks of winter-day usage. From this point it continued to climb during the entire day, reaching a peak at 5:00 p.m. that is about a third again as great as the heaviest winter loads. During the 24-hour period the utility had to provide service in a range that swung from about 2.6 million kilowatts at 4:00 a.m. to about 4.7 million kilowatts at 5:00 p.m.

Almost all the difference between the winter and summer loads is accounted for by one usage—air-conditioning, an amenity that barely existed before 1950 and that has obviously transformed our world in more ways than one. On summer days, commercial air-conditioning loads in the Washington area climb during the morning hours, reach a plateau between 11:30 a.m. and noon, remain there until about 4:30 in the afternoon, and then decline. Residential use continues to move up during the afternoon, peaking at around 7:00 p.m. The dual peak of the two categories of usage occurs between 4:00 and 5:00 p.m.

Utilizing Capacity More Efficiently

Let us consider some questions that are highlighted by the graphs. The lines showing the two winter days reveal that the utility is generally not under pressure during most of the

24-hour period. When demand drops from the twice-a-day peaks, the system has excess capacity that is not put to use.

When electricity was a cheap commodity, leveling off the peaks and valleys of usage was not a compelling issue. If peak loads reached the point of exceeding existing capacity, new plants could be built, with the virtual certainty that the added capacity would soon be fully used. Consumers of course paid indirectly for unused capacity, but the cost was virtually invisible and no one complained.

Now, when electricity is more expensive and new facilities are difficult to construct, the unutilized capacity of existing facilities has moved to the forefront of attention. Finding ways to smooth out the peaks and valleys of usage and create a more level profile has become a top-priority issue.

The problem has been made even more important by the fact that as utilities build progressively toward peak loads, the cost of generation increases. In providing electricity, utilities draw upon their least costly and most efficient facilities first. As the load increases, more costly and less efficient facilities are pressed into use.* In addition, the system is often under strain; brownouts or blackouts may occur, with further associated cost.

In the traditional method of pricing electricity, all these costs are bundled together, and consumers pay flat rates that cover the costs plus a regulated profit. This method has important deficiencies in the context of the new era that is described in this chapter. Flat rates offer little incentive for efforts to smooth out the peaks and valleys of usage. In fact, if anything, they actively penalize the conscientious consumer who would be willing to cooperate by reducing his usage during times of peak

---

* The general order of increasing cost for power plant operation is as follows: nuclear; coal; low-grade crude oil; better grades of crude oil; and natural gas.

load, but who must nevertheless subsidize less responsible behavior by others.

Time-of-Use Pricing

An obvious alternative to flat rates is time-of-use pricing, in which the prices charged for electricity at different times of the day bear a more direct relationship to the costs of generation. Time-of-use pricing can also provide an incentive for consumers to participate in smoothing out the peaks and valleys of usage.

This approach has been used by telephone companies since their earliest years. Few people make telephone calls during periods of highest cost, if it is possible to wait a few hours in order to take advantage of the off-peak rates. In the new era of more costly electrical power, the same approach to pricing is replacing flat rates.

An Experimental Program

Experiments and demonstrations in time-of-use pricing have begun. One of the most extensive experiments was launched in 1984 by Pacific Gas and Electric Company (PG&E), which serves San Francisco and the Bay area. PG&E's program is a relatively simple one; it establishes an "on-peak" rate that is charged between noon and 6 p.m. from Monday through Friday, and an "off-peak" rate that is charged at all other times. The rates, which were approved for the experimental program by the California Public Service Commission, are as follows:

	On-Peak Rate	Off-Peak Rate
Winter	10 cents/kw-hour	6.5 cents/kw-hour
Summer	21.6 cents/kw-hour	5.2 cents/kw-hour

With regard to the summer rates, the off-peak rate is obviously a substantial carrot, and the on-peak rate is a substantial stick, to persuade homeowners to help level off the air-conditioning peak.

In addition to these rates, participants in the experiment must pay an additional $4.50 per month for the new and more costly meters that must be used to deliver time-of-day service. Standard meters, including installation, cost the utility between $30 and $40; meters capable of providing the new service cost between $210 and $220.

The average home in PG&E's service area that uses gas appliances consumes about 250 kilowatt-hours of electricity per month. All-electric homes, and homes that make more substantial use of electricity, typically consume between 450 and 550 kilowatt-hours per month. Heavy users consume more.

By comparison with present flat rates, the break-even point with the experimental rates, including the monthly cost for the meter, is about 350 kilowatt-hours per month. Homes that use more can apply their savings either to reducing the cost of their electric bills or to buying more electricity.

Consumer response has been highly favorable. The experiment has laid to rest any question of whether ratepayers are interested in participating in such programs to help in energy conservation and/or to save money. By 1987 some 25,000 homes had requested and received time-of-use meters. Some civic groups have even asked the public utility commission to require PG&E to install the meters universally, and add their cost to the overall rate base. For its part, PG&E will install 4,500 of the new meters next year, which reflects the maximum up-front cost that has been assigned to the program, but which will not meet the demand.

The PEPCO Program

In the metropolitan area of Washington, D.C., Potomac Electric Power Company launched a special program in 1987 to deal with the problem shown in the PEPCO graph, Figure 18. In this program, residential customers agree to permit the power com-

pany to curtail power for a period not to exceed 13 minutes per half hour at peak load times when the utility is under pressure. Curtailment can occur during weekdays only, usually runs for no more than 3 to 4 hours, and is prohibited by the tariff filing to run more than 6 hours. The tariff also specifies that the utility can invoke the curtailment no more than 15 times per year.

In exchange for agreeing to participate in the program, the customer receives a credit of $35 per season on his electric bill. The utility has applied to the Public Service Commission to raise the credit to about $50; the application was pending before the commission as this was being written.

Customer response has been literally overwhelming. PEPCO had expected to sign up 8,000 customers during the program's first year, and an additional 17,000 in each of the immediately succeeding years. When PEPCO launched the program in the late spring of 1987, it had not yet been approved by the District of Columbia Public Service Commission, and customer signups could therefore be solicited only in the utility's service area in the Maryland suburbs. In the first two months, 30,000 people in Maryland signed up.

"I really believe," says Michael Maher, who heads energy management development at PEPCO, "that it isn't so much the money that is causing all these people to sign up. It's that people understand. They agree with the purpose and they want to participate."

The Contribution of Smart House

These approaches represent a good start, but they suffer from two shortcomings. One is the limited capability of the methods and technologies being employed. The other, which is closely related, is the low level of homeowner control, participation, and choice. "What we currently lack," says Brian Brady, manager

of energy management technical services for Southern California Edison Company, "is a reliable and economical technology for the utility-customer interface." This key problem will be solved with the coming of Smart House.

First, as already discussed, the Smart House will provide zoned temperature control in the home, which will in itself reduce energy consumption for heating, ventilation, and air-conditioning. The homeowner remains in control of the amount and stringency of the measures that he wishes to take to reduce costs. These decisions can be related to the cost of time-of-use offerings. They can also be temporarily changed at any time to accommodate special situations such as illness in the family, the needs and requirements of older persons, the arrival of visitors, or absence during holidays and vacations.

Second, the operation of certain appliances can be shifted so that these appliances will run automatically at hours when electricity is cheapest. Major appliances likely to be involved include dishwashers, clothes washers, and clothes dryers, which can be loaded at any time of the day; the Smart House can operate them when electric rates are lowest. Water heaters can be operated in the pre-dawn hours to have hot water ready for the morning. For families fortunate enough to have a swimming pool, the requisite skimming and filtering can usually be accomplished by running the filter pump no more than ten hours a day. The time or times for this operation can be chosen to coincide with the periods of low electric rates.

As was noted at the end of the last chapter, the compressors of heat pumps and home air-conditioning units are additional items whose operation could be controlled during on-peak hours. Also, frost-free refrigerators are likely to accumulate frost at increased rates during the summer months. If left to themselves, they are likely to defrost during peak-use hours, but, if

controlled by Smart House, their defrosting can be deferred to hours when electricity is cheaper.

In addition, the Smart House can incorporate capabilities that go well beyond anything that can now be done. These capabilities would involve the installation of a two-way communications link between the utility and the home. With such a link, consumers could be given monthly bills resembling those now received from the telephone company, with costs broken down by time of day and possibly by category of service such as lighting, water heating, and air-conditioning.

An approximation of the daily status of the consumer's account during the month could be called up anytime on the home TV screen. Thus, on the 15th of the month, husband and wife could sit down, look at their consumption of electricity for air-conditioning for the first half of the month, and decide whether or not to be a little tougher on themselves during the second half of the month to reduce costs.

Other cost-saving strategies are possible:

- The family could decide to spend no more than $5 a day on air-conditioning. So instructed, the Smart House system could do the rest, deciding the levels of temperatures in various zones, and making special allowance for comfort in such rooms as the dining room at lunch and dinnertime.

- The family could set up a monthly energy budget. The system could report if and when the budget was exceeded, and the family could then decide what steps to take.

- The system could inform the family how well it is controlling energy costs by comparison with last month or with the same or a similar day or month in previous years. For those who might like to be

talked to by their house, the system could say, "Congratulations! You made it through a 90-degree day on $5.20!"

The same link could be used to provide utilities with a clearer picture than they now possess of how electricity is used in the American home. Utilities know surprisingly little about the details of how electricity is used; they provide it as it is called for and send a bill at the end of the month. Efforts to learn more involve costly survey techniques that produce, at best, rough or approximate information. "Load research costs us a lot now," says Michael Maher. "With permission from a Smart House owner, we could learn a lot more about how power is used in the home and be able to set rates more appropriately and plan for the future more efficiently."

A communicating link between the utility and the Smart House would make possible two other improvements in utility performance. First, as system loads reached the danger point, the utility could reduce the amount of power available for selected applications in the home. The priority of power reduction could be worked out in advance and appropriate instructions given to the Smart House network. For example, it seems highly undesirable to heat water when no one is in the house to use it and when the utility is struggling.

With this communication and power reduction capability, the utility could move past its power-generating danger point with far less risk of a brownout or blackout. The same method could be used to ease system load for the performance of essential maintenence or at times of unanticipated breakdown, whether or not such breakdown was the result of heavy loads.

Second, if breakdown or failure should occur, service could be partially restored, with the most important applications receiving power first, as the utility progressively recovered its capability.

As we noted in a previous chapter, staged restoration of service would also protect the utility against the substantial problem of "inrush" when power is brought back on the line.

There is an additional technical problem experienced by utilities for which the Smart House provides effective answers. Disturbances can occur on power lines that, in today's environment, can be passed right through into the house. One type of disturbance, called a "spike," can be caused by lightning or by "back EMF (electromotive force)" fed into the power network by heavy electric equipment. Spikes can run as high as several hundred volts. "Surges," which are lower in voltage and of longer duration than spikes, can be caused by problems at the generating source. Either one, but especially spikes, can harm the semiconductors in home computers, TV sets, microwave ovens, VCRs, and other types of home equipment. The Smart House system can insulate the house from power irregularities that occur on the line, thereby protecting equipment in the home and improving the quality of the electrical service.

The Smart House system can also make a helpful contribution in securing maximum value and energy savings from alternate sources of power. Such sources include windmills and solar power generators.

All electrical uses in the ordinary home can usually be accommodated by 160 to 200 amperes of power. Alternate power sources will usually generate less power—generally, from 2 to 30 amperes—and such generation will occur irregularly. The Smart House system can factor this supplemental power into the house's total requirements, reducing the power requirement from the utility in the exact amount that the supplemental power is available. There can also be an automatic trip-over to the alternate power source if power from the utility fails, with the highest-priority needs for continuing power in the home being served first.

WOODBURY UNIVERSITY LIBRARY
7500 GLENOAKS BOULEVARD
BURBANK, CA 91510

An additional possibility that is causing substantial interest in technical circles is cogeneration. It would be well within the bounds of current technology to build a gas appliance that would serve simultaneously as a furnace and hot-water heater, and that could use some of the heat produced in these processes to run a small turbine that would generate electricity. This electricity could be fed into the house power circuit by the Smart House system in the fashion described above. Prototype cogeneration systems and appliances will be tested in the Laboratory Smart House sponsored by the Gas Research Institute.

It should be noted that many appliances and devices currently exist that can perform useful functions resembling one or more functions that can be performed by the Smart House. For example, sophisticated versions of modern clock thermostats can establish a range of comfort in the home on a 24-hour cycle designated by the user, with one cycle being set for weekdays and a different cycle for weekends.

Such devices have significant value, but they differ from Smart House in two respects. First, they are manually and mechanically set. Experience indicates that, after an initial period in which the homeowner adjusts and readjusts them, their more sophisticated capabilities often fall into disuse, and they are operated as regular thermostats. Second, such devices do not interact with other devices and appliances in the home.

"The key," says David MacFadyen, "is integration and interaction of all technologies. Nothing operates by itself, and all interaction is electronic. You give the system simple instructions about the things that you want it to do, and the system takes care of coordinating all the relevant items and appliances to achieve what you want."

This chapter might appropriately close with a look into the more distant future, and particularly at the relationship of Smart House to the evolving technology called superconductivity.

The term superconductivity refers to a change that takes place at low temperatures in some materials, in which they lose all their resistance to the passage of electricity. With superconductivity, electrical currents can be carried without the losses that are encountered today when such currents are carried by copper wire, or when they pass through the increasingly tiny circuits in electronic chips.

The phenomenon of superconductivity was discovered in 1911, but until very recently it appeared to have little commercial value. To achieve it, metals had to be cooled by means of liquid helium to within a few degrees of absolute zero, which is -460 degrees Fahrenheit. However, new materials now being discovered and produced become superconductive at much higher temperatures.

"It is conceivable," says Ross K. Heitzmann, executive director of system development for the Smart House Project, "that eventually, in a time span anywhere from 3 to 30 years from now, superconductivity will be attained at room temperatures, and that 10 to 40 years from now it will be possible to manufacture the required superconductive material at costs similar to those for copper. When that happens, all the rules will be changed for electrical engineers.

"Wire size can be very small, for very large currents. One can imagine a power level of 12 volts to run standard devices and appliances in the home.

"Motors of all types can be lighter, lower in cost, and more efficient. They won't need fans to cool, and they will be capable of very high performance. They will, however, require high starting current, and new designs will be needed.

"Higher efficiency motors could lead to more portable tools and appliances.

"Finally, demand for copper would decline. Pennies may become the only significant copper product."

As this manuscript is being written, advances are being made almost daily in superconductivity technology. There can already be little doubt that superconductivity will be used for certain large-scale applications that involve very high currents in a relatively confined space, such as particle accelerators for atomic research and transformers for electrical power distribution.

Superconductivity might make at least one contribution to the Smart House system itself. It might simplify the designing of the miniaturized switching power supply that is needed to distribute alternate forms of power in the Smart House system. (See Chapter 5, first footnote.)

The level of power that is ultimately decided on for residential applications of superconductivity could be delivered by the system where it is wanted and needed, with 120-volt service being maintained for other functions. It would therefore not be necessary to choose between two technologies, neither of which was best for all usages. Homes with Smart House wiring systems will be able to take selective advantage, not only of superconductivity, but of other technological advances that the future may bring.

8

Living in the Smart House

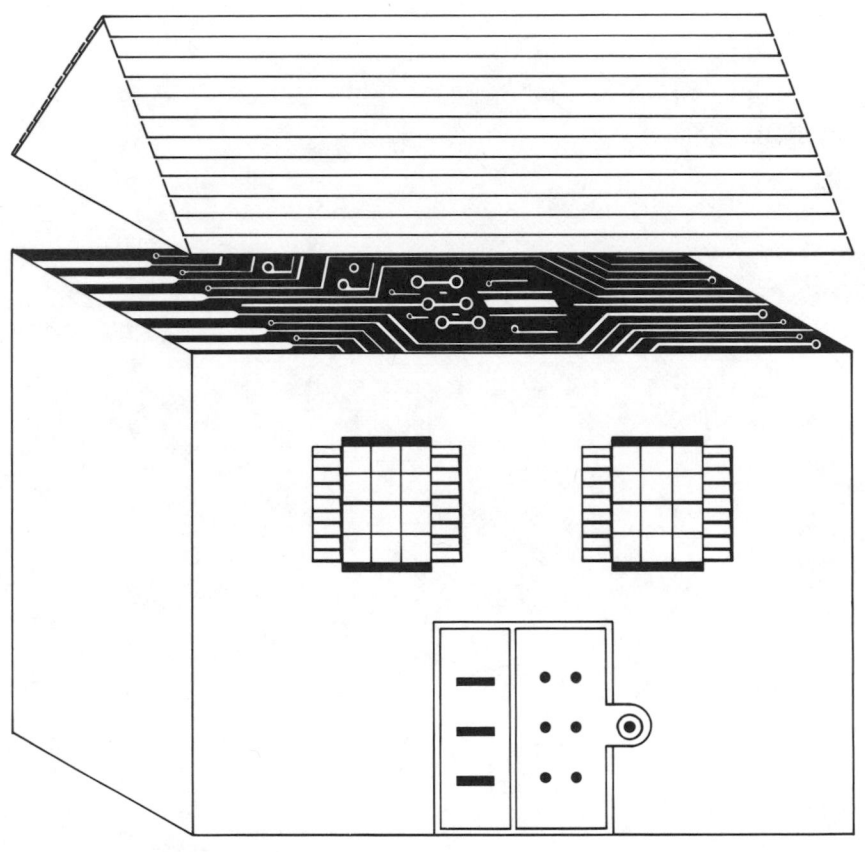

The coming of the Smart House will make it possible to do a number of things better than they can be done today, and will open up possibilities for doing some things that cannot now be done at all. Some of these possibilities will involve the development of new products and services, either through imaginative entrepreneurship or in response to pressures of consumer demand. Some of the foreseen areas of development and usage are described below.

A New Type of Gas Distribution

A consumer technology that can be greatly changed and expanded by the coming of the Smart House is the use of natural gas in the home. In today's homes that utilize natural gas, the piping network reaches one or two locations where the gas appliances are, for all practical purposes, permanently located. Moving these appliances involves reconfiguration of the piping, which is often no small matter after the house has been built. The piping network has little or no relationship to the electric and communications networks other than connection to switches and thermostats.

In the Smart House, the gas distribution system will consist of five subsystems: distribution, control, safety, monitoring, and communications. The network will serve a number of gas outlets located at various points in the home, some of which could even be configured as convenience outlets. Appliances attached to the network or plugged into the outlets will be simultaneously connected to the gas piping and to the Smart House network. A schematic diagram of the Smart House gas distribution system is shown in Figure 19.

Gas distribution will be centrally regulated by a controller/ monitor unit. This unit will control the flow of gas on the basis of information received from the appliances and from flow meters, valves, regulators, and sensors. Flow conditions and meter readings will be continuously monitored.

When an appliance is connected to the gas outlet and turned on, it sends a message to the controller/monitor unit via the Smart House network. In this message the appliance identifies itself and indicates its required flow rate. The controller then allows gas to flow to the outlet.

In the Smart House, indoor air quality can be constantly monitored. If it reaches an undesirable level in any zone in the house, fresh outdoor air can be brought in by using ventilation or through an air-to-air heat exchanger, found in some new homes, until an acceptable condition is restored.

The Changing World of Home Appliances

If and when appliances malfunction, the Smart House system can alert the home occupant in the house if he is present, or by phone if he is not. Both gas leaks and water leaks can be detected, and gas or water shuts off whether the home occupant is present or absent.

With the system in place, the home occupant can access it from outside the home—in fact, from anywhere in the world.

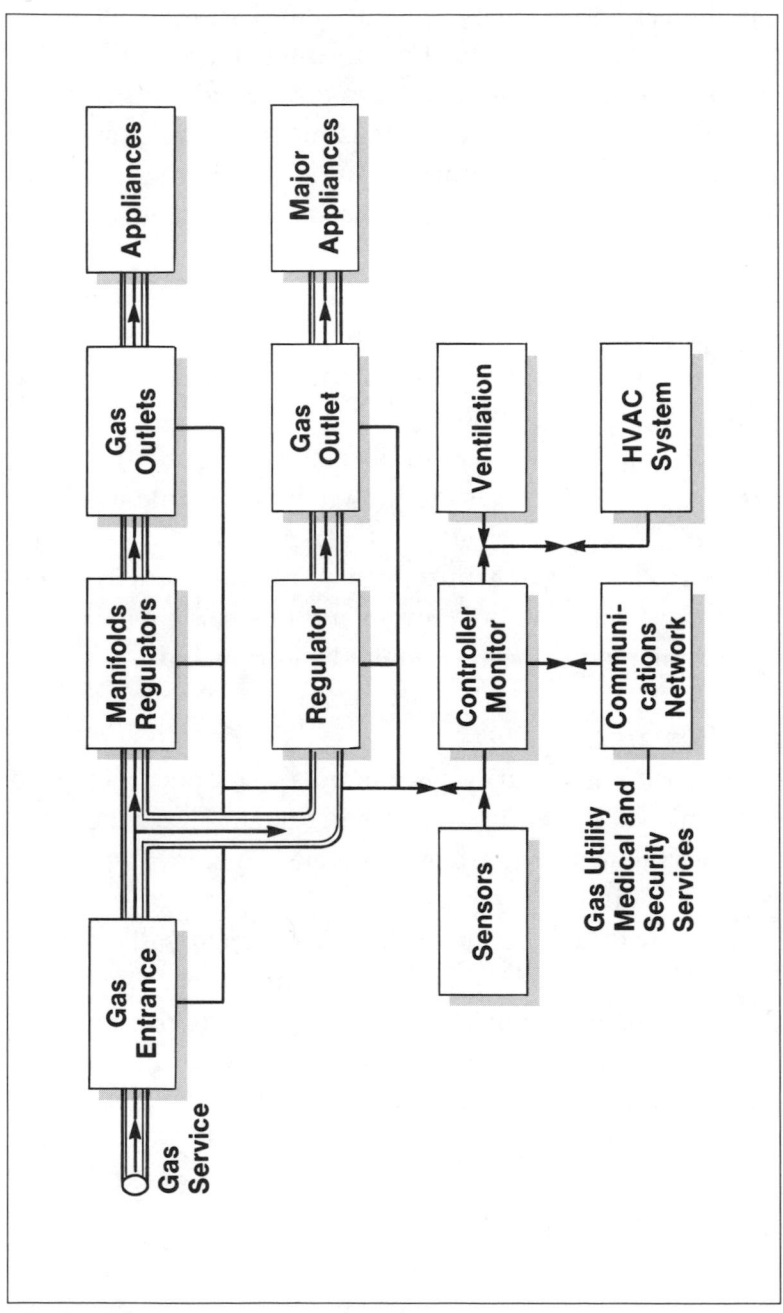

Figure 19. The Smart House gas distribution system

It will no longer be necessary to turn around an hour after one has started a vacation trip to be sure that doors are locked, thermostats properly set, or appliances turned off; inquiries and instructions of this type can be transmitted to the system by touch-tone telephone. From any location, the home occupant can learn if there are any problems at home, and can tell appliances what to do and when.

Potentially dangerous appliances such as stoves or power tools can be locked out of use when no parent is present to supervise children, or when a handicapped person is alone in the house for a period of time (Figure 20).

As was previously noted, a number of basic limitations can be overcome at such time as d.c. power may become available in the home. Appliances designed to operate on d.c. could be smaller, more efficient, and less costly to manufacture. Circuits and devices for conversion of current and mechanical transmissions for changing the speed can both be eliminated.

Security Systems

The cost of a home security system will be reduced since no special wiring will be required. The basic Smart House network will include a security system controller, and sensors in a number of areas of the house.

All systems will include fire and smoke detectors, the former being types of sensors that react to abrupt changes in temperature, and the latter being capable of detecting an increase in the number of ions of certain gases that result from combustion, such as carbon monoxide and carbon dioxide.

Sensors to detect occupancy and motion are currently undergoing a rapid increase in technological sophistication. The sensors are of two basic types. Infrared sensors can detect a change or disturbance in ambient heat patterns. Such changes, for example, are produced by body heat as a person moves around

Figure 20. Smart House childproofs a stove

in a room. Ultrasonic sensors emit high-frequency sound waves, and then "listen" for changes in the returning echo of these sound waves that are caused by movement in the room. Directional setting of these sensors can leave a zone near the floor through which pets can pass without setting off the alarm.

New sensors include types that combine the capabilities of infrared and ultrasonic sensors, or infrared sensors plus sensors that emit electronic microwaves rather than sound waves. Such sensors are controlled by a chip that requires both types of sensors in the device to agree that there has been movement in the room before permitting them to register an alarm.

Highly sophisticated systems employing video cameras are being developed for the home. Such a system, upon detecting an intruder, could make a full video record of his activities complete with time and date. Another technology called image analysis, which is now very costly, is likely to come down in price with advances in chip technology and could be used in home security systems. A system with image analysis will deal once and for all with the question of whether the motion detected in a room involves a household pet or a person who shouldn't be there.

Voice recognition, discussed below, will also be factored into security systems as the technology advances. Arming and disarming systems could be done by voice command, as could the direct activation of alarms by the homeowner.

When the system is armed for protection against intrusion, the security controller in the Smart House network will receive data from the sensors, accept supplementary commands and instructions from the home occupant, perform the necessary logical operations on the basis of the data received, and react in virtually any way that the home occupant may wish.

A central monitoring bureau of the type increasingly being used by security companies can receive the alarm automatically.

At the same time, if the intrusion occurred at night, the system could turn on the lights in the homeowner's bedroom, or in the room that has been entered, or both, and could announce to the intruder that his presence has been detected and that the police are being called. If the home occupants are absent— or even if they are present—the system could also flash all the lights in the house on and off and sound a highly audible alarm in addition to announcing to the intruder that his presence is known. If the homeowner wishes, the same kind of protection could be given to the perimeter of the house; a person coming close enough to look in a window could cause the system to respond.

During the day, when members of the household may be away, the system could activate an audible alarm that could be heard by neighbors, and could also place calls to the homeowner at his office and to designated neighbors in nearby homes.

Additional Uses and Applications

It will be possible to plug a TV screen into any outlet in the house to receive the output of a TV set, VCR, or security camera operating anywhere else in the house. There will be a similar capability for audio speakers to receive signals from any sound source.

A cordless computer keyboard would permit one to sit down in front of any TV screen to do word processing and letter writing. For persons with two- or three-track minds, the screen could have overlay windows in the upper corners, enabling the worker to watch a couple of TV programs without a sound component as he worked. If something looked especially interesting, he could postpone his work, turn on the sound, and watch the picture in full-screen size.

The Smart House could serve as a reminder calendar for all its residents. "Various software packages could keep your sched-

ule for you in various ways," says David MacFadyen. "For example, with voice recognition (discussed below), when you want to enter a future activity or appointment on your calendar, you can do it directly by voice. This could be done at home, or even by telephone from your car. At the beginning of each day, you could review the voice messages and reminders that you have stored for that day. The system could also make voice announcements during the day, such as 'It's time to take your pill,' or 'Your hairdresser's appointment is at 3 o'clock.'

"Another software package would make the same capability available as a visual display on your TV set. Entries could be made with a hand-held controller. At the beginning of each day you could sit down and review your schedule."

Special Needs of Special Groups

Certain capabilities of the Smart House have particular relevance to the needs of older persons and to problems of the handicapped.

One of these capabilities is voice recognition. At this writing, voice synthesis is well developed, and everyone has encountered it in such applications as the time-of-day information on the telephone network. Voice recognition is more difficult to achieve, but nevertheless it is just about to arrive.

While this book was being organized and written, a prototype car featuring voice control of windshield wipers, radio, heater, air conditioner, and windows was shown at a Paris auto show; a doll that recognizes 25 words and responds to about 100 phrases was shown at the New York Toy Fair; a wheelchair controlled by voice commands was being produced by a firm in California; and persistent rumors were circulating that one of the big computer firms was moving along with a word processor that can recognize 15,000 spoken words and put them into print with a minimum of error.

In a Smart House with voice recognition, the system will be capable of recognizing speech sounds and responding in ways for which the system has been programmed. Early voice recognition systems will probably be able to understand only one person's voice. These systems base their recognition on both the pattern of sound and the individual's "voice signature"— that is, the pitch, level, and dynamics of the individual speaker's voice. The speaker will "train" the system by speaking the required words a number of times, and the system will thereafter execute appropriate commands upon hearing these words in this voice.

Voice recognition systems for use in homes can be based on recognition of a small number of words, each of which can serve as an instruction to the system. This level of capability for voice recognition already exists. The network will be able to reply in synthesized speech, and to react in different ways to various specified answers.

Voice synthesis and voice recognition could both be used to serve the needs of special groups—for instance, the blind. Thus, the network could use voice synthesis to tell a blind person when he has left the stove on (Figure 21). It could also use voice recognition to execute various functions for blind persons upon voice command.

The ramifications of this capability are very great for older persons in the home. If an older person should fall and sustain injury or experience some other emergency when no one else is present, the person need only say "Help." The network could provide a programmed reply—for example, "Shall I call John at the office?" or "Shall I call Dr. Brown?" The answer "Yes" would cause the system to place the call, delivering a prearranged or prerecorded message (Figure 22). The system could be similarly programmed for persons with significant medical problems.

Figure 21. System sensors help blind people cope

Figure 22. System can summon help for the disabled

Demographic trends make it clear that there will be increasing demand for services of this type. The number of people over 65 is rising steadily, and so is their life expectancy. More and more of this older population is living alone; the current number is 8 million, of whom three-fourths are women. Those who do not live alone must nevertheless often be alone in the house for the regular hours of the school day and working day, when younger household members are either working or in school.

Various types of services are already being established for persons living at home who have serious health problems. These services usually involve small devices which the person can wear around his or her neck, or carry around. In an emergency, the person can push a button on the device, which sends a signal either to a hospital or to a privately run monitoring center via a unit attached to the telephone.

It is of course neither practical nor desirable to place panic button devices around the necks of every older person in America. And with Smart House it will not be necessary. Voice recognition systems can extend this kind of protection far more widely into the general population, combining normal living and freedom of movement with immediate protection in the event of emergency. The capability of the Smart House to receive and understand voice communication, and to respond to problems by communicating with the outside world, may emerge as the technology's most valued contribution to American life.

And of course, whether or not one has medical or other special reasons for having such a system, one could use the same microphone pickups, combined with available speakers, to hold a telephone conversation without moving from one's favorite easy chair.

9
From Idea to Reality

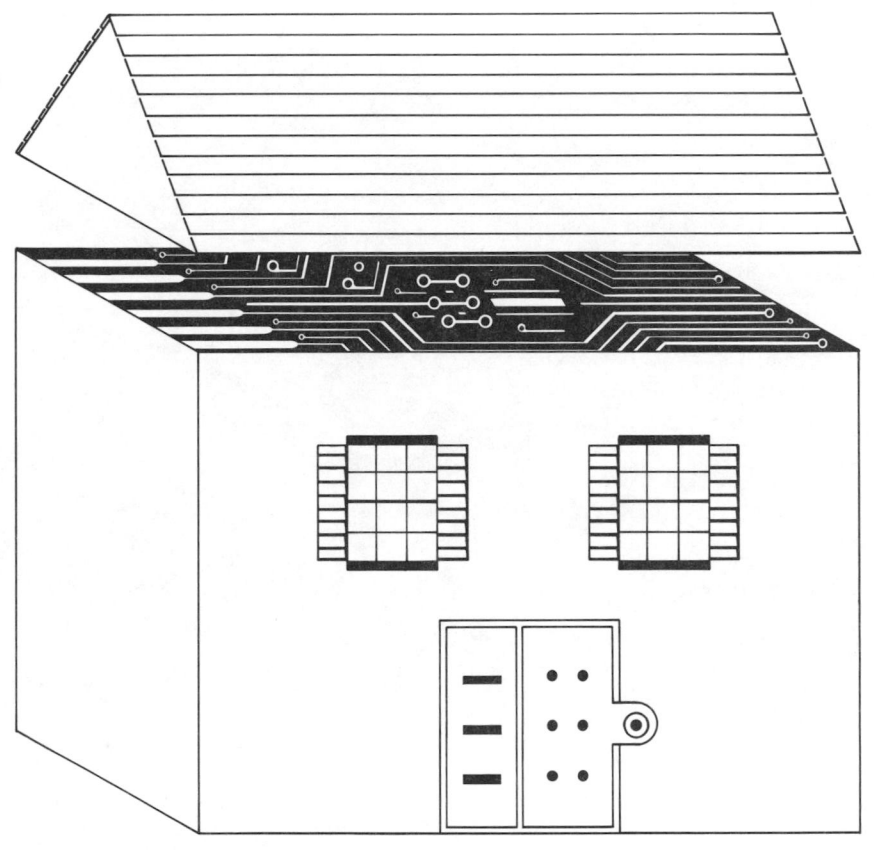

As is described in Chapter 3, Smart House was the first project filed with the Department of Justice under the National Cooperative Research Act of 1984. It was thus a highly novel undertaking, whose success would require a degree of coordination among firms in the building, electric, electronic, and gas industries that was without precedent in the experience of any of the participants. Finding the right organizational path posed at least as many problems as development of the technology itself. A brief description of the Venture and its plans was provided in Chapter 3. Here we will provide some additional information.

Participating Firms and Advisors

Forty manufacturing firms are participating in the Smart House project. They are:

AMP, Inc.

Apple Computer

ARCO Solar, Inc.

AT&T Technologies, Inc.

Bell Northern Research

Bose Corporation

BRIntec Corporation

Broan Mfg. Co., Inc.

Burndy Corporation

Carrier Corporation

Challenger Electrical
Equipment Corporation

Dukane Corporation
DuPont Connector Systems
Emerson Electric Company
General Electric Company
Honeywell Corporation
I-T-E Electric Products
Johnson Controls, Inc.
Kohler Company
Landis & Gyr Metering, Inc.
Lennox Industries, Inc.
National Semiconductor
  Corporation
NOMA, Inc.
North American Philips
Northern Telecom

NuTone Division–Scovill, Inc.
Onan Corporation
Pass & Seymour, Inc.
Robertshaw Controls Co.
Schlage Lock Company
Scott Instruments Corp.
Shell Development Company
Signetics Corporation
Slater Electric
Sola Electric
Southwire Company
Square D Company
Systems Control, Inc.
Whirlpool Corporation
Wiremold Company

As noted in Chapter 3, a number of firms and organizations that are not in the business of manufacturing products for use in the Smart House nevertheless expressed strong interest in the project and sought an avenue of involvement. These firms, which include a number of electric and gas utilities and telephone companies in the United States and Canada, and even an Italian energy firm (AgipPetroli), joined an Advisory Council which meets regularly to receive information on the project progress and to provide input. Members of the Advisory Council are:

AgipPetroli
American Gas Association
Baltimore Gas & Electric Co.
Bell Canada
Bell Communications
  Research
Bell of Pennsylvania
Boston Edison Company

Copper Development
  Association
Dayton Power and Light Co.
Delmarva Power & Light Co.
Duke Power Company
Electric Power Research
  Institute
Gas Research Institute

Hydro Quebec	Southwest Gas Corporation
Oklahoma Gas & Elec. Co.	Southwestern Bell Telephone
Ontario Hydro	Company
Potomac Electric Power Co.	U.S. Department of HUD
Professional Builder	Virginia Power
Magazine	Washington Gas Light Co.
So. California Edison Co.	Wisconsin Electric Power Co.

Of these firms and organizations, the Electric Power Research Institute and the Gas Research Institute, acting for their respective industries, have made substantial commitments to the funding of Smart House. In addition to being members of the Advisory Council, they have been designated as sponsors of the Smart House project.

The Role of the Venture

All participants agreed that certain overall responsibilities should be assigned to the Smart House Development Venture. They included general scheduling and coordination of the development work and assurance of technical quality.

An additional matter of central importance that was assigned to the Venture was the development of the common electronic language that would enable the Smart House network and all Smart House appliances to communicate with each other and operate as a unified system. The ability to recognize and use this language would be built into the "chips" in the Smart House network and all equipment and appliances that will attach to it. The Venture will develop and will hold the license for these chips.

As each manufacturer completes his development work, he will pass the license for the manufacture of his particular product to the Smart House Development Venture. The Venture will hold all of the licenses until such time as enough products are ready to enable simultaneous release of the system and associated

products. It will then license the products back to the firms that have developed them, telling all of them to begin production.

The Construction Program

The first laboratory Smart House, for which ground was broken in April 1987, is jointly sponsored by the Gas Research Institute and the NAHB National Research Center. In addition to serving as a test bed for technology matters of interest to GRI, the house will be used for component testing and system integration testing of initial versions of the Smart House wiring network, and for testing of initial versions of Smart House software and appliances. Study of human factors associated with the Smart House and its uses will also begin, to determine preferences in such matters as the best type or types of Smart House controllers.

Construction of the second group of Smart Houses, called prototype houses, is scheduled to begin in mid-1988. Several are planned in various locales throughout the United States. They will be co-funded by Advisory Council members, local home builders associations, local builders, and participating Smart House manufacturers.

The prototype houses will contain all the amenities of lived-in homes. They will be used to test advanced system integration and to develop operating features of the Smart House, including the capability for two-way communications with gas and electric utilities. They will also be used in designing and developing installer training programs and for conducting market research.

Most or all electric utilities, gas utilities, and telephone companies that are members of the Smart House Advisory Council have become involved because they believe the Smart House bears an important relationship to the improvement or expansion of services that they offer, and/or to the development of new types of service. In the prototype houses they will conduct technological research relating to new or expanded service offer-

ings and will also secure consumer reactions to new services and ideas.

Research in the prototype houses will continue through much of 1989. By then, the schedule calls for participating manufacturers to be ready with standard production models of supplies, materials, devices, and appliances. As the new decade approaches, the Smart House will move toward the marketplace.

About l00 demonstration houses will then be built by interested builders and developers, which will launch the Smart House on the national level. From that time on, persons living in the vicinity of builders and developers who are building the new type of house can ask for it and get it.

Cost of the Smart House

The exact cost of adding the Smart House network to a new home is not yet certain because products have not yet been developed and their prices are not known. However, initial costs are likely to be offset by operational advantages such as lower utility bills and lower rates for home hazard insurance. The value of the home will be permanently increased and the presence of the network will facilitate resale.

It costs some $5,000 to install the wiring system now used in homes. In the initial stages of production and installation of Smart House equipment, several thousand dollars will likely be added to this cost. As production runs of equipment and contractor experience in installation both increase, the differential between the costs of installing the existing type of wiring and the cost of installing a Smart House network will probably move toward insignificance.

The Coming Decade

The system is expected to gain rapid market acceptance, and, within ten years, to substantially supplant today's type of wiring

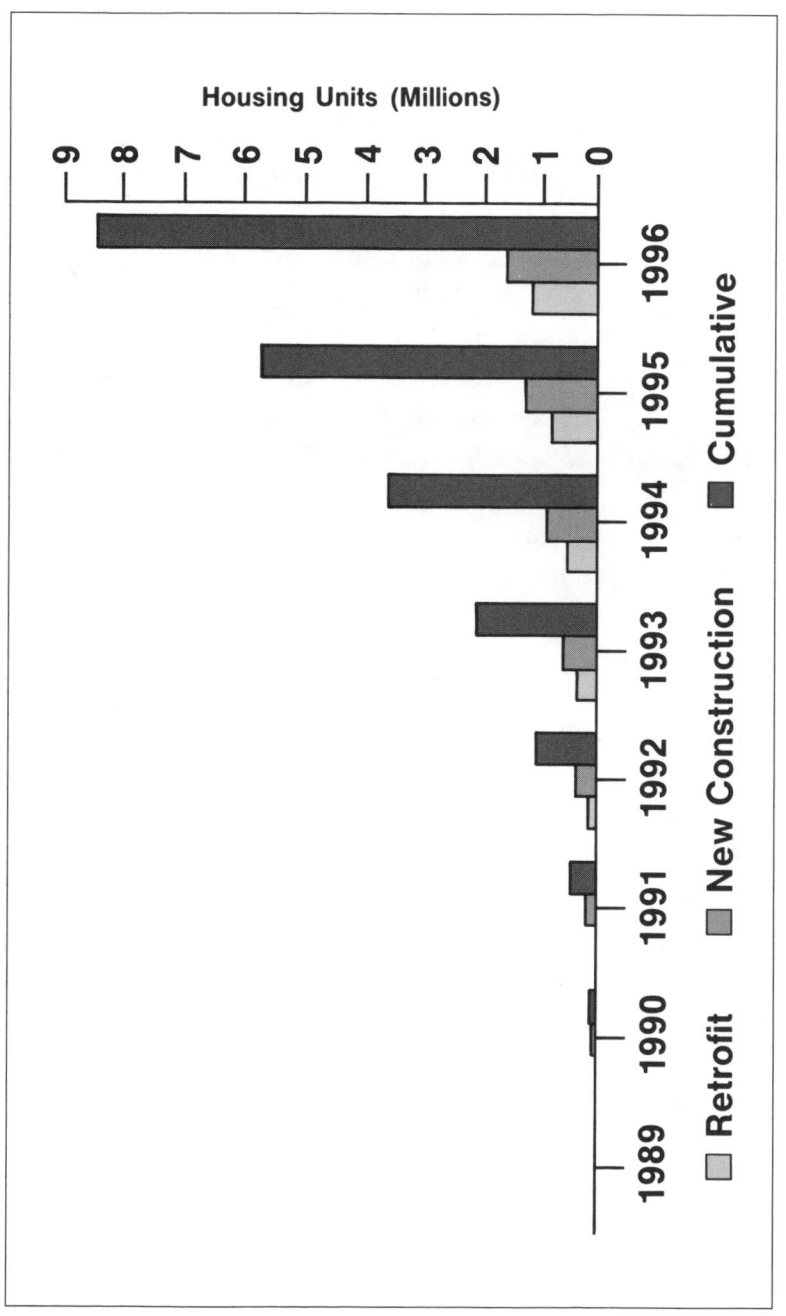

Figure 23. Projections for Smart House installations

in new home construction. At the same time, retrofit versions of Smart House hardware will be developed. It is not expected that the Smart House retrofit package will be installed in a major portion of the existing housing supply. Total rewiring of an existing home will always be a costly undertaking. However, at such time as a new room or wing is added or substantial renovation is undertaken, a certain number of homeowners will elect to modernize their wiring too.

The bar chart in Figure 23 shows projections for Smart House installations in both new and existing homes. As the 1990s draw to a close, a cumulative total of more than 8 million homes and light-frame buildings in the United States and Canada are projected to have the new wiring.

By then, the information age, long stalled at the front door of the home, will have moved comfortably inside. Thomas Edison would be pleased.

TH
4812
.S63
1988

Smith, Ralph Lee,
1927-

Smart house

WOODBURY UNIVERSITY LIBRARY

7500 Glenoaks Blvd.
Burbank, CA 91510

CARD OWNER IS RESPONSIBLE FOR ALL
LIBRARY MATERIAL ISSUED ON HIS CARD
RETURN BOOKS PROMPTLY — A fine is charged
for each day a book is overdue, except Satur-
days, Sundays, and holidays.

REPORT A LOST BOOK AT ONCE — The charge for
a lost book includes the cost of the book plus
fines.